The Nottingham China Policy Institute Series

Series Editors

Shujie Yao
School of Contemporary Chinese Studies
University of Nottingham
Nottingham, UK

Steve Tsang
School of Contemporary Chinese Studies
University of Nottingham
Nottingham, UK

Aims of the Series

The Nottingham China Policy Institute series brings cutting edge scholarship, policy relevance and accessibility together. It includes works on the economics, society, culture, politics, international relations, national security and history of the Chinese mainland, Taiwan and Hong Kong in the twentieth and twenty-first centuries. Books in this series are written in an accessible style though they are based on meticulous research. They put forward exciting ideas and research findings that specialist academics need to take note of while policy makers and opinion leaders will find inspiring. They represent innovative multidisciplinary scholarship at its best in the study of contemporary China.

More information about this series at
http://www.springer.com/series/14423

Steve Tsang • Honghua Men
Editors

China in the Xi Jinping Era

palgrave
macmillan

Editors
Steve Tsang
School of Contemporary Chinese Studies
University of Nottingham
United Kingdom

Honghua Men
Central Party School, Beijing and
Tongji University, Shanghai
China

Translation from the Chinese language edition: *China's Strategy in the Coming Decade* by Honghua Men and Steve Tsang, © China Economics Publishers 2015. All Rights Reserved.

The Nottingham China Policy Institute Series
ISBN 978-3-319-29548-0 ISBN 978-3-319-29549-7 (eBook)
DOI 10.1007/978-3-319-29549-7

Library of Congress Control Number: 2016943532

Printed on acid-free paper

This Palgrave Macmillan imprint is published by Springer Nature
The registered company is Springer International Publishing AG Switzerland

Preface

This book is the product of a collaborative project between the China Policy Institute at the School of Contemporary Chinese Studies at the University of Nottingham and the Institute for International Strategic Studies at the Central Party School of the Communist Party of China. It started as delegates from the Central Party School and Nottingham engaged in frank and constructive dialogues beyond the formal proceedings of a Wilton Park conference in December 2012. What triggered this discussion were the invaluable and timely exchanges that constituted the formal proceedings of the conference entitled 'Implications and Opportunities of the 18th Congress of the Communist Party of China'.

It was at Wilton Park that Steve Tsang and Honghua Men worked out a preliminary plan to conduct a joint project to examine the strategic directions that the Xi Jinping Administration would follow, and to explore options and opportunities that it might like to or should consider. This proposal quickly received the support of Professor Baojiang Han, then the Director of the Chinese Institute for International Strategic Studies. The focus of this book and the end product is to examine and explain the thinking of the Chinese leadership, the forces within China that shape their approach, and where and how further improvements can be made during the Xi Jinping decade. It is not about whether contributors approve or disapprove of the Chinese approach.

The collaboration took Tsang to the Central Party School. A group of colleagues from there and a few highly selected others from different Chinese institutions then gathered in Nottingham for intensive brainstorming and research. The working language for the exchanges and collaboration was Mandarin. The exchanges and debates were open, critical, and frank. The atmosphere was friendly and highly conducive to debate; and debate we did. All members of the research team regardless of nationality presented their research findings and received direct and critical comments in a respectful and highly constructive spirit. Both sides take the view that it was Sino-British intellectual cooperation at its best.

The papers that form the main body of this volume were presented at a conference in Nottingham in early 2014. They were subsequently revised, some quite substantially, after taking into account the debates that took place at the Si Yuan Centre at the University of Nottingham. In addition to the colleagues from the Central Party School and the China Policy Institute who were directly involved in this collaborative project, a number of other delegates from outside the two hosting institutions were also invited to join this special conference, conducted behind closed doors under the Chatham House rule. The contributions by the Chinese colleagues were written in Chinese and translated into English. Those contributions by British colleagues were written in English and then translated for a Chinese edition of this book.

The contributions by our Chinese colleagues, particularly those based at the Central Party School, also enable readers to understand better the thinking and arguments of an important group of scholars who work in an institution that supports the Central Committee of the Communist Party of China. Readers should not assume that views articulated by professors at the Central Party School represent that of the School or the Chinese leadership. They do not. What their contributions provide, in addition to the scholarly insights, is how the particular subjects are being approached by leading Chinese scholars whose views are generally taken very seriously by top level policy makers in China. Their style of presentation also differs from that taken regularly by scholars working at leading universities in the English-speaking world, but they adopt such a style because it is more effective in China, the context in which they work on a daily basis. Providing a glimpse into this is an additional value of this volume.

As we bring this collaborative project to its logical conclusion, we, as editors, decided to publish this book in both the Chinese language and the English language. The Chinese edition was released first under the title *China's Strategy in the Coming Decade* by China Economic Publishing House in June 2015. The two editions are not identical as the different timeframes for finalising the text gave scope for some updating and adjustments to be made in the English edition. We have also organized and structured the two editions slightly differently. The Chinese edition was also able to be released sooner as the publication cycle in China is much shorter than that for academic volumes in the English speaking world, which we were particularly keen to ensure in order to make the insights gained available to the Chinese authorities, colleagues, and general readers as soon as possible. We and our fellow contributors are specialists on China and fully committed to help China develop and move forward in the best possible way, and to assist readers not familiar with some elements of the inner workings of the Chinese system. We see our work in this volume as a contribution to this cause.

In conducting the research and bringing the findings to print, we have received generous support and help from various individuals and institutions. Above all, we would like to thank Baojiang Han, the former Director of the Institute for International Strategic Studies at the Central Party School. He not only contributed intellectually as a member of the research team and as an author to this volume but also lent the institutional support that made this collaboration possible. We are also deeply grateful to all our colleagues on the research team whose contributions constitute the main body of this book. They have responded promptly and efficiently to queries about their works and other editorial matters repeatedly in a spirit of understanding and forbearance.

We are much indebted to those colleagues who shared their critical comments on our preliminary findings at the Nottingham conference. They are Julie Chen, Miwa Hirono, Niv Horesh, Hong-yi Lai, Chun-yi Lee, Nicola Macbean, Tyler Rooker, Ian Seckington, Lina Song, Jonathan Sullivan, Patricia Thornton, Zhengxu Wang, Peter Wickenden, Qianlan Wu, Qing Yang, and Shujie Yao. We are also grateful to Hua Geddes, Tessa Schofield, and the incredibly able and reliable team of administrators at the School of Contemporary Chinese Studies who ensured this project and the conference worked like clockwork. Louise Woodward also helped with the preparation of the final typescript. Last but not least, we would like to thank Royal Dutch Shell and the Foreign and Commonwealth Office for providing support for the Nottingham Conference. Cho Khong in particular was invaluable in helping to secure the funding from Shell. Their generous support for scholarship and Sino-British research collaboration has enabled this project to progress well and come to fruition.

Steve Tsang
Honghua Men

Contents

Notes on Contributors

Andreas Fulda is a senior fellow at the China Policy Institute and an assistant professor at the School of Contemporary Chinese Studies, both at the University of Nottingham. He is also the Coordinator for the School's Centre for Contemporary Chinese Politics. Between 2011 and 2014 he ran a major EU funded project called the EU–China Civil Society Dialogue at the China Policy Institute. He had also helped to design and implement two major capacity building initiatives for Chinese civil society organizations: the Participatory Urban Governance Programme for Migrant Integration (2006–2007), and the Social Policy Advocacy Coalition for Healthy and Sustainable Communities (2009–2011).

Baojiang Han is a professor and Director of the Economics Department at the Central Party School of the Communist Party of China. He was the director of the Institute of International Strategic Studies at the Central Party School (2012–2015). He is an expert on the reform of economic systems, state-owned enterprise reforms, income allocation, labour relations, economic globalization, and intra-county economies. He has written or edited more than 20 books and textbooks, such as *China Outlook: Considerations on the future of China's Development (2013)*, and published more than 200 articles in leading journals, periodicals, and newspapers, such as *Study on Economics* and *The People's Daily*.

Christopher R. Hughes is Professor of International Relations and Head of the Department of International Relations at the London School of Economics and Political Science. He has published extensively on the international relations and politics of the Chinese Mainland and Taiwan. His most important books include *Chinese Nationalism in the Global Era* (London, 2006) and *Taiwan and Chinese Nationalism: National Identity and Status in International Society* (London, 1997).

Honghua Men is Distinguished University Professor, President of the Institute for China Strategic Studies, and Dean of the School of Political Science & International Relations at Tongji University in Shanghai, and is concurrently the KF Chair Professor at the Central Party School in Beijing. He is Deputy Secretary General of the Chinese Association of Asia Pacific Studies, Board Member of the Standing Committee of the China National Association for International Studies, and a non-resident senior fellow of the China Policy Institute at the University of Nottingham. He has also been a senior visiting scholar at the University of Tokyo (Japan Foundation Scholar, 2015), Pembroke College at the University of Oxford (Chevening Scholar, 2013–2014), the Eisenhower Fellowships (Eisenhower Fellow, 2011), the Japan Centre for Economic Research (Nikkei Economist, 2006–2007), Taiwan Chengchi University (2005), and the Carnegie Endowment for International Peace (Kimsey Fellow, 2003). He is a leading expert in strategic studies in China and has published very extensively on IR theory and grand strategy, including over 40 books of which nine are single authored.

Shiping Qi is a PhD candidate in economics at the Central Party School of the Communist Party of China in Beijing. His main areas of research are China's changing economic development model and the evolution of the global economy.

Yingchun Sun is Professor of Intercultural Communication and International Relations at the Communication University of China, a research fellow of the Culture & Communication Institute at Peking University, and a board member of the China Communication Association. His research mainly focuses on intercultural communication, culture, and international relations. He has published 15 works and translations in Mainland China and Taiwan. His articles have been published in numerous scholarly journals and anthologies. His works *Intercultural Communication: Global and Indigenous Perspectives* (Peking University Press, 2015) and *Intercultural Communication: Theories and Analysis* (Peking University Press, 2008) are currently the most popular and widely used textbooks of this area in universities in Mainland China.

Steve Tsang is Professor of Contemporary Chinese Studies at the University of Nottingham. He had previously served as Director of the China Policy Institute at the University of Nottingham, and as Professorial Fellow, Dean, and Director of the Asian Studies Centre at St Antony's College, Oxford University. He has published very extensively on the politics, international relations, security, and history of the Chinese Mainland, Taiwan, and Hong Kong. They include 16 books of which five are single authored.

Lifeng Wang is a professor in the Faculty of Political Science & Law and Director of the Research Centre for Human Rights of the Central Party School. His main research field focuses on legal and political philosophy. He has published widely, including monographs such as *Philosophy of Punishment* (Tsinghua University Press, 2006), *Politics and Morality: Machiavelli and the Prince* (China Legal Publishing House, 2012), *Political Philosophy of Human Rights* (China Social Sciences Publishing House, 2012), *Political Parties in Government: The Relationship between the Chinese Communist Party and the Government* (China Legal Publishing House, 2013), and *Rule of Law in China* (People's Publishing House, 2014). He is also a co-author of the *China Law Development Report* (Chinese Renmin University Press, 2008).

Xi Xiao is Kuang Yamíng Chair Professor and Head of the Department of International Politics at the School of Administration, Jilin University in Changchun. She was a visiting scholar at Cornell University (2007–2008), Oxford University (2013–2014), and Waseda University (2014–2015). She is Distinguished Professor in IR studies of Jilin Province, Deputy Secretary General of the National Association for International Politics of Chinese Universities, and Board Member of the Chinese Association of Political Science. Her papers have been published in *China: An International Journal*, *Social Sciences in China*, and other leading journals.

Jing Zhang is an assistant professor at the School of Contemporary Chinese Studies and a senior fellow of the China Policy Institute, both at the University of Nottingham. She is also an executive board member of the Chinese Economic Association UK. Her research mainly focuses on globalisation, economic development, and the environment in China. Her works have been published in journals such as the *Journal of Regional Science* and *World Development*. Her most recent book is *Foreign Direct Investment, Governance, and the Environment in China* (Palgrave Macmillan, 2013).

Lei Zhao is a professor and Deputy Director of the International Relations Department at the Institute for International Strategic Studies of the Party

School of the Central Committee of the Communist Party of China. He was in charge of the projects 'Practice of Constructing a Harmonious World: China's Participation in Peacekeeping Operations' and 'Ethnic Conflict Management in an International Perspective'. His area of research and expertise covers China's foreign policy, crisis management, as well as soft power, especially China's security contribution to global governance. Articles include 'Two Pillars of China's Global Peace Engagement Strategy: UN Peacekeeping and International Peacebuilding', published in *International Peacekeeping*.

Tianyong Zhou is a professor and Deputy Director of the Institute for International Strategic Studies at the Central Party School of the Communist Party of China. He also serves as an adjunct professor at the Graduate School of the Chinese Academy of Social Sciences, the Beijing University of Science & Technology, and the North-eastern University of Finance. Zhou is a leading economist in China and is well-known for his work on the theoretical basis for socialist economic development and macroeconomics. He is the author or editor of over 30 books, including *The China Dream and the China Road* (2011).

List of Abbreviations and Acronyms

ACFTA	ASEAN–China Free Trade Area
ADIZ	Air Defence Identification Zone
APEC	Asia-Pacific Economic Cooperation
ARF	ASEAN Regional Forum
ASEAN	Association of Southeast Asian Nations
BBC	British Broadcasting Corporation
BRICS	Brazil, Russia, India, China and South Africa
CCCP	Centre for Contemporary Chinese Studies
CIIS	China Institute of International Studies
CO2	carbon dioxide
COD	chemical oxygen demand
CPC	Communist Party of China
CPPCC	Chinese People's Consultative Political Conference
CPSU	Communist Party of the Soviet Union
EKC	Environmental Kuznets Curve
EU	European Union
FOCAC	Forum on China–Africa Cooperation
G2	Group of Two
GATT	General Agreement on Tariffs and Trade
GDP	gross domestic product
HDI	Human Development Index

HSBC PMI	Hong Kong and Shanghai Banking Corporation Purchasing Managers' Index
INGO	international non-governmental organization
ISO	International Organisation for Standardisation
LSGDR	Leading Small Group for Deepening Reform
MENA	Middle East and North Africa
MEP	Ministry of Environmental Protection
NATO	North Atlantic Treaty Organization
NBS	National Bureau of Statistics
NBS PMI	National Bureau of Statistics Purchasing Managers' Index
NDRC	National Development and Reform Commission
NGO	non-governmental organization
NO2	nitrogen dioxide
NPC	National People's Congress
NPL	non-performing loans
PLA	People's Liberation Army
PM10	particulate matter 10 micrometres
PM2.5	particulate matter 2.5 micrometres
PMI	Purchasing Managers' Index
PRC	People's Republic of China
PV	Photovoltaic
R&D	research and development
RMB	Renminbi
RoC	Republic of China
SCE	standard coal equivalent
SCO	Shanghai Cooperation Organisation
SDP	Social Democratic Party
SEPA	State Environmental Protection Administration
SME	small and medium-sized enterprise
SO2	sulphur dioxide
SOE	state-owned enterprises
SSC	State Security Council
UAE	United Arab Emirates
UK	United Kingdom
UN	United Nations
UNCLOS	United Nations Convention on the Law of the Sea

UNSC	United Nations Security Council
US	United States
USA	United States of America
USD	United States Dollar
VAT	Value Added Tax
WHO	World Health Organization
WTO	World Trade Organization

List of Figures

List of Tables

1

Genesis of a Pivotal Decade

Honghua Men and Steve Tsang

As Xi Jinping took the reins of the Communist Party of China (CPC) as its General Secretary at the 18th Party Congress in November 2012, he made it clear he would take the People's Republic of China to a new stage of development—one of deepening reform. This was not just about rebalancing the economy but also about substantially improving governance and enhancing the role China would play in the world. Xi's accession to power at the 18th Congress marked the turning of a new chapter in the era of post-Mao reforms.

H. Men (✉)
School of Political Science and International Relations, Tongji University, Shanghai, China
e-mail: menhonghuacanran@163.com

S. Tsang
School of Contemporary Chinese Studies, University of Nottingham, Nottingham, UK
e-mail: steve.tsang@nottingham.ac.uk

S. Tsang, H. Men (eds.), *China in the Xi Jinping Era*,
The Nottingham China Policy Institute Series,
DOI 10.1007/978-3-319-29549-7_1

The decade under Xi's leadership, from 2012 to 2022, is going to be a pivotal one as he is determined to lead China towards national rejuvenation at a time when sustaining a fast rate of growth is becoming increasingly challenging. China's reforms have reached a stage where a crucial decision has to be made. Just prior to Xi taking over in 2012, when all Chinese leaders were reformers, it was not clear where that reform was heading or what the next stage would look like. China could stay the course or embark on an ambitious process of rebalancing the economy, with all the potential benefits and risks this would entail. As top leader Xi is not happy to rest on his laurels or muddle through. He is determined to use his decade in power to leave his mark.

As China steps into the second decade of the 21st century, it has already greatly enhanced its overall national strength. It is the second ranking power in the world by this measure or, for that matter, by economic prowess. It has become the top trading country and the fastest growing major industrial economy. But the need to rebalance the economy, after the benefits of the established model had been nearly exhausted in the decade under Hu Jintao, meant fresh impetus to sustain the economic miracle would need to be found. Full of confidence and determined to face this challenge squarely, Xi takes to heart an axiom of one of the great Chinese classics: 'Great achievements cannot be attained without ambition; success is impossible without hard work'.[1] Xi thus promptly put forth the concept of 'the China Dream' to encapsulate the ambitions he had for the country, and has since then been driving the Party hard to pursue them. There is no doubt that China faces a complex and difficult decade during which changes and challenges, both domestic and global, will be daunting. But Xi is committed to lead a rapidly rising and confident China to overcome them.[2]

By the end of the decade of his presidency, Xi intends to turn the rhetoric of the China Dream into reality. More specifically this means converting the country into a moderately prosperous society, giving the amazingly rapid economic growth a new lease of life, and preparing it to transform itself from a regional power into a superpower, or at least a leading global power. The domestic and external goals are intertwined, and reaching them will have

[1] Ctext, "The Classics of Zhou."

[2] Hu, *Minzhu juece*, 184.

profound implications, both for the country and for the world. The prospect of the Xi transformation is therefore a matter of great significance and is the central focus of this book. How it shapes China's approach to dealing with the rest of the world is the subject of Chap. 12 by Honghua Men.

Opportunities and Challenges

China is in the midst of a great transformation. It has already changed from being a regional power to a global power and is on a trajectory to become a superpower. As it does so, its global interests and capabilities are developing fast.[3] The rise or, depending on one's perspective, reemergence of China and the changes this brings is increasingly becoming a subject of great interest in the world (see Chap. 10 by Xi Xiao). Its rise from being one of the major regional powers to one of the leading global powers is making other great powers readjust strategically. This gives rise to risks and opportunities and makes the international situation more complex and complicated (see Chap. 11 by Christopher Hughes).

Under Xi, China is making the most of the capacities and progress it made in the last three decades of reform to seek new opportunities for further development and advancement. The steady improvement in the living conditions of its citizens and landmark achievements, such as becoming the second largest economy in the world, have helped the Chinese leadership to refine its objectives. What Xi's administration aims to achieve by 2022 is to double the size of the gross domestic product (GDP) both nationally and on a per capita basis, whether in the urban centres or in the rural regions. This is what becoming a moderately prosperous society is intended to mean. The Party plans to build a strong national consensus around its commitment to make the China Dream a reality, and to use this process to galvanize everyone to join the efforts to build a rich, powerful, socialist-democratic, civil, and harmonious country. This approach is meant to shape the development strategy for the next three decades (see Chap. 8 by Tianyong Zhou).

[3] Men, "Zhongguo guojia rentong bianqian," 54–66.

At the same time, Xi seeks to improve China's relations with the great powers and its neighbours. China is already the largest trading partner of nearly 130 countries and plans to build on this to promote mutually beneficial collaboration. The setback to economic advancement in the world brought about by the global financial crisis has been seized on by China as an opportunity to leave its mark. Its commitment to sustained growth has prevented the global economy from slipping further and led to it expanding its investment and interests far and wide. Since the global financial crisis, China is contributing to improvement in infrastructure and industrial capacity, not only domestically but also elsewhere through its outward investment. In its efforts to reach out, China is creating new opportunities and challenges for others.

The environment in which China needs to achieve its ambitions is tough and testing. The successful reforms of the previous three decades have also produced deep economic and societal contradictions. This is recognized by Xi:

> In development, China faces a series of sharp contradictions and challenges, which means there are plenty of problems and difficulties in the way forward. They include the lack of balance, co-ordination and sustainability in development, inadequate capacity in innovation, irrational industrial structure, the lack of clarity and precision on how to develop the country, wide disparity in development and income between the cities and rural regions, and the increase in social contradictions … To solve these problems the key lies in deepening reform.[4]

Since the 18th Party Congress, China has embarked on the journey to rebalance the economy and seek a 'new normal' for sustainable growth and development. How to do so is the crux of the matter (see Chap. 6 by Baojiang Han and Shiping Qi).

The wider international and strategic condition is even more complex. There is a gap between China's capacity to fulfil its wish to take on more international responsibilities and what the wider international community expects of it. This has given rise to suspicion about its intentions. The rise of 'the China threat' narrative and the contradicting demand that China should be 'a responsible stakeholder' has made the task more

[4] Xi, *Zhiguo lizheng*, 71–2.

daunting. As the advanced countries led by the United States of America (USA) seek to tighten rules and conventions in the international community to tame a rising China, China's neighbours also become concerned. They have consequently heightened cooperation with the USA. In other words, the more China develops rapidly, the more others suspect and worry about its intentions, and their responses in turn pose extra challenges and difficulties for China (see Chap. 10 by Xiao, Chap. 11 by Hughes, and Chap. 12 by Men).

Putting the domestic and external challenges and opportunities together, the Chinese Government still sees scope to seize the opportunities despite the difficult environment. As the celebrated poet Su Dongpo of the Song Dynasty observed: 'not letting something that lands on your hand slip away is good timing; not letting someone who passes by go unutilized is seizing the moment'.[5] Under Xi, China is taking a proactive approach, looking carefully at the domestic and international environment to make the most of the opportunities and to confront the challenges as they arise. This means staying true to the bottom line and focusing on planning at the top level, as it presses on with deepening reform across the board. This spirit was summed up by Xi in a speech delivered at the Institute for International Relations at Moscow on 23 March 2013: 'we must march in sync with progress brought about by the age we live in, which means that in the 21st century we must not retain a mind-set of the past—mentally stay in the era of colonial expansion, think the thoughts of the Cold War period or retain the zero-sum mentality'.[6]

Strategic Framework for Comprehensively Deepening Reform

Xi has advocated the upholding of the bottom line and high level planning from when he came to power. As members of the Politburo Standing Committee of the 18th Congress attended 'The Road to National Revival' exhibition in November 2012, Xi declared a commitment to implementing the China Dream. He said: 'the China dream is about turning national

[5] 360 Doc, "Xiang Yuci."

[6] Xi, *Zhiguo lizheng*, 273.

revival, the greatest aspiration of the Chinese people in the modern era, into a reality'.[7] In his conception, 'the goal of making China into a moderately prosperous society will be met by the centenary year of the CPC [2021]. The objective of transforming it into a rich, powerful, democratic, civil and harmonious modern socialist country will be met by the centenary year of the People's Republic of China (PRC) [2049]. The China dream will be turned into reality'.[8] While the Chinese leadership takes both a very long and a shorter view of strategic planning, its policies are in fact guided by the latter. This was clarified by Xi in 'the decision of the CPC central leadership on comprehensively deepening reform', in which he said 'the missions of the reform should be implemented by 2020'. This means the most important goal is that of making China into a moderately prosperous society by 2021. As Xi takes charge he is confident of the guiding principles behind reform, of the direction of reform, and of the strength of the political system (see Chap. 2 by Steve Tsang). He is also keen to make the most of China's cultural inheritance (see Chap. 9 by Yingchun Sun). Xi sees Communism and Chinese civilization as complementary, and the blending of them a great asset for national revival.

Based on the above guiding principles, the Chinese leadership is seriously pressing forward with further reform to strengthen the political system and enhance governance capacity (see Chap. 2). In November 2013, the Party held the Third Plenum of its 18th Congress and passed 'the decision of the CPC central leadership on comprehensively deepening reform'. What is striking about this document is the commitment to go beyond economic reform. Based on the needs identified at the 18th Party Congress, it outlines an overall plan for the first half of the 21st century, focusing in particular upon the coming decade. This involves a 'five combined into one' approach to deepen reform comprehensively, consisting of political, economic, social, cultural, and environmental dimensions.[9] In accordance with 'the decision of the CPC central leadership on comprehensively deepening reform', China will use economic development as the focal point to promote socialist economic construction, political development, cultural enhancement,

[7] Xi, "*Fuxing zhilu jianghua.*"

[8] Ibid.

[9] Hu, "Shenhua gaige feifan yiyi."

social construction, and environmental advancement. The leadership should deepen reform and opening up, push forward scientific development, and unrelentingly build up the material foundation for implementing the China Dream. According to Xi Jinping, 'the overall goal of the Third Plenum in deepening reform was to prefect the system of socialism with Chinese characteristics' and improve the governing system and governing capacity through modernization'.[10] The commitment to realizing this approach was reinforced at the Fourth Plenum of the 18th Congress, held in October 2014. This plenum focused on the promotion of rule by law. It issued an action plan for legal reform under which 'building a socialist legal system with Chinese characteristics and constructing a socialist country with rule by law' became the overall goal (see Chap. 3 by Lifeng Wang). This commitment to deepening reform and constructing a country governed by law is meant to deliver long term stability and good order, as well as laying the foundation for another 'thirty years of glorious development'.[11]

The Chinese Government now takes a proactive approach in international affairs, particularly over global economic governance and improving the international order. As China continues to rise it is taking on more of a leadership role—the founding of the Asian Infrastructure and Investment Bank being an example. According to Wang Yizhou, 'the raising of the curtain for domestic reforms has led to not only progressive changes within China but also a transformation of how China manages its foreign relations'.[12] Indeed, Chinese leaders have come up with new ideas that are being incorporated into the thinking of China's foreign policy establishment.

China under Xi appears more assertive to the outside world. But, as far as the government is concerned, it still adheres to a peaceful development strategy, modified by an open commitment to take a very robust stance over the territorial integrity of the country and uphold the right for the Party to decide what is best for China. When Xi was speaking to colleagues of the Politburo in January 2013, he said:

---

[10] Xi, *Zhiguo lizheng*, 104.

[11] Chi, "Fazhi Zhongguo gaige luxian," 169.

[12] Wang, "Waijiao zhanlue qige guanjianci," 22–4.

> We must steadfastly take the peaceful development road, but this does not mean we do not protect our legitimate rights and definitely not scarifying our core national interest. Any foreign power that thinks it can get China to do a deal over its core national interest is delusional. It should not think China will ever compromise on sovereignty, national security and development rights.[13]

The Chinese leadership is aware of the discomfort many other countries feel about China's rise. To reassure them it promotes the notion that all can be winners. It also puts emphasis on mutually beneficial international collaboration so that it can play greater roles in world affairs that it can comfortably perform. This is what is behind its policy to promote mutual interest, shared responsibilities, and a shared fate in international affairs (see Chap. 12). This approach manifests itself in the advocating of a new kind of great power relationship, 'the maritime silk road' and 'the silk road economic belt', now popularized as the 'one belt one road' strategy. However they are received by the outside world, they are policies designed to ensure both China and its partners benefit from its assertiveness and developing strategic partnerships among them.

The Chinese encapsulate their approach in a concept which they call 'the bottom line thinking'. What this means is that they start off by thinking about the worst case scenario but strive to get the best possible results in order to ensure they are prepared for all contingencies and hold the initiative in their hands. The Chinese Government works on the premise that the coming decade will be trying and hazardous for its reform programme but it is committed to confront the challenges squarely, hold tight to its bottom line, and keep the initiative.[14]

Five Strategic Measures for Deepening Reform

Strengthening Governance and Anti-corruption

The incorporation of a commitment to strengthen political institutions, particularly the party machinery, and enhance their efficacy into Xi's approach to deepening reform was made at the 18th Party Congress, as

[13] Xi, *Zhiguo lizheng*, 249.

[14] Du, "Shenhua gaige de fangfalun."

soon as Xi took on the leadership of the CPC (see Chap. 2). The blueprint was issued at the Third Plenum (2013), which outlined six major areas for enhancement, namely economics, politics, culture, society, the environment, and national security. In line with this approach the State Security Council was created to complement the state security apparatus, coordinate the national security strategy, and protect state security. The Leading Small Group for Comprehensively Deepening Reform was likewise formed to take charge of the overall design, coordination, promotion, and implementation of the reforms. Since the Fourth Plenum (2014) the objective is to build and strengthen the institution for 'governing the country according to the constitution' so that rule by law will prevail. This strengthening of the legal and judicial framework also implies a commitment to build what the Party sees as a harmonious relationship among the ethnic groups in China (see Chap. 5 by Lei Zhao). Since the 18th Party Congress, the anti-corruption campaign has been put in place and widened and deepened to a level never seen in the reform era to create a better political environment that will enhance governance capacity and efficacy.

Building the New Normal and Maintaining Social Stability

The concept of the new normal was put forward by Xi to guide China in striking a balance between promoting growth and environmental protection (see Chap. 7 by Jing Zhang), so that the government can improve people's livelihood and maintain stability and good order in the country. This strategic approach to rebalance the economy requires a lowering of the growth rate to between 6.9 and 7.6 % in the rest of the decade. In Xi's conception, 'in the foreseeable future, China is still in an upward trajectory … and through hard work its economy can still maintain a relatively high level of growth'.[15] More specifically, what Xi has in mind is:

> China's growth is slowing down and it is the result of government direction. To achieve the objective of doubling the 2010 per capita GDP by 2020, a growth rate of 7 % will suffice. This is based on our calculation as we drew up the medium and long term plans. We recognize that in order

[15] Xi, *Zhiguo lizheng*, 113.

> to address in a fundamental way the basic issues for long term economic development, we must resolutely implement structural reform, though this would require reducing the growth rate. In all matters we must take into account both the long and the short term requirements as we plan carefully and reflect deeply. Methods that maximize short-term returns at the expense of long-term gains are not sustainable.[16]

What the new normal means is that the Chinese leadership will steer the economy to grow at medium to high speed, with a better balance and new impetus for growth. It also implies structural reforms are to be implemented to place greater emphasis on sustainability and quality of growth, which requires scope being given to allow the market to play a decisive role so that resources are used effectively to support the government's objectives (see Chap. 3).[17] In parallel to this adjustment, the Chinese Government plans to use the law as the basic instrument to govern the country and society. It sees social justice as a core value, and its efforts to provide a safe and 'harmonious' environment for ordinary people to live and work as crucial for its policy of social governance and stability (see Chap. 6).

Uphold Core Values and Promote a Revival of the Chinese Culture

The Chinese leadership under Xi values soft power and seeks to build it by reviving elements of traditional Chinese culture and blending this with the country's socialist core values. At a Politburo study meeting in December 2013, Xi made this clear. As he sees it, to achieve the goals encapsulated in 'the two centenaries'—that of the founding of the CPC and of the PRC—or the implementation of the China Dream, China must make the most of the beauty and appeal of its civilization to enhance its soft power.[18] To Xi, a country's core values are what make soft power, and the way to promote and project socialist core values is to dress it in the civilization of China, which he believes is in the DNA of its people—something that

[16] Xi, "Yatai fenghui yanjiang."

[17] Xi, *Zhiguo lizheng*, 116.

[18] Xi, "Tigao guojia wenhua ruanshili."

determines how they think and behave (see Chap. 9). Thus, for China to transform its core values into soft power, it must project the Chinese culture as full of life and impact, one that strives to build a better future by drawing on the great qualities from a magnificent civilization.

Enhance the National Security System Through New Thinking and Institution Building

From the perspective of the Chinese leadership the complexity and challenges that China needs to face as it rises are increasing substantially. In a globalized world that is constantly evolving, the leadership finds it necessary and useful to set up a new state-level overarching body to ensure China has the capacity to enhance its national security strategy and to plan and prepare to meet whatever challenges it may face (see Chap. 10). This underpinned the creation of the State Security Council at the Third Plenum (2013), which was tasked with making and coordinating policies that affect the security of the state, as well as enhancing its capacity to respond effectively to unexpected challenges. The areas that fall within its remit include territorial integrity, maritime security, foreign affairs, military matters, resource security, the economy, and people's livelihood—the last two imply that social stability is within its remit as well. At the inaugural meeting of the State Security Council, held on 15 April 2014, Xi pointed out that its mission was to devise an approach to national security with Chinese characteristics. This requires the putting in place of a comprehensive national security strategy that treats the security of the people as its calling. The starting point of this strategy is the security of the state. Economic security is to be treated as a matter of core importance, the protection of which requires maintaining military security, social security, and cultural security.[19] Xi added the importance of building on a sustainable basis a shared Asian security framework that promotes comprehensive cooperation in the region at a meeting of the Conference on Interaction and Confidence Building Measures in Asia, held in Shanghai a week later.[20]

[19] Xi, *Zhiguo lizheng*, 200–1.

[20] Ibid., 354.

The ultimate aim of the Chinese national security strategy is to further the security and interests of the state as China marches towards superpower status and seeks to enhance global security. The coming decade is going to be a testing one for it as it advances in this direction. To succeed, the national security strategy devised is intended to meet the following objectives in the remaining period of Xi's leadership:

- To protect territorial integrity and maritime rights;
- To pre-empt independence movements and promote unification;
- To maintain or create an international environment conducive to China's policy of peaceful development;
- To defend and enlarge the scope for advancing China's strategic interests;
- To build up military capabilities to ensure the security of the state.

Advance Strategic Interests by Emphasizing Mutual Benefits

Xi takes a proactive approach to managing relations with the rest of the world. In the first two years as leader he visited 32 countries across Asia, Australia, Africa, Europe, North America, and Latin America. The message he has tried to deliver is China's commitment to seek cooperation and promote mutually beneficial ties, as well as a willingness to contribute to improving the international order and global governance. As China puts forth various proposals for bilateral relations, regional cooperation, and other developments, it incrementally asserts its right to speak on regional and global matters.

The centrepiece of Xi's new look diplomacy is the promotion of a 'new kind of great power relationship' with the USA. He introduced this concept to the world at the Sunnylands summit with American President Barack Obama in California in June 2013. This was a landmark event as Xi proactively produced a basis for developing a healthy relationship between the two leading powers. The guiding principles he presented were to avoid clashes and confrontation and to promote mutual respect and mutually beneficial relations. He intended his proposal to form the basis for reaching a consensus for forging a new kind of relationship between the two, thus avoiding the Thucydides' Trap. Scholars and analysts outside of China and the governments of its neighbouring countries do not all share or accept such an interpretation of its policy or Xi's intentions. Their reservation notwithstanding, the fact that Xi took such an initiative is significant. The relationship between China and the USA is a highly complex one, with competition and beneficial interests interwoven at every level, bilaterally, regionally, and globally. The consequences of this most important bilateral relationship being mismanaged could be dire. In making this démarche at Sunnylands Xi was presenting a formal welcome to the USA to play a positive role in the peace and development of the region, and as an effort to contribute to stability and improvement in Sino-American ties on Chinese terms.[21]

Aware that the rise of China is causing concern around the world, the leadership do try to reassure others that it remains committed to the peaceful development approach. It has reached out to European countries in particular, attempting to improve relations, promote cooperation, and move their relationship to a higher level. It is also deepening its strategic partnership with Russia and actively supports the working of the BRICS (Brazil, Russia, India, China, and South Africa) as a multilateral cooperation organization.

As to China's neighbours, Xi takes them seriously. Indeed, eastern Asia remains the strategically most important region in the thinking of the government, a reality not changed by the steady transformation of China from being a regional power to a global power. In a working meeting of the Party Central held on 24 October 2013, Xi laid down the guiding principles for managing ties with the region: insist on kindness and building friendships with neighbours, and reassure and enrich them in line with a policy of promoting closeness, sincerity, benefits, and tolerance.[22] This was translated in policy terms into a plan to upgrade relations with the Association of Southeast Asian Nations (ASEAN) through the founding of the Asian Infrastructure and Investment Bank and the building of a 'silk-road economic belt' and a modern 'maritime silk road', so that all will benefit from being part of a 'coalition of a shared future'. The

---

[21] Men, "Zhanlue renzhi,"11–24.

[22] Xi, *Zhiguo lizheng*, 297.

Chinese Government is also exploring the scope for upgrading its involvement and contribution to the region and its neighbouring countries. It focuses on the forming or upgrading of free trade areas, supporting infrastructural development in South East Asia, and potentially constructing a China–Burma–India economic corridor. Such efforts have been made to reduce suspicion and concern of China's rise among ASEAN countries, and are intended to contribute to the forging of a stable and prosperous order in the region.[23]

Contextualization

The decade under Xi Jinping's leadership is and will be an important and eventful one. The developmental progress China had made by 2012 put it in a place where its leadership had to make strategic decisions as to which direction it should move forward. The developmental approach it had followed after Deng Xiaoping inaugurated the reforms in late 1978 was by then losing steam. The 'golden decade' of the Hu Jintao–Wen Jiabao partnership marked the high point of what the old approach could deliver. The prospect of stretching and extending it for another decade was poor. The international environment was changing, the economic landscape was evolving, demographic advantages were being eroding fast, environmental pressures were mounting, public expectations were rising, and the relationships among ethnic groups were becoming testing. The Chinese Government had to take a more dynamic approach or risk such challenges getting out of hand. Whoever succeeded Hu Jintao would have found himself—there was no female successor in sight—presiding over an important and eventful decade.

By the time of the leadership succession at the 18th Congress, whether the established approach to reform could be revitalized by minor tweaking or needed to be substantially overhauled by a bold effort to make major changes was the central question that needed to be addressed. Abandoning China's chosen developmental path and adopt a Western democratic developmental model was not an option taken seriously by

[23] Men, "Dongya zhixu," 56–62.

any Chinese policy maker. But the exclusion of this as an option does not make it much easier for the leadership to decide on the strategic direction to follow.

What is defining the direction of change in the Xi decade is not the general condition of the country and the need for change, but the personality and vision of Xi Jinping himself. Whether Xi could have done what Hu Jintao did and try to keep the ship of state on an even keel without rocking it is a moot point. Xi did not consider this an option. From the time he took over the leadership of the CPC, he immediately put his own stamp on the Party and the country, and pushed hard for changes. His chosen approach was to deepen reform—not to change course but to press on way beyond what had previously been attempted in order to revitalize the reforms started under Deng Xiaoping. More specifically it means making full use of the Party as the instrument for deepening reform, for which he promptly started a rectification campaign to rid it of the ineffective and unreliable elements and strengthen its capacity to work through the anti-corruption campaign. This campaign was also launched to rally public support to his cause. Whether Xi will succeed or not, history will tell. What is certain is that Xi has already left his mark in shaping the strategic direction of China's development, be it in domestic policies or in foreign affairs.

Bibliography

360 Doc. 2015. Su Shi. Dai Hougong shuo Xiang Yuci. [online]. Available at http://www.360doc.com/content/14/0709/16/2561833_393213393.shtml. Accessed 31 July 2015.

Chi, F. L. 2015. Jianshe fazhi Zhongguo de gaige luxian. In *Zhongguo guoqing yanjiang lu*, ed. H.H. Men, 169. Beijing: Zhongguo jingji chubanshe.

CText. 2015. The classics of Zhou. In *Shangshu* (*Book of ancient documents*). [online]. Available at http://ctext.org/shang-shu/officers-of-zhou/zhs. Accessed 3 Aug 2015.

Du, F. J. 2014. Xí Jinping guanyu quanmian shenhua gaige de fangfalun. *Renminwang*. [online]. Available at http://theory.people.com.cn/n/2013/1218/c112851-23877798.htm. Accessed 10 Dec 2014.

Hu, A. G. 2013. Quanmian shenhua gaige de feifan yiyi. *Beijing Ribiao* 18 November.

Hu, A. G. 2014. *Minzhu juece: Zhongguo ji ti lingdao tizhi*. Beijing: Zhongguo renmin daxue chubanshe.

Men, H. H. 2013. Liangge daju shijiao xia de Zhongguo guojia rentong bianqian (1982–2012). *Zhongguo shehui kexue* 9: 54–66.

——— 2014. Zhongguo dui Meiguo dezhuliu zhanlue renzhi. *Guoji guancha* 1: 11–24.

——— 2015. Lun Dongya zhixu jiangou de qianjing. *Jiaoxue yu yanjiu* 2: 56–62.

People's Daily. 2014. Xi Jinping, Jianshe shehui zhuyi wenhua qiangguo zhuoli tigao guojia wenhua ruanshili. *Renmin Ribao*. [online]. Available at http://cpc.people.com.cn/n/2014/0101/c64094-23995307.html. Accessed 28 July 2015.

Wang, Y. Z. 2014. Xinyijie lingdaoren waijiao zhanlue qige guanjianci. *Renmin Luntan* 6: 22–24.

Xi, J. P. 2012. Zai canguan fuxing zhilu zhanlan shi de jianghua. *Renmin Ribao*. 1st edn.

——— 2013. Shenhua gaige kaifang gongchuang meihao Yatai – zai Yatai jinghe zuzhi gongshang lingdaoren fenghui shang de yangjiang. *Renmin Ribao*. [online]. Available at http://news.xinhuanet.com/world/2013-10/08/c_125490697.htm. Accessed 28 July 2015.

Xi, J. P. 2014. *Xi Jinping tan zhiguo lizheng*. Beijing: Waiwen chubanshe.

2

Consolidating Political and Governance Strength

Steve Tsang

By the time Xi Jinping completed his two terms as General Secretary of the Communist Party of China (CPC) in the autumn of 2022 the Party will have celebrated its centenary (2021), and the People's Republic of China (PRC) will have outlasted the Soviet Union by four years. These forthcoming landmarks are important points of reference for Xi. As China's leader he is committed to pre-empt a Soviet style implosion and to revive the Party and the country during his watch. The general direction to which he would like to take China is encapsulated in the China Dream, which he articulated in public for the first time at 'The Road to Revival' exhibition at the National Museum in Beijing, shortly after he took power in November 2012. This determination was affirmed at the Third Plenum of the 18th Party Congress held in November 2013. Although the Fourth

S. Tsang (✉)
School of Contemporary Chinese Studies, University of Nottingham, Nottingham, UK
e-mail: steve.tsang@nottingham.ac.uk

S. Tsang, H. Men (eds.), *China in the Xi Jinping Era*,
The Nottingham China Policy Institute Series,
DOI 10.1007/978-3-319-29549-7_2

Plenum (October 2014) focused on 'comprehensively advancing the rule of law', the overall objective of Xi was not changed.[1]

Essentially Xi is committed to restore China to greatness by building on 'socialism with Chinese characteristics'.[2] He is keenly aware of the weaknesses within the political system, which makes it potentially vulnerable. While Xi acknowledges the risk that the PRC could follow the footsteps of other former Communist states and implode, he does not share the worry Party leaders had in the early 1990s. Xi exudes immense confidence in China's political system and its prospects.[3] To him the system is not fundamentally weak or faulted but it needs a good shake up and a strong leadership to function as an effective machinery for governance that delivers the national revival to which he is committed. The system that he has inherited is a consultative Leninist one, which took shape under the leadership of Jiang Zemin and Hu Jintao. The focus of reforms in the political arena is to reinforce and strengthen this system, not to replace it by an alternative system such as liberal democracy or by a restoration of Maoist totalitarianism or by a dictatorship.

The term 'consultative Leninism' was first used by Richard Baum in a paper published by the French Centre for International Studies and Research in 2007.[4] I used the same term and developed it independently into an analytical framework for understanding the nature of the political system in the PRC in an article in the *Journal of Contemporary China* in 2009.[5] The same analytical framework is used in this chapter to assess the direction and scope of changes in the political sphere in the coming decade.

The changes that Xi would like to introduce in the political sphere are tied closely to the goals encapsulated in the China Dream. In essence it is about restoring China's greatness as a rich country supported by a powerful modern military. The primary instrument to deliver the China Dream is the Communist Party, which Xi plans to reinvigorate through two mutually supportive initiatives. The first is to revitalize the Party as a Leninist instrument of control and governance. The anti-corruption

[1] China.org, "4th plenary session communique."

[2] Xinhua Net, "Fuxing mubiao fenyong qianjin."

[3] Yu, "Xi Jinping the man."

[4] Baum, "Limits of authoritarian resilience."

[5] Tsang, "Consultative Leninism." 865–80.

drive is intended primarily to deliver this, in addition to restoring the reputation and credibility of the Party countrywide. The revival of the Maoist principle of 'the mass line' is adopted to enable the Party to direct public opinion and secure public support after it has ostensibly reached out to the general public for their views. The second initiative is to reassert the Party's narrative of history and reaffirm its legitimacy based on its 'great historical achievements' with the great tragedies that happened under Mao appropriately contextualized.

The consultative Leninist system Xi inherited from Hu has demonstrated its resilience. It has withstood two generational leadership successions, in 2002 and 2012, as well as a major potential crisis, as the global financial crisis of 2007–2009 threatened to engulf China. The public commitment by successive leaders including Xi to deepen reform reveals the system's inherent requirement that it must constantly adapt to sustain its resilience.

It is a system that reaffirms the basic Leninist nature of the political system as it greatly strengthens its capacity to respond to public demands, shapes public opinions, and builds up a strong sense of national pride. While this involves introducing considerable changes in the political arena, this system is meant to enable the CPC to reject Western or liberal democracy as a model for China. 'Chinese democracy' as interpreted and implemented under Xi does not tolerate any scope for the Party to lose power. When the Party refers to 'political reform' it does not imply changes that will lead to democratization as it is usually understood in Europe and North America. In the PRC it generally implies governance changes to strengthen the capacity of the Party to rule more effectively and efficiently or deepen 'socialist democracy'.

Following the analytical framework I put forth in 2009, this consultative Leninist system blends together the Leninist instrument of control with innovations from other sources.[6] It has five defining characteristics:

1. The Communist Party is first and foremost focused on staying in power, for which maintaining stability in the country and preemptively eliminating threats to its political supremacy are deemed essential.

---

[6] Ibid., 866.

2. A focus on governance reform both within the Party and in the state apparatus in order to pre-empt public demands for democratization in the Western sense of the word.
3. A commitment to enhance the Party's capacity to elicit, respond to, and direct changing public opinion.
4. A commitment to sustain rapid growth and economic development by whatever means the party leadership deems politically expedient.
5. The promotion of a brand of nationalism that integrates a sense of national pride in a tightly guided narrative that stresses the greatness of China's history and its civilization under the leadership of the Party.

Preservation of Party Leadership

Under the leadership of Xi Jinping, the Party reaffirms its right to rule on the basis that it will transform the China Dream from rhetoric into reality. The provision in the state constitution for the Party to play the leading role in the PRC remains the basic principle that underpins the political system.[7] Xi is determined that the Party will continue as the 'vanguard party' and 'guardian of the people'. As such he will ensure it maintains, indeed strengthens, its long standing capacity to deal with dissent as well as to devise and implement a development model that seeks to deliver growth, employment, stability, order, prosperity, and improved governance for ordinary people. Under Xi, the CPC will keep its Leninist structure, ethos, and organizational principles and will remain totally dedicated to staying in power and exercising supervision over the state institutions and the media.

Notwithstanding expectations that the Third Plenum of the 18th Central Committee (2013) would usher in a new phase of reform, there is a strong continuity with the pattern set over the last two decades. With the passing of Deng Xiaoping as the last strong man in the PRC in 1997, Jiang Zemin stressed that 'the whole Party must always maintain the spirit of advancing with the times and constantly extend Marxist theory into new realms … give top priority to development in governing and invigorating the country and constantly break new ground and

[7] *People's Daily*, "Constitution of China."

open up a new prospect in the modernization drive … [and] improve its Party building in a spirit of reform and constantly inject new vitality into itself.'[8] This marked the start of consultative Leninism. Xi is just as committed to making the Party adapt in order to stay in power. This is to be achieved, when the general conditions in the country are benign, by the Party supervising the government machinery in delivering improvements in governance, strengthening the authorities' narrative of developments in the country, reaching out to the general public, redressing public grievances, and improving living conditions.

In the leadership change year of 2012, there was strong pent up public discontent over the scale and reach of corruption which caught the public imagination as the powerful leader of Chongqing and Politburo member Bo Xilai was removed from office.[9] Xi clearly saw this as a major challenge to the Party's governance capacity since corruption is highly corrosive of the Party's Leninist discipline and therefore its ability to respond to challenges effectively. It is also damaging to the Party's credibility and legitimacy. Hence, Xi took up the anti-corruption cause as soon as he took over power by promptly appointing Wang Qishan, widely seen as the member of the new Politburo Standing Committee most able to tackle corruption, to spearhead such a campaign.[10] While it is questionable whether the anti-corruption drive will be able to eradicate systemic corruption, it already has a powerful salutary effect in dramatically curbing lavish official entertainment and ostentatious displays of ill-gotten wealth by officials at all levels.[11] The anti-corruption drive is essentially part of a party rectification operation designed to reinvigorate the consultative Leninist system, something Xi will keep going or even institutionalize; it should not be seen as a political campaign, which always gets wound down after a period of time.

The anti-corruption policy should reduce and contain the abuse of power but it will not change the nature of the political system. Indeed, the resultant enhancement to the governance capacity and credibility of the Party is meant to pre-empt popular demand for liberal democracy or

[8] *People's Daily*, "Three represents."
[9] AFP, "Calls for transparency."
[10] *Economist*, "A corruption fighter."
[11] Coonan, "Communist officials sidestep."

constitutionalism.[12] Under Xi, the Party will sustain a benevolent and efficient monopoly of power while it practises democratic centralism. As a consultative Leninist system China under Xi will seek to use precision or well-focused repression and inducement to eliminate or neutralize challenges to the Party as soon as such challenges are detected. This should pre-empt or reduce the need to resort to dramatic large scale or summary repression. It does not mean that summary repression as a tactic will not be applied if the top leadership should see a challenge to the security and unity of the state. This applies not only in the western regions with a heavy concentration of minorities but also to the rest of the country. The perceived rise of a serious terrorist challenge of the Islamist kind in Xinjiang following a series of bombings in Urumqi in the spring of 2014 is likely to result in the wider use of summary, rather than precision, repression there.[13] But precision repression remains the preferred option in the rest of the country.

Enhancing Governance

Consultative Leninism promotes 'good governance with Chinese characteristics'. What this means needs to be contextualized. 'Chineseness' in this formulation should not be confused with traditional Chinese culture or the original Confucian values. The traditional Chinese concept of 'the ideal government … is one which is efficient, fair, honest and paternalistic, yet non-intrusive vis-à-vis the life of the ordinary people'.[14] The last requirement contradicts the basic nature of the Party as a Leninist institution, which is about proactively leading, directing, and mobilizing the general population to support all aspects of development as the Party sees fit.

In defining good governance with Chinese characteristics the Party looks back into both its own relatively short history and China's long history for inspiration. It also examines ideas and experience from outside

[12] Zheng, "Renqing 'xianzheng' de benzhi."

[13] Xinhua, "President Xi vows punishment."

[14] Tsang, *Documentary History Hong Kong*, 5.

of China as it constructs an alternative to democratization that is suited to the 'special conditions of China'. In Xi's words, 'with regard to our cultural tradition and those from outside the country, we must make the old serve the present and those originating in the West useful for China' today.[15] Thus, while Xi advocates a revival of the Confucian tradition, Leninism—a Russian import—is deemed no less Chinese for this purpose.

A particularly important set of lessons Xi insists on the Party learning is that from the implosion of Communism in the Soviet Union and Eastern Europe.[16] Xi felt that the most essential one was that nobody in the Communist Party of the Soviet Union (CPSU) 'was man enough to stand up and resist' the likes of Mikhail Gorbachev.[17] Since he took office Xi has stressed the importance of returning to traditional Leninist discipline to pre-empt the risk of the Party following the fate of the CPSU.[18] The Party has further examined the experience of the 'Asian tiger economies' under authoritarian rule, particularly that of Singapore.[19] The final product is, however, what the Party chooses to put together regardless of their origins, which it labels as a distinctly modern Chinese approach. The Party's definition of what is Chinese is meant to be final.

The instrument to deliver good governance is the Party itself. As such it requires constant reform and updating. The Party seeks to do this by 'promoting a new generation of leaders, reformulating its ideological content, appealing to nationalist impulses in society, strengthening its organizational apparatus throughout the country, and opening the channels of discourse within the party and between the party-state and society.'[20] Such an approach, which is reinforced by increasing institutionalization and merit based promotion, has continued under Xi.

More specifically the Party has introduced reforms in the political arena aimed at enhancing its own capacity and that of the state to govern effectively. The Party uses 'a mix of measures to shore up popular support, resolve

[15] *People's Daily*, "Xionghuai daju."

[16] Fewsmith, *China Since Tiananmen*, 52–3.

[17] *China Digital Times*, "Leaked speech."

[18] Buckley, "Vows of change."

[19] Chen, "Xinjiapo Remin Xindongdang," 5–10.

[20] Shambaugh, *China's Communist Party*, 9.

local protests, and incorporate the beneficiaries of economic reform into the political system'.[21] After Hu Jintao succeeded Jiang Zemin the Party quietly started to re-emphasize selectively some Maoist ideas or practices, for example the principle of democratic centralism.[22] Hu saw a greater need for the Party to deliver social justice in order to pre-empt discontent in the countryside from developing into a major source of instability.[23] He publicly advocated that the Party should 'devote themselves in building a government "by the people, for the people", and one that ensures all Chinese enjoy the fruits of the country's economic development'.[24] He took the view that 'the biggest danger to the Party … has been losing touch with the masses' and the Party leadership must therefore 'focus on the core issue of the inextricable link between the Party and the masses'.[25] Xi has embraced this approach with a vengeance and is not promoting a full scale Maoist restoration. He can see how effective some of the Maoist mobilization and propaganda methods were and intends to make the most of them. He and his cohort who, in an important sense, inherited power from their parents are not apologetic about their inheritance and are comfortable using Maoist methods as they see fit.

Increasing Institutionalization

Consultative Leninism relies on institutionalization to make Chinese politics less volatile. The most important achievement in this regard is the introduction of an institutionalized way to manage succession. When Jiang Zemin's 'third generation' leadership handed over to Hu Jintao's 'fourth generation' leaders in 2002–2003 it was the first time that an heir apparent successfully took over as planned. This is a significant landmark as all previously anointed successors, from Liu Shaoqi to Zhao Ziyang, ended their careers in dramatic and in most cases tragic circumstances. Hu's relatively uneventful succession to Jiang set a precedent.

---

[21] Dickson, "Populist authoritarianism," 37.

[22] Wang, *Ganbu zhidu jianshe*, 354.

[23] Shambaugh, *China's Communist Party*, 114–15.

[24] *People's Daily*, "President urges improved service."

[25] Nathan and Gilley, *China's New Rulers*, 193–4.

This practice was followed and indeed strengthened at the 18th Party Congress a decade later. On this occasion, Hu passed on both the offices of General Secretary of the Party and the Chair of the Central Military Commission to Xi and formally retired. In contrast, his predecessor Jiang hung on to the latter position for two years after relinquishing the Party leadership in 2002. The period 2012–2013 was also the first time in the history of the PRC when the new party chairman and premier emerged from an agreement reached in the previous Party Congress five years earlier, and was not the result of having been anointed by a strongman. Even by the standards of the post-Mao era this is a major landmark, as Deng had in fact anointed three direct and one indirect successor. Among those directly anointed, namely Hu Yaobang, Zhao Ziyang, and Jiang Zemin, only the last completed his term of office without having been removed by fiat. The indirect successor was Hu Jintao himself.

Despite all the drama and rumours that appeared in the media ahead of the 18th Party Congress (2012) and the intensity of tough bargaining behind the scenes, the politics of succession has become sufficiently institutionalized that it is now nearly predictable, at least for the headship of the Party and of the State Council. The old practice of the paramount leader anointing a successor has now been replaced by a new one, which is still at the early stages of being institutionalized. It involves the existing top leadership collectively choosing their key successors and placing them in an apprenticeship for five years before ascending to the top offices, as General Secretary of the Party and Premier of the state. The handing over of power is not democratic in the Western sense but it is structured, stable, and basically predictable—indeed, much more predictable than possible in a democratic system. As a political system, consultative Leninism supports collective leadership with an identifiable top leader but limits (though it cannot eliminate) the scope for the rise of a strongman.

At the third plenum of 2013, Xi strengthened the institutionalization of policy making on the most important challenges the PRC will face by creating two new top level agencies. The first is the State Security Council (SSC); the other is the Leading Small Group for Deepening Reform (LSGDR). By taking charge of them personally Xi ensures that he, as the leader of both the Party and the country, coordinates and directs the most important policy issues. While Xi has already proved that he is a more assertive and powerful leader than Hu after only one year in office, he is apparently seeking to exercise such authority through the two new institutions rather than asserting himself by fiat as a strongman normally would.

Although details on how the two new agencies work in practice are not yet available, it is almost certain that the SSC will be responsible for both internal and external security. Whether internal or external security takes precedent is a moot point, as both are essential for the legitimacy and continuation of the Party in power. Internal security will in reality take precedent mainly because the PRC does not face any external threat in the foreseeable future, whereas the risk of an internal threat cannot be eliminated fully. Xi's awareness of the vital significance of internal security was fully revealed in his stress of the need to pre-empt the rise of a Gorbarchev figure and of his commitment to tighten control over the media and dissidents. In December 2013, the Party issued new guidelines to strengthen management of the media. This was for 'bolstering core socialist values and pooling positive energy to realize the Chinese dream of national rejuvenation'.[26] This focus on domestic security was reinforced by the introduction, in parallel, of an Air Defence Identification Zone (ADIZ) a month earlier. Given the implications for China's relations with its neighbours and the rest of the world, it was impossible for the ADIZ to have been introduced without Xi's approval, though there is no evidence to suggest this was the first act of the SSC. The pushback from China's neighbours to the ADIZ underlines the importance for setting up a top level coordinating body for state security. The SSC is undoubtedly intended to fulfil such a purpose in coordinating all relevant government and party organs to ensure matters of state security are implemented in accordance with the decisions of the top leadership.

Xi's taking charge of the LSGDR was formally announced at the end of 2013, and this confirmed his commitment to use the Party as the key instrument to take reform forward. The most notable change thus introduced is to assign this portfolio not to the Premier, who is primarily responsible for managing the economy, but to the Party General Secretary, whose primary focus is politics and setting the general direction of development. This represents either a diminishing of the Premiership or a new

[26] Xinhua Net, "China focus."

emphasis on reform not being primarily a technical matter of managing the economy. It is easy to see this as reflecting the former, implying a factional seizure of power, since Xi and Premier Li Keqiang do not share the same factional power base.[27] However, there is no sign of serious tension between Xi and Li over this new arrangement. It is more likely that the change reflects a re-emphasis on the Leninist tradition of the Party, in line with the trend since the 18th Party Congress. As far as can be ascertained General Secretary Xi is taking personal charge to ensure the Party will greatly strengthen its own capacity to deepen reform by first imposing tight discipline on party members, with Li keeping his position as the number two ranking leader. It implies that the top leadership under Xi intends a reinvigorated party to take the lead and direct the next stage of reform—in tune with the consultative Leninist system.[28]

Strengthening Consultative Capacity

The Party's formal commitment to and its assertion that it already practises 'democracy' needs to be put in context. 'Socialist democracy' in China requires electoral outcomes to be predictable and to deliver results approved by the Party beforehand. The chief mechanism the Party relies on to secure this is the principle of democratic centralism, which governs 'intra-party democracy'. Under Xi this mechanism is to be reinforced by 'the mass line', based on the Maoist principle of 'from the masses and to the masses'. In essence this means the Party must go to the masses or 'patriotic citizens' to collect and collate ideas from them, organize and otherwise add new input to produce a coherent and constructive set of policies, take them back to the masses, then educate and otherwise induce them to embrace such ideas as their own.[29] As far as the Party

[27] Huang, "Reform panel."

[28] Xinhua Net, "Shenhua gaige lingdao xiaozu."

[29] Saich, *Governance Politics of China*, 44. The concept of 'the masses' is essentially a Maoist concept. The nearest meaning to such a term is 'patriotic' citizens, with the Communist Party holding the right to define what 'patriotic' means. The issue of patriotism is examined further towards the end of this chapter.

is concerned its leadership 'is a fundamental guarantee for the Chinese people to be masters in managing the affairs of their own country'.[30]

Consultative Leninism is meant to pre-empt democratization as the term is understood by political scientists in the West. What it is designed to deliver is 'consultative democracy'. This is deemed 'a special advantage that China enjoys under socialist democracy', and a 'manifestation of the mass line'.[31] As is explained in a Third Plenum document, 'policy decisions are not made and implemented without first conducting widespread consultation under the leadership of the Party, which will focus on the important problems of socio-economic development, and bear in mind the practical issues of the interests of the masses'.[32] Under Xi, the Party is committed to resurrect fully the mass line.

It should not be assumed that deepening the Party's version of 'consultative democracy' that includes the reintroduction of some Maoist practices is incompatible with features commonly seen in democratization. Indeed, the Party is interested not only in expanding good governance practices but also in allowing for a greater scope for civil liberties and for political participation for the overwhelming majority of the citizenry. Dissidents who are deemed by the Party as subversive of the national interest are excluded. Indeed, they have their scope to do so more tightly restricted than previously, as the Party itself becomes more effective as an instrument to govern under Xi. But the number of dissidents in China who fall into such a category is a small fraction of the total population.

In terms of greater political participation the most important general elections in China are not those for the National People's Congress but for the Communist Party's national congress. At the 17th Party Congress, held in October 2007, the party leadership allowed 15 % of nominees to fail to get elected.[33] At the 18th Party Congress of November 2012, 9.3 % of those nominated for Central Committee membership were required to accept 'electoral' defeat, whereas the percentage was set at the higher figure of 11.3 for those nominated as alternative members of

[30] Brown, *Ballot Box China*, 40.

[31] Xinhua Net, "Shenhua gaige wenti jueding."

[32] Ibid.

[33] Thornton, "Long time coming," 8–9.

the Central Committee.[34] The government has also experimented with township level elections since the turn of the century on the basis of the experimentation with village level elections introduced in the 1980s.[35] Such developments do not amount to genuine democratic exercises as defined in the West, since the Party can and generally does secure its desired electoral outcomes, but they do enlarge the scope for election.[36]

The Party has also made a point of consulting individuals and organizations outside itself than before. Important gestures underlining the Party and the government's commitment to do so range from reaffirming the right of existing consultative institutions to criticize specific government policies, to using the new media as an opinion forum, to allowing greater scope for civil society to operate.[37] Indeed, the Party revived the Chinese People's Consultative Political Conference (CPPCC), which includes other political parties, as an institution of consultation. As such the CPPCC is now asked by top level leaders like Yu Zhengsheng 'to better exert its role as a political consultative body'.[38] Non-Communist individuals of considerable personal achievements have also been co-opted to join the central government. Dr Wan Gang, President of Tongji University, has consequently served as Minister of Science and Technology since 2007. Likewise, Dr Chen Zhu, a haematologist and Vice President of the Chinese Academy of Sciences, was appointed Minister of Health from 2007 to 2013. Although such appointments represent primarily the application of a classic United Front idea to 'attract outstanding individuals from all over for the cause of the Party and country', it was a significant step in strengthening the non-exclusive element of consultative Leninism.[39]

---

[34] Xinhua, "New party leadership elected."

[35] Shi, "Rural China," 244–6.

[36] Deliberative and incremental steps in increasing the element of elections are part of democratization. In the case of Taiwan, for example, local elections from the 1950s onwards helped the democratization process once the Kuomintang authoritarian regime under Chiang Ching-kuo accepted the need to democratize in the late 1980s, even though such elections in the 1950s were not particularly democratic or meaningful at the time.

[37] For enlarging the scope for civil society, see discussions below regarding the rescue and relief efforts during the Sichuan earthquake of 2008.

[38] Xinhua, "CPPCC play bigger role."

[39] China.org, "18th CPC National Congress."

As to the new media, which can be an important instrument for undermining authoritarian regimes, the Chinese authorities not only monitor and control it vigorously but also adopt it for consultation or reaching out to the masses. Starting in 2007 the State Council has used its official website to collect opinions on draft laws and regulations. Even top leaders prefer to project an image of accessibility via the new media. When he was Premier, Wen Jiabao maintained a presence on Facebook.[40] As General Secretary of the Party Hu Jintao held online discussions in the *Renmin Ribao*'s 'Strong Country Forum' in 2008.[41] Xi Jinping approached this differently. In an importance sense he went further by allowing photographs of him buying and eating a meal of steamed buns and sharing a table with citizens of Beijing in a local restaurant being circulated on Weibo, before it was showcased on Xinhuanet in late 2013.[42]

Xi is keen to ensure the Party plays a leadership role in directing the efforts of non-government organizations (NGOs). The approach adopted is to treat NGOs collectively like a bird in a cage. The Party is prepared to enlarge the cage as it sees fit, but a cage is nonetheless maintained. This is to give NGOs sufficient scope to operate in the non-critical realm while its ambition to extend its scope to the critical realm is contained, so that genuine civil society cannot emerge and pose a threat to the Party.[43]

Economic Pragmatism

In reiterating the Party's commitment to deepen reform and rebalance the economy, Xi has acted in line with the requirement of consultative Leninism and adhered to economic pragmatism. The 'bird cage approach' for managing the economy, as expounded by Party elder Chen Yun in the Dengist period, is still practised, though the cage has already been enlarged so much that it is not normally noticeable to most ordinary Chinese citizens. The basic principle remains that the

[40] Wen, Facebook.

[41] Danwei, "Chat with Hu Jintao."

[42] Xinhua Net, "Xi paidui mai baozi."

[43] Although the term 'civil society' is among seven concepts that are now required not to be used in universities, NGOs are not in fact banned under Xi. Lam, "Seven 'speak-not' subjects ban."

Party will enlarge the cage as long as the performance of the bird (or the economy) justifies it and it is safe to do so. But the Party will reduce the cage should it become necessary to sustain the consultative Leninist system in place. A key limitation of this approach is that it is essentially a blunt instrument, as reducing the size of the cage invariably causes unintended consequences. This being the case, the enlargement of the cage has only been allowed on a carefully calibrated incremental basis. The scale of changes so far is the result of over 30 years of carefully managed expansion.

Notwithstanding the dramatic transformation over three decades of reform, China's economy is still, by design, not a free market, though it is also no longer a command economy. It is a mixed one where private capital now has huge scope to invest in almost whatever it deems the most profitable lines of manufacturing, trade, or service provision. It is also one where state or publicly owned enterprises enjoy great privileges and government patronage, and are still subject to government direction. In a nutshell the Party has enlarged the bird cage so much that the bird has largely developed without finding itself seriously constrained by the cage most of the time. But the cage has not been and will not be removed.

As Xi leads the way to rework the strategy to rebalance the economy in the coming decade, he is exploring ways to manage the bird cage in a smarter way. There is no doubt that under Xi the Party will continue to consult the country's best economists and others with the requisite expertise, but the Leninist nature of the Party will also assert itself. The creation of the LSGDR should strengthen the capacity of the Party to control and take bolder steps forward in rebalancing the economy. This was reflected in the Third Plenum's commitment to allow the market to play not just a 'basic' but 'a decisive role in resource allocation' in order to 'give better play to the role of government'.[44]

To rebalance the economy essentially means making it much more efficient as well as less dependent on growth driven by export and infrastructural investments, and more dependent on domestic consumption and the market. This is not a new realization. When he was Premier, Wen Jiabao publicly acknowledged this. What are needed are:

[44] Xinhua, "Boost economic efficiency."

1. Widening the social safety net and raising household incomes and, ultimately, consumption;
2. Removing the distortions in relative prices—mainly in the exchange rate and input costs—to exploit real comparative advantages and make the model more robust;
3. Reducing the government's interference in the allocation of resources;
4. Liberalizing the financial system, which would allow for a more efficient and effective intermediation of savings.[45]

What is getting more pressing is for the Chinese Government to deal with the debt problems that mushroomed as a corollary of the economic stimulus packages since the global financial crisis threatened China. A majority of the loans taken out for this purpose that has matured has only been rolled over, not repaid.[46] They will need to be settled in the next few years. What it will take to rebalance the economy is not unknown to the Party. The difficulty is in implementing them without putting the stability of the system at risk.

Whether under Xi's leadership the consultative Leninist system will be able to do what Hu and Wen failed to deliver in this regard in the previous decade remains to be seen. Xi has chosen to strengthen the Party and his grip over it as the prerequisite for this endeavour. What is being put in place is a capacity to manage the enlargement of the birdcage in a smarter way. The intention is to enlarge the birdcage substantially, but not in every direction, so that the market can indeed play a 'decisive role' but without posing a threat to the integrity of the consultative Leninist system.

Nationalism as the New Ideology

The last defining feature of consultative Leninism is the promotion of nationalism as the ideological force that binds the country together under the leadership of the Party. Xi is a nationalist. His advocacy of the China

[45] Dorrucci, Pula and Santabárbara, "Growth and rebalancing," 45.

[46] Rabinovitch, "Local debt audit."

Dream takes the Party sponsorship of nationalism to a level higher than hitherto. But in so doing he is merely reinforcing an existing trend. This process started as Communism in effect ceased to function as the state ideology after 1989. This was in part a reaction to the events in Eastern Europe and the Soviet Union as the Chinese establishment feared social and national disintegration following 'the decline of the traditional ideology'.[47] It was also because the Party intended to pre-empt Western values and beliefs from captivating Chinese citizens living in an ideological void.[48] With consultative Leninism replacing the strongman politics of Deng Xiaoping, the promotion of this new ideological binding force was essential to keep the system function effectively. Xi Jinping seeks to use 'traditional faiths in the hope these will help fill a [moral] vacuum created by the country's breakneck growth and rush to get rich'.[49]

The choice of nationalism as the new, though informal, state ideology is meant to enhance the Party's capacity to stay in power by two mutually reinforcing ways: to provide a new basis for legitimacy and to serve as a new rallying force to develop a national aspiration around the leadership. After 1989 the Party 'moved quickly to position themselves as the defenders of China's national pride' and unity.[50] The historical narrative chosen for this purpose is a pan-Chinese one. It is, however, based on a Han-centric view of the history of greater China. The nationalism thus promoted encourages Chinese nationals to identify with a rising China under the leadership of the Party in juxtaposition to the West that is portrayed as being uncomfortable with the country's resurgence and historic unity.[51]

This has not been diminished under Xi despite his commitment to defend the Maoist heritage of the Party and the PRC, which should not be confused with an attempt to revive Communism as the state ideology. On the contrary Xi uses nationalism, not Maoism, as the ideological base

[47] Zheng, *Discovering Nationalism in China*, 51.

[48] Chen, "Minzu zhuyi," 74.

[49] Lim and Blanchard, "Traditional faiths."

[50] Zhao, "China's Pragmatic Nationalism," 134.

[51] The large public outburst of nationalism when the Olympic torch relay outside of China met with large scale public protests in April 2008. For a strong representation of some Chinese nationalists' frustrations, see *China Digital Times*, "What do you want."

for the Party's legitimacy. Within a month of his elevation, Xi explained to sailors in Guangzhou that the China Dream was about national revival and about building a strong country and powerful armed forces that should be totally loyal to the Party.[52] His invocation of national victimhood in China's 'century of humiliation' has led to foreign observers seeing him as unashamedly appealing to emotion.[53] As elaborated in the Party's theoretical journal, *Qiushi*, the China Dream is about 'merging the dreams of individuals with the dream of the country, of the nation, and of the people, and to put the interest of the individual, of the country, of the nation, and of the people together as a whole'.[54] This focus on national revival suggests that he is even more committed than his predecessor to use nationalism as the state ideology to galvanize the country in support of consultative Leninism.

Under Xi the Party continues to use an extensive propaganda and educational campaign to indoctrinate the people in patriotism. It is one that requires the citizens of the PRC to participate in affirming 'the rightness and acceptability of the state, its values, policies and agencies'.[55] The core of this campaign is to emphasize 'how China's unique national conditions make it unsuitable to adopt Western style liberal democracy' and how China's existing political system helps to 'maintain political stability, a prerequisite for rapid economic development'.[56] By 'reinforcing China's national confidence and turning past humiliation and current weakness into a driving force for China's modernization' the Party has transformed nationalism into 'an effective instrument for enhancing [its] legitimacy'.[57] The intention is to instil in the mind of the people a sense of pride in China and its development that is inseparable from the leadership of the Party or a strong feeling of 'my government right or wrong'. The pursuit of the China Dream and the sustaining of the consultative Leninist system require this.

---

[52] Xinhua, "Xi kaocha Nanhai jiandui."

[53] *Economist*, "Xi and Chinese dream."

[54] *QS Theory*, "Ningju Zhongguo Liliang."

[55] Kelly, "Citizen movements," 201.

[56] Zhao, "China's pragmatic nationalism," 135.

[57] Ibid.

Conclusions

Xi Jinping clearly intends to leave his mark. Since he assumed power, he has embraced consultative Leninism as the basis to build the China Dream. All the indications so far are that he will develop the potential of the consultative Leninist system to the full. He has shown that he appreciates the advantages of this system. It gives China arguably as resilient a political system as it can have without democracy, a resilience that is rooted in the capacity to control and that is inherent in what remains an essentially Leninist political machinery. It is strengthened by incorporating various consultative elements and a new ideology that has much more ready appeal than Communism. By modernizing the regime's capabilities to monitor and direct public opinion and instil a sense of patriotic duty on its citizens to support the government, the Party has built up a significant capacity to deflect public discontent away from itself. By enhancing its ability to detect challenges as they emerge and remove most of them, either by co-optation or by relatively well-focused repression, before they become major threats to the system, consultative Leninism lowers the need to resort to large scale summary repression. This, in turn, reduces exposure to risks that could destabilize the system in a fundamental way.

Xi is committed to make the consultative Leninist system work better. He understands that it is not a static system but one that needs to adapt to the changing environment so that the Party will stay in power and direct China's development. The big differences between his approach and that of Hu Jintao lies in his willingness to drive the Party much harder to make the China Dream a reality within a decade, and to take risks. Xi appears ambitious and driven. He articulates confidence in the system's ability to form the foundation for China to secure its re-emergence as a great power of the first league. He seeks to do this by reinvigorating the Party so that it can perform as a Leninist instrument for control and for directing the next stage of reform as well as for reaching out to the masses more effectively. The launch of the anti-corruption drive after the 18th Congress was but the first step in this process. Xi is committed to strengthen further the capacity and effectiveness of the Party, the state apparatus, and the armed forces, such as by the 2015 plan to reduce 300,000 officers and other ranks from the People's Liberation Army (PLA) in order to streamline its organization and strengthen its combat readiness.

As Xi asserts himself as the new leader he has not behaved like a strong man but acted in line with the consultative Leninist political system, which favours an institutionalized collective leadership. In dealing with highly sensitive and potentially divisive issues, such as the bringing of the disgraced former Politburo member Bo Xilai to trial and in the investigations into alleged misdeeds of the retired Politburo Standing Committee member Zhou Yongkang, Xi has moved with great deliberation. There is little doubt that Xi is in the driving seat but he has apparently not imposed his will on his colleagues in the Politburo and its Standing Committee in a way that would provoke an immediate backlash. What Xi has so far demonstrated is an attempt to lead from the front and yet preserve a collective leadership. He also seeks to institutionalize this by the creation of the SSC and the LSGDR. Xi will stay the course, but whether vested interests will attempt to fight back remains to be seen.

As consultative Leninism consolidates and the Party under Xi gains further in confidence and competence, it is likely to take bolder steps to deepen reform. This should imply greater scope being given to NGOs and private citizens to operate as long as they pose no challenge to the Party while the scope of dissidents to articulate themselves will be restricted more tightly. Reinvigoration of specific Maoist or highly modified Confucian ideas will be adopted where the Party believes they can enhance its ability to govern or improve its moral authority. But they will not lead to a full scale restoration of either Maoism or Confucianism as the state ideology. The bottom line remains unchanged—the dominance of the Party, even if intra-party reforms, such as greater 'inner party democracy', may appear to make the top leader more responsive to others than his predecessors. Indeed, the increased scope for debate among party leaders is one of the means through which the Party enhances consultative Leninism and improves on its development model. Xi will also maximize the value of the mass line and associated consultative elements to strengthen the Party's capacity to reach out to the masses. These considerations will drive political development in China that is meant to deliver a national rejuvenation in the coming decade.

Bibliography

AFP. 2012. Anti-corruption tsar hears calls for transparency. *South China Morning Post*. [online]. Available at http://www.scmp.com/news/china/article/1096511/anti-corruption-tsar-hears-calls-transparency. Accessed 31 May 2013.

Baum, R. 2007. The limits of authoritarian resilience. [online]. Available at http://www.stephen-t.com/pdf/the%20limits%20of%20authoritarian%20resilience%20-%20Baum.pdf. Accessed 31 May 2013.

Brown, K. 2011. *Ballot box China: Grassroots democracy in the final major one-party state*. London and New York: Zed Books.

Buckley, C. 2013. Vows of change in China belie private warning. *New York Times*. [online]. Available at http://www.nytimes.com/2013/02/15/world/asia/vowing-reform-chinas-leader-xi-jinping-airs-other-message-in-private.html?pagewanted=all&_r=0. Accessed 31 May 2013.

Chen, F. 1993. Xinjiapo Remin Xindongdang minzhu shehuizhuyi mowu jichi jiejian yiyi. *Guoji Gongyun Shi Yanjiu* 1: 5–10.

Chen, S. M. 1996. Minzu zhuyi: Fuxing zhi dao. *Dong Fang* 2: 74.

China Digital Times. 2008. My friends, what do you want from us? [online]. Available at http://chinadigitaltimes.net/2008/04/my-friends-what-do-you-want-from-us/. Accessed 2 June 2014.

———. 2013. Leaked speech shows Xi Jinping's opposition to reform. [online]. Available at http://chinadigitaltimes.net/2013/01/leaked-speech-shows-xi-jinpings-opposition-to-reform/. Accessed 3 June 2013.

China.org. 2012. Report of Hu Jintao to the 18th CPC National Congress. [online]. Available at http://www.china.org.cn/china/18th_cpc_congress/2012-11/16/content_27137540_12.htm. Accessed 2 June 2014.

———. 2014a. Communique of the 4th Plenary Session of the 18th Central Committee of CPC. [online]. Available at http://www.china.org.cn/china/fourth_plenary_session/2014-12/02/content_34208801.htm. Accessed 7 Aug 2015.

———. 2014b. President Xi vows severe punishment on terrorists. [online]. Available at http://www.china.org.cn/china/2014-05/22/content_32460524.htm. Accessed 2 June 2014.

Coonan, C. 2013. Communist officials sidestep Xi's anti-corruption efforts. *The Irish Times*. [online]. Available at http://www.irishtimes.com/news/world/asia-pacific/communist-officials-sidestep-xi-s-anti-corruption-efforts-1.1380894. Accessed 30 May 2013.

Danwei. 2008. Online chat with Hu Jintao. [online]. Available at http://www.danwei.org/internet/president_hu_jintao_talks_to_n.php. Assessed 2 June 2014.

Dickson, B. 2005. Populist authoritarianism: China's domestic political scene. David Shambaugh (2008) China's Communist Party: Atrophy and Adaptation (Washignton DC: Woodrew Wilson Center Press).

Dorrucci, E., G. Pula, and D. Santabárbara. 2013. China's economic growth and rebalancing. *ECB Occasional Paper* 142: 45.

Economist. 2013a. A corruption fighter: Calling Fire Chief Wang. *The Economist.* [online]. Available at http://www.economist.com/news/china/21574022-wang-qishan-has-one-crucial-advantage-fighting-corruption-calling-fire-chief-wang. Accessed 31 May 2013.

———. 2013b. Xi Jinping and the Chinese dream. *The Economist.* [online]. Available at http://www.economist.com/news/leaders/21577070-vision-chinas-new-president-should-serve-his-people-not-nationalist-state-xi-jinping. Accessed 31 May 2013.

Fewsmith, J. 2001. *China since Tiananmen: The politics of transition.* Cambridge: Cambridge University Press.

Huang, G. 2013. Xi Jinping to head reform panel, taking another role from premier. *South China Morning Post.* [online]. Available at http://www.scmp.com/news/china/article/1393479/xi-jinping-head-reform-panel-taking-another-role-premier. Accessed 31 Dec 2013.

Kelly, D. 2006. Citizen movements and China's public intellectuals in the Hu-Wen era. *Pacific Affairs* 79(2): 201.

Lam, O. W. 2014. Chinese government bans seven 'speak-not' subjects. [online]. Available at http://globalvoicesonline.org/2013/05/16/chinese-government-bans-seven-speak-not-school-subjects/. Accessed 2 Jan 2014.

Lim, B. K., and B. Blanchard. 2013. Xi Jinping hopes traditional faiths can fill moral void in China. [online]. Available at http://uk.reuters.com/article/2013/09/29/us-china-politics-vacuum-idUSBRE98S0GS20130929. Accessed 2 June 2014.

Nathan, A. J., and B. Gilley, eds. 2002. *China's new rulers: The secret files.* London: Granta Books.

People's Daily. 1982. Constitution of the People's Republic of China. [online]. Available at http://english.people.com.cn/constitution/constitution.html. Accessed 2 June 2014.

———. 2006. Three represents. [online]. Available at http://english.cpc.people.com.cn/66739/4521344.html Accessed 2 June 2014.

———. 2008. Chinese president urges improved public service in gov't. [online]. Available at http://english.people.com.cn/90001/90776/6359481.html. Accessed 2 June 2014.
———. 2013. Xí Jinping: Xionghuai daju bawo dashi zhuoyan dashi nuli ba xuanchuan sixiang gongzuo zuode genghao. [online]. Available at http://cpc.people.com.cn/n/2013/0821/c64094-22636876.html. Accessed 27 Aug 2015.
QS Theory. 2013. Zhongguo shehuikexue yuan Zhongguotese shehuizhuyi lilun tixiyanjiu zhongxin, Ningju Zhongguo liliang shixian weida mengxiang. [online]. Available at http://www.qstheory.cn/zxdk/2013/201311/201305/t20130527_234345.htm. Accessed 3 June 2013.
Rabinovitch, S. 2013. China confident it aced local debt audit exam. *The Financial Times*. [online]. Available at http://www.ft.com/cms/s/0/88b02c30-71c3-11e3-adbd-00144feabdc0.html#axzz2p9GgH0wJ. Accessed 1 Jan 2014.
Saich, T. 2004. *Governance and politics of China*, 2nd edn. Basingstoke: Palgrave Macmillan.
Shambaugh, D. 2008. *China's Communist Party: Atrophy and adaptation*. Washignton: Woodrew Wilson Center Press.
Shi, T. J. 2000. Economic development and village elections in rural China. In *China and democracy: Reconsidering the prospects for a democratic China*, ed. S.S. Zhao, 244–246. New York: Routledge.
Thornton, J. L. 2008. Long time coming: Prospect for democracy in China. *Foreign Affairs* 87(1): 8–9.
Tsang, S., ed. 1995. *A documentary history of Hong Kong: Government and politics*. Hong Kong: Hong Kong University Press.
——— 2009. Consultative Leninism: China's new political framework. *Journal of Contemporary China* 18(62): 865–880.
Wang, Y. 2006. *Xin shiqi Dang de ganbu zhidu jianshe*. Beijing: Zhonggong dangshi chubanshe.
Wen, J. B. 2009. [Facebook]. Available at http://en-gb.facebook.com/pages/-Wen-Jia-bao/13823116911. Accessed 12 Feb 2009.
Xinhua. 2012a. New China Party leadership elected. [online]. Available at http://www.china.org.cn/china/18th_cpc_congress/2012-11/14/content_27108963.htm. Accessed 31 May 2013.
———. 2012b. Xi Jinping kaocha Nanhai jiandui, guanmo junyan yu guanbing gongjin wucan. [online]. Available at http://bbs.tiexue.net/post_6465710_1.html. Accessed 31 May 2013.

———. 2013a. China's emphasis on market's 'decisive' role to boost economic efficiency. [online]. Available at http://english.people.com.cn/business/8456596.html. Accessed 1 Jan 2014.
———. 2013b. CPPCC urged to play bigger role. [online]. Available at http://english.peopledaily.com.cn/90785/8187228.html. Accessed 2 June 2014.
Xinhua Net. 2012. Xi Jinping, Chengqian qihou jiwang kailai jixu chaozhe zhonghuanminzu weida fuxing mubiao fenyong qianjin. [online]. Available at http://news.xinhuanet.com/politics/2012-11/29/c_113852724.htm. Accessed 30 May 2013.
———. 2013a. China focus: China promotes core socialist values. [online]. Available at http://news.xinhuanet.com/english/china/2013-12/24/c_132990379.htm. Accessed 30 Dec 2013.
———. 2013b. Shouquan fabu: Zhonggong zhongyang guanyu zhongyang quanmian shenhua gaige ruoganzhongda wenti de jueding. [online]. Available at http://news.xinhuanet.com/politics/2013-11/15/c_118164235.htm. Accessed 30 Dec 2013.
———. 2013c. Xi Jingping paidui mai baozi, jizi maidan duanpanzi. [online]. Available at http://news.ifeng.com/mainland/detail_2013_12/28/32553245_0.shtml. Accessed 31 Dec 2013.
———. 2013d. Zhonggong zhongyang zhengzhiju jueding chengli zhongyang quanmian shenhua gaige lingdao xiaozu. [online]. Available at http://news.xinhuanet.com/politics/2013-12/30/c_118771223.htm. Accessed 30 Dec 2013.
Yu, G. 2013. Beijing observation: Xi Jinping the man. [online]. Available at http://seeingredinchina.com/2013/01/26/beijing-observation-xi-jinping-the-man-by-gao-yu/. Accessed 26 Nov 2013.
Zhao, S. S. 2005–2006. China's pragmatic nationalism: Is it manageable? *The Washington Quarterly* 29(1): 134.
Zheng, Y. N. 1999. *Discovering Chinese nationalism in China: Modernization, identity, and international relations*. Cambridge: Cambridge University Press.
Zheng, Z. X. 2013. Renqing "xianzheng" de benzhi. [online]. Available at http://theory.people.com.cn/n/2013/0529/c83855-21652535.html. Accessed 29 May 2013.

3

Enhancing Credibility and Transparency Through Judicial Reforms

Lifeng Wang

At the Third Plenum of the 18th Central Committee in November 2013, the Communist Party of China (CPC) announced a decision to reform its judicial system.[1] It emphasized 'exercising jurisdiction and prosecutorial power in an independent and impartial manner in accordance with the law', and improving the mechanism for exercising judicial power. In particular, it stipulated that 'public trials and prosecutorial work must be made more transparent' and to 'press ahead with publicizing court judgment documents that have come into effect'.[2] This was an important, though not wholly new, departure.

[1] Decision on Some Major Issues Concerning Comprehensively Deepening the Reform.

[2] Third Plenary Session of the 18th CPC Central Committee, "Decision of CCCPC," 33–4.

L. Wang (✉)
Department of Political Science and Law, Central Party School, Beijing, China
e-mail: wanglf@ccps.gov.cn

S. Tsang, H. Men (eds.), *China in the Xi Jinping Era*,
The Nottingham China Policy Institute Series,
DOI 10.1007/978-3-319-29549-7_3

In a bid to create more judicial transparency, the Chinese courts had already introduced a series of reforms. For example, the Supreme People's Court had brought out several publications[3] with a view to promoting judicial transparency to 'safeguard people's rights to know, participate in, express and oversee the work of the People's Courts, protect the legitimate rights and interests of the litigants, improve the level of judicial democracy, regulate judicial acts, and promote judicial impartiality'.[4] They also aimed to 'protect fully the litigation rights of the litigants, willingly accept the supervision by litigants, take the initiative to invite the National People's Congress (NPC) and its Standing Committee to supervise its work, appropriately deal with public opinion supervision by the media, and build a fair, efficient and authoritative socialist justice system by enhancing transparency in court trials'.[5] Enhancing judicial transparency would, it was thought, improve relations between the courts and society.

In compliance with the people's requirements, the courts are expected to expand the scope, as well as diversify the forms, of judicial transparency. The Chinese courts need to strengthen their judicial legitimacy because they are facing a crisis of confidence. To counter this and build judicial credibility, it is essential to establish legitimacy. Therefore, one of the key tasks facing the courts is how to establish judicial legitimacy through transparency within the existing political framework.

'Legitimacy' is a complex concept. In that judicial legitimacy encompasses both law-based and socially recognized legitimacy, which one should we consider more important? It is generally believed that judicial legitimacy should be based on *legality*, yet legality is nothing other than law-based legitimacy, namely the procedural legitimacy of the justice system. Therefore, exemplifying the courts' search for procedural legitimacy is the fact that they (the courts) regard the regulation of judicial acts as an important objective of judicial transparency. At the same time, however, the courts also seek socially recognized legitimacy, although to a more

[3] Regulations on Strictly Implementing the System of Public Trials (1999), Several Opinions on Enhancing Transparency in Trials in the People's Courts and Provisions on Transparency in Enforcement in the People's Courts (2007), and Six Provisions on Judicial Transparency (December 2009).

[4] China.com, "Judicial Transparency."

[5] Lawtime, "Opinions on Enhancing Transparency."

limited extent. Judicial transparency is not only an important means by which the courts seek to please society and ensure judicial authority, but it is also a way of regulating the political acts of other state organs and, by promoting political reforms through social forces, ensuring the authority of the justice system within the political framework. By advocating judicial transparency, the courts are in effect seeking socially recognized legitimacy, which I shall here call 'substantive legitimacy'. In this regard, the courts need to answer a number of important questions. For example, why are they pursuing both procedural and substantive legitimacy? What value lies in establishing legitimacy, and what are its limitations? And how are the courts supposed to set about enhancing judicial transparency?

In this chapter, I first analyse the concept of legitimacy before going on to discuss the value and limitations of procedural and substantive legitimacy in the justice system. I then look at some of the problems confronting judicial transparency in China and the strategies that Xi Jinping's regime are using to enhance it.

The Meanings of Judicial Legitimacy

The Concept of Legitimacy

Judicial transparency is about legitimacy. Judicial legitimacy is essential to both the justice system and to social relations, but the concept of legitimacy is complex. In an empirical sense, judicial legitimacy exists where judicial procedures are in place and the public recognizes it as such. If a judicial authority is unable effectively to control the trial process and the outcomes of trials, such trials will be in name only and the system will be unsustainable. Society has no need for an incompetent judicial authority controlled by external forces. A judicial authority must reinforce the establishment of legitimacy if it is to acquire authority. We should not confuse judicial legitimacy with the operational capacity of the justice system, for a judiciary with relatively strong judicial capacity does not necessarily carry sufficient legitimacy. If a court has legitimacy, the trials conducted in it are in conformity with the law and the public recognizes and respects its decisions.

The importance of the concept of 'legitimacy' is self-evident. Coicaud states that 'the importance of the notion of legitimacy is recognized, as is attested to by the fact that the observers of political life cannot prevent themselves from referring to it. But this recognition goes hand in hand with a reluctance to broach the question of political judgment'.[6] As Habermas commented, 'political theories occupied themselves with the issue of the rise and fall of legitimate domination, at the latest since Aristotle, if not since Solon'.[7] Although the concept of legitimacy is frequently used, it has very vague meanings and there is a lack of clear definition.[8] From a descriptive viewpoint, however, legitimacy at least highlights that one cannot rely on coercive power alone to sustain a regime. There is a vast difference between a regime that the people recognize wholeheartedly and one that forces them to obey its authority—the former has legitimacy, the latter does not. Political practices in human society show that, although political domination is inseparable from violence or material force, resorting to violent coercion alone only achieves a temporary conquest, rather than effective long-term domination. Any kind of coercive force has to be tested against the criteria of legitimacy, otherwise it will degenerate into violent coercion, which means that its effectiveness will not last. Therefore, stable authorities are always seeking to legitimize their domination. Only by establishing legitimacy can coercive power become a meaningful and legitimate form of state power.

'Legitimacy' refers mainly to the fact that people recognize the political power. It conveys two levels of meaning—being legitimate and being legal. Being legitimate means to conform to established legal norms based on the doctrine of legal positivism. It also, however, implies the people's support of and loyalty to the political power because of its compliance with value-based norms, which goes beyond legal positivism. As Habermas noted:

---

[6] Coicaud, *Legitimacy and Politics*, 1–2.

[7] Habermas, *Communication and Evolution*, 186–7.

[8] Przeworski believes that the notion of legitimacy is so vague that it lacks any substantive content, and therefore should be abandoned(Przeworski, *Transition to Democracy*, 47–63). Stillman also points out that the concept of political legitimacy needs to be reviewed, because people have not been aware of the significant arbitrariness and prejudice contained therein (Stillman, "The Concept of Legitimacy", 32–56).

> Legitimacy means that there are good arguments for a political order's claim to be recognized as right and just; a legitimate order deserves recognition. Legitimacy means a political order's worthiness to be recognized. This definition highlights the fact that legitimacy is a contestable validity claim; the stability of the order of domination (also) depends on its (at least) de facto recognition.[9]

However, 'if belief in legitimacy is conceived as an empirical phenomenon without an imminent relation to truth, the ground[s] upon which it is explicitly based have only psychological significance'.[10] From the above discussion it is clear that legitimacy entails a value judgement from a normative perspective.

It must be pointed out that, although legitimacy has a normative value orientation, it does not simplistically refer to the idea of conformity to a particular value. Undoubtedly, all societies have their established values, but legitimacy cannot be inferred by relying solely on such values. Parsons argues that any action relies on established norms, values, and belief systems;[11] however, these are abstract, general, and imperfect, therefore they may not be used as guidelines for specific actions under particular circumstances and conditions. Parsons defines 'legitimation' as a process by which actions in specific situations are appraised in terms of established values, norms, and beliefs that are based on specific provisions under particular situations.[12] For an action to be recognized by others, it must be explained with the aid of established beliefs, values, and norms. In fact, such an explanation may not be related to the true motives of the action, but rather its purpose is only to allow the action to be accepted by others. Therefore, legitimacy cannot be acquired by purely relying on established beliefs, values and, norms, but can only be achieved when the specific situations under which established beliefs, values, and norms are applicable have been taken into consideration. It should be clear from the above that the establishment of legitimacy is a dynamic process rather than just a set of static values. All societies have their established values,

---

[9] Habermas, *Communication and Evolution*, 206.

[10] Habermas, *Legitimation Crisis*, 97.

[11] Parsons, *Structure and Process*.

[12] Ibid., 175.

but relying on these alone will not infer legitimacy. For an authority to have legitimacy, it is essential to consider the relationship between established values and the specific social context. It is of paramount importance to recognize the above argument, otherwise the emphasis on legitimacy will collapse into dogmatism and a resultant crisis of legitimacy.

Procedural Legitimacy of the Justice System

Law plays a decisive role in modern societies where the procedural legitimacy of the justice system is mainly manifested in the form of 'legality'. The rule of law is the most important basis on which legitimacy is established in modern Western societies. This is what Weber defines as 'rational-legal authority'. 'Rules are a potent resource of legitimating power. They fix with precision the scope and limit of official authority, thus offering seemingly clear tests of accountability.'[13] The very nature of the rule of law establishes legitimacy for authorities to exercise their power. The public can express its level of recognition and obedience to the political and legal systems by assessing the deviation between individual actions and the legal rules prescribed by the state, based on their inner value systems. In view of the value of the legal system, the public can also understand why the state is entitled to regulate individual actions by exercising its power. Weber believes that in today's Western society, 'the most common form of legitimacy is the belief in legality, the compliance with enactments which are formally correct and which have been made in the accustomed manner'.[14] Under rational-legal authority, the political consensus is mainly achieved between the ruling regime and those being ruled by way of procedures and systems. If a political decision is made, or an action taken in accordance with established systems and procedures, and the operation completed through the prescribed channels, it is naturally legitimate to comply with and support such a decision or action. Whether the people support a judicial authority depends on how it is run, how orders are made, and the nature of the procedures and outcomes. What kind of judicial processes are needed to acquire legitimacy?

[13] Nonet and Selznick, *Law and Society*, 68.

[14] Weber, *Economy and Society*, 37.

Well, it all comes down to passing judgments in accordance with the law and insisting on procedural fairness. Procedural fairness, that is legality, is the most important factor in winning people's support.

Why is law so important for a modern political authority? The Weberian interpretation is that the transformation from a traditional to a modern society is a process of secularization and rationalization, as well as a process during which people become disenchanted with former world views. In a secular society, the law has to be evoked to defend any social order. The formal rules and procedures embedded in the legal community are sufficient to legalize political decisions. The law itself requires no further legalization; it does not even need substantive support. Fuller identified eight principles about laws: (1) they must be designed in a manner that can generally be applied; (2) they must be widely promulgated; (3) they should be prospective rather than retroactive; (4) they must be clear; (5) they must be non-contradictory; (6) they must not impose impossible standards; (7) they should remain relatively constant; and (8) there must be congruence between the actions of law enforcement officials and the laws.[15] From the above characteristics, it is clear that the fundamental feature of the rule of law is that it overcomes arbitrariness. One of the main reasons why a judicial procedure fails to realize its prescribed functions or has limited effects is that the system lacks adequate authority, with the result that the rules are not strictly and conscientiously implemented. To achieve greater judicial legitimacy, the actions of the judicial authority should be legalized and judicial actions strictly regulated.

The procedural legitimacy of the justice system is important because the latter is stable and constant. Judicial actions should consist of predictable judicial decisions based on a stable system rather than on the interests of individuals or on a utilitarian calculation of benefits. A judicial action is not stable if it is built on utilitarianism, or if a judicial decision is accepted only because it is beneficial to the community. This is because changes in people's interests always occur faster than the interests of a stable system. Rather than inclining towards the changing interests of various parties, a judicial authority needs to rely on a stable legal system to maintain long-term legitimacy. How can a stable judicial

---

[15] Shen, *Modern Western Jurisprudence*, 58–62.

system be created? Douglas suggests that the fundamental principle in creating stable concepts or institutions is the naturalization of social classifications so that they become normal, undoubted, and acceptable. After being naturalized, institutions become part of the universe and are therefore ready to stand as the grounds of argument for other issues.[16] Douglas discussed three specific mechanisms for achieving naturalization, namely that institutions should (i) confer identity and shape people's thinking habits, (ii) enable social groups to remember and forget, and (iii) make classifications and put things into different categories. Once law becomes a faith, the legal system will attain stability and, quite naturally, the justice system will acquire long-term legitimacy.

Procedural legitimacy of the justice system is very important because it emphasizes the value of procedural fairness. As social value systems become more diverse, the importance of procedures as the basis of judicial legitimacy becomes increasingly more apparent. Without procedures, it is impossible to achieve a fair justice system and judicial adjudication becomes out of the question. Judicial legitimacy not only implies that the community desires, or at least accepts, the result of a judicial ruling, but also that such a result is achieved through certain procedures that are acceptable to the community. Procedural fairness is of paramount importance. Some judicial decisions may achieve the desired social influence, but if the procedural rules have been violated, such judicial actions will lack legitimacy. Conversely, a judicial action that follows the procedural rules may be ineffective if it fails to achieve satisfactory results; but, nevertheless, it will have legitimacy.

Legitimacy is based on people's subjective evaluation of the judicial process. When the public evaluates the legitimacy of judicial actions, its main concern is whether the procedures used in reaching judicial decisions are fair. The judicial outcomes themselves are not the psychological basis on which legitimacy is evaluated.[17] Procedural fairness is the most important principle of judicial actions. It means that people can participate in the procedures in an equal manner and that the procedures

---

[16] Douglas, *How Institutions*, 82–3.

[17] The reason why gamblers accept the results regardless of winning or losing the game is because gambling has fair procedures. See Rawls, *A Theory of Justice*, 80–3.

are transparent. Therefore, the legitimacy of China's judiciary should centre on the procedural fairness of the justice system. Only by acting fairly and in accordance with the procedures and rules can the judiciary acquire legitimacy.

It is evident that procedural legitimacy is very important and rests on some kind of established judicial system. Hamilton et al. pointed out that:

> The judiciary, on the contrary, has no influence over either the sword or the purse; no direction either of the strength or of the wealth of the society; and can take no active resolution whatever. It may truly be said to have neither force nor will, but merely judgment; and must ultimately depend upon the aid of the executive arm even for the efficacy of its judgments.[18]

The above assertion acknowledges that the legitimacy of the judicial system is very important and does not come from external coercive forces, such as violence or financial power, but from a specific system based on the principles of democracy, neutrality, and impartiality. Similarly, judicial legitimacy does not come from elections, for it is not based on majority rule. In this sense, the will of the people or public opinion must not influence judicial judgments. Judicial legitimacy has to come exclusively from the fact that the people have voluntarily accepted it. It is self-evident that every citizen has a moral obligation to obey judicial decisions.

Although procedural legitimacy is a vital part of the establishment of judicial legitimacy, we must recognize that it also has its limitations. From the perspective of *law as it ought to be*, too much emphasis on the procedural legitimacy of the judiciary may eventually move towards legal positivism. However, legal positivism cannot explain how positive laws acquire legitimacy and is likely to equate legitimacy with legality. Therefore, the limitations of procedural legitimacy have to be recognized. The laws upon which the justice system is based can only acquire legitimacy if they reflect values the public recognizes and cater for the interests of the community. As Unger noted, 'some precautions are needed at the outset. First, formality is always a matter of degree: law is never purely

[18] Hamilton, Madison and Jay, *Federalist Papers*, 391.

formal, nor can formality ever vanish'.[19] He discussed the limitations of formality by examining the relationship between formality and equity:

> The more equity is sacrificed to the logic of rules, the greater the distance between official law and the lay sentiment of right. As a result, the law loses its intelligibility as well as its legitimacy in the eyes of the layman; he knows it either as a chest of magical tools to be used by the well-placed or as a series of lightning bolts falling randomly on the righteous and the wicked.[20]

Therefore, procedural legitimacy is not equivalent to legitimate procedures or legitimacy. All judicial systems require procedures and legal forms to a certain extent, but for a judicial authority to be recognized by the people, substantive legitimacy must be considered.

Substantive Legitimacy of the Justice System

It is widely believed that judicial legitimacy arises from compliance with established procedures and legal principles; however, this is far from satisfactory in a sociological sense. Judicial legitimacy cannot simply be understood as legality, nor can it be classified as being purely an issue of judicial procedures. From a sociological perspective, in addition to adhering to procedural fairness, the courts should present an image to the public of being fair and impartial during trials. This depends on both the ability of the court to present its fair image, and on the public's perception of, and preference for, what constitutes a fair action by the court. As stated in the documents published by the Supreme Court, justice should be 'visible justice', judicial efficiency should be 'efficiency that can be felt', and judicial authorities should be 'authorities that have been recognized'.[21] Not only does a judicial action need to be fair, but such fairness should also be visible and felt. Therefore, judicial legitimacy involves both procedural and substantive legitimacy. The notion of substantive legitimacy refers to

[19] Unger, *Law in Modern Society*, 190.

[20] Ibid., 191.

[21] Lawtime, "Opinions on Enhancing Transparency."

the public perception of the judicial system, and such perception relies on judicial democracy. In modern democratic societies, judicial legitimacy must be established through designated procedures or mechanisms if it is to achieve transparency and prudence, and it must meet the needs of the public. That democracy is being increasingly considered as a factor of judicial legitimacy means that the values and beliefs of the citizens must be taken into account when making court judgments.

The focus of substantive legitimacy is judicial democracy. Judicial legitimacy is mainly manifested through people having real faith in the judicial authority, or giving de facto recognition to the judiciary through their actions. Democratic discourses and democratic procedures thus become the most powerful evidence of these conditions. In a rational modern society, where 'God has died' and the sanctity of religion can no longer be relied on to justify the legitimacy of modern politics, democracy is taking over. Historical evidence suggests that, throughout the 20th century, democracy had become a universal value as well as the main driving force behind political and social development in the world. Democracy is not a perfect system, for social inequality in the real world hampers its realization. Participatory democracy and deliberative democracy are constantly emerging, but political legitimacy is the reason why democracy has continued to thrive. There is a Chinese saying that 'win the people's support and you will win the world'. In today's world where the concept of equality is deeply rooted, it is very difficult to win people's support and sustain it in the absence of democracy. Therefore, democracy must be incorporated into the system to establish judicial legitimacy and harmonize the relationship between the judiciary and society, with an emphasis on judicial democracy.

Taiwanese scholar Lian-Gong Chiu asserts that judges should serve the litigants, and so must step down from their 'pedestal' to do so. This is a system in which the judiciary is meant to serve the public: the judges are regarded as the litigants' servants and the justice system is perceived of as warm and humane.[22] The courts are places where people come to resolve disputes; in other words, they are the courts of the people. Because the people grant the judges their jurisdiction, they should exercise it for the

[22] Chiu, *Judicial Modernization*, 17.

people's benefit. As such, the judges must abandon the principle of *ex officio* in terms of their professional ideologies. They must respect all parties involved in the litigation and treat litigants from all parties equally, if they are to achieve real transparency at every stage of the trial rather than superficial transparency aimed at litigants.

Substantive legitimacy, which deals with the relationship between the judiciary and society, requires judicial neutrality. The logic of the justice system is that the courts and litigants from both sides form a triangle during the dispute resolution stage. Such a relationship is subject to continuing tensions because the courts are always under pressure from the litigants. Ideally, the courts should act independently as a third party and acquire legitimacy through their judgments. However, a court has to decide which side to support, so it cannot satisfy the litigants on both sides. Judicial neutrality becomes particularly important under such circumstances, which is why it forms the basis of judicial legitimacy.

Substantive legitimacy also requires the courts to be responsive; in other words they need to demonstrate their openness to society through judicial transparency and open procedures. If they adhere to these standards, the courts acquire legitimacy and the judicial system becomes more democratic. Courts of law must always remember that judicial legitimacy originates from judicial neutrality and not from punitive forces, elections, or fiscal policies. Therefore, the establishment of judicial legitimacy should be based on fair procedures rather than on external power. As a system or power built on a thin definition of democracy, the judiciary must be responsive. In a democratic society, the justice system should incorporate responsive courts and respond to the needs of society in a timely manner.

It is evident that judicial transparency is essential to achieving substantive legitimacy. Generally, public trust in the judiciary depends on the extent to which procedures are predictable, which in turn depends on how transparent and stable they are. Decisions made through predictable and controllable procedures are more likely to be accepted. Although fair procedures do not necessarily result in fair outcomes, they are under normal circumstances more likely to produce fairer outcomes than opaque ones. This is because the fairness of litigation procedures ensures that all parties to the litigation are able to participate equally in the process, thus protecting the dominant position of the litigants and allowing them to accept the legitimacy of the judgment. Fair procedures are manageable, transparent, and able to be monitored. They are the prerequisites to achieving substantive fairness because they can restrict the self-expansion of jurisdiction and reduce interference in judicial judgments from extra-legal influences. The level of judicial transparency and the commitment to achieving it directly determine whether the public perceives the justice system as fair and just. As the German jurist Gustav Radbruch commented:

> The series of principles adopted in litigation, including the adversarial principle, principle of orality, principle of direct trial and principle of concentration, in essence boil down to transparency. In particular, they need to be supervised by the press and the parliament. Judicial transparency should not be aimed at supervision only. The fact that the public are actively involved in legal activities will gain people's trust in the legal system. Meanwhile, such trust is the prerequisite for them to participate in these activities, such as jury trials, autonomy and the parliamentary system.[23]

In summary, although different people interpret the concept of legitimacy differently, judicial legitimacy undoubtedly involves institutional legitimacy in cases where complying with a system is the only means of acquiring legitimacy. Not only should the courts respect procedural fairness, but they should also show society that they do. As a form of political power, the justice system is weak and neutral in that it has to build its image of impartiality and neutrality through procedures. As such, the only way forward is to promote a prudential and transparent judicial system through judicial transparency.

Characteristics and Challenges of Judicial Transparency in China

Characteristics of Judicial Transparency

Because of the value of judicial transparency in enhancing judicial legitimacy, since 2009 the Chinese courts have been actively exploring new ways to push judicial transparency towards all round transparency, full procedural transparency, and substantive transparency.

[23] Radbruch, *Introduction to Legal Science*, 125–6.

The first stage is to advance from procedural to substantive transparency. Procedural transparency involves admitting members of the public to hearings in public galleries and allowing them to access the judgment papers of cases held in a closed court. It also entails permitting journalists to report the cases openly in the media. Substantive transparency involves granting the public open access to information, such as admissible evidence, findings of fact, and judgments on liability. To implement these reforms, the courts are gradually improving their methods of pre-trial evidence exchange and regulating the way judges are able to control actions during trials. This is with a view to enabling the litigants to present disputed facts, adduce evidence, and have a full debate on disputed matters and liabilities in court in an open and comprehensive manner. A system whereby witnesses in criminal cases are required to give evidence in court has also been developed and now, to ensure transparency and objectivity in evidence submission and cross-examination, key witnesses and expert witnesses must attend court. Four procedures on public hearings[24] have been enacted and implemented. These stipulate that reviews of major litigation matters involving retrial applications submitted by litigants, objections to enforcement actions, requests for state compensation, and applications for reduced sentences and parole for offenders shall all take place in public hearings. The purpose of having open, transparent, and equitable hearing procedures is to protect the litigants' rights to know, participate, and oversee, to safeguard the litigation rights of the litigants effectively, and to defend the interests of all parties involved in the litigation in an equal manner.

The second stage is the move from transparency in the litigation process to transparency in the grounds for reaching judgments. The former entails elucidating the specific stages of the litigation process, including initiating the court case, submitting evidence, and the court debate. The latter consists of ensuring that the process of reaching decisions, the reasons for making those decisions, and the grounds on which they are made become more transparent. This is to ensure that the litigants are fully informed and aware of the procedures throughout the process. Some courts have laid down their opinions on how to resolve several important

[24] These include regulations on the application for a public hearing or for rehearing cases.

issues concerning the paperwork arising from the court's judgments. These include the stipulation that the judgment papers should fully reflect the hearing procedures of the cases, should accurately summarize the disputes between the parties, and fully elucidate the grounds for determining whether or not evidence is admissible. They should also clarify how facts are obtained and describe the basis on which laws are applicable; if the litigants are to understand exactly what is going on they need access to a proper analysis of the laws and regulations in language that is easily accessible to them. There is also a case for regulating the interpretation stage of the hearing process by requiring judges to provide full and reasonable explanations during case hearings, regardless of the type of case, how it is closed, or what queries the litigants have raised. This is to ensure that the litigants are 'able to make sense of the decisions' and are 'fully aware of the reasons for winning or losing the case'.

The third stage is to advance from open access to information to litigation guidance. There is a clear need to revamp the judicial concepts and replace the narrow pursuit of an authoritative judgment with a more people-oriented approach to justice. It is also necessary to change working methods by replacing the old inquisitorial system based on an *ex officio* authority with an adversarial system emphasizing litigation guidance. In addition to keeping the litigants informed of the litigation matters and workflows, it is necessary to take active measures to provide guidance, for instance by distributing leaflets on litigation risks and regulating the way information is divulged and interpreted. This is to ensure that litigants are well informed of their rights and obligations as well as the risks at various stages of the case's initiation, preservation, hearing, and enforcement. By helping litigants exercise their rights properly, such as the right to apply for relevant persons to be excluded to avoid conflicts of interest and the right to appeal, it is hoped that unfavourable outcomes caused by the litigants' lack of knowledge can be largely prevented.

The fourth stage of introducing transparency is to take it from court trials to judicial affairs. There should be more transparency in trial procedures, processes, outcomes, and the grounds for making decisions. More transparency in judicial affairs would allow the public to participate in the proceedings in a better informed, more appropriate, and timely manner and would ensure a more equal and more efficient distribution of legal aid. Relevant measures include:

- Providing case updates via a quick search service to keep litigants abreast of information relating to their cases;
- Hearing processes and case transferrals;
- Regularly publishing the names of retired staff and lawyers excluded from making legal representation in particular courts (this is to guarantee the right of litigants to apply for the exclusion of certain relevant people);
- Posting notice of a hearing on the Internet so that the public can observe cases when the court is sitting;
- Helping litigants make enquiries by providing them with the office phone numbers of the judges in their cases and posting the duty officer contact numbers of all courtrooms and other service departments on the Internet;
- Providing the public with prompt information about trial updates and other relevant matters by holding news conferences and broadcasting information on the Internet.

The fifth and final stage is to proceed from granting the litigants full rights to information to allowing open access to the public. The former allows the litigants to retrieve the relevant information and to participate fully and effectively in the proceedings, whereas the latter allows the wider public to access and scrutinize the judicial work. The following measures are under consideration:

- Establish working mechanisms such as allowing the public to observe cases freely when the court is sitting;
- Invite appropriate people to observe case hearings;
- Raise public awareness of the laws and regulations;
- Fully implement jury supervision and law enforcement supervision by electing people's jurors and appointing special law enforcement supervisors;
- Provide updates on trials in a timely, objective, and comprehensive manner by actively exploring different ways of publicizing legal activities, such as live coverage of trials, webcast and newspaper articles;

- Enhance the transparency and credibility of judicial work by publishing judgment documents of closed cases on the Internet.

Challenges Facing Judicial Transparency

For more than a decade now the Chinese courts have been introducing reforms with a view to improving judicial transparency. A publication entitled *Essentials of the Five-Year Reform Programme for the People's Courts* proposed the full implementation of a system of public trials. Since then, the Supreme People's Court has published a number of other documents on the subject.[25] Transparency in court trials has advanced considerably since the days when it was confined solely to public hearings. In 2013, the Supreme People's Court brought out several publications with a view to implementing the decisions of the Third Plenary Session of the 18th CPC Central Committee.[26] Although the reform on judicial transparency is in full swing and has made significant progress, it still faces social, political, and technological challenges.

The social challenges, in the form of doubts about judicial credibility and the public's unwillingness to recognize the courts, are rooted in the conflicts accompanying the transitional period and the increase in public political participation that the Internet age unleashed. In fact, society's lack of respect for the judiciary and defiance of the law have become matters of concern, with the number of court cases across China more than doubling from 825,405 in 1992 to 2,508,242 in 2010. At the same time, the compulsory enforcement rate of the courts remains at a high level of around 20 % (see Fig. 3.1). Fuelled by 'a primitive sense of justice', public dissatisfaction with court decisions will always, to a greater or lesser extent, raise questions about judicial legitimacy: the public cannot help but suspect the presence of judicial corruption and wonder about

[25] These include Regulations on Strictly Implementing the System of Public Trials (1999); Several Opinions on Enhancing Transparency in Court Trials in the People's Courts (2007); Provisions on Transparency in Enforcement in the People's Courts (2007); and Six Provisions on Judicial Transparency (December 2009).

[26] Several Opinions on the Effective Implementation of Justice for the People; Vigorously Strengthening a Fair Judiciary and Continuously Enhancing Judicial Credibility; and Opinions on Promoting the Construction of Three Major Platforms of Judicial Transparency.

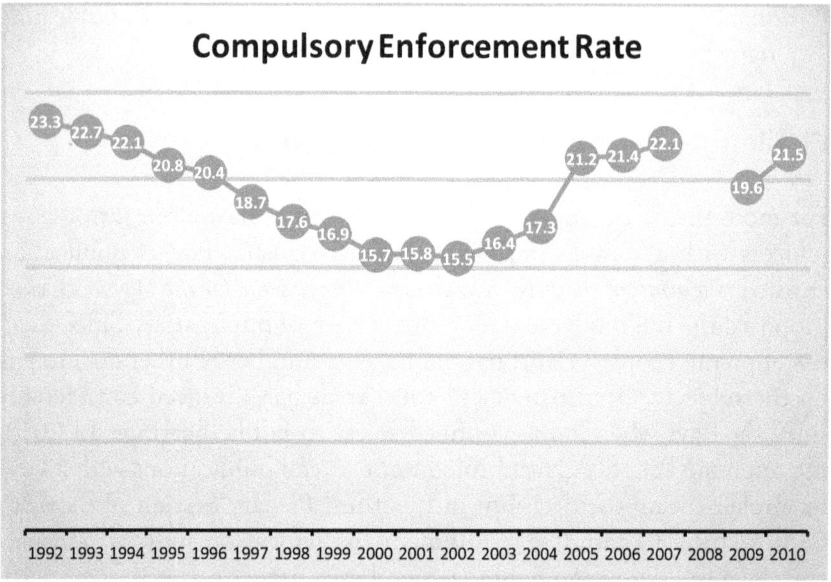

Fig. 3.1 National compulsory enforcement rate of the courts, 1992–2010 (%)

its independence. In other words, society has lost faith in its legal system; the issue is about legal culture and the establishment of a society based on the rule of law. The judiciary and society have a shared responsibility to tackle the low credibility of the laws and the justice system. The only way to retrieve such credibility would be through the joint efforts of the state and society, through practising the rule of law and extensive education.

On the second issue of political challenges, judicial transparency undoubtedly not only has a significant effect on judicial trials and judicial administration, but it also impinges on judicial politics. Since the 16th National Congress of the Communist Party of China, 'exercising state power in accordance with the law' has become the fundamental mode of governance of the CPC in the new historical period. What has always been a difficult issue is the need for careful consideration about how to improve the way the CPC leads the judiciary to achieve the organic unity of the principle of 'ruling the country in accordance with the law' and adherence to CPC leadership. On the one hand, the concept of judicial transparency has impinged on the judicial and political systems as it helps the judiciary resist interference from external political forces. On the other hand, judicial transparency inevitably calls on the CPC and judiciary to adopt new leadership styles. In terms of the scope and mode of judicial transparency, the Party Committee and Politics and Law Commission make recommendations in accordance with the law rather than interfere with individual judicial cases. Therefore, in the context of 'exercising state power in accordance with the law', the impending task is to resolve the problems in the judicial system brought about by judicial transparency and further promote judicial reforms.

The third issue concerns technological challenges. With the advent of the Internet age, achieving an open and transparent trial process via online broadcasting is not only an objective requirement of justice, but also a new requirement. Now the public is supposed to participate in the justice system, understand justice, and supervise the judiciary. At present, although many courts have opened accounts on micro-blogging sites to publish information, overall the courts are reacting slowly to the rapid development of the new media.

The judiciary faces a major dilemma in attempting to achieve transparency in this new situation, for it has to maintain neutrality while simultaneously considering online public opinion. In the light of this, the courts should consider how to manage online public opinion about unforeseen events and how to enhance public confidence in the judiciary via micro-blogging.

The fourth issue is in relation to judicial challenges. By examining first-instance judgments[27] between 1987 and 2010, almost 3 % were deemed to have been wrongly judged, as ruled by second-instance trial judges (see Fig. 3.2). The rehearing correction rate[28] of criminal retrial cases jumped from 26.1 % in 1988 to 54.9 % in 2010, while the statistics for civil rehearing cases multiplied from 18.9 to 50.6 %, and the rehearing correction rate of administrative rehearing cases increased

[27] The error rate of first-instance judgments is the ratio of all cases where amended sentences, retrials, or settlements via mediation took place to the total number of closed first-instance cases, which reflects the quality of judgment in the first-instance cases.

[28] The rehearing correction rate is the ratio of all closed rehearing cases where amended sentences, retrials, or settlements via mediation took place to the total number of closed rehearing cases, which reflects the quality of judgment in first-instance, second-instance, or rehearing cases.

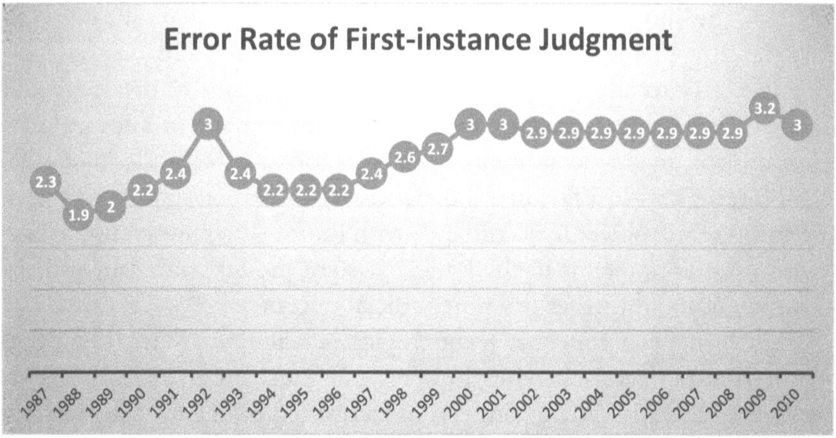

Fig. 3.2 Error rate of first-instance judgments by the courts, 1987–2010 (%)

from 17.8 to 36.6 % (see Fig. 3.3). The number of rehearing cases rose more than 3.9 times from 1,168,715 in 1988 to 5,730,722 in 2010.[29] The high judgment error rate and rehearing correction rate indicate that the judgments are of substandard quality. It also reveals the underlying reality of judicial corruption or the lack of operational capacity of the judiciary. This creates a huge challenge for judicial transparency, especially open access to court case files.

The Principles of China's Reform on Judicial Transparency

China's reform on judicial transparency should uphold the following principles. First, the leadership of the CPC must be upheld. In China, the historical tasks of the Chinese nation and the advanced nature of the CPC are what determine the leadership and governance of the latter. Only by being reassured of the power of the CPC can China successfully

[29] The data cited in this report are obtained from
Law Yearbook Editorial Committee,
Law Yearbook of China.
Zhu, *Towards Pluralist Legal Practice.*
Zhu, *Professionalization of Legal Workers*, unless otherwise specified.

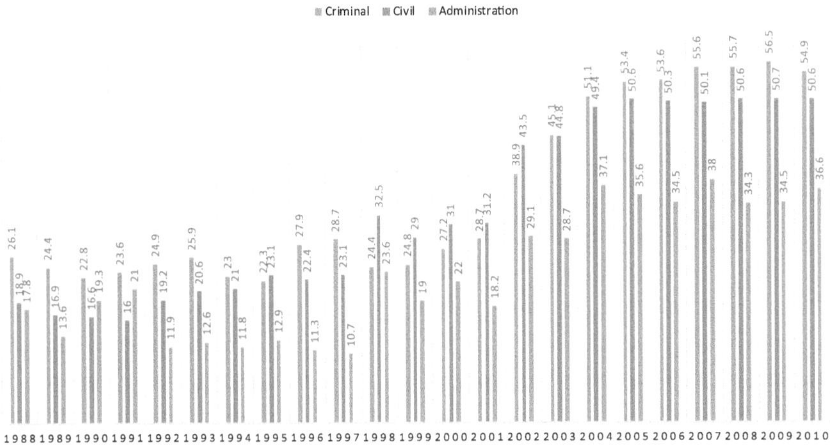

Fig. 3.3 Rehearing correction rate of the courts, 1988–2010 (%)

realize its various modernization tasks.[30] On the one hand, reforms or system improvements in the judicial field require the leadership and support of the CPC. Therefore, the CPC leadership must support and guarantee the reform on judicial transparency, though this concerns judicial politics as well as trials and administration. Placing undue emphasis on achieving a completely transparent justice system will inevitably affect the judicial and political systems and undermine the relationship between the judiciary and the political parties or other state organs. Although it is necessary to stress the importance of judicial transparency, it should by no means sway the leadership of the CPC. Therefore, the principle of upholding the leadership and ruling status of the CPC should not be abandoned or weakened by reforms or innovations of any kind, and judicial transparency is no exception.

The second principle is to adhere to procedural legitimacy when trying to achieve judicial transparency. The purpose of the innovations in the field of judicial transparency is to safeguard the rights of the litigants during the litigation process. Not only is judicial transparency backed by laws, such as the constitution, the procedural laws, and the Organic Law, but judicial power must also be exercised in accordance with the law. Reforms and innovations on judicial transparency must follow the

[30] Wang, *Political Parties in Government*, Chap. 3.

principle of 'ruling the country in accordance with the law', and ensuring that the exercise of judicial power can be regulated by laws. The laws shall specify which institutions are subject to judicial transparency and confirm its scope and boundaries, as well as its associated procedures, processes, and outcomes. The laws must also stipulate who is responsible for implementing it.

The third principle is to adopt a prudent and steady approach. Reforms and innovations on judicial transparency are not only concerned with the interaction between the judiciary and society, they are also related to many areas of the judicial system and the relationship between the judiciary and other state organs. As such, a gradual and steady approach should be adopted, rather than allowing no flexibility by trying to change the system completely in one attempt. Judicial transparency both relies on and influences judicial reforms. However, not only is it hindered by traditional values, but it also requires the judges to improve their professional standards further. In view of the above, judicial transparency is also a judicial reform in the new era, which should follow a proactive and steady approach under the leadership of the CPC. Being proactive means having the determination to overcome difficulties once the necessity and legitimacy of the reforms have been recognized. Being steady means promoting the reforms in a prudent manner after careful consideration. A proactive and steady approach involves starting the easy tasks first before moving on to the more difficult ones; in other words, one should wade across the stream by feeling the way. It also means expecting and accommodating ups and downs during the reforms.

The judiciaries across China have very different characteristics. Their financial capacity and the judges' professional standards vary greatly. The blind pursuit of judicial transparency at a time when the judiciary is not fully prepared for the changes will damage its credibility. This is especially true when there is an increase in the number of court cases, for the pursuit of judicial transparency inevitably brings numerous social conflicts into the judiciary when it still lacks the human, material, and financial resources to deal with them. Therefore, we should be cautious about the feasibility of transparency as well as its associated measures.

The fourth principle is to tailor the reforms to China's national conditions. China and Western countries are at different stages of social development. The judicial transparency needs of Chinese society differ from those of the West. While Western judicial systems are already in the post-modern era, the development of the rule of law in China is still immature and China's task is to build a modern judicial system.[31] Therefore, it is inappropriate simply to compare and contrast the experience of other societies with that of China, or to use criteria from other countries to assess the situation in China. In addition, since there is no uniform or universal model for judicial transparency in the world, and since significant differences exist between civil law and common law systems, the Western model must not be copied in a simplistic manner. The functions of the courts vary across different countries; courts have legislative functions in common law countries, whereas in civil law countries they only deal with dispute resolution; therefore the focus of judicial transparency also varies across countries. If a court assumes legislative functions, it is bound to grant the public greater open access to information. By briefly observing the current situation of the Chinese People's Courts at all levels, it is clear that the main tasks facing China's current judicial reforms are to: improve the legal knowledge and social status of judges and other relevant personnel; achieve true judicial independence; and, by way of procedural rationality, firmly prevent judicial corruption.

The fifth principle is to focus primarily on procedural transparency while considering granting the public open access to information. Judicial transparency has two orientations—society-oriented open access to information and litigant-oriented procedural transparency. A longstanding weakness of China's judicial system is that it has always been subject to intervention from external forces, making it difficult to resolve problems effectively. If too much emphasis is put on granting the public open access to information, it will inevitably have a negative impact on the independent exercise of judicial power in accordance with the law. As such, at a time when the rule of law is still being developed, the guidelines should focus mainly on procedural transparency. Therefore, the fundamental tasks facing China's judicial transparency at present should

[31] According to the reports of the 16th National Congress of the Communist Party of China, China will have completed the building of a moderately prosperous society by 2020. It may be anticipated that, prior to this time, the building of the rule of law will still be at its development stage, rather than at the reinforcement or simplification stage.

be the implementation of the three main procedural laws, focusing primarily on procedural transparency. The fundamental and key purpose of judicial transparency is effectively to protect the rights of the litigants and representatives as granted by the procedural laws, and to promote and guide the work of judicial transparency through procedural transparency. Although judicial transparency has the function of raising legal awareness and being close to the people, given that the Chinese courts do not currently engage in social policy development and legislation, the value of granting the public open access to information is not significant. Even if open access to information is to be emphasized, the scope of such access would still be limited. Therefore, the guidelines should focus primarily on procedural transparency while considering granting the public open access to information.

Strategies for Enhancing Judicial Transparency

The first strategy is to define clearly the basis of judicial transparency and revisit the procedural laws. The fundamental mission of the justice system is to protect human rights. Judicial credibility can naturally be achieved if human rights have been protected. Therefore, it makes sense that the International Covenant on Civil and Political Rights has made extremely detailed provisions for judicial transparency. Considering that China is at a stage where the rule of law is still being developed, the current priority is to implement the relevant procedural laws and protect the rights of the litigants. Therefore, judicial transparency is based on political rather than legal needs. China's reform on judicial transparency should be built on the constitution, the procedural laws and the Organic Law of the People's Courts. The emphasis should be on the protection of litigation rights at various stages, including transparency in case initiation, hearings, enforcement, and judicial affairs, with a view to promoting judicial reforms effectively, maintain justice, and enhance the authority of the judiciary. Without support from the legal system, the exploration of judicial transparency will lose legitimacy. This is especially true of the restrictions placed on judicial transparency, because not only is it difficult to achieve transparency without a clear legal basis, but misunderstandings will also arise. Therefore, to enhance judicial transparency, it is necessary to define clearly its basis and revisit the procedural laws. The second strategy is to protect the rights of the litigants on the basis of transparency in proceedings.

Timely disclosure of information. To achieve transparency, the judiciary must strictly follow the disclosure timetables stipulated by the laws and judicial interpretations and ensure timely and complete disclosure of information within the statutory timeframes in accordance with the law. In cases where no disclosure timetable is prescribed, the judiciary should disclose relevant information as soon as possible within a reasonable timeframe. This is to ensure that the litigants and the public are informed of the work of the courts so that they can strengthen supervision in a targeted manner. Therefore, it is necessary to ensure the timeliness of judicial information disclosure in a legislative sense by developing timeframe standards for information upload through legislation. The courts at all levels should also implement the principle of timely disclosure in their practices of judicial transparency. This is the only way to protect better the public's right to know and participate.

Clearly specify the scope of transparency. By far the most comprehensive judicial interpretation of the scope of judicial transparency in China is the Six Provisions of the Supreme People's Court on Judicial Transparency. The Standards for Demonstrative Courts for Judicial Transparency, which is based on the aforementioned provisions, further refines the contents of judicial transparency and has become one of the specific bases on which it may be implemented by the courts. However, it is still not possible to define its scope by relying only on the constitution, the three procedural laws, or the relevant judicial interpretations issued by the Supreme People's Court, for there are still many unanswered questions. The existing laws and the Six Provisions have not made any comprehensive or specific provision on the disclosures of information in relation to court staff. China should further refine the provisions on the aforementioned disclosures during its legislative and judicial practices. Judicial transparency must not impede the judiciary's legitimate and independent exercise of jurisdiction. When judicial information is publicly disclosed, it is necessary to protect the lawful rights and interests of the litigants and participants in the proceedings.

Emphasizing transparency in case initiation. In recent years, significant progress has been made in court trials from the perspective of procedural transparency, but more still needs to be done to ensure transparency in case initiation. Because Chinese society is in transition, the introduction of some legislation, such as the Criminal Procedure (Amendment) Law and the Administrative Enforcement Law, is likely to cause new social problems. If the judiciary restricts access to documents during the case initiation process by arbitrarily setting criteria and denying public access to information, it will inevitably lead to controversy. Therefore, judicial documents on case initiation should be open to the public upon approval by the People's Congress.

The third strategy is to focus on professional ethics and the professional development of judges. The premise of judicial transparency is the capability of achieving transparency. Judicial transparency would be of no value if there were frequent miscarriages of justice or if the judgment documents were roughly drafted. Such value can be obtained only if fair trials are carried out and if judgment documents are written in a scientific, legitimate, and stringent way. A convincing judgment document can achieve the desired legal and social effects or even academic value by clearly presenting its standpoints, grounds of argument, and reasoning. Otherwise, not only will the case-specific information be withheld from the public, but also the attitude and capacity of the caseworkers will be doubted. Therefore, training a team of judicial professionals is the first critical step towards establishing a modern justice system and realizing transparency. Improving the professional standards of judicial officers will help them to withstand undue influence from external forces and to achieve independence. A professional judicial workforce is required to support the expansion of the scope of judicial information disclosure. The current work on transparency should focus on the professional development of officers and the establishment of professional ethics.

The fourth strategy is to rationalize the relationship between the Party Committee and the judiciary in line with the principle of 'exercising state power in accordance with the law'. Judicial reforms can only be of practical value in the wider context of political reforms. At present, the priority is for the courts to revert to exercising jurisdiction and resolving social disputes through judicial adjudication. The legitimate and independent exercise of judicial power is significant. If the Party Committee, the Politics and Law Commission, or the Standing Committee of the National Congress were to supervise individual cases, other authorities in society would also be able to supervise individual judicial cases, which would invalidate the authority and legitimacy of the justice system. Therefore, it is of paramount importance to promote judicial reforms in accordance with the principle of 'exercising state power in accordance with the law'.

The fifth strategy is to foster a culture of respect for the rule of law by granting the public open access to information. In fact, judicial transparency effectively raises legal awareness. It allows judges, prosecutors, and lawyers, through their activities inside and outside the court, to transmit their legal knowledge to the public, thus achieving the best result in social education at the lowest cost. To promote open access to information for the public, the judiciary should focus on building court websites and publishing material on the Internet. There should be two online judicial transparency facilities, the one offering open access and the other restricted access. The open access one would provide information relating to trials, such as booklets on litigation, case initiation information, notices of hearings, live broadcasts of trials, enforcement information, appraisals, auctions, judgment documents, case studies, and updates on high-profile trials. It may also include information on judicial affairs, such as unclassified judicial statistics, reports and updates on the work of the courts, information on court staff, normative documents, and press releases. The restricted access one would be open to litigants only and would allow them to request updates on the progress of a case and view electronic documents. Both facilities should have a built-in review module so that members of the public could express their opinions by leaving comments and suggestions relating to the work on judicial transparency.

The sixth strategy is to enhance transparency by gradually granting the public open access to written judgments. Apart from freely allowing the public to observe cases when the court is sitting, another way of enhancing judicial transparency would be to ensure that everyone has access to written judgments and details of the trials. This is undoubtedly a good way of providing transparency to the public. Understandably, many people would like the courts to make all written judgments public, but this idea is clearly unfeasible. First, even foreign courts do not publicly disclose all their written judgments. Instead, these are published on a selective basis. Second, it is very costly to provide open access to all written judgments. For example, the courts in Beijing deal with as many as 400,000–500,000 cases a year. If the names were to be edited out from all written judgments, the courts would have to cope with an unprecedented workload with which they have neither the financial nor human resources to deal. Third, the professional standards of the judges vary greatly, which means that not every written judgment is of high quality. Therefore, providing every citizen with the opportunity to read written judgments by granting open access to these documents is a task that should be implemented gradually with the privacy of the litigants duly protected. When making written judgments publicly accessible, the personal details and full names of the litigants and relevant persons need not and should not be published, for example, this may be achieved by omitting one character from litigants' names.

On 17 February 2014, Xi Jinping delivered an important speech to the opening ceremony of the Symposium for Provincial Leaders and Cadres on Learning and Implementing the Spirit of the Third Plenary Session of the 18th CPC Central Committee. He pointed out that the overall objective of deepening the reforms was to improve and develop a characteristically Chinese socialist system and to promote the modernization of China's governing system and capabilities. The tasks the Chinese government faces for the next decade include deepening the reform on judicial transparency by establishing judicial legitimacy, improving the judicial systems and mechanisms, and enhancing judicial credibility. The successful completion of these tasks will contribute significantly to modernizing China's governing system and capabilities. Judicial transparency aims to manage the relationship between the courts and society; in other words, to serve the requirements of the people the people's courts need to expand the scope of judicial transparency and diversify its forms. In essence, this is a matter of judicial legitimacy. As stated in the documents published by the Supreme Court, justice should be 'visible justice', judicial efficiency should be 'efficiency that can be felt', and judicial authorities should be 'authorities that have been recognized'.[32] However, the emphasis on judicial

[32] Lawtime, "Opinions on Enhancing Transparency."

legitimacy reveals the real problem confronting China's judiciary, which is that the courts are facing a crisis of confidence in society. To ease this and build credibility, it is essential to establish legitimacy. Therefore, the government guidelines should focus primarily on procedural transparency while considering granting the public open access to information. It is also necessary to adopt a prudent and steady approach, tailor the reforms to China's national conditions, and promote the reform on judicial transparency. The current priorities are as follows:

- To define clearly the basis of judicial transparency and revisit the procedural laws;
- To protect the rights of litigants on the basis of transparency in proceedings;
- To focus on professional ethics and the professional development of judges;
- To rationalize the relationship between the Party Committee and the judiciary in accordance with the principle of 'exercising state power in accordance with the law';
- To foster a culture where the rule of law is highly regarded in society by granting the public open access to information;
- To enhance transparency by gradually granting the public open access to written judgments.

Bibliography

China.com. 2009. The six provisions of the Supreme People's Court on judicial transparency. [online]. Available at http://www.china.com.cn/policy/txt/2009-12/23/content_19120679.htm. Accessed 27 Aug 2015.

Chiu, L. G. 1992. *Judicial modernization and procedural laws*. Taipei: San Min Book Co., Ltd..

Coicaud, J. M. 2002. *Legitimacy and politics: A contribution to the study of political right and political responsibility*. Cambridge: Cambridge University Press.

Douglas, M. 1986. *How institutions think*. New York: Syracuse University Press, cited in Zhou, M. 2003. *Ten lectures on organizational sociology*, pp. 82–83. Beijing: Social Sciences Academic Press.

Habermas, J. 1975. *Legitimation crisis*. Boston: Beacon Press.

——— 1989. *Communication and the evolution of society*. Chongqing: Chongqing Publishing House.

Hamilton, A., J. Madison, and J. Jay. 2006. *Federalist papers*. Beijing: The Commercial Press.

Lawtime. 2010. Notice of the Supreme People's Court on several opinions on enhancing transparency in court trials in the People's Courts. [online]. Available at http://www.lawtime.cn/info/zhaiquan/zhaiquanzhaiwufagui/20100902/6392.html. Accessed 27 Aug 2015.

Law Yearbook Editorial Committee, ed. 1987–2010. *Law yearbook of China*. Beijing: China Law Yearbook Press.

Nonet, P., and P. Selznick. 1994. *Law and society in transition: Towards responsive law*. Beijing: China University of Political Science and Law Press.

Parsons, T. 1958. *Structure and process in modern societies*. Glencoe: Free Press.

Przeworski, A. 1986. Some problems in the study of the transition to democracy. In *Transition to democracy*, eds. P.C. Schmitter, and L. Whitehead, 47–63. Baltimore: Johns Hopkins University Press.

Radbruch, G. 1997. *Introduction to legal science*. Beijing: Encyclopedia of China Publishing House.

Rawls, J. 1988. *A theory of justice*. Beijing: China Social Sciences Press.

Shen, Z. 1996. *Modern Western jurisprudence*. Beijing: Peking University Press.

Stillman, P. G. 1974. The concept of legitimacy. *Polity* 8: 32–56.

Third Plenary Session of the 18th CPC Central Committee. 2013. *Decision of the CCCPC on some major issues concerning comprehensively deepening the reform*. Beijing: People's Publishing House.

Unger, R. M. (1994) [1976]. *Law in modern society*. Beijing: China University of Political Science and Law Press.

Wang, L. 2013. *Political parties in the government*. Beijing: China Legal Publishing House.

Weber, M. 1978. *Economy and society: An outline of interpretive sociology*, eds. G. Roth, and C. Wittich. Trans. E. Fischoff, H. Gerth, A. M. Henderson, F. Kolegar, C. W. Mills, T. Parsons, M. Rheinstein, G. Roth, E. Shils, and C. Wittich, 2 vols. Berkeley: University of California Press.

Zhu, J. W., ed. 2011. *Report on legal development in China: Towards pluralist legal practice*. Beijing: China Renmin University Press.

———, ed. 2012. *Report on legal development in China: Professionalization of China's legal workers*. Beijing: China Renmin University Press.

4

The Logic and Limits of the Party's Social Management Approach in Maintaining Stability: Lessons from Bismarck

Andreas Fulda

Lessons from European History for the Communist Party of China?

Following the leadership transition in Autumn 2012, Politburo Standing Committee member Wang Qishan recommended party members to read the book *The Old Regime and the Revolution* by Alexis de Tocqueville.[1] Reflecting on the causes of the French Revolution, Tocqueville argued in his seminal work that a social revolution was more likely when living

Andreas Fulda is lecturer at the School of Contemporary Chinese Studies and senior fellow at the China Policy Institute, University of Nottingham. He is also coordinator of the School's Centre for Contemporary Chinese Politics (CCCP). The author would like to thank Bernhard Fulda, Gerhard Fulda, Steve Tsang, Niv Horesh, Jeremy Taylor, Baojiang Han, Sun Yingchun, Wang Lifeng, and Zhao Lei for comments and suggestions for revision of this research paper.

[1] Caixin, "Tocqueville in China."

A. Fulda (✉)
School of Contemporary Chinese Studies, University of Nottingham, Nottingham, UK
e-mail:andreas.fulda@nottingham.ac.uk

S. Tsang, H. Men (eds.), *China in the Xi Jinping Era*,
The Nottingham China Policy Institute Series,
DOI 10.1007/978-3-319-29549-7_4

conditions are improving and dissatisfaction with the old regime is rising. Chinese academic He Qinglian has argued that '[Wang Qishan] meant to warn the ruling clique that, according to the Tocqueville Law, reform might not be fun, "the most dangerous time for a bad regime is not when it is most evil, but is when it begins to reform", the so-called "reform" is no different from seeking death.'[2] He Qinglian further stated that 'from this we could guess that for the next five (or even ten) years, China's political direction would be maintaining the status quo, making minor repairs here and there, insisting not to go back to the old path (Mao's path) or walk down the evil path (democratization)'. If He's analysis is correct, and Wang Qishan was indeed interested in upholding the status quo, he could have also recommended cadres to learn more about another European country in the 19th century, namely Otto von Bismarck's German Empire. Known for his balance-of-power realpolitik, Bismarck unified the country in 1871 and laid the foundations for the modern German welfare state. In this chapter I will argue that Bismarck's rule could provide a useful historical analogy to discuss China's socio-political trajectory, past, present, and future. I concur with Roxann Prazniak that '[the] histories of Europe and China offer rich opportunities for exploring aspects of the diversity and common experience of human history'[3] and that '[the] history of Western Europe illuminates facets of the historical experience that often remained in the shadows or side currents of the Chinese experience. Conversely, Chinese historical patterns have often developed possibilities that remained untapped or dormant in the European context'.[4]

I will begin by comparing and contrasting key socio-political developments in the German Empire under Bismarck (1862–1890) with the People's Republic of China (PRC) during the Mao (1949–1976) and post-Mao period (1976–). I argue that there are more similarities than differences between Bismarck's approach to social and political stability in the 19th century and China's social management approach in the late 20th and early 21st century. Both the German Empire and the PRC were

[2] He, "Tocqueville and political predicament."

[3] Prazniak, *Dialogues Across Civilizations*, 2.

[4] Ibid.

late-comers to nation-building. In both cases the Industrial Revolution and urbanization were initiated top-down under authoritarian political leadership. Economic modernization led to societal diversification and the rise of new economic and social interest groups seeking political representation.

Similar to China since the reform and opening up period, the German Empire under Bismarck was marked by decades of relative political stability and increasing economic prosperity. This stability was the outcome of political rule which can be likened to an iron fist in a velvet glove. While Bismarck persecuted political opponents such as German Catholics, the Polish minority in Prussia, as well as social democrats, he simultaneously also laid the foundation for a modern welfare state. By introducing health insurance, accident insurance, and old age pensions Bismarck attempted to limit the revolutionary potential of the German workforce. As my discussion will show, Bismarck's approach to social and political stability failed to succeed.

In the rest of the chapter Bismarck's social legislation will be contrasted with the introduction of social policies in the fields of social security, labour, health, education, and housing in post-Maoist China. Distinguishing between social policy and social management, often understood to mean stability preservation (*wei wen*),[5] I argue that such efforts have at best led to the establishment of a rudimentary welfare state in China. The lack of success of Bismarck's social legislation suggests that social policies limited in scope and ambition may enhance regime stability in the short term, but that they are likely to fail in the medium to long term since they do not address deep-seated questions about social, political, and economic justice in China.

This chapter thus centres around the question to what extent the approach of the Communist Party of China (CPC) to social management in post-Maoist China can be explained with reference to Bismarck's political statesmanship in the late 19th century. If the historical analogy provides illuminating insights and if historical lessons can be drawn from the comparison of the political history of the two different nations during different periods of time, this would be highly significant. Given

[5] Qian, "Preserving stability."

the uncertainty of mainland China's political transition,[6] which has been described by Minxin Pei as 'trapped',[7] the question of how China will deal with the social question is relevant not only for researchers studying China but also for Chinese decision makers as well as the general Chinese public. It is hoped that by pausing 'to step to the side of one historical tradition to examine issues from another historical perspective interrupts the construction of a central authoritative narrative'.[8] and by juxtaposing 'the cultural spheres of Western Europe and China reveals more about the human historical experience than either one alone can offer and opens each to the experiences of other historically conditioned situations'.[9]

In my conclusion I will argue that while Bismarck's social legislation succeeded in temporarily slowing the ascent of Germany's Social Democratic Party, he ultimately failed to contain their rise to power. In terms of the historical lessons from Imperial Germany a deepening of social policies in China would not only contribute to enhanced social safety nets but also help lay the foundations for state-led reconciliation of interests between different parties. As a necessary precondition for such a development the CPC would need to open up gradually the political process for non-state actors. Such a reform strategy would allow the CPC to continue steering China's transition, albeit with the help of civil society actors and greater public participation.

Bismarck's Approach vs China's Social Management Approach: Similarities and Differences

While it should not surprise anyone that a newly industrializing middle European country like the German Empire in the 19th century differs in many ways from the PRC since its foundation in 1949, there are nevertheless remarkable similarities in terms of the nature of the political system and the effects it has on societal development in both countries.

[6] Waldron, *China's Directionless Transition.*

[7] Pei, *Limits of Developmental Autocracy.*

[8] Prazniak, *Dialogues Across Civilizations*, 2.

[9] Ibid.

Findings from a comparative historical study will inform my critique of the CPC's social management approach later in the chapter.

Germany and China as Late-Comers to Nation-Building

One of the most striking similarities between Germany and China is that both are late-comers to nation-building. The German Empire came into existence after the Prussian victory over France at Sedan in 1871.[10] Hans-Peter Ullmann described its form of governance as 'hegemonial federalism'. Among the 27 constituent territories the Kingdom of Prussia played a leading role. The German Empire was ruled by four organs, the Emperor and Chancellor, as well as the two bodies of parliament, the Reichstag on the national level and the Bundesrat on the federal level. As a constitutional monarchy with a strong Prussian-dominated administration, the new German nation-state adopted the rule of law and allowed competitive elections among political parties.[11]

The German Empire had the features of an authoritarian nation-state, with the executive branch of government dominating the legislature. While playing a largely symbolic role, the Emperor was also in charge of the military. He authorized the Prussian wars against Denmark in 1864, Austria in 1866, and France in 1870–1871. The Chancellor, on the other hand, played a more significant role in the day-to-day domestic administration of the country. As the nominal head of the Bundesrat, the Chancellor had to garner support for his national policies in the German Reichstag. The Reichstag was initially elected every three years (after 1888 every five years) by male Germans above the age of 25. It could establish laws and approve budgets.[12]

Forty years after the establishment of the German Empire China's revolution in 1911 led to the foundation of the Republic of China (RoC). The RoC emerged as the successor of the Qing Empire in 1912. Experiments with constitutional democracy failed in the early years of the Republic.[13]

---

[10] Pulzer, *Politics, State Formation, War*, 15.

[11] Ullmann, *Politik im deutschen Kaiserreich*, 3–7.

[12] Ibid.

[13] Zhao, *A Tragedy of History*, 33–51.

The subsequent first half of the 20th century was marked by warlordism and civil war between the CPC and the ruling Kuomintang. In 1949 the PRC emerged as the successor of the RoC. In quick succession the PRC extended its territory and incorporated Xinjiang in 1949 and Tibet in 1951, creating a unitary multi-ethnic state under Leninist party rule, with Mao Zedong as the paramount leader until his death in 1976.

According to Frederick Teiwes the Maoist state was a 'totalistic state', 'one which may have fallen short of the idealized totalitarian model, but which nevertheless achieved a remarkable degree of penetration of society'.[14] The key governing organs consisted of a trinity of party, state, and military (*dang zheng jun*). Representative bodies such as the National People's Congress (NPC) had no independent power and its key functions were communication and propaganda as well as the articulation of limited interests. The second representative body of the Chinese People's Political Consultative Conference (CPPCC) played an important role in creating a united front. Its democratic parties were not autonomous nor could they influence national policies.[15]

In the post-Mao era, the 'totalistic functions performed by the Maoist state'[16] changed to those such as 'playing multiple roles normally left to the private sector in many countries: employer, saver, investor, manager, economic planner, price setter, social provider, and redistributor of social and economic resources'.[17] According to David Shambaugh, 'Deng's program changed the very nature of the state from being a proactive agent of social-political change to being a more passive facilitator of economic change and reactive arbiter of social-political tensions'.[18] China's political system evolved from an autocratic and highly personalized system under Mao to a more consensus-based, bureaucratic form of authoritarianism based on Leninist party rule.[19]

A comparison of the political systems of the German Empire and the PRC reveals both similarities and differences. In terms of similarities

---

[14] Teiwes, *The Maoist State*, 106.

[15] Ibid., 113–128.

[16] Shambaugh, *The Chinese State*, 161.

[17] Ibid.

[18] Ibid., 163.

[19] Ibid., 172–173.

leaders such as Bismarck, Mao or Deng perceived themselves as a political avant-garde with the mission to modernize their respective countries. In the case of Imperial Germany political leadership under Bismarck has been described as authoritarian.[20] In China, autocratic rule under Mao turned to a more paternalistic and authoritarian style under Deng.[21] In terms of differences, national policies in the German Empire were debated publicly and at times subject to electoral outcomes. In the PRC policies have been largely confined to internal party deliberations and thus can be considered party policies.

State-Led Industrialization in Germany

In comparison with its European neighbours Britain and France, Germany's industrial revolution started comparatively late. According to Hans Mottek industrialization unfolded from 1834 until 1873 and differed from other European nation-states also in other significant ways. Ralf Dahrendorf identified five phenomena that were characteristic of the special development in Germany. He points to: the role of large-sized banks and their support for major companies; state-led top-down industrialization; state ownership of railways and canals as well as key industries such as mining, iron, electricity, gas, water, and transportation; state socialism in the form of the three insurances for health, accident, as well as old age and disability; and a strong emphasis on nationalism as the dominant spirit of the time (zeitgeist).[22]

As a late-comer to industrialization the German Empire did not have to engage in a bottom-up experimentation and could learn from the experiences of neighbouring countries. It did so, however, in a highly selective way. According to Dahrendorf, the German Empire was able to 'borrow the achievements of its western neighbours, despite the latter being incompatible with its own social and cultural context. It was able to appropriate the acquired to meet its own ends, to meet the ends of its obsolete institutions'.[23]

---

[20] Seligmann and McLean, *Germany, Reich to Republic*, 21.

[21] Shambaugh, *The Chinese State*, 162.

[22] Dahrendorf, *Gesellschaft und Demokratie*, 39–55.

[23] Ibid., 50.

The combination of modern economic forms and an authoritarian political order led to a peculiar form of capitalism in which the state played a dominant role in the economy. While it enabled the German Empire to industrialize 'quickly and thoroughly',[24] the state-led nature of the process also hampered the growth of small and medium sized companies, prevented the rise of a broad-based and politically conscious bourgeoisie, and undermined the emergence of a citizen society.[25]

Industrialization in China: Catching Up with the United Kingdom?

In the case of China, industrialization started in the first half of the 20th century during the republican period. Industrialization during the Nanking decade, however, occurred highly unevenly, with the lower Yangtze Delta and part of the Wuhan area taking a lead. Manchuria under Japanese occupation also industrialized more quickly than other parts of north-west China. After the foundation of the PRC the first attempts by Mao Zedong to catch up with the United Kingdom's steel production during the Great Leap Forward in the 1950s ended in famine.[26] Only with the disbanding of the people's communes after the Cultural Revolution (1966–1976) in the early 1980s did China embark successfully and in a sustained way on large scale industrialization. In the context of the four modernizations, the CPC: prioritized agriculture, light industry, national defence, and science and technology; decollectivized land in order to enhance rural productivity; allowed foreign investment in some sectors of the economy; and strengthened the higher education system with the establishment of eight key universities.[27]

Just as the 'ancient' regime in the German Empire of the 19th century, Chinese decision-makers in the late 20th and early 21st century engaged in instrumental learning and selective adaptation. The approach of

[24] Ibid., 54.

[25] Ibid., XX.

[26] Yang, *Tombstone.*

[27] Spence, *Search for Modern China*, 618–646.

'utilising Western techniques whilst maintaining a Chinese core' (*yi xixue weiyong, yi zhongxue wei ti*), first popularized by reformers during the late Qing dynasty (1644–1911), was characteristic of China's embrace of market reforms after 1978. He Qinglian identified four key characteristic features of China's reform process under Deng: a continued over-concentration of political, economic, cultural, and military might in the hands of the CPC; a privatization of previously collectively held assets (*hua gong wei si*); a turn to pragmatism as the only guiding principle; and incremental economic reforms without political structural reforms.[28]

The comparison of state-led industrialization in Imperial Germany and the post-Maoist period in the PRC reveals some remarkable similarities. In both cases the political elites could employ the full weight of the state machinery to promote industrialization from the top down. As late comers, both in Germany and China commercial practices were introduced without adjusting the existing political institutions to the newly adopted models of capitalism. Finally, the strong emphasis on the state as a key developmental actor reduced the space for a more independent private sector and civil society. As the following discussion will show, the late but state-led industrialization and urbanization had a profound influence on societal development.

Social Responses to State-Led Modernization in Imperial Germany

Industrialization and urbanization in the German Empire led to occupational differentiation. Whereas in 1871 almost half of the German population were employed in agriculture, this dropped to one-third by the beginning of the First World War.[29] Industrialization fundamentally altered family structures, in particular among the working class. Industrial work disciplined the workforce and led to long working hours for men, women, and children. When industrial accidents happened, workers were often left without compensation and fell back

[28] He, *China in der Modernisierungsfalle*, 461–507.

[29] Dahrendorf, *Gesellschaft und Demokratie*, 56–57.

into poverty. Access to health and education prior to Bismarck's social reforms was limited.[30] Economically successful members of the middle class, on the other hand, such as wealthy industrialists, bankers, and leading administrators integrated themselves into the upper aristocratic class. Dahrendorf argues that the emerging German bourgeoisie was characterized by individuals in competition with one another, unable to instigate a citizen-led revolution and to make demands for a new political class.[31]

A born aristocrat himself, Bismarck relied during his liberal era on the parliamentary support of the National Liberal Party (1871–1879), followed by a conservative turn in 1880, when he started working with the conservatives and a reformed and more right-wing National Liberal Party (1880–1890). He was deeply concerned about the Social Democratic Party (SDP) and its ability to garner more and more votes from workers in Reichstag elections.[32] He also perceived the Polish minority in the eastern part of Prussia to be a threat to the unity of the new German Empire. He was also suspicious of German Catholics and their loyalty to the Roman Church, which he considered a threat to the integrity of the German Empire.

Historians have explained Bismarck's approach towards minorities as one of 'negative integration'. Hans-Ulrich Wehler described it as 'a manipulative strategy on the part of the Chancellor, designed to safeguard the authoritarian system in an age of rapid social and economic change by focusing the attention of ordinary Germans on a common enemy, large enough to be credible, but not serious enough to threaten the Reich's political survival'.[33] Bismarck repeatedly rallied the public against perceived enemies of the empire (*Reichsfeinde*) to pursue his policy goals. Such political manoeuvring came at the expense of developing the German monarchic and bureaucratic state into a parliamentary state based on civic and liberal premises.[34]

[30] Specht, *Social-Politik*, 415–417.

[31] Ibid., 57–60.

[32] Craig, *Germany. 1866–1945*.

[33] Seligmann and McLean, *Germany, Reich to Republic*, 21.

[34] Ullmann, *Politik im deutschen Kaiserreich*.

Bismarck's relentless persecution of social democrats in the form of the Anti-Socialist Law (1878–1890) only temporarily slowed their ascent. Seligman and McLean argue that 'what cannot be contested is that the Anti-Socialist Law backfired disastrously … The same sense of unity developed among Socialists as a result of official persecution as had emerged in similar conditions among Catholics and Poles'.[35] During the 1912 Reichstag election the SDP emerged as the strongest parliamentary group and garnered 110 seats.[36] Seligman and McLean further conclude that 'his strategies of persecuting minorities polarized German politics, contributed to the atomization of society in the Reich, and set a dangerous precedent of official intolerance which, lamentably, was followed by the governments of both Wilhelm II and Adolf Hitler'.[37] Political conservatism and societal dynamism thus characterized state–society relations in the German Empire towards the end of the 19th century.

In the following, I will contrast the social responses to state-led modernization in Imperial Germany with social developments in both Maoist China (1949–1976) as well as the post-Maoist period (1976–). This distinction is necessary to do justice to the historical particularities of the Chinese case. Arguably, there are also important ideological differences to consider. Whereas Bismarck fought against the perceived danger of socialism, the Chinese leadership after Mao had to reinvent Communism after the failures of the Great Leap Forward (1958–1960) and the Cultural Revolution (1966–1976). Whereas previous discussions showed more similarities than differences between the two time periods, it can be argued that societal development in China followed a different path from the German Empire.

Social Cellularization in Maoist China

Social stratification in China followed very different trajectories during the Maoist and post-Maoist period. Andrew Nathan has pointed out that Maoism 'was highly stratified in several ways: by the class status system,

[35] Seligmann and McLean, *Germany, Reich to Republic*, 26.

[36] Ullmann, *Politik im deutschen Kaiserreich*, 40.

[37] Ibid., 27.

by the system of bureaucratic ranks, and by the social cleavages between rural and urban residents and between state and non-state employees'.[38] He maintains that 'the system of control mechanisms (units, class labels, political campaigns, the party network) added up to a unique achievement in the social technology of control'.[39] Chinese farmers were kept in their place and in a significant way tied to the land with the help of the household registration system (*hukou zhidu*), whereas the urban Chinese became dependent on the work unit (*danwei*) in the allocation of resources. According to Vivienne Shue societal demands had to be channelled through the party-state bureaucracy and 'articulated in the categories of the state's own ideology – categories of class struggle and revolutionary purity, anti-imperialism and antirevisionism'.[40] Shue maintains that the 'party-state relied on its organs of mass mobilization – the peasant associations, labor unions, the women's federation, the youth league, and so on – to press these categories of social analysis and concern into the popular mind'.[41] Nathan described the Maoist social structure as one which 'forced individuals into dependency on party secretaries in their work units in order to enforce social conformity'.[42]

The economic failure of the Great Leap Forward and the political violence during the Great Proletarian Cultural Revolution posed an existential threat to the CPC. Teiwes maintains that 'Mao Zedong left a difficult legacy for the post-Mao state: a fractured and grievance-riddled society, a party-state with reduced legitimacy and weakened dominance over society, faction-infested institutions, ambiguous official norms and a divided top leadership'.[43] Nathan outlines the key concerns of Deng as thus to 'reform economic institutions so as to increase living standards and efficiency; to redress the grievances of individuals who had been harmed under Mao; to create a new legitimacy based on economic performance rather than a vision of a future utopia; and to institutionalize the Party's own decision making processes to improve the quality of its leadership'.[44]

[38] Nathan, *China's Transition*, 50.
[39] Ibid.
[40] Shue, *State Power Social Organization*, 69.
[41] Ibid.
[42] Nathan, *China's Transition*, 54.
[43] Teiwes, *The Maoist State*, 159.
[44] Nathan, *China's Transition*, 59.

Social Stratification and New Social Cleavages in Post-Maoist China

Societal development during the post-Mao era was a result of top-down economic modernization and bottom-up entrepreneurialism of the people. As Shue outlines, '[expanded] markets in commodities, labor, services, money, and knowledge have presented people in almost all walks of life with new opportunities to provide for their own welfare by working or investing in ventures outside the scope of their home units'.[45] Economic reforms after 1978 created both winners and losers. While rural people briefly benefited from relaxed price controls in the early 1980s, their income progressively declined in comparison to urban wages.[46] Rising income inequalities are just one of the social ills that have plagued China since 1978.

While Shue argues that 'thanks to all the splendid opportunities – and to all the terrible risks – that come with marketization of social relations, a great many people in China today are less dependent on the very contained local communities that characterized Chinese social life in the recent past',[47] it can equally be argued that top-down economic modernization alone failed to solve persistent social problems such as income inequality, gender inequality, uneven regional development, and mass migration.[48] Chan, Ngok, and Phillips have pointed out that 'economic benefits have not been equally shared by all citizens, and inequalities have widened between social classes, between rich and poor provinces and between urban and rural areas'.[49] Economic modernization has benefited a relatively small but growing middle class in China, which remains highly dependent on official patronage. According to Peter Hefele, 'the main difference between the Western and Chinese concept of a middle class lies in the unique role played by party functionaries as a result of their having access to power and resources. Working in the state sector is seen as a key factor in becoming part of the middle class, and having a

---

[45] Shue, *State Power Social Organization*, 74.

[46] Young "China development brief."

[47] Shue, *State Power Social Organization*, 75.

[48] Young "China development brief".

[49] Chan, Ngok and Phillips, *Social Policy in China*, 5.

close relationship with the political elite can have a significant impact on financial success'.[50]

This mirrors the development in Imperial Germany where the emerging bourgeoisie was unable to press for bottom-up reform and create a new political class. This can at least partly explain why widening inequalities and societal discontent so far has not posed a direct threat to the continued rule of the CPC. As Saich argues, it is 'clear that no coherent alternative vision has emerged that would fashion either a civil society or a rapid construction of a democratic political order'.[51] At the same time, he points out that 'from the party's view, what is lurking in the shadows waiting to pounce on any opening that would allow freedom of expression is revivalism, religion, linguistic division, regional and non-Han ethnic loyalties'.[52] Similar to Bismarck's approach of 'negative integration', the CPC in post-Maoist China has continuously emphasized the dangers of greater pluralism, rather than accepting the latter as a necessary precondition for social and political liberalization. As the German case showed, such official intolerance is likely to lead to societal atomization and fragmentation, thereby undermining bottom-up efforts to strengthen social cohesion through self-organization and democratic self-government.

Logic and Limits of Social Management in Maintaining Stability

The discussion so far has compared socio-political developments in the German Empire under Bismarck and the PRC during the Mao and post-Mao period. It has revealed both similarities in the nature of political control and the effects of industrialization and urbanization on societal development in both countries. I will now discuss in more detail the logic and limits of China's social management approach in maintaining stability in the late 20th and early 21st century.

[50] Hefele, "China's middle class."

[51] Saich, *Governance and Politics*, 204.

[52] Ibid.

Political or Social Stability?

Despite challenges to its legitimacy, the CPC has been governing China from 1949 until the present day. According to Gunter Schubert it has achieved this feat not only by relying on economic development and nationalism but also by building legitimacy through incremental political reform, more specifically by gradually developing its ideology, adjusting its administrative structures, and by enhancing the personal authority of officials.[53] Such 'authoritarian resilience' in the post-Mao period resembles Bismarck's rule in the German Empire, which can be likened to an iron fist in a velvet glove. A key to understanding why the CPC has been able to hold onto power is the stability among its political leadership.

Duncan Freeman argues that 'the quest for stability is arguably at the very centre of the Chinese concept of politics'.[54] Drawing on speeches by Hu Jintao, Wen Jiabao, and Jiang Zemin, Freeman points out that 'the statements from China's leaders invoke the double connotation of stability, considered as political stability (stability of the state, the party and ultimately the Chinese nation) and social stability (stability of society in the wider sense, including law and order)'.[55] According to this logic, the stability of the political system and social stability are two sides of the same coin. Drawing on Jiang's political thinking Freeman summarizes the official position to mean that 'stability is both a prerequisite for and a result of reform and development'.[56]

This seemingly contradictory view is also mirrored in the CPC's social management (*shehui guanli*) concept. While Chinese academic Yu Keping has interpreted its emergence to signify that 'the Party and government have in fact already begun to see the existence and role of civil society as an important basis for decision making'[57], Zhou Benshun, a secretary of the Party's Central Politics and Law Commission, warned that

---

[53] Schubert, "One-party rule," 195.

[54] Freeman, *Stability and Change*, 145.

[55] Ibid.

[56] Ibid. Eberhard Sandschneider has argued to the contrary that instability should be considered a key driver for reform in China. See Sandschneider, "Chinas Zukunft," 10–16.

[57] Qian, "Society lost."

some people have had two misunderstandings about social management overseas. The first is the idea of 'small government—large society', that the bulk of social management should be taken on by society. In fact, not all developed nations follow this 'small government—large society' model, and quite a number of large nations have large governments with the government taking on the principal tasks of social management. Second is the idea that social organizations are a 'third sector', independent of the government and of the social management system. In fact, the vast majority of nongovernmental organizations overseas have government backgrounds, and all are under the effective management of the government. In our country, we must properly regulate conduct in fostering and developing social organizations, first putting 'safety valves' in place, thereby preventing the propagation of social organizations with ulterior motives.[58]

While Yu sees social management as a stepping stone towards inclusive social governance[59] Zhou Benshun's interpretation appears to be less benign. The official's emphasis on 'safety valves' can also be interpreted to mean 'stability preservation' (*wei wen*). According to Qian Gang this political term gained currency in the second half of the Hu/Wen administration and can be understood as 'a coded reference to social disorder—which is to say, social disorder must be avoided at all costs'.[60] Based on such an official understanding of stability, social harmony therefore is not only to be achieved by social policies alone but also with the help of a strong party-state capable of initiating political campaigns and employing law enforcement agencies such as the notorious City Urban Administrative and Law Enforcement Bureaus (*chengguan*), police departments (*gonganju*), as well as the People's Armed Police (*renmin wuzhuang jingcha*) in times of crisis.

The CPC's two-pronged approach of influencing societal development with a combination of social services and increasingly heavy handed policing strategies[61] strongly resembles Bismarck's approach of utilizing

58 Ibid.

59 Yu, "Shift towards social governance."

60 Qian, "Preserving stability."

61 For a critical discussion of the CPC's approach to stability preservation see Yu, "Reassessing rigid stability."

social legislation to appease the growing working classes' demand for participation and representation, while at the same time employing the Anti-Socialist Law (*Sozialistengesetz*) to harass and persecute active members of the German SDP. As our previous discussion revealed, Bismarck's strategic approach only yielded short-term results and could not prevent the rise of the SDP. The latter were repeatedly labelled as enemies of the state (*Reichsfeinde*), thereby creating resentment of the *ancien régime* among large swathes of the German working class. A similar development may also be taking place in post-Mao China, 'where ethnic minority questions are especially often portrayed … as a threat to national sovereignty, unity and stability'.[62]

Logic and Limits of Building Legitimacy Through Social Policy

Pitman Potter argues that the CPC has also been trying to 'build legitimacy through social policy'.[63] Reforms became necessary during the transition from the Maoist period, when social welfare was 'an integral part of economic policy and planning, rather than a separate residual sector'.[64] According to Sarah Cook 'a major feature of the system was the division between the "iron rice bowl" (and arm-chair) security provided to urban state workers (and officials) and much less generous programs of relief and social assistance for the remainder of the population—the minority of urban residents who fell outside the work unit system, and the majority of the rural population'.[65] This level of social welfare became unsustainable in the subsequent reform period.

In the post-Maoist period 'the government has been transferring back to society and family many welfare functions for which it previously had taken responsibility'.[66] Chan, Ngok, and Phillips argue that slow economic restructuring and the dismantling of state-owned enterprises

[62] Freeman, *Stability and Change*, 145.

[63] Potter, "Belief in control," 318.

[64] Cook, *After Iron Rice Bowl*, 73.

[65] Ibid., 74.

[66] Ibid., 73.

(SOE) during the 1990s 'almost completely destroyed China's socialist welfare system centred on the welfare activities of communes and state-owned enterprises'.[67] Sarah Cook argues that 'the government's concern [was] with "perfecting" the social security system, principally as a means to smooth the reform of the state enterprise sector, maintain social stability, and reduce the costs on the state'.[68]

Social welfare reforms thus went hand in hand with the introduction of new social policies. The latter were designed to pre-empt societal challenges to economic policies by co-opting politically significant parts of the Chinese population. Whereas 'urban workers received a wide range of social protections including old age insurance, medical insurance and discounts on the sale of public housing',[69] Chan, Ngok, and Phillips point out that 'poorer families, especially those in rural areas, as well as migrant workers, received inadequate support with public assistance, housing, education and health'.[70] Björn Gustafsson, Li Shi, and Terry Sicular have argued that 'concerns … arise if segments of the population are left behind with insufficient resources to meet basic needs or entitlements'.[71]

Reviewing the government's efforts in the field of social security, labour, health, education, and housing policies, Chan, Ngok, and Phillips conclude that 'China's welfare reforms focused on the privatisation of public welfare and the localisation of welfare provisions that accelerated social divisions of welfare, threatening the equal value of citizens'.[72] They go on to argue that 'the development of social policy over the past three decades, revealed from market-oriented welfare provisions, the exclusion of migrant workers from basic needs, and the welfare gap between men and women, shows that China's traditional socialist welfare values centred on equality and human needs have been severely suppressed'.[73]

The picture that emerges from the discussion of social policies and social services as a key element in China's social management approach

---

[67] Chan, Ngok, and Phillips, *Social Policy in China*, 27.

[68] Cook, *After Iron Rice Bowl*, 88.

[69] Chan, Ngok, and Phillips, *Social Policy in China*, 217.

[70] Gustafsson, Shi, and Sicular, *Inequality and Public Policy*, 1.

[71] Chan, Ngok, and Phillips, *Social Policy in China*, 217.

[72] Ibid.

[73] Ibid.

both differs and resembles the situation in 19th century Germany. Whereas the challenge for the CPC in post-Maoist China was 'to reform and dismantle certain structures, thus reducing entitlements for some, while replacing and extending others',[74] Bismarck's social legislation created social safety nets where there had been none before. Bismarck's concern was to reduce the dissatisfaction of the workers by insuring the life risks of sickness, accidents, disability, and old age.[75] From 1883 until 1889 he introduced health insurance, accident insurance, and old age pensions.[76]

A co-author of Bismarck's social legislation, Theodor Lohmann (1831–1905) described why the attempt to combine state repression with welfare ultimately failed. He mused that

the real social dissatisfaction is not simply a lack of material conditions … but the desire for true equality before the law and the ability to participate in cultural affairs. Dissatisfied workers will only be satisfied if they have a feeling of genuine equality with the owning classes (e.g. in terms of the right to associations and the right to assembly) and by providing them with an orderly family life (regulation of the working hours for women, during nights, and on Sundays), thereby allowing them to gain access to a higher quality of life.[77]

Lohmann's comment is illuminating insofar as it highlights the inherent limits of building legitimacy through social policy. Whereas Bismarck's social policy can be described as too little, too late, the post-Maoist dismantling of the traditional welfare state and the accompanying privatization could equally be described as too much, too soon. In both instances, the resulting welfare states were rudimentary at best, providing only limited safety nets for vulnerable groups. As the German case has shown, the strategic use of social policy as a means to upholding political stability was thus rather short-lived. If the CPC wants to avoid a similar demise as Bismarck's *ancien régime* its political strategists may need to go back to the policy drawing board. One possible first step for

[74] Ibid., 59.

[75] Specht, *Social-Politik*, 416.

[76] Ibid.

[77] Ibid.

CPC decision makers would be to acknowledge that economic reforms in China have brought about a multitude of new interest groups. In order to give Chinese citizens a better chance to articulate their various interests and defend and extend their particular values, the CPC should consider creating the legal-administrative framework conditions for civil society to participate in the policy process.

Learning from Bismarck?

This chapter has raised the question to what extent the CPC's current approach to social management can be explained with reference to Bismarck's political statesmanship in the late 19th century. In order to address this question I have compared the political history in the German Empire under Bismarck with the PRC during the Mao and post-Mao period. This historical comparison has revealed a number of similarities as well as a few differences. Both Germany and China were late-comers to nation-building. Whereas the German Empire had the features of an authoritarian nation-state, the PRC developed from a totalistic state under Mao to a more paternalistic and authoritarian state under Deng Xiaoping. State-led industrialization in Imperial Germany and the post-Maoist period in China reveal remarkable similarities. In both cases, commercial practices were introduced without adjusting the existing political institutions to the newly adopted models of capitalism.

Social responses to state-led modernization in Imperial Germany and China also exhibit some degree of similarity. In both cases the working class had to bear the brunt of rapid industrialization and urbanization. Members of the emerging middle classes in both cases aimed to improve their economic situation and thus became dependent on the good will of the upper aristocratic class in the German Empire and government bureaucrats in the PRC respectively. Both political systems responded in similar ways to the increasing demands of a diversifying society. Bismarck employed manipulative strategies to focus the attention of Germans on perceived common enemies, both home and abroad. Such political manoeuvring yielded short-term political gains during Reichstag elections, but also set a precedence of official intolerance towards minorities. A similar phenomenon can be observed in the case of China, where the fear of religion, linguistic division, and ethnic conflict has led to the blanket curtailment of freedom of expression.

I have also discussed in more detail the logic and limits of China's social management approach in maintaining stability in the late 20th and early 21st century. The discussion revealed that leading proponents of the CPC regard the stability of the political system and social stability as two sides of the same coin. Social management has either been understood to signify an opportunity for the inclusion of non-state actors in the development process or as a call to arms for an empowered bureaucracy to intervene actively in societal development. Upon closer inspection it became evident that the CPC's approach to social management combines social policies with increasingly heavy handed policing strategies.

The subsequent discussion centred around the question to what degree the CPC has been able to build legitimacy through social policy. While social policies have so far been successful in co-opting politically significant parts of the population, the preferential treatment of urban workers over rural Chinese and migrant workers also raises serious questions about social, political, and economic justice in China. According to a study conducted by Göbel and Ong '[social] unrest in China has been increasing at an alarming rate. Few incidents of public demonstrations, disruptive action or riots occurred in the 1980s, but 8,700 "mass incidents" were recorded in 1993 alone. By 2005, their number had grown tenfold to 87,000, and estimates for the number of public protests in 2010 range between 180,000 and 230,000'.[78] The costs of maintaining social order through domestic policing has also dramatically increased. According to a study conducted by Tsinghua University, the budget for internal security in 2010 surpassed spending on national defence.[79] Such developments suggest that the CPC's current social management approach to maintaining stability is not sustainable. One of the historical lessons from Bismarck's approach to social and political stability is that his repression of societal demands was ultimately unsuccessful. So what could be done by the CPC to escape the political predicament of the German Empire, which imploded in 1918?

[78] Göbel and Ong, "Social unrest in China."

[79] Kelly, "Costs of maintaining stability."

While none of the Chinese political leaders in the post-Maoist era have attained the historical status of Otto von Bismarck, it can be argued that the CPC as a Leninist party is already playing by his book. Pre-empting societal demands for political reform by establishing a rudimentary form of welfare state has helped enhance the party-state's legitimacy. China's current political leaders should, however, not be too self-congratulatory and simply assume that their social management approach will also work in the future. Bismarck ultimately failed to win over the hearts and minds of German workers. I have argued that he failed due to the limited scope and ambition of his social legislation. He also failed to develop the political institutions of the German Empire to meet the needs of a diversifying society.

In conclusion I argue that a deepening of social policies in China would not only contribute to enhanced social safety nets but also help lay the foundations for state-led reconciliation of interests between different parties. The Xi Jinping Administration can also learn another historical lesson from Imperial Germany, that it is in its organizational self-interest to gradually open up the political process to non-state actors and to become more inclusive. Such a reform strategy would allow the Xi Administration to continue steering China's transition, albeit with the help of civil society actors and greater public participation.

In 2012 Chinese academic Yu Jianrong put forward a ten-year plan for social and political reforms which provides details of how such a political opening could be achieved. In a first reform phase from October 2012 until December 2015 he suggests that China's new political leadership should '[achieve] basic social equality and justice, with the adjustment of public welfare policies as the premise and the protection of people's rights as the foundation'.[80] During a second phase from January 2016 to September 2022 he suggests that the Xi Administration in its second term should '[promote] the transition of the country to a constitutional democracy, with political reform as the premise and civil rights as the foundation'.[81] As I have argued before, 'Yu's plan is the most notable reform agenda to emerge since the Charter 08'[82] and 'signifies a willingness

---

[80] Bandurski, "social and political reform."

[81] Ibid.

[82] Fulda, "China's political reform."

among party-state officials to engage in open-ended discussions about democracy and human rights in China'. Yu has been 'working within the system to advocate incremental political reform and is frequently invited to lecture officials at training seminars funded by the Communist Party'.[83]

The 'Decision on Major Issues Concerning Comprehensively Deepening Reforms' published by the CPC on 15 November 2013 in the wake of the Third Plenum of the 18th CPC Congress suggests that Yu's message is not entirely falling on deaf ears. While some commentators have lauded the document as evidence that 'the Communist Party has indeed produced its most wide-ranging and reform-tinged proposals for economic and social change in many years',[84] there seems to be a great deal of continuation of the former social management approach under Xi Jinping. As Alice Miller has pointed out, 9 of the 60 reform proposals address 'social services and "social management" reform'.[85] Miller has furthermore argued that the goal of China's new Central State Security Committee, another outcome of the Third Plenum, is to 'improve national security strategy and its work mechanism to keep high vigilance against and resolutely forestall activities of separatism, infiltration and subversion carried out by hostile forces to ensure national security'.[86] Such continued emphasis on a few social policy carrots and a big political control stick does not bode well for China's future. If the CPC wanted to avoid the predicament of Bismarck's *ancien régime* and if the new Xi Administration was to adopt Yu Jianrong's ten-year plan for social and political reforms, either wholesale or in part, it may once again prove the naysayers wrong and continue to steer China's political future.

Bibliography

Bandurski, D. 2012. Scholar posts 10-year plan for social and political reform. China Media Project. [online]. Available at http://cmp.hku.hk/2012/03/26/20910/. Accessed 26 Mar 2012.

[83] Fulda, "China's reformers within."

[84] *Economist*, "Reform in China."

[85] Miller, "How strong is Xi?"

[86] Ibid.

Chan, C. K., K. L. Ngok, and D. Phillips. 2008. *Social policy in China. Development and well-being*. Bristol: Policy Press.
Cook, S. 2003. After the iron rice bowl: Extending the safety net in China. In *Social protection in Asia*, eds. S. Cook, N. Kabeer, and G. Suwannarat, 73. New Delhi: Har-Anand Publications Pvt Ltd..
Craig, G. A. 1981. *Germany. 1866–1945*. Oxford: Oxford University Press.
Dahrendorf, R. 1971. *Gesellschaft und Demokratie in Deutschland*. München: Deutscher Taschenbuch Verlag.
Caixin. 2013. Tocqueville in China. [online]. Available at http://english.caixin.com/2012-09-14/100438129.html?p1. Accessed 3 Oct 2013.
Freeman, D. 2012. Stability and change: The EU, China and perceptions of stability. In *Conceptual gaps in China-EU relations. Global governance, human rights and strategic partnerships*, ed. Z.Q. Pan, 145. Basingstoke: Palgrave Macmillan.
Fulda, A. 2012a. A convergence of China's political reform agendas. China Policy Institute Policy Paper 2012: No. 3. [online]. Available at http://www.nottingham.ac.uk/cpi/documents/policy-papers/policy-paper-2012-03.pdf. Accessed 13 Oct 2013.
——— 2012b. China's reformers within. *South China Morning Post*. [online]. Available at http://www.scmp.com/comment/insight-opinion/article/1135292/chinas-reformers-within. Accessed 13 Oct 2013.
Göbel, C., and L. H. Ong. 2012. Social unrest in China. Europe China Research and Advice Network. [online]. Available at http://www.euecran.eu/Long%20Papers/ECRAN%20Social%20Unrest%20in%20China_%20Christian%20Gobel%20and%20Lynette%20H.%20Ong.pdf. Accessed 13 Oct 2013.
Gustafsson, B., L. Shi, and T. Sicular, eds. 2010. *Inequality and public policy in China*. New York: Cambridge University Press.
He, Q. L. 2006. *China in der Modernisierungsfalle*. Bonn: Bundeszentrale für politische Bildung.
He, Q. L. 2012. Tocqueville and China's political predicament. [online]. Available at http://hqlenglish.blogspot.com/2013/01/chinas-political-predicament.html. Accessed 12 Aug 2013.
Hefele, P. 2011. China's middle class: A driving force for more democratic change or guarantor of the status quo? KAS International Reports. [online]. Available at http://www.kas.de/wf/doc/kas_29625-544-2-30.pdf?111205133611. Accessed 13 Oct 2013.
Kelly, D. 2010. Costs of maintaining stability in China. [online]. Available at http://www.eastasiaforum.org/2010/05/23/costs-of-maintaining-stability-in-china/. Accessed 13 Oct 2013.

Miller, A. 2014. How strong is Xi Jinping? *China Leadership Monito* 43 [online]. Available at http://media.hoover.org/sites/default/files/documents/CLM43AM-2.pdf. Accessed 4 June 2014.
Nathan, A. 1997. *China's transition*. New York: Columbia University Press.
Pei, M. X. 2006. *China's trapped transition. The limits of developmental autocracy*. London: Harvard University Press.
Potter, P. B. 2003. Belief in control: Regulation of religion in China. *The China Quarterly* 174: 318.
Prazniak, R. 1996. *Dialogues across civilizations. Sketches in world history from the Chinese and European experiences*. Taipei: SMC Publishing Inc.
Pulzer, P. 1997. *Germany, 1870–1945, politics, state formation, and war*. Oxford: Oxford University Press.
Qian, G. 2012a. Preserving stability. China Media Project. [online]. Available at http://cmp.hku.hk/2012/09/14/27074/. Accessed 6 Oct 2013.
——— 2012b. Society lost. China Media Project. [online]. Available at http://cmp.hku.hk/2012/09/27/27630/. Accessed 9 Oct 2013.
Saich, T. 2001. *Governance and politics of China*. New York: Palgrave.
Sandschneider, E. 2003. Chinas Zukunft. Projektion und Wirklichkeit. *Internationale Politik* 53: 10–16.
Schubert, G. 2008. One-party rule and the question of legitimacy in contemporary China: Preliminary thoughts on setting up a new research agenda. *Journal of Contemporary China* 17(54): 195.
Seligmann, M. S., and F. R. McLean. 2000. *Germany from Reich to republic, 1871–1918*. London: Macmillan Press Ltd.
Shambaugh, D. 2000. The Chinese state in the post-Mao era. In *The modern Chinese state*, ed. David Shambaugh, 161. Cambridge: Cambridge University Press.
Shue, V. 1994. State power and social organization in China. In *State power and social forces. Domination and transformation in the third world*, eds. J.S. Migdal, A. Kohli, and V. Shue, 69. Cambridge: Cambridge University Press.
Specht, A. V. 1990. Social-Politik. In *1990, Bismarck – Preussen, Deutschland und Europa, Nicolaische Verlangsbuchhandlung*, ed. Deutsches Historisches Museum, 415–417. Berlin: Beuermann GmbH.
Spence, J. 1999. *The search for modern China*, 2nd edn. New York: W. W. Norton & Company.
Teiwes, F. C. 2000. The Maoist state. In *The modern Chinese state*, ed. David Shambaugh, 106. Cambridge: Cambridge University Press.

The Economist. 2013. Reform in China. The party's new blueprint. [online]. Available at http://www.economist.com/blogs/analects/2013/11/reform-china. Accessed 4 June 2014.

Ullmann, H. P. 1999. *Politik im deutschen Kaiserreich, 1871–1918*. München: R. Oldenbourg Verlag.

Waldron, A. 2004. China's directionless transition: A commentary, Asia Media Archives. [online]. Available at http://www.asiamedia.ucla.edu/article.asp?parentid=8157. Accessed 6 Oct 2013.

Yang, J. S. 2008. *Tombstone. The untold story of Mao's great famine*. London: Allen Lane.

Young, N. 2007. How much inequality can China stand? A special report from China Development Brief. [online]. Available at http://www.chinadevelopmentbrief.com/node/1001. Accessed 6 Oct 2013.

Yu, K. P. 2011. A shift towards social governance in China. East Asia Forum. [online]. Available at http://www.eastasiaforum.org/2011/09/09/a-shift-towards-social-governance-in-china/. Accessed 9 Oct 2013.

Yu, J. R. 2013. Reassessing Chinese society's "rigid stability" stability preservation through pressure, its predicament and the way out. [online]. Available at http://www.thechinastory.org/2013/01/chinas-rigid-stability-an-analysis-of-a-predicament-by-yu-jianrong-. Accessed 15 Oct 2013.

Zhao, S. S. 2000. A tragedy of history, China's search for democracy in the twentieth century. In *China and democracy. Reconsidering the prospects for a democratic China*, ed. S. S. Zhao, 33–51. New York: Routledge.

5

Forging a Harmonious Relationship Among the Ethnic Groups

Lei Zhao

China has been a unified multi-ethnic country for more than 200 years, which Professor Fei Xiaotong's depiction of 'the pluralistic unity of the Chinese nation' encapsulates so well. However, because of a variety of historical and contemporary factors, more specifically colonialism and imperialism in the last two centuries, ethnic relations in China's border regions are beset with complex and sensitive problems. As China attempts to forge harmonious relations among its many ethnic groups, it should face the crux of the matter head on and actively learn from the experience of other societies. As an old Chinese saying goes, 'there are stones in other mountains that can be polished into our jade'—China can benefit from drawing on the positive experiences of other nations in dealing with ethnic relations.

L. Zhao (✉)
Institute for International Strategic Studies, Central Party School,
Beijing, China
e-mail: m13021080517@163.com

S. Tsang, H. Men (eds.), *China in the Xi Jinping Era*,
The Nottingham China Policy Institute Series,
DOI 10.1007/978-3-319-29549-7_5

Lessons in Promoting Harmonious Ethnic Relations Outside China

Among the 230 plus countries and regions in the world with diverse ethnic populations, it is possible to define four main types:

- Immigrant countries such as the USA, Canada, and Australia;
- Western industrialized countries such as the United Kingdom, France, and Germany;
- Traditional multi-ethnic countries such as Russia, or India;
- Small countries such as Singapore and Switzerland.

After encountering different challenges and difficulties, all these countries have accumulated fruitful experience in promoting harmony among ethnic groups.

Lessons from Immigrant Countries

Immigrant countries like the USA, Canada, Australia, and New Zealand were established mainly by European settlers. During the colonization period, the settlers killed off many or most of the indigenous people and the minority that remained were usually completely marginalized.

As new immigrant countries, they are mostly built by immigrants from all over the world. Because of the structural characteristics of their populations and the great diversity of their peoples, these countries focus primarily on relations between different immigrant groups. For example, the early immigrants to the USA came predominately from Western Europe, but were later joined by slaves from Africa, settlers from the Middle East, Scandinavia, and Eastern Europe, and labourers from Asia. In its early history, democracy, freedom, and equality were only available to white American communities. These white Americans worked together and forged a new identity as American, which supported economic development and territorial exploration. Not until after the civil rights movement in the 1960s were the principles of democracy and equality applied to every citizen irrespective of race, colour, language, or religion.

Immigrant countries generally rely on their constitution to manage their ethnic relations. They seek to weaken the immigrants' connections with their kinship and ethnic ties to the countries of origin and, instead, cultivate a sense of citizenship based on rights and an awareness of their new national identity. The concept of multi-culturalism was adopted to ease ethnic tensions. Since immigrants come from many different nations, they have different cultural identities and senses of belonging. Their host countries forge a common nationality by demanding that new immigrants embrace the constitution and the rights and duties of citizenship. In other words, they maintain social stability and political unity among ethnic groups by treating their language, religion, and customs as purely cultural differences, which are not allowed to be elevated to a political level.

Intermarriages in these countries have helped to harmonize ethnic relations. Between 1980 and 2008, the rate of intermarriages between white and black Americans increased dramatically and exceeded the rate of intermarriage between white and other ethnic Americans. For example, in 1980, only 5 % of African American males married white American females. In 2008, this increased to 14 %. However, the total number of black and white American intermarriages is still lower than white and other ethnic Americans, with 38 % of Asian and Latino American males marrying white women in 2008. Recently, the structure of the American population has changed dramatically. Between July 2010 and July 2011 the number of ethnic minority newborn babies accounted for more than half of those born in the USA, in which Latino Americans occupied the most. By contrast, the number of white newborns has dropped to below half for the first time in American history.

This demographic change has caused new and increasing generational differences among Americans. The older generations are mainly white, whereas the younger ones are mostly Latino. This leads to tension on how appropriately to allocate insufficient resources across the ethnic divides. Consequently, the biggest challenge to managing ethnic relations becomes one of de-Americanization, meaning that some ethnic groups are becoming more loyal to their countries of origin than to the USA. To counter this problem and promote social harmony among immigrants and long established Americans, the US government has established a 'new Americanization' programme, for which it seeks support from both the private and public sectors.[1]

Lessons from Western Industrialized Countries

The UK, France, and Germany are typical Western industrialized countries; the notions of nationality, nationalist movements, and nation-states originated in these countries. In the process of building their respective nation-states, they have already comprehensively integrated their politics, economy, culture, and language with their ethnic groups. Their people approve of the new nations and solve ethnic problems within this framework. Therefore, they have stronger national productivity and a more dominant military than traditional multi-cultural countries. This type of model has spread to Scandinavia and Eastern Europe and even all over the world.

However, it should be emphasized that European countries cannot be single nation-states. Despite nationalism being introduced through government policies in the 19th century, the whole of Europe has been a multi-ethnic region since ancient times. 'One nation, one country' does not actually exist. Even Germany, which is supposed to be ethnically the least diverse of these European countries, still has to contend with political conflicts arising from differences between High German and regional dialects, as well as tensions between Protestants and Catholics. In the UK, the Anglicization of the Irish has a long history. The teaching of the Irish language was removed from Ireland's school curriculum in 1831. Children who spoke Gaelic at school would be ridiculed and punished by their schoolmates and teachers alike. Even after the establishment of the state of Northern Ireland in 1921, Gaelic was banned from use on the radio and television for another 50 years.

After the Second World War, British policies on ethnic minorities were eased. The Belfast Agreement of 1998 granted Welsh and Scottish Gaelic equal status with English. In 2000, the UK signed the European Charter for Regional or Minority Languages and agreed that 'the British should cherish and utilize their language diversity'. In 2006, the British and Irish

[1] Huntington, "American national interests," 24.

governments signed the St Andrews Agreement, which committed them to legalize a series of protections to the Gaelic language. However, as a result of long-term assimilation, only a few people in Northern Ireland now speak Gaelic.

During the era of industrialization and colonization, the UK, France, and Germany were major sources of emigrants who settled in their colonies. In contrast, after the Second World War, because of shortages of labour, these major Western European countries imported a large number of workers from South Asia, the Middle East, and North Africa to help rebuild their nations. The arrival of new immigrants raised new issues on ethnic relations.

In response, the Western European countries introduced multi-cultural policies. In 1983, the British Commission for Racial Equality encouraged the media to promote ethnic harmony. The British Broadcasting Corporation (BBC) then promised to produce more programmes to reflect the diversity of British society. They interviewed groups from different ethnicities, cultures, and religions, including atheists, and introduced their thoughts and customs to the British people. Today, titles such as 'black', 'Arabs', and 'Asian' are rarely mentioned on official documents. Identity documents purposely avoid ethnic identification by only stating the birthplace of an individual. No other ethnic information is included.

After a series of 'honour killings' by Muslim immigrants and the 7 July 2005 terrorist outrage in London, European countries started to review their policies on ethnic relations. Leaders in Germany, the UK and France admitted that their multi-cultural policies had failed and started to implement a new cultural policy based on integration. There are now two main immigration trends in Western Europe. First, immigration from undeveloped countries has skyrocketed. Second their Muslim population is rising dramatically, having doubled in the past three decades.

This immigration problem differs from that of the USA, which is a traditional immigrant country where mainstream society is mentally prepared for the arrival of new immigrants. They are integrated and arranged properly by a series of systems and policies. Western Europe, by contrast, regards new immigrants as providing a temporary solution to the shortage of domestic labour. Mainstream society does not believe that new immigrants should be given the same citizenship as themselves. Some of the countries do not even grant citizenship to the new immigrants and their offspring.[2] Such a discriminatory attitude inevitably leads to ethnic conflicts and resentment from the new immigrants. In September 2014, an independence referendum in Scotland highlighted the problem of incomplete national policies in Western Europe.

Lessons from Traditional Multi-cultural Countries

Multi-cultural countries like Russia and India have long histories, vast territories, and powerful civilizations. They are like ethnic museums and share many similarities with China in dealing with ethnic relations.

Historically, during its tsarist period, Russia allowed indigenous Russians, who accounted for only 43 % of the total population, to enjoy various privileges. This left the majority labelled as belonging to non-Russian ethnicity and thus ineligible for political office. Economically, the ethnic minority areas were regarded as producers of raw materials and sales markets. The tsar then implemented mandatory 'Russification' to promote one nation, one country, one emperor, one religion, and one language, stopped ethnic minorities from using their own languages, and converted them to the Russian Orthodox Church.

With various measures, tsarist Russia strove throughout the 19th century to implement its Russification policy. First, it actively promoted a Russian political and cultural identity in all border areas and ethnic minority regions. It endorsed a theory about and political identity for Slavic people. The tsar attempted to unite the Slavic groups, including Ukraine and Belarus, into one 'super ethnicity', namely the Russian ethnicity that embraced diversity within its unity.[3] Second, it created provinces in ethnic minority regions to reduce the various ethnic groups' ties to their territorial heritage.[4] Third, it co-opted a select few from the various ethnic groups to join Russia's elites.

---

[2] For example, Germany still does not treat Turkish immigrants as national citizens. This is due to the requirements of citizenship including language and ancestry, and therefore immigrant children cannot be granted German citizenship despite being born in Germany. This changed in 2000.

[3] Guo, *Russia's Messiah Consciousness*, 148.

[4] Liu, *Reform and Revolution*, 169.

The above measures show how the tsar strove to build a modern nation-state by integrating minorities into a unified polity. However, the transition was not successfully completed before the socialist revolution. During the Soviet period, Nikita Khrushchev proposed the introduction of a higher identity than an ethnic-based one. This new identity as 'people of the Soviet Union' did not, however, take root among the ethnic groups, despite being regularly propagated by the state organs.

Once the Russian Federation had approved its new constitution on 12 December 1993, the new state pursued a policy of building a multicultural unitary national identity. In place of the privileges that individual republics had enjoyed under the former Soviet Union, the constitution enshrined the principle of equal rights for all federal states. Autonomy among the nationalities became a cultural rather than a political right. Meanwhile, intellectuals and politicians reviewed and reflected on the old Soviet policies on ethnicity and nationality, and proposed a new set incorporating the following. First, on the principle of equality for all nationalities, the unity of Russia is emphasized. This included the removal of the right to secede from constituent republics in the 1993 constitution. Second, it puts human and civil rights above ethnic rights. In 1991, the Russian Federation promulgated a 'Civil Code' specifying that citizens from different ethnic groups should share the same rights, freedom, and obligations. Third, it decreased the importance of ethnicity and ends the 1934 requirement to put one's nationality or ethnicity on identity documents. Fourth, to pre-empt extreme nationalism, the state introduced new laws to punish behaviour inciting ethnic hostility or provoking ethnic conflicts. A new set of regulations known as an outline of the Russian Federation's Nationality Policy was introduced in 1996 to prohibit activities that undermined national security, or incited social, racial, ethnic, or religious conflicts.[5] Henceforth, ethnic policy sought to develop civil society and construct a unified Russian nation.[6] In 1994, a charter for harmonious relations among Russian citizens was passed to promote peaceful coexistence among different ethnic groups. In 2004,

[5] Xiong and He, "Minzu chongtu," 19–21.

[6] Zuo, "Eluosi de minzu wenti."

the Russian Labour Code was modified to make 4 November a national solidarity day and a statutory holiday.

Lessons from Small Countries

In terms of size and population, Switzerland and Singapore are undoubtedly small countries. However, their practices and theories on dealing with ethnic conflicts, from which China can draw inspiration, are more progressive than those of other countries.

Despite the country's conspicuous ethnic diversity, Switzerland's ethnic groups enjoy respectable and harmonious relations with one another and no serious ethnic conflicts have ever occurred there. In Switzerland, people only describe themselves as 'Swiss citizens' and do not use words such as 'ethnic' or 'minority'. So what kinds of ethnic groups does Switzerland have? In their own words, 'the country is constructed by people who came to Switzerland because they did not want to live in their original country'. The majority originated from Germany, France, and Italy. Multiculturalism is reflected in every aspect of society. Under the egalitarian social system, the Swiss people tolerate and respect considerable differences in culture and religion among the different regions. Consequently, no interference or structural social conflict has arisen.[7] Scholars describe this as citizen-based federalism, which has the following characteristics.[8]

First, the political foundation of the Swiss constitution is based on citizens rather than ethnicity. None of the 26 cantons allows special rights for their citizens, and no special arrangement has been established for specific ethnic groups. The constitution lays stress on citizenship to reinforce civic equality and political participation.

Second, the most important feature of Swiss democracy is its citizens' involvement in making policy rather than relying on the electoral mechanism or representation. By giving its citizens from different ethnic groups ample opportunities to participate regularly at different levels of government decision making, the system grooms mature and sensible 'federal citizens' who can surpass the constraints and narrow interests of their

[7] Guan, "Multiculturalism."

[8] Tian, "Ruishi zuqun zhili moshi," 98–107.

own ethnic groups. Direct democracy further diminishes citizens' dependence on political parties and factions.

Third, it promotes social equilibrium and cohesion. The preamble of the 1999 Swiss constitution states that 'the strength of a country is measured by welfare received by its weakest member'. The federal government is responsible for promoting social and economic development between different units, thus removing gaps and inequality among ethnic groups. Its economic or financial policies do not favour ethnic groups, and its constitution is focused on promoting citizenship without any ethnic undertones. Consequently, Switzerland does not have 'ethnic privileges' or 'ethnic divisions', just 'self-government by citizens' and 'equality before the constitution'.

Problems and Solutions to Ethnic Relations in China

Ethnic relations in China should be examined in accordance with the facts on the ground. Its practices are neither the worst nor the best in the world. Adjectives such as good or bad are inappropriate for describing and evaluating the current situation. It is better to ascertain what the problems are and then seek solutions to put Chinese ethnic relations on a healthier track. This is how China should project soft power during its peaceful rise in the 21st century.

A policy of 'ethnic compartmentalization' merely serves to strengthen ethnic awareness and deepen demographic and cultural distinctions between ethnic groups. After the establishment of the People's Republic of China (PRC) in 1949, China emulated the Soviet Union by introducing classification and recognition along ethnic lines with a view to laying the foundation for promoting autonomy in ethnic minority regions and supporting the development of minorities. Consequently, ethnic groups used their identity to secure privileges offered by the government, which reinforced their identity along demographic and cultural lines.[9]

Meanwhile, the central government established 'autonomous regions' based on the population sizes and settlement patterns of recognized

[9] Ma, "Scene of secession," 101–102.

ethnic groups. These constitute 65 % of the total landmass in China. Each autonomous region is identifiable by the main ethnic group in the area and has a stable administrative region and clear boundary. The ethnic groups that enjoy autonomous status are a minority in the population but they are granted various privileges, for example, in terms of the 'one child policy', entrance requirements to universities, or application for civil service posts. This preferential treatment nurtures and strengthens ethnic awareness among different ethnic groups and causes inter-ethnic estrangement and conflicts.[10]

Ethnic awareness has been strengthened and manifests itself in the following ways:

- People from other ethnic groups are not welcome in various autonomous areas;
- Ethnic languages are protected at schools, particularly where there is concern about low use of the mother tongue in the region;
- There is a desire to develop an ethnic local economy;
- The reinforcement of ethnic awareness and ethnic cohesion through religion, customs, history, and education is so great that it hinders the harmonization of different ethnic groups on the basis of equality.[11]

Furthermore, streaming cadres along ethnic lines creates an artificial ceiling. For example, some outstanding ethnic cadres from minorities find themselves in an awkward position as they pursue self-development to achieve their personal goals. They would like to join the ranks of the national elite and serve their country and society, but the current environment and system in place prevents this from happening, for it designates them as cadres from specific ethnic groups. As a result, they are constantly being reminded of 'what they are' and 'what position is or is not reserved for them'.[12]

Second, not all problems that occur in ethnic regions are 'ethnic problems'. Only when ethnic problems and problems in ethnic regions are

[10] Ibid., 102.
[11] Ibid., 103.
[12] Ibid., 105.

differentiated can the government correctly judge the current situation and future trends on ethnic relations. Livelihood and identity issues are the two main types of problems in the western minority regions. In terms of livelihood issues they also happen in Han regions, where they suffer from corruption, tense relations between cadres and citizens, and even vicious riots such as the '2008 Weng'an incident'. However, if the same things happened in Xinjiang or Tibet, the local people would see them through a prism of ethnic interests and would cause them to manifest in different ways and result in different consequences. Do the local ethnic groups and the Han settlers have separate ethnic identities? Do members of ethnic groups identify more with the Chinese than with their own ethnic group?[13]

Identity issues, especially intergenerational identity, should be a high priority in minority regions. The younger generations in these regions may well not share the same values and frames of references as their parents. In the era of globalization, population migration increases difficulties in social management. Globally, there is a tendency for public problems (such as high unemployment and inequality in education and job opportunities) to be transformed into political issues.[14] Ethnic problems have received more attention in Chinese politics since the start of the reform period. While the minorities have been offered more privileges, their capacity for social management and for balancing competing interests has weakened, as a result of which many youths from ethnic minorities are discriminated against and put in disadvantaged positions. In the past, the work-unit system operated in cities and the commune system in rural areas, which meant that population movements were controlled as part of the planned economy. Today, people can move freely, so the demands on social management mechanisms are much higher. Moreover, information is now disseminated differently. Young people from ethnic minorities now primarily obtain information online, which raises a new challenge for China's social management systems.

Third, ethnic relations in China are facing both domestic and international pressure. In the 20th century ethnic and religious problems in

---

[13] Ibid.

[14] Yu, "Liangxing zhili."

most countries were primarily about responding to external pressure, about opposing separatism, as well as safeguarding sovereignty and territorial integrity. In the early 21st century, the pressure is mostly domestic and to do with such things as cultural identity, ethnic integration, and equality. While ethnic and religious problems have always existed in the world, the causes have changed significantly.

With China's rise in the 21st century, the pressure on ethnic relations comes mainly from the outside world, from places such as the USA and Europe, but it is also intensifying domestically. For instance, when the ecological migration project required Tibetan herdsmen to relocate from the grasslands to the cities, a significant change occurred in their culture and ethnic identity. They started to have employment difficulties because the majority of herdsmen did not speak Chinese and they had no knowledge or experience of earning a living in a city. In their original pastoral environment, they had felt no different from others, but this changed significantly when they moved to the cities and interacted with Han people there. They felt estranged from the Han and could not identify with the cities or with anyone in them. They found their sense of marginalization distressing and such alienation can easily lead to conflict. If it gets politicized, it nurtures mistrust in the government and allows hostile external forces to take advantage of them.

Fourth, Chinese government policies for supporting minority regions still need to be improved. On the one hand, many cadres and citizens in Han populated provinces believe that the economic conditions in their region are insufficiently strong to offer support to Tibet and Xinjiang. Consequently, their policy commitments to support the minority regions are all talk but no action. On the other hand, the ethnic minority cadres and citizens are unhappy. They claim that Han culture is no better than theirs and since their regions are endowed with ample resources, they see need of help from the Han. They are also anxious that the government's policy to support minority regions might lead to the plundering of their resources and damage to their environment. Furthermore, they are concerned that such a policy will eventually make ethnic minority regions too dependent on central government. In other words, they fear that as soon as the central government withdraws its assistance from the minority regions, their economies, administrations, and social orders will collapse. The government should therefore realize that devising a policy in good faith cannot guarantee that it will achieve its desired goal.

Long-term stability cannot be secured merely by strengthening efforts to support minority regions. It can only be established by implementing a new comprehensive policy on ethnic relations that delivers equality across the ethnic groups. Some Chinese scholars suggest applying preferential policies to regions rather than specific ethnic groups. This means making preferential treatment available to all citizens living in the western regions and ethnic minority areas, rather than to minorities who live in large cities or developed areas. In addition, comprehensive development projects should not be confined to Tibet and Xinjiang but should cover the entire western region of China. If the central government gives preferential treatment to an ethnic area whenever it experiences a riot, it will only create an incentive for further rioting. Hence, the policy to support ethnic minority regions must be implemented carefully to avoid unnecessary comparisons and feelings of inequality that could trigger further conflicts in ethnic minority areas.

In fact, members of ethnic minorities hold two different views on this policy. The elite ones view the support from the central government as excessive and discriminating, whereas those from the lower and middle strata think that the support is insufficient and that they have been ignored. Furthermore, the Chinese government should not really confine its policy on Xinjiang to the Uighurs because more than 50 other ethnic groups also inhabit the region. The reality is that young people from the ethnic minorities who receive their education in China proper often go back to Xinjiang after graduation, whereas the Han youths who do the same are more likely to remain in China proper than to return to Xinjiang. This has implications for the social stability and ethnic unity of Xinjiang. It also raises questions about who really constitute the minorities in ethnic areas. For example, Hotan Prefecture in Xinjiang has a population of 1.95 million, consisting of 22 ethnic groups including the Uyghur, Han, Hui, Tajik, and Kirgiz. The Uyghur make up 96.3 % of the population, the Han 3.5 %, and other ethnic groups the remaining 0.2 %. Government policy should therefore take into account the actual situation in ethnic areas, taking care of 'relative minorities' there rather than focusing on the 'absolute minority' in China as a whole.

Finally, it is necessary to clarify that ethnic policies should not focus exclusively on maintaining social stability. Social stability, ethnic unity, and anti-separatism are all important for the happiness of all ethnic groups. If the government concentrates only on economic development and growth, it will create a whole range of other problems.

Promoting Ethnic Integration

Ethnic integration is a sensitive issue that cannot be enforced by administrative fiat. Ethnic groups must develop their prosperity collectively, and on this subject there are profound lessons to be drawn from China's history. In the late 1950s, a leftist approach inappropriately and hastily raised the 'great ethnic integration' slogan and a campaign was launched to that effect. The Cultural Revolution, under the banner of *Fēng-zī-xiū* (anti-feudalism, anti-capitalism, and anti-revisionism), sought to undermine the customs, languages, economic arrangements, ways of life, and cultures of all the ethnic minorities. During that period China saw ethnic genealogies burnt, temples demolished, and, among other things, Muslim people forced to raise pigs. These actions naturally inflicted deep wounds and long-lasting resentment among the members of those ethnic minorities.[15]

Even now, well after the start of the reform period, certain policies and practices concerning ethnic relations still need rethinking. For example, is it really wise to create a written language for an ethnic group that has never previously had one? Surely such a move will merely create artificial divisions and estrangements that can only harm inter-ethnic interaction and integration. Also, do minorities still warrant exemption from the one child policy? Given that demographics have changed significantly in the last two decades, with ethnic minorities increasing dramatically from 5 to 10 % of the total Chinese population, it was ill advised to encourage minorities in deprived and backward areas to have more children. Such a policy is no longer appropriate. The rapid population growth among the minorities has affected economic development, employment opportunities,

[15] Zhu, "Thoughts on nationality issue."

and education and, as a result, it has become more difficult to improve people's quality of life and eradicate poverty. Today, social inequality is not among ethnic groups but between different regions, with little disparity between different ethnic groups in the same area.[16]

To promote integration, respect, tolerance of difference, and diversity among ethnic groups, a growing number of scholars and experts are suggesting that it would improve ethnic relations if the government were to remove ethnic information from identity cards, promote ethnically mixed schools, and stop increasing the number of regional ethnic autonomies.[17] Ethnic integration should definitely not be about 'Sinicization', but about the various ethnic groups sharing their virtues and strengths across the board. More specifically, ethnic integration should include intermarriage, the coordination of economic interests, and ideological harmonization through education.

First, it is universally accepted that intermarriages effectively enhance communication between ethnic groups and promote social integration. In China, centuries of close kinships among some ethnic groups have resulted in there being little noticeable physical or ethnic differences between them. In reality, religious prohibitions are the main obstacles to intermarriage. Islamic laws explicitly prohibit marriages between Muslims and non-Muslims. Muslim men can marry Ahl al-Kitab (Christian and Jewish women), though she must convert to her husband's religion and follow all the religious customs. A Muslim woman cannot marry a non-Muslim man unless he converts to Islam. From a practical viewpoint, ethnic intermarriage is a prototype of religious marriage. For example, 99 % of China's Uygur, Kazak, and Kirgiz people live in Xinjiang and account for 53 % of the total Xinjiang population. However, they have the lowest rate of intermarriage among China's 55 minorities, with only 1.05 % of Uighurs, 2.21 % of Kazaks, and 5.15 % of Kirgiz marrying outside their own ethnic group.[18]

Policy orientation is also a key factor in influencing inter-ethnic marriages. In the 1950s, intermarriage was frowned upon in Xinjiang if either

[16] Mo, "Makesi zhuyi minzu ronghe," 136.

[17] Zhu, "Thoughts on nationality issue."

[18] Li, 'Xinjiang zu ji hunyin," 87.

ethnic group objected to it. It was considered damaging to ethnic unity and people were expected to sacrifice their personal feelings for the good of the minority group, which was clearly not conducive to social integration. Furthermore, it gave the general public a negative impression of the government's view on intermarriage and limited their understanding and choices on such a matter. Such a situation is not conducive to the protection of personal autonomy in marriage, social integration, or harmonious ethnic relations.[19]

The Marriage Law of the People's Republic of China, introduced on 1 January 1981, again put the issue of intermarriage onto the agenda. Some ethnic autonomous regions legislated to prohibit interference in the freedom of intermarriage. Under the Marriage Registration Management Regulations of the Xinjiang Uygur Autonomous Region (1996), the Xinjiang Uygur Autonomous Region People's Government Order No. 62 states that 'men and women from different ethnicities or religions can legally register for marriage by their own accord, and any other act of interference to the freedom of marriage shall be prohibited'. This repealed the old requirement that prohibited intermarriages, and people in Xinjiang started to share the same marriage registration procedures practised elsewhere in China. Since then, the number of intermarriages in Xinjiang has increased; and a higher incidence has taken place in the north than in the south, in urban than in rural areas, and in mixed rather than single ethnic neighbourhoods. People of Han ethnicity intermarry most, particularly to the Hui group. People who do not live in ethnically segregated areas, but in places such as Urumqi, Ghulja, and Xibe district in Tacheng City, generally have a higher rate of intermarriage. Ethnic groups that share a similar cultural heritage, as do the Uygur, Kazak, and Uzbek, the Tatar, Han, and Manchu, and the Mongo and Xibe, also intermarry more.[20]

In Xinjiang, intermarriage is least common between the Uyghur and Han. Their increasingly frequent interaction over the last 20 years has done nothing to break down the barriers between them. On the contrary, it has intensified their differences. Since religion exerts such a deep

[19] Li, "Hunyin zhuangkuang de yingxiang," 109.
[20] Li, 'Xinjiang zu ji hunyin," 83.

influence over the daily lives of Uyghur people, intermarriage is enormously stressful in their society. This is undoubtedly due to propaganda from ethnic separatist and religious extremist groups, but it also shows that improvements in material circumstances or increased interethnic mingling are not enough to guarantee deep integration across ethnic groups.

Since the nature of intermarriage is complicated, the government should always respect individual choices and refrain from interference in any form. It should support every citizen's legal right to marry and should advocate personal freedom of choice; the entire society should place more value on the interest of the individual over that of the group.[21] In short, government policies should meet the needs of social development, which includes intermarriage and ethnic integration.

Second, economic complementarity provides the material foundation with which to unite ethnic groups. Some scholars believe that ethnic integration cannot rely on instilling friendship and rationality among groups, and a successful outcome requires economic development. However, this is not a panacea. Although sharing economic interests and economic space places different ethnic groups together, we should not ignore market forces. The former Soviet Union ignored the market economy for a long time, using administrative fiat to manage labour and the economy, but this was not conducive to economic development.[22]

A World Bank study of Chinese poverty undertaken in 2009 concluded that poverty was concentrated in rural areas, with the rate in remote mountainous areas two to three times that in urban areas; also, ethnic minorities were two to three times more likely than the Han race to suffer from poverty.[23] Furthermore, a kind of occupational stratification exists among ethnic groups in industry and the professions, which is not only a major obstacle to economic unity but also a huge impediment to ethnic integration.

In general, the regions that ethnic minorities populate have harsh natural conditions; they have underdeveloped infrastructures, a limited

[21] Li, "Hunyin zhuangkuang de yingxiang," 109.

[22] Zuo, "Minzu zhengce,"145.

[23] *Wall Street Journal*, "Zhongguo pinkun wenti."

capacity for self-development, as well as inadequate education, social security, and social development. In 2012, nearly 40 million people living in rural ethnic minority populated areas suffered from poverty. In Guangxi, 80 % of those in poverty are from ethnic minorities. In fact, there are two 80 % benchmarks in Xinjiang. In the south 80 % live below the poverty line, whereas the 80 % of those living in poverty in the north are from ethnic minorities. Therefore, the national policy to target poverty alleviation among minorities, pursued since the 1950s, was the right approach. This has proved essential and brought about notable changes.

In light of the existing ethnic distribution, ethnic and regional factors will remain crucial in shaping government policies in the foreseeable future. However, due to the gradual increase in mixed residence among ethnic groups and improvements in their quality of life and education, the government should place more emphasis on regional factors. In other words, financial support should not be directed to specific ethnic groups but to people who live in a harsh natural environment or in a particularly poverty-stricken area. This can be accommodated by existing schemes such as 'Develop the West' and the 'Frontier Action Plan'. By focusing on helping deprived regions, ethnic minorities who live there will still benefit, though a different political course will be provided.[24]

Third, there is a need to promote ideological integration through education. Before 1949, there was no formal higher education institute dedicated to teaching minorities, and the enrolment rate of school-age children from minority groups was extremely low. For example, in 1928 only 2 % of school-age children in Xinjiang attended a school; in 1949, this was 10 % in Ningxia and 2 % in Tibet. This led to a high rate of illiteracy among the minorities and in regions heavily populated by minorities. During the1930s and 1940s, 22 of the ethnic minorities had an illiteracy rate of more than 95 %. Even among the more literate minorities such as the Koreans, Mongos, and Uzbeks, illiteracy rates ranged between 40 and 60 %.[25] It was not until

[24] Zhu, "Thoughts on nationality issue."

[25] Yang, *Northwest Ethnic Minority*, 63.

September 1951 that the Ministry of Education held its first national conference on ethnic minority education in Beijing. There it adopted a policy to educate the minorities and to establish a dedicated unit for ethnic education at the department of education, with branches in the provinces.

The big change took place in 2002 when the State Council issued its 'decision to deepen reform and accelerate the development of minority education', setting clear objectives and requirements. Since then, minority education has been significantly improved as the government introduced a series of vital measures, which narrowed the differences in education provision between minority populated regions and the rest of the country. In the transitional period it remains essential to give extra support to ethnic groups through preferential policies because the historical legacy of different provision of educational resources needs to be overcome. For this purpose, the Outline Plan for Medium and Long-term Education Reform and Development (2010–2020) was issued in July 2010 to ensure that educational resources would be preferentially invested in minority populated regions.

Indeed, the plan requires educational support to be allocated to support the policy. At the beginning of the 1980s, some key national universities started to cooperate with relevant provinces and autonomous regions to hold preparatory classes for them. Special classes and schools for Tibetans have been provided in the mainland since 1984, followed by similar provisions for Xinjiang's ethnic groups in 1987, which was extended to include provisions in high schools in 2000. These special policies and measures have undoubtedly improved education and social development in ethnic regions. However, for social, historical, and environmental reasons, their progress has been slow compared with educational growth in the more developed coastal and mainland regions. The number and quality of their graduates are wanting and there is still a severe shortage of high-level professionals with post-graduate qualifications in the eastern regions. In comparison with the rest of China, professionals in the western regions reach only 20.4 % of the national average, senior technical personnel 13.6 %, and academics a mere 8.3 %. Among them few are from a minority background, with only 15.4 % of the senior technical personnel in engineering and 8.8 % in scientific research being a member of any minority group.[26] Therefore, the government must implement, as a matter of urgency, special measures to improve ethnic equality and to train members of minorities to take on high-level professional jobs.

There are other problems associated with implementing government policy. In some autonomous regions, certain ethnic minorities actually share the same language with the Han, and their culture and traditions are largely similar. They are educated at the same schools or equally good schools, but students from ethnic minority backgrounds receive preferential treatment when they apply for admission to university. This goes against the basic spirit of equality.[27] Admittedly, a policy of positive discrimination is needed, but it also increases minority students' dependence on state support. The real problem in the varying quality of educational resource allocation is caused by the difference in stages of development within a region. Therefore, what is needed in the long term is a policy to allocate educational resources based on regional variations, rather than ethnic differences.

Equality across ethnic divides also requires equality in the treatment of languages. Indeed, there is a close relationship between policies in language and education. Bilingual education must be an essential part of education in ethnic areas. It enables ethnic minorities not only to acquire the ability to use their own languages but also to learn to use Mandarin. This enables them both to keep their ethnic traditions alive and to meet the challenges brought forth by globalization. Any language (irrespective of whether or not it has a written form) is a valuable historical legacy and deserves protection and respect. By learning different languages, students can understand and respect the diversity of cultures. It improves their communication skills, increases their tolerance, and helps them understand themselves better, as well as learn about others. It is important not to emphasize politics in bilingual education. It is not meant to undermine the diversity of ethnic groups but to enhance communication and connection between them. Following the above principle and based on their actual needs, ethnic groups should be able to choose what language they want to learn.

[26] Jiaoyu bu, "Shaoshu minzu gugan rencai."

[27] Li, "Shaoshu minzu youhui zhengce," 79.

From Ethnic Communities to a Community of Shared Values

Given the continuous progress of socialist modernization, the movement towards integration in the distribution, communication, and development of ethnic groups in China has now reached the progressive stage of 'embedded development'. The future challenge is to establish a common set of values that all ethnic groups can embrace and that can unite all the people in China (Fig. 5.1).

In the age of the nation-state, a nation is the basis for a sovereign state, meaning 'a nation is normally presented as a country'.[28] The coincidence of nation with state implies that it is natural to rely on nationalism to define the identity and meaning of a country.[29] A nation-state is usually defined as 'a political community that is constituted by the same nation

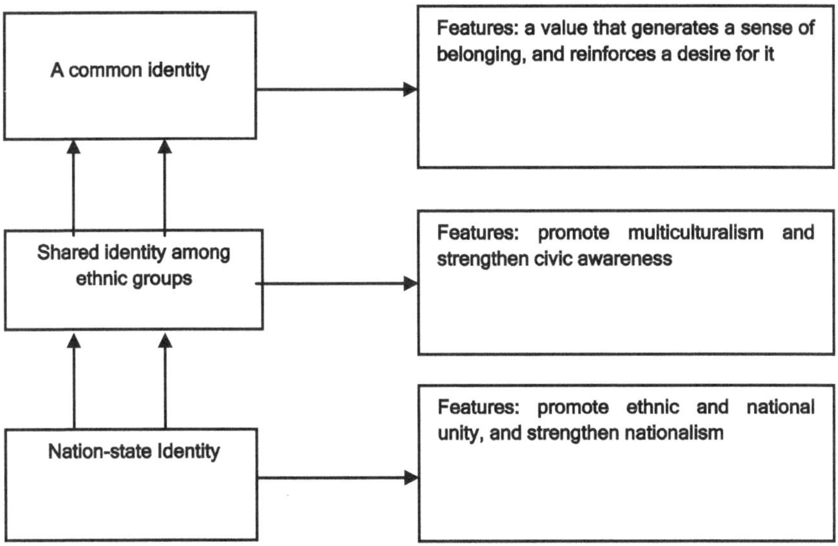

Fig. 5.1 Three stages in forging an ethnic and national identity

[28] Xu, *Nationalism*, 13.

[29] Jiang, *Liberalism, Nationalism, National Identity*, 139.

(or primarily by one nation)'. Therefore, national identity is inevitably connected with ethnic awareness or nationalism. Nevertheless, in the process of putting the nation and state together, almost every country has to confront the challenge of separatism. The international community, however, has now largely abandoned the ideal of ethnic and national unity.

For a multi-ethnic country to forge a common identity, it needs to base its legitimacy on the leaders and citizens belonging to the same multi-ethnic community and sharing in all its benefits. This implies that the citizens' sense of belonging is not to a nation-state but to a multi-ethnic country and that they no longer seek unity between ethnicity and the state. The political focus is not on serving an ethnic community but on the multi-ethnic country to which all its citizens feel enduring enthusiasm and loyalty. This shared identity should be the source of political authority and the basis for resolving conflicts among the various ethnic groups and for establishing stability and consistency in the community. Admittedly, building a multi-ethnic country is much more difficult than building a single ethnic one. For instance, to achieve equal rights for all, citizens from minority backgrounds need to make extra efforts to learn the national language and to absorb the common culture.[30]

In China, forging a shared identity is about strengthening Chinese national identity. To do so, we should learn the lessons of the collapse of the Soviet Union and of the impact of Soviet ethnic theories on China. We must instill in all citizens a strong sense of identity and civic duty to China as a sovereign state. At the same time we must respect and protect the traditional culture and languages of ethnic minorities where appropriate and support their rights as citizens if they need special help.

In reality, the creation of a shared identity of ethnic communities will not lead to the wholesale replacement of ethnicity with nationality. The general pattern is that people increasingly want to assert their sense of history, culture, religion, ethnicity, and historical origins. In other

[30] Zhu and Guan, "Zhengzhi yinsu."

words, people need to affirm their identities and historical memories.[31] Establishing a shared identity, or community of shared values, is not only about protecting cultural heritage but also about improving cohesion among ethnic groups through forging common values vis-à-vis others in the international context.

In the process of forging national values, the various ethnic groups must share their own values and work together to develop a common value that all will embrace sincerely.

In the first two stages, namely building first a nation-state identity and then a shared identity among ethnic groups, the Chinese state has, in its attempt to avoid conflicts caused by ethnic heterogeneity, tried to deal with matters related to territorial integrity and sovereignty by focusing on commonalities. The common identity to be created in the third stage is not based on the value of the dominant ethnic group but on the shared values of all ethnic groups. More specifically, this has two requirements. The first is to incorporate as much as possible the different ethnic cultures into the new common one from which all ethnic groups will be able to trace their personal heritages. The second is to ensure that the new common identity has a philosophical core and values that all the constituent ethnic groups will find acceptable.[32]

In China, the basis for developing common values derives from the personal relationships, friendliness, and care that people are able to show for one another. This Chinese ideal is fundamentally different from the American dream, which is essentially about the USA being a platform from which individuals who come from different backgrounds can fulfil their ambitions. It places emphasis on individuals (such as individual freedom and equality), and quantifiable achievements (such as a black person becoming president). The Chinese ideal is about human relationships and inner qualities. It is something that needs to be appreciated by and should be shared with the rest of the world. This is because modernization and information technology have created disengagement, distance, emptiness, and loneliness. By promoting traditional Chinese

---

[31] Grumman, *Nationalism and Territory*, 27–28.

[32] Han, "Minzu renting," 6.

culture, Chinese diplomacy can work to redress such negativities in the world. In other words, by forging a common ideal in China, the Chinese people can also contribute to the world by offering to share its wonderful culture with others.

Bibliography

Grumman, J. N. 2009. *Nationalism and territory*. Beijing: Central University for Nationalities.

Guan, K. 2004. Multiculturalism and the national regional autonomy: Analysis of the international experiences of ethnic policies (continued). *N.W. Ethno-National Studies* 2: 41–42.

Guo, X. L. 2009. *Russia's messiah consciousness*. Beijing: People's Publishing House.

Han, Y. 2011. Cong minzu renting dao xianfa renting – lixian zhuyi shijiao xia minzu yu guo jia guanxi zhi fansi yu zhong gou. *Faxue pinglun* 3: 6.

Huntington, S. P. 1997. The erosion of American national interests. *Diplomacy*. October. Cited in Sun, D. Y. 1999. Jieshi minzu chongtu de san zhong lilun tu shi. *GuiZhou Ethnic Studies* 3: 24.

Jiang, Y. H. 1998. *Liberalism, nationalism and national identity*. Taipei: Yangzhi wenhua shiye.

Jiaoyu bu. 2004. Jiaoyu bu, guojia fazhan gaige wei, guojia min wei, caizheng bu, renshi bu guanyu dali peiyang shaoshu minzu gao cengci gugan rencai de yijian. *Zhonghua renmin gongheguo jiaoyu bu gongbao* (9). 8 July, 2004.

Li, X. X. 2005. Xinjiang gaoxiao zhaosheng zhong de shaoshu minzu kaosheng youhui zhengce fenxi. *Xinjiang daxue xuebao* 1: 79.

——— 2008a. Xinjiang zu ji hunyin de diaochao yu fenxi. *Xinjiang daxue xuebao – renwen shehui kexue ban* 3: 87.

——— 2008b. Xinjiang zu ji hunyin de diaochao yu fenxi. *Xinjiang daxue xuebao – renwen shehui kexue ban* 3: 83.

——— 2010. Guojia zhengce dui zu ji hunyin zhuangkuang de yingxiang. *Xinjiang shehui kexue* 5: 109.

Liu, Z. X. 2001. *Reform and revolution – Russian modernisation research*. Beijing: Peking University Press.

Ma, R. 2011a. How to view the current issue of ethnic relations in China. *Leader* 2: 105.

——— 2011b. Whether there will be a scene of secession in China in the 21st century. *Leader* 2: 101–105.

Mo, Y. Y. 2011. Makesi zhuyi minzu ronghe lilun de dang dai sikao – jian lun liweihan dui minzu ronghe de lilun gongxian. *Guangdong she hui kexue* 6: 136.

Tian, F. L. 2010. Ruishi zuqun zhili moshi pingshuo – jiyu xianfa aiguo zhuyi de gongmin lianbang zhi. *Faxue* 10: 98–107.

Wall Street Journal. 2009. Zhongguo pinkun wenti mei name jiandan. [online]. Available at http://www.cn.wsj.com/gb/20090414/chj135948.asp. Accessed 14 Apr 2009.

Xiong, K. X., and J. R. He. 2007. Xiandai guoji minzu chongtu yu minzu hejie anli fenxi. *Heilongjiang National Series* 6: 19–21.

Xu, X. 2005. *Nationalism.* Beijing: China Social Sciences Publishing House.

Yang, J. 2006. *Northwest ethnic minority development of elementary education.* Beijing: Ethnic Publishing House.

Yu, H. Y. 2012. Liangxing zhili: Weihu minzu guojia tizhi he huajie minzu chongtu de qianti. *Zhongguo minzu bao.*

Zhu, W. Q. 2012. Some thoughts on the current nationality issue. *Study Times.*

Zhu, L., and K. Guan. 2007. Zhengzhi yinsu yiran shi minzu wenti de shouyao yuanyin. *Zhongguo minzu bao.*

Zuo, F. R. 2010. Minzu zhengce yu suilian jieti. *Contemporary World & Socialism* 2: 145.

Zuo, F. R. 2011. Xianjin eluosi de minzu wenti yu minzu zhengce. *Study Time.*

6

Ageing, Urbanization, and the Search for a Sustainable Development Model

Baojiang Han and Shiping Qi

Rapid urbanization and dramatic population ageing are two of the main characteristics of China's current economic and social situation. These two features, which interact with and affect each other, are having a major impact on the country's ability to pursue sustainable development.

According to the 'Statistical Communiqué of the People's Republic of China on National Economic and Social Development in 2013' (hereafter 'the 2013 Statistical Communiqué') issued by the National Bureau of Statistics (NBS) in 2014, the number of people in China aged 60 and over had reached 202 million by the end of 2013, accounting for 14.9 % of the total population, 1.64 percentage points higher than in 2010. These figures show that the process of population ageing in China is accelerating and this, of course, will have a significant effect on the supply of workers to its economy. The proportion of young people is decreasing,

B. Han (✉) • S. Qi
Department of Economics, Central Party School, Beijing, China
e-mail: Hanbj@ccps.gov.cn; Qishiping@163.com

S. Tsang, H. Men (eds.), *China in the Xi Jinping Era*,
The Nottingham China Policy Institute Series,
DOI 10.1007/978-3-319-29549-7_6

while that of old people is increasing. The consequent shrinking of the labour force will trigger a labour shortage, while a decrease in public resources providing healthcare, long-term care, and income support for an older population will lead to further strains on these facilities. With this acceleration of population ageing, the maintenance of sustainable economic and social development presents a major challenge for China.

Meanwhile, urbanization is accelerating rapidly. According to the 2013 Statistical Communiqué, there were 731 million permanent urban residents at the end of 2013, accounting for 53.73 % of the total population, 1.16 percentage points higher than the previous year. The rapid acceleration of urbanization brings opportunities as well as challenges. On the one hand, it will lead to the development of certain industries in China, which will stimulate domestic demand, boost growth in domestic consumption, attract private investment, spur investment demand, improve tertiary industry, and facilitate an upgrade of the industrial structure. This acceleration of urbanization will lead to a huge increase in demand for housing, infrastructure, and a variety of other durable consumer goods, which will become an important focus for China with regard to stimulating domestic demand. On the other hand, the country will face the challenge of 'poor quality' urbanization. China's sixth population census shows that its floating population has reached 260 million. However, this transfer of rural labour to urban centres poses special problems. Because most migrants from rural areas working in cities are still registered as rural residents, they are not entitled to receive the same treatment as urban residents or enjoy the same access as they do to public services. This means that China's urbanization is based on an unsound foundation.

Sustainable development is a relatively broad concept, but population and urbanization, which closely impinge on one another, are two of its most important components, along with demographic shifts such as population ageing. Because the main feeder for China's urbanization is the migration of its rural population to urban areas, the rapid increase in the number of older people has led to fewer rural migrants moving to urban areas, thereby decreasing the supply and increasing the cost of labour. The pace at which the rural population ages affects the speed of urbanization, which causes a negative correlation, or in other words the faster the rural population ages, the slower the process of urbanization becomes and vice versa. An ageing population increases the economic pressures on urbanization, reduces the vitality of the labour force in cities, and lessens the overall efficiency of the urbanization process. At the same time, urbanization has produced a better infrastructure with which to cater for an ageing population because the services that elderly people require are increasingly being provided in urban areas. It is noteworthy that China has not yet developed a full-blown 'silver industry', namely the business sector designed specifically to produce products and services for senior citizens. This sector lags behind China's other service industries and its underdevelopment is not conducive to harmonious social and economic development. Promoting a 'silver industry' should therefore be one of the main areas of focus for China's urbanization in the future.

Building a moderately prosperous society in an all-round manner in China is, in essence, about achieving sustainable economic and social development. China needs to resolve its problems associated with an ageing population and urbanization in a coordinated manner to ensure positive interaction between them.

China's Ageing Population and Loss of 'Demographic Dividend'

Its ageing population is an important social phenomenon in China and it needs proper handling to ensure the smooth development of the country's modernization programme. As numerous scholars have testified, 'the ageing of China's population will pose a huge challenge to its rise in the twenty-first century'.[1] Jackson and Howe believe that 'how China deals with the challenges of its ageing population will determine whether it will be able to transform itself into a prosperous and stable modern country'.[2] Zhang Guilian and Wang Yonglian state that 'the demographic transition and the ageing of its population have brought great pressure to bear on China's economic and social development, resulting in a shortage

[1] OECD, *Economic Surveys.*

[2] Jackson and Howe, *Graying of Middle Kingdom.*

of labour and an increase in pressure on its social security'.[3] Forming a scientific understanding of the economic and social pressures caused by its ageing population is an important prerequisite to dealing properly with these challenges.

The Current Situation and Characteristics of China's Ageing Population

China is a large, populous country and population issues have always been at the heart of its economic and social development. To ease the pressure of population growth during the 1970s and 1980s, China successfully implemented a family planning policy that effectively curbed the over rapid expansion of its population. However, while this policy brought down the birth rate, it also very quickly changed the demographic structure to one in which the proportion of elderly people became much greater than ever before, with the consequence that it has become an ageing society earlier than expected.

The old-age dependency ratio, the ratio of those aged 65 or over to the rest of the population, is an important indicator of whether a country or region is considered relatively old or young. In general, a society is considered relatively old when the ratio exceeds 7 %. However, simply using one measure is insufficient and it is necessary to take a combination of various other ratios into account as well. These include: the child dependency ratio, which is the proportion of the population aged under 15; the ageing index, which measures the population over 65 as a proportion of the population under 15; and the median age, which is the average age of the population. All four of the above-mentioned measures place China as a relatively old country by international criteria (see Table 6.1).

According to criteria formulated by Swedish demographer Elin Sandberg, the age composition of China's population in reproductive terms is decreasing. The child population ratio was 16.46, while the ratio for its population aged 50 or above was 26.19, showing a relatively strong correlation with the category of 'decreasing' (see Table 6.2). In summary,

[3] Zhang and Wang, "Zhongguo laoling hua," 48–53.

Table 6.1 Categories of age composition of China's population at the end of 2013

	Categories of a nation according to international criteria measuring age composition			
Different population age groups	Young	Adult	Ageing	Age composition of China's population at the end of 2013
Aged under 15 (%)	Over 40	30–40	Under 30	17.5
Aged over 64 (%)	Under 4	4–6	Over 7	9.7
Ageing index (%)	Under 15	15–30	Over 30	55.12
Median age	Under 20	20–30	Over 30	36.5

Source: Based on data from 2013 Statistical Communiqué

Table 6.2 Categories of age composition of China's population in terms of population reproduction in 2012

	Categories of a nation according to the population division criteria formulated by Sandberg			
Population age groups	Increasing (%)	Stable (%)	Decreasing (%)	Age composition of China's population in 2012 (%)
Aged under 15	40	26.5	20	16.46
Aged 15–49	50	50.5	50	57.36
Aged over 50	10	23	30	26.19

Source: China Statistical Yearbook 2013

the age composition of China's population falls into the parameters of one that is both ageing and decreasing, and it can no longer be thought of as a young country.

China is the most heavily populated country in the world with vast regions in which there is relatively uneven economic and social development. Its ageing population, which is a recent development but one that has evolved rather quickly and with distinct and unique characteristics, is China's greatest challenge.

First, China has experienced a quick demographic transition with a rapidly ageing population. Taking only the old-age dependency ratio into account, namely measuring the proportion of people aged over 64, in the 1970s the population shifted from being 'young' to being 'adult'. In 2001 this ratio reached 7.1 %, which pushed it into the 'ageing' category. China's demographic transition differs from those of European countries in that the latter were not distorted by a mandatory population policy. It took nearly a century for most European countries to complete the transformation from 'young' to 'ageing', including a period of between 50 and 80 years to transform from 'adult' to 'ageing' (Graph 6.1).

The starting point of China's demographic shift to an older society took place 29 years later than Japan's, 69 years later than the UK's, 54 years later than the USA's and 134 years later than that of France. The rate of this change was also much faster than in these countries. It took 12 years for China's old-age density ratio to increase from 7 to 10 %, faster than the four previously mentioned countries by 3, 8, 18, and 63 years respectively. In addition to a decrease in the mortality rate and an increase in life expectancy, China's family planning policy, which resulted in a sharp decline in the fertility rate, played an important role in accelerating the speed of its ageing process and the resultant changes in its population structure. These changes included a decrease in the number of new-born babies and a rapid increase in the proportion of elderly people.

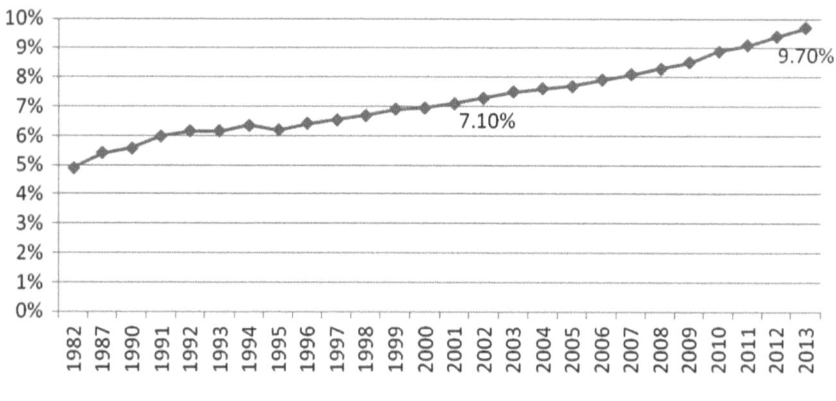

Fig. 6.1 The development trend of the aged population ratio in China (1982–2013) (*Source*: Data for 1982–2012 is from the China Statistical Yearbook 2013; data from 2013 is from the 2013 Statistical Communiqué)

Second, there is a disjuncture between ageing and economic development in China in that the usual link found in developed countries does not apply. When the developed countries began to become ageing societies, all of them had already completed their processes of modernization. They are countries that either became rich before growing old or became rich while growing old. In Japan, for example, the percentage of the population aged 65 or over reached 7 % when GDP per capita was $1,967, 10 % when it was $11,335, and 14 % when it was $38,555. China, by comparison, became an ageing society when its economy was still underdeveloped, making it a country that is growing old before it gets rich. In 2000, when its population aged 65 or over reached nearly 7 %, its GDP per capita was only $840, less than 20 % of the global average and ranking 109th in the world. In 2005, when its GDP per capita was just over $1,000, 7.69 % of its population was aged 65 or over. Therefore, China has become an ageing society while it is still relatively weak economically and lacks a solid material foundation, which obviously puts a huge strain on its social and economic development.

Third, there are significant regional variations. A higher percentage of elderly people live in rural than in urban regions. In general, population ageing and economic development happen simultaneously. Both have relatively high uniformity, meaning that the faster the economic development is in one region, the more rapidly the age dependency ratio increases. There are prominent regional differences in China's economic development and, therefore, regional differences in the speeds at which their populations age. The rate of ageing in different regions is broadly in descending order from east to west, meaning that, with some obvious regional variations, the rate in the western regions is significantly slower than that in the eastern ones (see Table 6.3). The sixth population census in 2010 showed that the percentages of elderly people in 12 provincial units were higher than the national average, including Shanghai, Jiangsu, Zhejiang, Chongqing, Tianjin, and Liaoning. Most of these units are in economically developed eastern regions; in Shanghai, for instance, 10.13 % of the people are aged 65 or over. Meanwhile, the results also show that the percentages of elderly people in 19 other provincial units were lower than the national average; these are mainly inland in the central and western regions. In Tibet, for example, just 5.09 % of the people are 65 or over. As Table 6.3 shows, China's provinces can be divided into three

Table 6.3 China's provincial distribution of percentages of people aged 65 or over in 2010

Aged population ratios	Provinces
Above 9%	Zhejiang, Hubei, Hunan, Guangxi, Liaoning, Shanghai, Jiangsu, Anhui, Chongqing, Sichuan
7–9%	Beijing, Tianjin, Hebei, Shanxi, Inner Mongolia, Jilin, Heilongjiang, Fujian, Jiangxi, Henan, Hainan, Guizhou, Yunnan, Shaanxi, Gansu
Under 7%	Guangdong, Tibet, Qinghai, Ningxia, Xinjiang

Source: The Sixth Population Census in China

categories according to their age density ratios—regions not yet ageing; regions in the preliminary stage of ageing; and regions in the middle and advanced stages of ageing.

China's sixth population census also shows that 10.06 % of rural residents are aged 65 or over. This is higher than for the residents of cities (7.68 %) and towns (7.98 %). In fact, more than two-thirds of people aged 65 or over live in rural rather than urban areas. The distribution of elderly people between rural and urban areas has an inverted relationship with the rate of development. Because the rapid development of urbanization in China attracted many young rural residents to work and live in the cities, there were dramatic changes in the demographic structures of the latter, but also a higher old-age dependency ratio and faster rate of population ageing in rural areas. The age dependency ratio in rural areas is predicted to continue to rise, thus making population ageing in these areas an even more serious challenge than it is in urban areas.

What Effect Has Population Ageing Had on China?

For a start, ageing has changed the employment structure, leading directly to a decrease in the working-age population. The labour force is important to economic development, which requires a stable supply of large numbers of high quality workers. Population ageing means that the percentage of the elderly population is increasing and that of the working-age population decreasing. It is projected that by the middle of the 21st century 336 million people in China will be aged 65 or over, or a quarter of the total population. The rapid ageing of a population, whether through an increase in the overall adult population, particularly those aged 65 or over, a decline in the population aged between 15 and 49, or a decline in the child population, will inevitably lead to a decrease in the working age population and a change in the structure of the group. Ageing makes it more difficult to improve labour productivity and slows down economic growth.

Population ageing can in fact have two apparently contradictory effects on a nation's economic development. On the one hand, when population size, technological capabilities, and economic strength remain unchanged, population ageing leads to a corresponding increase in the employment rate. On the other hand, population ageing can cause an insufficient supply of labour. Although there is currently no shortage of labour in China, it will not be able to enjoy its 'demographic dividend' forever. Because of its family planning policy, population growth is now quite slow. But ageing will lead to a decrease in the working-age population, which in turn will cause a relative shortage of labour. In addition, the re-employment of older people will affect employment opportunities for the working-age population. Overall, ageing will change China's employment structure and cause a drop in labour productivity and growth.

Second, an ageing population will have an effect on Chinese industry and consumption patterns. When China started to age, its economy was relatively underdeveloped. Getting old before becoming rich has seriously challenged the country's industrial structure. An ageing society requires a relatively developed service sector to support it, but the tertiary sector is lagging behind and cannot keep up with the demands of its older population. There are two major issues to address in taking care of the elderly. Who is responsible for providing financial and material support? And who is responsible for providing their healthcare? Most elderly rural residents depend on their children, so both the level of economic development in their region and the relative wealth of their families have a bearing on the quality of their living standards. However, most elderly urban residents receive a pension and are, therefore, less reliant on their children, though certain factors can make it difficult for them too to maintain their standard of living. For example, some pensions are tied to the financial wellbeing of the company that provides them; some are fixed in value and payable only for a defined period of time; and inflation can erode the value of them all. The economy is in a period of transition, which involves many adjustments of various interests, which will increase the risk of poverty in the older population. The picture is bleaker in terms of health, particularly for the rural elderly, as few of them have access to subsidized healthcare. In short, ageing has diverted resources from investment to consumption, which is hardly conducive to sustaining economic development.

Third, ageing has increased the old-age dependency ratio. In addition, the country has to allocate more of its social resources towards caring for the elderly, which will inevitably put increased pressure on business and society and seriously hinder its harmonious social and economic development. The old-age dependency ratio in China is currently 0.1, meaning that there are approximately nine working-age people to support one older person. If we divide the mortality rate into low and medium categories to calculate the future old-age dependency ratio, several conclusions can be drawn. If the calculation is based on a low mortality rate, the dependency ratio in 2020 will reach 0.19, 72.7 % higher than in 2000, meaning that there will be approximately five working-age people to support one elderly person. If the calculation is based on a medium mortality rate, the dependency ratio in 2020 will reach 0.17, 54.5 % higher than in 2000, meaning that there will be about six working-age people to support one elderly person. Based on these two mortality rates, the old-age dependency ratio in 2050 will reach 0.45 or 0.37 respectively, 4.1 or 3.4 times higher than in 2000. With China's current family planning policy, the number of working-age people will rapidly decrease and the 'demographic dividend' brought by the generation of baby boomers born in the 1950s and 1960s will disappear. The country will face a severe labour market shortage and population ageing will seriously challenge its economic development, thereby threatening the entire society.

How Long Will China's Demographic Window of Opportunity Last?

Chinese academics have been fiercely debating the question of how long the demographic dividend will last in China and have come up with a variety of views. Some believe that its total dependency ratio fell to its lowest point in about 2013 and that, as this ratio begins to rise, its demographic dividend will gradually disappear. Others argue that after this ratio falls to its lowest point, the demographic dividend will continue for another 20 years.

The demographic dividend, also known as the demographic window of opportunity, refers to a period when a nation's working-age population is high compared with its general population, so it has a relatively low total dependency ratio. At such a time the demographic conditions are favourable for economic development because the overall economy is experiencing high savings rates, high levels of investment, and rapid growth. Therefore, discussions on the demographic dividend are as much about economic development as about demographics.

As their projections show, many scholars believe that the total dependency ratio reached its lowest point in around 2013, after which it will gradually begin to rise and the demographic window of opportunity will close. Some have estimated the period of demographic dividend and found that every 1 % decrease in its total dependency ratio has resulted in a 0.115 % increase in GDP per capita (Cai and Wang, 2005). If this is correct, on the basis of the changes in the total dependency ratio, one can assume that China's demographic dividend will disappear.

Others focus on the absolute level of the total dependency ratio, which gives a different assessment. They argue that, even though after 2013 the ratio began to rise, by 2030 its absolute level will still be similar to that of the mid-1990s, which was relatively low. Therefore, they believe that the demographic dividend will continue to last for about another 20 years, or possibly longer. If the criteria measuring this ratio are further loosened, meaning that they still regard the 1990 level as able to provide China with a demographic dividend, the window of opportunity will continue to last until around 2030. The three leading projections are those of Hu Ying, Wang Guangzhou, and the United Nations, which provides projected figures every five years.[4] Notwithstanding specific differences,

[4] Hu, "Shierwu renkou fazhan qushi."

Wang and Zhang "Shengyu qianli guji."

United Nations Population Division Department of Economic and Social Affairs, "World Population Prospects."

all three show similar development trends, with the total dependency ratio in China reaching its lowest point between 2010 and 2015 before rising again.

Obviously, if the earlier assessment of the link between an increased total dependency ratio and a decreased GDP per capita are correct, then the demographic window of opportunity will gradually close in the coming years. However, if the assessments based on the absolute level of the total dependency ratio are correct, with a ratio of 45 % being regarded as a relatively low level, China will continue to enjoy its demographic dividend until 2030. Furthermore, if a total dependency ratio of 50 % could be considered to be the threshold, the 'demographic window of opportunity' will not close until around 2035.

Different judgements about the potential duration of China's demographic dividend will obviously yield different policies. Policy makers who believe the dividend will continue for a long time rather than disappear immediately are likely to hold the view that the country's family planning policy does not need to be adjusted in the short term. However, those who believe that the window of opportunity has ended are more likely to emphasize the urgent need to reform the policy. If we understand the relationship between population structure and economic development, as well as recognize the effect of the disappearance of China's demographic dividend on its sustainable development, it becomes clear that the focus of the discussion should centre on the urgency of reforming the country's model of economic development rather than on whether the family planning policy should be adjusted.

How Will China Develop Its Economy After the Demographic Dividend?

It is inevitable that China's demographic dividend will end at some stage and that the impetus for its current economic development will gradually disappear, thus increasing the burden of supporting an ageing population. How will the country achieve sustainable development when the era of the demographic dividend has ended?

Some believe that the disappearance of the dividend will not necessarily have a wholly negative effect on the economy and that, so long as certain conditions are met, it is possible for an ageing society to usher in a second demographic dividend, which usually occur when, in the society's early stage of ageing, the older members of the population accumulate relatively large amounts of capital and savings and the working-age ones are able to put aside a relatively high percentage of their earnings for the future. The accumulated savings then become available for use as capital for the next cycle of production, thereby stimulating economic output and growth. However, this only happens if the savings are used as capital for investment or production. If not, they would merely be used to support the economy through increased consumption.

To generate a second demographic dividend, the rate of investment returns on pension funds must be higher than the direct and indirect effects of these funds on the wider economy. Otherwise, it is impossible to generate this dividend. How can a country ensure that this rate of investment return will increase? On the one hand, its economy must maintain a relatively high level of growth; on the other hand, it must accelerate the upgrade of its industrial structure and improve the output elasticity of capital, which mainly involves improving the quality of the labour force, increasing the investment in manpower capital, and promoting technological progress. Some scholars believe that in an ageing society the decline in the number of young people results in a decrease in the speed of the dissemination of knowledge and new technologies, with the result that the spread of technology becomes very slow. They conclude, therefore, that this will weaken the positive effect of its technological progress on economic growth. However, other scholars believe that the decline in the working-age population in an ageing society puts pressure on business and society to promote technology, which then results in an acceleration of technological progress. Therefore, to generate its second demographic dividend, an ageing nation must encourage constant learning and innovation.

The demographic structure of an ageing society shifts the investment focus from physical capital to human capital. A demographic dividend will make the transition to a human resource dividend, thus potentially increasing the productivity rate. Therefore, the labour force should be upgraded to increase output per capita and to offset the impact of the fall in the working-age population.

The full exploitation of potential positive factors during the transition of China's population structure is not only an important prerequisite for sustainable economic development but it is also a pressing matter for a country which is becoming an ageing society. To achieve this, China should first regulate its pension schemes better, as well as accumulate capital to generate a 'second demographic dividend' and secure relatively high yields. Second, it should accelerate its industrial upgrading. This will not only increase businesses' investment return rates, meet the investment demands of their employees' pension funds, and facilitate a second demographic dividend, but will also match the future supply of the major factors of production for healthy economic growth. Third, China should accelerate the accumulation of human capital. Improving the quality of the labour force will enhance productivity, solve the demographic problems, and sustain economic development.

Urbanization and Sustainable Development

Characteristics of China's Urbanization

China's urbanization started late and developed quickly, but the quality of development is poor. However, once the reform and opening up had begun, urbanization began to accelerate rapidly and make significant progress. In 1978 China was 17.9 % urbanized, but by 2013 this figure had risen to 53.73 %. Thus, in 34 years the level of urbanization increased by 34.7 percentage points, an increase of more than 1 percentage point per year (Graph 6.2).

The urbanization of the country since the founding of the PRC can be divided roughly into three phases—steady advancement, stagnation, and rapid development. The steady advancement phase, from 1953 to

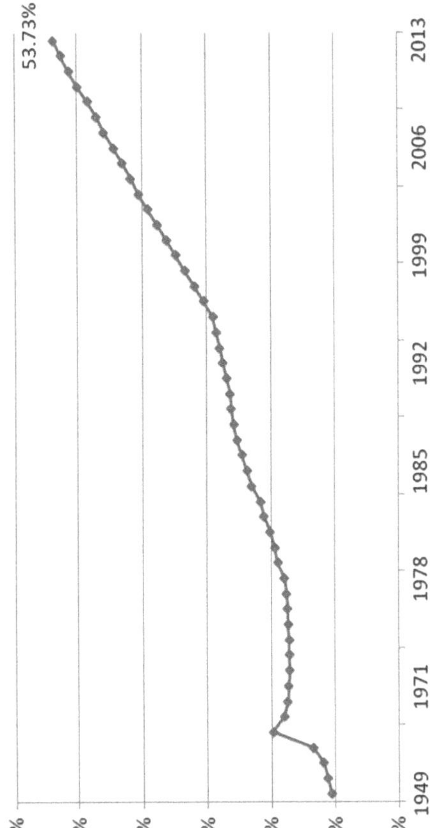

Fig. 6.2 Development of China's urbanization between 1949 and 2013
(*Source*: Data for 1949–2012 are from the China Statistical Yearbook 2013; data for 2013 are from the 2013 Statistical Communiqué)

1958, was typical of a planned economy: large numbers of farmers were transferred from rural areas to cities to work on the extensive industrialization programme and service the urban economy. Development during this phase was planned and advanced steadily. The urbanization rate rose from 10.6 to 16.3 %, an average annual increase of 0.63 percentage points.

During the second phase, from 1958 to 1978, urbanization was characterized by stagnation due to the impact of the 'Great Leap Forward' and the 'Cultural Revolution'. In fact, so great was the indecisiveness and confusion of this phase that the government even tried a policy of 'non-urbanized industrialization'. The urbanization rate during these two decades rose by just 1.6 percentage points, or an average annual increase of 0.08 percentage points, with several years actually recording negative growth.

The third phase, since 1978, is one of rapid development. The urbanization rate had risen to 53.73 % by 2013, delivering an average annual increase of 1.02 percentage points. This resulted from two factors. The first was the Central Committee of the Communist Party of China's (CPC) decision that urbanization would provide the solution to 'three rural issues' agriculture, the countryside, and farmers. The second was the implementation of the tenth five-year plan, which unambiguously promoted urbanization and so adjusted the various restrictions and policies that had previously discouraged farmers from working or living in cities.

Challenges Facing China's Urbanization

Urbanization is not only a symbol of economic prosperity but also a powerful driving force for economic development. Since the start of its reform and opening up phase, China has made significant progress in developing urbanization, but there are still some quite serious problems. These include unscientific urban planning, an unsound industrial structure, inadequate provision of infrastructure in some urban areas, high energy consumption, high emissions, and urban traffic congestion. The sustainable development of China's urbanization therefore faces many difficulties and challenges.

First, there is a mismatch between its urbanization and industrialization: the latter is a prerequisite of the former. In other words, urbanization generally follows industrialization, implying a high correlation between the two. When the urbanization rate is divided by the industrialization rate the result is usually greater than one, meaning that the urbanization rate is generally higher than the industrialization rate, especially when both rates reach around 13 %. However, because of the negative impact of its planned economy and system of household registration, this does not apply.

After the founding of the PRC, priority was given to developing heavy industry, and rural residents were not allowed to move to the cities. In addition, the policy of sending 'educated youth' to work and live in the countryside distorted the relationship between urbanization and industrialization. Thus, China's urbanization lagged far behind its industrialization. However, since the reform and opening up China has been experiencing rapid urbanization—it exceeded 53 % in 2013—and the uneven development between the two has lessened considerably.

Nonetheless, China's manufacturing sector remains relatively unsophisticated by global standards. Even though it is now called the 'factory of the world', there remains a significant development gap between it and the UK and the USA. To improve the quality of its urbanization, China needs first to upgrade its industrialization and ensure that they complement one another.

Second, the urban–rural dual economic structure, which refers to uneven economic development between cities and rural areas, as well as between cities and towns, is becoming stronger and more rigid. The focus on industrialization at the expense of agriculture and the peasantry resulted in urbanization lagging behind economic development and the rural–urban divide becoming more pronounced. It has also meant that the development of small towns is falling behind that of large and medium-sized cities. In recent years, there has been an increased effort to support rural development and to get industrial development to support agricultural advancement. While this has improved farmers' living standards and to some extent narrowed the gap between the urban and rural economic structures, the progress is insufficient to have changed the basic nature of the problem.

With rapid urbanization, a large amount of capital continues to flow from rural areas to cities. Through the operation of an unreasonable and unfair land use policy, more of the revenue generated from land is going to cities and government organizations dealing with non-agricultural issues than to rural areas and government organizations dealing with agricultural matters. Similarly, with an equally unreasonable and unfair income distribution policy still in place, migrant workers are classified as rural residents even though they work in cities and are paid less than their urban counterparts, thus holding back the overall increase in earnings in the rural population. In addition, the public expenditure policy still favours cities over rural areas, which causes a disparity in infrastructural development and in the provision of social security. Thus, instead of reducing it has increased the gap between urban and rural areas, making the 'three rural issues' even more pressing.

Third, China's rural population faces increasing pressure as its government still implements a discriminatory policy that favours urban over rural populations, particularly in the areas of household registration, land, social security, employment, and education. Although migrant workers live and work in cities, they do not enjoy equal status or rights in terms of living conditions and employment opportunities with those who have urban registration, *hukou*. This dampens their enthusiasm to move to a city and increases the pressure in their lives. Migrant workers should have been at the heart of China's urbanization, but the household registration policy prevents that from happening. Consequently, migrant workers generally have to take on the hardest, dirtiest, and worst-paid jobs and, because they cannot settle down as permanent urban residents, they have to move between cities like 'migrant birds'. Compared with their urban counterparts, migrant workers suffer from various disadvantages. These include: low social status; low pay; fewer employment opportunities; difficulties accessing healthcare; unequal access to education for their children; and difficulties obtaining social assistance in the event of significant problems arising, such as unpaid salary or uncompensated work injuries.

Fourth, despite the acceleration of China's urbanization, the capacity of its urban centres to accommodate larger populations remains weak. Urbanization is a systemic process that can only run smoothly and in an orderly manner when several factors, such as the infrastructure, ecological environment, housing, education, and healthcare, work together in a complementary way. Indeed, urbanization consumes substantial natural resources and creates a great deal of pollution. With urbanization continuing and urban populations rising, China needs to improve its infrastructure, public services, environmental protection, and housing. Because of its different historical approach to development, urban planning and construction has lagged far behind that of advanced countries. With their poor infrastructure and insufficient facilities, including urban transport, underground pipelines, power and water supplies, pollution control, education, housing, and healthcare, China's cities cannot keep up with the rate of urbanization. Consequently, many of its large and medium-sized cities are beset with problems like traffic congestion, environmental pollution, and social disorder. These 'urban diseases' have become challenges that the country has to address if it is to achieve sustainable development.

China has now reached a critical stage of urbanization and must confront some serious challenges, particularly the inefficiency of its urban carrying capacity with respect to resources and the environment. Land, water, and energy are important material foundations for urbanization, but China's cultivable land and water availability per capita are much lower than the world average. Furthermore, its public utility services are weak and lag behind the pace of its urbanization, all of which is making it increasingly difficult for the country to keep up with the accelerating pace of that urbanization.[5]

China Must Develop a New Type of Urbanization

The term 'urbanization' has a Latin origin, *urbs*, which means city. As a modern concept it was first used in 1867 by Spanish civil engineer Ildefons Cerdà[6] to describe the process of transforming predominantly rural areas into urban ones. The term gained wide acceptance in the world during the 20th century and was introduced to China in the late 1970s,

[5] Du, "Zhongguo chengzhen hua," 5–9.

[6] Cerdà, *Teoría General Urbanización.*

and translated as '*chengshi hua*' or '*chengzhen hua*', originally without a clear distinction between them in the academic community. The term '*chengzhen hua*' is now widely used in the Communist Party and government documents, with an increasing number of scholars also favouring it. It has a specific meaning that differs from the commonly understood definition of 'urbanization' used outside China, which is closer to *chengshi hua*. In this term, '*cheng*' means city and '*zhen*' means town. In legal terms, both cities and towns are collectively referred to as 'city' in China, but they differ administratively. The distinction between a 'city' and 'town' in China lies in the difference between their administrative systems rather than in their size or population numbers. China's urbanization includes both '*cheng hua*', which refers to rural residents flowing into cities as well as the resultant development of these cities, and '*zhen hua*', which refers to the similar process occurring in towns. Therefore, China's urbanization is not simply the growth of big cities or of small towns.[7] Outside the country, the distinction between 'city' and 'town' is primarily based on size and population. The larger areas with more non-agricultural residents are called cities, while the smaller areas with fewer non-agricultural residents are called towns.

Because of the difference of character between the terms '*chengzhen hua*' and '*chengshi hua*', Chinese urbanization will differ from that of other countries. Although the urbanization rate is now 53.73 %, its quality remains low. The floating population which consists mainly of migrant workers and their families numbers 260 million; they live in cities and towns, and, as we mentioned earlier, these people do not have the same access to public services as registered urban residents. To solve these problems, various arrangements need to change, including the household registration scheme, land law, and the administrative division system.

The 17th National Congress of the Communist Party recommended the introduction of a fundamentally Chinese version of urbanization, which Premier Wen Jiabao reaffirmed in May 2007. During the Central Work Conference on Urbanization held at the end of 2013, Wen's successor Li Keqiang took the recommendation a step further with a view to tackling

[7] Du, "Zhongguo chengzhen hua," 5–9.

the huge problems arising from the rapid urbanization. Undoubtedly, this version, which is different from previous urbanization as well as from anything seen in any other country, will usher in a new historical approach.

The new approach intends to take on board the lessons learnt from the previous period of rapid urbanization. To do so successfully, it will need to address the existing policy that restricts migrants from integrating into China's cities and towns. It should also shift its focus from managing expansion to providing and improving public services. The urbanization of a nation needs to be coordinated with its social and economic development because, irrespective of whether a country's urbanization is too slow or too fast, this will eventually affect the sustainability of its economy and society. China must take stock of its current economic and social situation, abide by the rules, and promote healthy urbanization in an active and steady manner in accordance with the policy put forward at the 18th Party Congress. This policy declares that:

> China should adhere to the path of developing a new type of industrialization, informatization, urbanization, and agricultural modernization with Chinese characteristics. We should promote the further integration between informatization and industrialization, the positive interaction between industrialization and urbanization, and the coordination between urbanization and agricultural modernization, promoting the synchronous development of those four areas.[8]

To achieve its declared objectives, China needs to promote synchronous, positive, and interactional development between urbanization and industrialization. If a nation's pace of urbanization is faster than that of its industrialization, it is guilty of what is defined as 'excessive urbanization'. If the nation's urbanization is slower than that of its industrialization, there is 'insufficient urbanization'. Both are unhealthy situations that will hinder the coordinated development of the country's economy and society. Only if China promotes positive and coordinated interaction between urbanization and industrialization will it be able to achieve sustainable urbanization.

---

[8] Hu, "Shiba ci daibiao dahui."

China needs to promote synchronous and positive interaction between urbanization and its new type of industrialization by closely coordinating the latter and information technology with urbanization. The same applies to the interaction between urbanization and agricultural modernization. The latter implies increasing China's rural human resource reserves, improving the modes of production in rural areas, guiding and supporting agricultural industrialization, raising agricultural productivity, increasing farmers' incomes, and consolidating the material foundations of urbanization. Meanwhile, China should formulate rational policies to increase the flow to rural areas of key resources such as knowledge, capital, skilled urban workers, and management experience. This will promote the exchange of ideas between rural and urban regions, increase the links between their respective industrial structures, and introduce new modes of production and lifestyles into the rural areas. Such measures will no doubt improve the agricultural structure and raise the value added of agricultural products.

Urbanization should also involve urban–rural integration to avoid the spread of so-called 'urban diseases', particularly the formation of slums, and to ensure that developing industry does not imply neglecting agriculture. As outlined at the 18th CPC National Congress:

> China should accelerate the process to put in place a mechanism for integrating urban–rural development, with a focus on integrating urban and rural planning, infrastructure and public services, promoting urban–rural exchange on an equal footing as well as balanced allocation of public resources. The objective is to establish a new type of relationship between agriculture and industry as well as between rural and urban areas. This new type of relationship includes making industrial development support agricultural development, making urban development promote rural development. In other words, it is about securing synergy between agriculture and industry as well as between the urban and rural sectors.[9]

Urban–rural integration is a systemic process involving society, the economy, ecology, and law and requiring coordinated development across

---

[9] Ibid.

these areas, overall planning at the highest level, and improvements to various administrative systems. First, to integrate urban and rural strategic development planning, China should optimize the allocation of resources between urban and rural areas through a two-way exchange of labour, capital, land, and technology. It needs to approach its urban and rural areas as a single unit if it is to coordinate research and planning and integrate the social and economic developments of these areas, including their industrial structures.

Second, to achieve unified planning and management in the fields of household registration, social security policies, and public services, China should improve its various administrative systems across the urban–rural divide. To allocate resources better, to promote a closer linkage between production and the lives of urban and rural residents, and to forge a unified market between the two areas, China should also encourage the efficient flow of the major elements of production.

Third, China should integrate its urban and rural policies and regulations. This means formulating and improving all policies (fiscal, taxation, credit, land, trade, price, investment, distribution) associated with coordinating the development of urban and rural areas. Policies that discriminate against rural residents in terms of access to housing, education, healthcare, employment, and social security should of course be abolished. Laws must be put in place to ensure equality between urban and rural residents, between industry and agriculture, and between urban and rural development.

Last but not least China should seek to transform its cities and towns into highly efficient, eco-friendly, and technology-oriented smart urban centres. Rapid urbanization is putting increasing pressure on the ecological environment and natural resources, so it must speed up the transformation of its urban development model to create conditions conducive to low consumption, low emissions, high efficiency, and recycling. It should aim to optimize the use of its resources, make urban planning more scientific, and rationalize urban layout. This will increase the efficiency of urban management and the carrying capacity of its urban centres. To achieve this goal, China should take a holistic approach so that the potential of its urban development on economic and social development can be exploited to the full. It should continue to improve its urban public service system, its infrastructure, and avoid repeating the mistakes of the previous urban development model, which encouraged exponential urban sprawl.

Small towns should be helped to play more of a role in trying to achieve a complementary and rational distribution between large, medium-sized, and small urban centres. China's urban areas need to become more eco-friendly, land-efficient, beautiful, harmonious, and pleasant places in which to live. To achieve this, the country must improve its ecological environment, expand its afforestation programmes, protect its eco-landscapes, establish and improve its ecological compensation schemes, and guarantee financial and political support to remedy environmental pollution. It should also improve energy efficiency, reduce carbon dioxide emissions, increase the use of renewable energy, and get rid of inefficient production facilities. Turning China's urban centres into smart, technology-oriented places will make urban living more convenient, particularly when innovations such as the Internet of Things and MultiNets are brought into play.

Urbanization, Population Ageing and Promoting Sustainable Development

Relationship Between Population Ageing and Urbanization

The mutually reinforcing processes of rapid population ageing and urbanization raise important issues for China's social and economic development. Currently, 26 provinces have an age-dependency ratio higher than 7 % and this process is gathering momentum. If China cannot properly handle the social and economic problems caused by population ageing, its whole urbanization programme will be in jeopardy.

Population ageing is having a three-fold effect on Chinese society. First, urbanization is affected by the migration of rural residents, which mainly drives it. The people who migrate are usually aged between 15 and 49, the age group supplying the main source of industrial labour and the major force behind urbanization. Population ageing will gradually reduce the size of this group, causing a decline in labour supply, an increase in labour costs, a restriction in the development potential of urbanization, and various other problems. Second, population ageing increases the economic cost of urbanization because the social and economic problems associated with it inevitably require extra social services and the consequent increase in social spending will have a direct impact on the next cycle of production. Third, population ageing reduces the vitality of urban labour and the efficiency of urbanization. With an increasing proportion of the population getting older, a higher percentage will find it difficult to accept innovation and thus cause a fall in efficiency. The ageing of China's population will lead to a decline in the vitality of its labour, which will impact negatively on its production and economic activity.

An ageing population needs well-developed health, fitness, and recreational facilities, which urban centres, with their superior carrying capacity, are better able to supply than rural areas. However, as we mentioned earlier, China has yet to create a 'silver industry' dedicated to servicing the elderly, which is a challenge to harmonious social and economic development.

Harnessing Urbanization and Population Ageing to Promote Sustainable Development

To build a moderately prosperous society and achieve sustainable development, China must handle the complications of population ageing and urbanization in a coordinated manner. Building a new type of urbanization should be given the same weight as solving the problems of population ageing. To ensure a rational distribution of its population China should improve the quality of its urbanization and regulate the orderly flow of migrants. It should reform its household registration system and seek better ways to meet its stated aim of 'three synchronized changes' (in location, occupation, and identification) for its migrant population. When people move from rural to urban areas and change their occupations from farmers to industrial labourers, there is no reason why they should be prevented from registering their new status in the *hukou*.

To achieve its objectives, China should take the following three actions:

1. While leaving the fertility rate unchanged in rural areas, it should increase it in urban areas to prevent a rise in the number of 'four-two-one' families (four grandparents, two parents and one child). This would slow down population ageing in urban areas and reduce China's overall old-age dependency ratio, thereby controlling population growth, preventing excessive population ageing, and producing synergy between population ageing and urbanization.
2. China should exploit the important potential of its 'silver industry' to improve domestic demand, stimulate consumption, ease employment pressure, and promote economic prosperity. It should take advantage of the significant differences in population ageing that exist between regions to achieve an efficient flow of labour. Before population ageing reaches its peak, China should take advantage of its 'golden period' to accumulate capital reserves and fully exploit the potential of its 'second demographic dividend'.
3. To mitigate labour shortages and stimulate economic development, China should exploit the economic potential of productive elderly people by allowing them to work beyond their retirement age. To this end, China should raise the retirement age, encourage people aged between 60 and 70 to seek re-employment, and promote the health of its ageing population.

Bibliography

Cerdà, I. 1967. Teoría General de la Urbanización. [General Theory of Urbanization].

Du, R. H. 2013. Zhongguo chengzhen hua ke chixu fazhan de kunjing yu pojie. [Challenges and solutions to the sustainable development of China's urbanization]. *Modern Economic Research* 6: 5–9.

Fang Cai and Dewen Wang. 2005. "Changes of Economic Growth Factors and the Sources of Farmer's Income". *Management World*, 5: 77–83.

Hu, Y. 2010. Shierwu shiqi renkou bianhua ji weilai renkou fazhan qushi yuce. In *Zhongguo renkou yu laodongli wenti baogao: hou weiji shiqi de laodong li shichang tiaozhan*, ed. F. Cai. Shehui kexue wenxian chubanshe: Guangzhou.

Hu, J. T. (2012) *Jianding bu yi yanzhe Zhongguo tese shehui zhuyi daolu qianjin wei quanmian jiancheng xiaokang shehui er fendou – zai Zhongguo Gongchandang di shiba ci quanguo daibiao dahui shang de baogao (2012 nian 11 yue 8 ri.* [Firmly March on the path of socialism with Chinese characteristics and strive to complete the building of a moderately prosperous society in all respects – Report to the Eighteenth National Congress of the Communist Party of China on November 8, 2012]. Beijing: People's Publishing House.

Jackson, R., and H. Howe. 2004. *The graying of the middle kingdom: The demographics and economics of retirement policy in China*. Washington: CSIS and Prudential Foundation.

OECD. 2005. *OECD economic surveys*. Paris: OECD.

United Nations Population Division Department of Economic and Social Affairs. 2012. World population prospects: The 2012 revision. [online]. Available at http://menschliche-entwicklung-staerken.dgvn.de/fileadmin/user_upload/menschl_entwicklung/FD/Dokumente/UN-Report_Bev_2013.pdf. Accessed 7 Aug 2015.

Wang, G. Z., and L. P. Zhang. 2012. Daodi neng sheng daoshao haizi?—Zhongguoren de zhengce shengyu qianli guji. *Shehui Xue yanjiu* 5: 119–140.

Zhang, G. L., and Y. L. Wang. 2010. Zhongguo laoling hua dui jingji fazhan de yingxiang fenxi. [Analysis of the impact of China's population ageing on its economic development]. *Population Journal* 5: 48–53.

7

Striking a Balance Between Environmental Protection and Rapid Development

Jing Zhang

Introduction

Rapid economic growth enhanced by the expansion of industrial production and consumption has had a significant effect on pollution in China. The high level of air pollution leading to thick smog in many cities has led to an unprecedented number of environmental crises, which have forced the government and the new leader Xi Jinping to make environmental protection their top priority. According to the China Environment Bulletin 2013 published by the Ministry of Environmental Protection

---

Research funding from the British Academy (SG110318) is gratefully acknowledged. Parts of the chapter come from Chaps 6 and 13 in J. Zhang (2014) *Foreign Direct Investment, Governance, and the Environment in China: Regional Dimensions* (Palgrave Macmillan), reproduced with permission of the publisher.

J. Zhang (✉)
School of Contemporary Chinese Studies, University of Nottingham, Nottingham, UK
e-mail: J.Zhang@nottingham.ac.uk

S. Tsang, H. Men (eds.), *China in the Xi Jinping Era*,
The Nottingham China Policy Institute Series,
DOI 10.1007/978-3-319-29549-7_7

(MEP, 2014), China had an average of 35.9 smog days in 2013, the highest level since 1961. Some cities in Central and Eastern regions had on average 50–100 days of smog a year, others experienced more than this. The surrounding Beijing-Tianjin-Hebei area experienced high air pollution on more than 60% of days on average. Among the 320 cities at prefecture level and above, 74 cities firstly adopted the new Air Quality Standards in 2013. However, only three cities (4.1%), namely Haikou, Zhoushan, and Lasa, met the new standards, while 69.5% of the other 256 cities met the old standards that do not measure $PM_{2.5}$.[1]

In April 2013, The *New York Times* published findings from a study conducted by the University of Washington, the World Health Organization (WHO), and several other universities which showed that in 2010 outdoor air pollution contributed to 1.2 million premature deaths in China, about 40 % of the global total of premature deaths from air pollution.[2] This figure is three times higher than estimated in 2007 when it was predicted, in a study carried out by the World Bank and the Chinese State Environmental Protection Administration (SEPA), the predecessor to the MEP, that between 350,000 and 400,000 people would die prematurely in China each year due to outdoor air pollution.

The condition of water quality is also challenging in China. The 2013 Environment Bulletin showed that surface water is lightly polluted and some river stream segments in cities are heavily polluted.[3] The quality of groundwater is cause for concern as 59.6 % of 4,778 monitoring sites are polluted or heavily polluted. Water pollution has also been a source of public anger after a series of scandals, including a leak of chemical aniline into a river in Shanxi Province, the incident in which 20,000 dead pigs were found in the Huangpu River, and the red well water incident in Hebei Province.

According to a joint report from the World Bank and the Chinese government in 2007, the health costs of air and water pollution account

---

[1] China's current air quality standards (GB3095-1996) were published in 1996 and revised in 2000. The updated standards (GB3095-2012) has been firstly adopted in 74 cities since 2013 and extended to all cities in 2016. The new standards include the standard of concentration of $PM_{2.5}$, which refers to tiny pollutant particles smaller than 2.5 microns that can penetrate deep into the lungs and blood stream and hence cause serious health problems, such as heart attacks and premature death.

[2] Wong, "Air Pollution."

[3] Ministry of Environmental Protection, "China Environment Bulletin 2013."

for 4.3 % of China's national gross domestic product (GDP) and the total cost of air and water pollution is about 5.8 % of GDP.[4] According to the Chinese Environmental and Economic Accounting Report made by the MEP and the National Bureau of Statistics (NBS), the total environmental cost, measured by the cost of environmental degradation and losses from ecological destruction, was about RMB1391.62 billion (about $204 billion) in 2009, equivalent to 3.8 % of that year's GDP.[5] The report also shows that poor regions are disproportionately affected by pollution and environmental degradation and usually have a vulnerable ecological system.

Whilst China's recent annual GDP growth has remained at about 8 %, the above estimations of the costs of economic growth indicate that the real growth would be 4 % or less, even negative, after offsetting pollution related losses, such as damages to natural resources, associated health problems, damages to agriculture and industry, and other negative impacts to the economy and society. Therefore, the costs incurred by the current levels of pollution, as well as the serious environmental issues, mean that it is no longer viable for China to continue its current system of economic growth.

There have been numerous theoretical and empirical studies that examine the relationship between economic growth and pollution. The theory of the Environmental Kuznets Curve (EKC) suggests an inverted relationship between pollution and economic growth, indicating that when income increases, pollution initially grows, reaches a peak, and then falls.[6] Severe air pollution has tended to occur during periods of rapid industrialization such as in early 20th century London (the UK), the Meuse Valley (Belgium), and St. Louis and Donora (both in the USA). Air quality in these countries subsequently improved with further economic development. Does it mean that the turning point of pollution will be achieved automatically if China simply focuses on economic

[4] The World Bank and The Government of the People's Republic of China, "Cost of Pollution."

[5] Latest news of environmental and economic accounting reports can be found at the website of the MEP's Chinese Academy for Environmental Planning. CAEP, "Environmental and economic accounting reports."

[6] Grossman and Krueger, "Environmental Impacts."

development, without paying special attention to the environment itself? The answer is an unequivocal 'no'.

In London, for example, stricter environmental regulations, such as the City of London Act (1954) and the Clean Air Acts (1956 and 1968), were implemented after the Great Smog in 1952 to reduce air pollution. Financial incentives were also provided to encourage householders to change to central heating, using gas, electricity, or other fuel. Policy intervention at an earlier stage of development is crucial as it could bring the turning point of the EKC forward and at a lower level of accumulated environmental cost. In order to achieve sustainable development there must be no delay in carrying out environmental protection and pollution treatment.[7] The current environmental crisis has forced the new leaders led by Xi Jinping to rethink air pollution and its future economic development model. Chinese economic reform since 1978 has generated a previously unimaginable scale of wealth. In 2010, China overtook Japan to become the second largest economy in the world which marked the success of its economic reforms. It is predicted that China's nominal GDP will exceed that of the United States by 2020.[8] Therefore, its great wealth and the present stage of its development enable China to put greater focus on environmental protection, as was done in other developed countries such as the UK and the USA.

China's new leaders have vowed to make the environment a top priority. In March 2014, Premier Li Keqiang said that they would wage 'war against pollution and fight it with the same determination [that they] battled poverty'.[9] China will 'take strong measures to strengthen pollution prevention and control' and will 'fully implement the plan for preventing and controlling air pollution, with the focus on mega cities and regions with frequent occurrence of smog'. Some steps have already been taken. The Action Plan on Prevention and Control of Air Pollution was issued by the State Council in September 2013 followed by the Trial Assessment Methods for the Implementation of the Action Plan published in May 2014; the Environmental Protection Law was revised and promulgated in

[7] Zhang, *Foreign Direct Investment*, 47.

[8] Yao and Zhang, "Chinese Economy 2010."

[9] Li, "Work of Government Report."

April 2014; Beijing announced its investment of RNB760 billion (about $121.5 billion) to improve the city's air quality by 2017; and action plans on soil and water pollution will soon be introduced. These signalled an intensified effort by the top leaders to protect the environment.

Heavy reliance on burning fossil fuels in industrial production and transportation has been the major source of air pollution in China, while industrial production and household usage have contributed to water pollution. Li Keqiang pointed out that improving the industrial infrastructure and raising energy efficiency are crucial to reduce pollution emissions. However, how does China achieve visible improvement in the environment over the next decade? What are the challenges in changing the industrial infrastructure and implementing stricter environmental regulations? How does China strike the balance between economic growth and environmental protection? This chapter provides some policy recommendations on sustainable development in China over the coming decade under Xi Jinping's leadership through analysing the challenges the country faces and the reasons behind them. Due to the scale of the topic, this chapter will focus on issues related to industrial infrastructure and the implementation of environmental regulations.

First, I introduce energy efficiency and environmental quality as it relates to China; this is followed by the achievement's of the country regarding environmental protection in the first decade of the 21st century. I then examine the challenges of environmental protection and analyse the reasons for inefficiency in implementing environmental regulations. I then provide some suggestions on the way to balance economic growth and environmental protection.

Environmental Quality in China

The extensive use of fossil fuels in China has caused heavy air pollution. China is the largest energy consumer in the world but energy is used inefficiently. The increasing expansion in production and consumption has sped up the exploitation of natural resources. In 2011, China's energy consumption reached 3.480 billion tonnes of standard coal equivalent (SCE) and its electricity consumption was 4.7 trillion Kwh. In terms of the composition of energy consumption, about 70 % of energy has been produced from coal which is cheap but extremely pollution intensive and the main source of acid rain.

Table 7.1 shows that the annual growth rate of energy consumption was quicker than that of the real GDP in the early 2000s and slowed down from 2006. However, the growth rate of electricity consumption has been more than that of GDP from 2000 to 2010, indicating a big waste of electricity use. Table 7.1 also reports that the energy intensity, measured by tonnes of SCE per unit of GDP, has tended to decline over recent years, though this cannot compensate for the increase in overall energy consumption. China's energy efficiency was much lower than that in developed countries. For example, in 2010, China's energy consumption per unit of GDP was only one-third of that in the USA and one-quarter of that in the EU and Japan.[10]

Due to the inefficient use of energy, China has been the largest emitter of carbon dioxide (CO_2) since 2006. Acid rain caused by sulphur

Table 7.1 Annual growth rates of energy consumption

Year	Growth of energy consumption (%)	Growth of electricity consumption (%)	Real GDP growth (%)	Energy intensity (tonnes of SCE per RMB10,000)*	Change of energy intensity (%)
2000	3.5	10.6	8.4	1.5	–4.5
2001	3.3	7.5	8.3	1.4	–4.6
2002	6.0	11.6	9.1	1.4	–2.8
2003	15.3	16.5	10.0	1.4	4.8
2004	16.1	15.4	10.1	1.5	5.5
2005	10.6	12.7	11.3	1.5	–0.7
2006	9.6	15.5	12.7	1.5	–2.7
2007	8.4	14.4	14.2	1.4	–5.0
2008	3.9	5.0	9.6	1.3	–5.2
2009	5.2	6.5	9.2	1.3	–3.7
2010	6.0	14.8	10.4	1.2	–4.1

* GDP at 2000 prices
Source: Based on China Statistical Yearbook, various years

[10] Yao, Luo and Rooker, "Energy Efficiency Economic Growth," 99–121.

Table 7.2 Air quality in Chinese cities in 2011 and air quality standard

		Ambient air quality standards		
Unit: mg/m^3	Annual concentration	China (class II)	EU	USA
SO_2	0.003–0.084 (0.020–0.060)	Annual: 0.06 24-hour: 0.15	Annual: N/A 24-hour:0.125	Annual: 0.08 24-hour:0.365
NO_2	0.004–0.068 (0.015–0.040)	Annual: 0.04 24-hour:0.08	Annual:0.04 24-hour: N/A	Annual: 0.10 24-hour: N/A
PM_{10}	0.025–0.352 (0.060–0.100)	Annual: 0.07 24-hour: 0.15	Annual: 0.04 24-hour: 0.05	Annual: N/A 24-hour: 0.15

Note: The concentration of pollutants in major cities are reported in brackets
Sources: Air quality in Chinese cities from China Environment Yearbook (2012); China's standards from MEP at http://kjs.mep.gov.cn/hjbhbz/bzwb/dqhjbh/; EU standards from the European Commission at http://ec.europa.eu/environment/air/quality/standards.htm; US standards from the Environmental Protection Agency of the United States at http://www.epa.gov/air/criteria.html

dioxide (SO_2) emissions falls on about one-third of China's cities.[11] Table 7.2 shows the range of annual concentrations of the major air pollutants (SO_2, Nitrogen Dioxide (NO_2), and particulate matter) in Chinese cities at prefecture level and above, as well as the comparison of air quality standards in China, the EU, and the USA. China's air quality standards for SO_2 and NO_2 are similar to those of the EU and the USA but the standards for PM_{10} are much lower than Western countries. While the majority of Chinese cities meet national standards of SO_2 and NO_2, they have a serious problem with PM_{10} pollution. Since 2012, the northern areas have frequently been affected by polluted smog, which is mainly caused by the high concentration of PM_{10} combined with the emissions of SO_2 and NO_2. Chronic exposure to these pollutants may increase the risk of developing respiratory and heart diseases, which are the leading causes of death in China. In addition to the impact on health, air pollution has a negative impact on other areas of the economy and society, for example acid rain which can reduce agricultural yields and damage forests, buildings, and production materials.

[11] China Environment Yearbook (2011).

China suffers from both water shortages and water pollution. It has 20 % of the world's population but only 7 % of the world's water resources, so its water per capita is only 25 % of the world average. The geographical distribution of water resources are not evenly distributed, with about 80 % concentrated in the south. Natural disasters such as drought and floods frequently hit the country and further affect the supply of water. Uneven distribution and shortages in supply are combined with an increase in water demand due to population growth and rapid economic development. The increasing demand and lax environmental controls both contribute to the reduction of water quality. By the end of 2010 almost all of China's rivers and lakes were polluted to some degree.[12] Rivers in northern China are more polluted than those in the south, while enclosed lakes in cities are more polluted than other freshwater lakes. Pollution in rivers and lakes has resulted in 60 % of China's total sea area being polluted to various extents.

Water pollution can significantly affect human health, leading to diarrhoea and other digestive diseases, and even reduced intelligence due to heavy metals and toxins (such as lead, cadmium, and mercury), to which more attention has been paid by Chinese citizens in recent years. In addition, since polluted water is widely used for irrigation and industrial production, it, along with water scarcity, has affected the quantity and quality of agricultural output and increased the costs of the industry.

Surface water pollution has increased the depletion of groundwater. In locations where groundwater cannot be replenished it increases the risk of seawater intrusion and land subsidence. Nowadays many northern cities rely on groundwater; however, the 'China Environmental Bulletin 2013' shows severe pollution in groundwater.[13]

China has recognized the deterioration of environmental quality and, for many years, has attempted to reduce pollution and to increase energy efficiency. The '*Jie neng jian pai*' (energy conservation and emission reduction) policy was formally introduced in China's 11th Five-Year Plan (2006–2010), and set binding targets to reduce energy intensity by

---

[12] Zhang, *Foreign Direct Investment*, 36–39.

[13] Ministry of Environmental Protection, "China Environment Bulletin 2013."

20 % and the emission of key pollutants by 10 %. More actions were put forward in the 12th Five-Year Plan from 2011 to 2015. The binding targets of energy conservation and emission reduction in the 11th and 12th Five-Year Plan demonstrate the determination and commitment of the government to improve the environment.

Over the past decade China has made great improvements in environmental protection and pollution treatment; however, the situation is still severe, mainly due to failure to implement the environmental management system. Although it has been recognized that reforms are needed in many areas, such as economic restructuring, improvement of legal systems, and internal changes to the government, China has not found a way to strike a balance between environmental protection on the one hand, and sustaining a high rate of growth and energy needs on the other.

Achievements in Environmental Protection in China 2000–2010

China started to implement its sustainable development strategy in 1979 when the provisional Environment Protection Law (for Trial Implementation) was introduced (officially promulgated in 1989). In 1983, the government announced that environmental protection would be one of the country's fundamental policies. One year later the National Environmental Protection Agency was established and subsequently upgraded to ministerial level in 2008. Over the past three decades, China has gradually established an administrative system of environmental protection. By the end of 2011, there were 13,842 units of environmental protection organizations with 201,161 personnel at five administrative levels: national, provincial, prefecture, county, and town.[14] Environmental organizations consist of environmental protection bureaus, monitoring stations, supervisory organizations, research institutions, propaganda and education organizations, information organizations, and others.

[14] *China Environment Yearbook* (2012).

China has established a comprehensive and systematic environmental regulation framework, including 24 laws on environmental protection and resource conservation, more than 50 rulings, and over 1,300 environmental standards. The MEP is responsible for setting up national environmental quality standards and monitoring systems, formulating the monitoring standards, and strengthening monitoring management. Local government is responsible for the implementation of environmental regulations and investigating and assessing the environmental situations within their jurisdiction.[15] The main features of environmental policy went through the following three phrases: end-of-pipe management and concentration based control (from 1972 to early 1991); source oriented pollution prevention and total emission control (1992–2001); and integrated and comprehensive management, cleaner production, and life cycle control (2002 onwards).[16] In recent years, China has tended to transform its growth path to the so-called scientific development, aiming to establish a harmonious, stable, and prosperous society in an all-inclusive way. This indicates that environmental protection and resource conservation are of equal importance to economic development; hence, sustainable development strategy should integrate both environmental and economic goals.

In addition to building up administrative and legislative systems, China has made significant investments in environmental pollution treatment, particularly after 2006 (Fig. 7.1). In 2011, China invested RMB659 billion (1.39 % of the national GDP) in tackling pollution, which was more than six times the total invested in 2000. Out of the investment 52.6 % was used for urban environmental infrastructure construction, such as gas supplies, central heating, drainage works, gardening and greening/planting, and environmental sanitation; 6.7 % was used for the treatment of industrial pollutants, including wastewater, waste gas, solid wastes, noise, and others; the remaining 40.6 % was the so-called 'three simultaneities' investment for a new project, which refers to the design, construction, and operation of the environmental protection

[15] Zhang, *Foreign Direct Investment*, 114–116.

[16] He et al., "Changes and Challenges", 25–38.

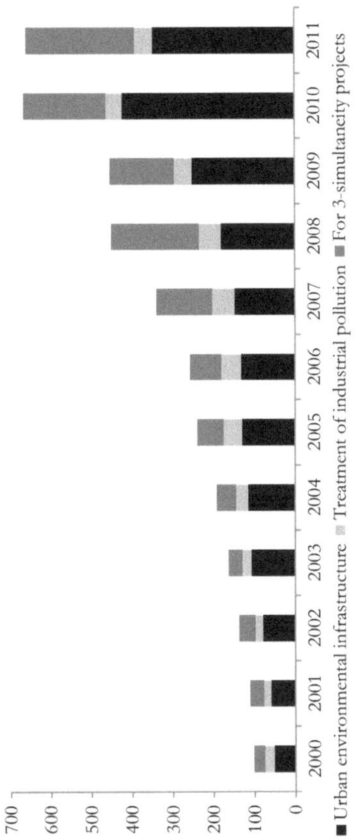

Fig. 7.1 Investment in environmental pollution treatment 2000–2011 (*Source*: Zhang (2014) and China Environment Yearbook (2012))

facilities that are required to be simultaneous with the design, construction, and operation of the new projects.

China's environmental protection has achieved success in many areas. First, as shown in Table 7.1, the growth rate of energy consumption peaked in 2004 but subsequently went into an overall decline. During the 11th Five-Year Plan period (2005–2010), the average growth rate was 6.6 %, much lower than the average GDP growth rate of 11.2 %. Simultaneously, energy intensity declined by 20.7 % during these five years, opposite to the increase in the previous three years.

Similarly, both household and industrial emissions of main pollutants peaked in the mid-2000s and then declined from 2006 to 2010 (Table 7.3). For example, chemical oxygen demand (COD), SO_2, and Ammonia Nitrogen emissions declined on average by 3–4 % a year during the 11th Five-Year Plan period, while the reductions of soot, industrial dust, and industrial solid wastes was much faster, with an average rate of decrease of 7, 13, and 21 % respectively. The emission levels of all pollutants in 2010, except SO_2, were lower than those in 2000, whereas the country's GDP has increased by three times in nominal terms and almost doubled in real terms during the same period. In addition to the changes in economic structure, one important reason is that of the enhanced capacity to deal with pollution emissions. Table 7.4 shows that the efficiency of

Table 7.3 Emissions of main pollutants in China 2000–2010 (million tonnes)

Year	COD	Ammonia Nitrogen	SO_2	Soot	Industrial dust	Industrial solid wastes
2000	14.45		19.95	11.65	10.92	31.86
2001	14.05	1.25	19.47	10.70	9.91	28.94
2002	13.67	1.29	19.27	10.13	9.41	26.35
2003	13.34	1.30	21.59	10.49	10.21	19.41
2004	13.39	1.33	22.55	10.95	9.05	17.62
2005	14.14	1.50	25.49	11.83	9.11	16.55
2006	14.28	1.41	25.89	10.89	8.08	13.02
2007	13.82	1.32	24.68	9.87	6.99	11.97
2008	13.21	1.27	23.21	9.02	5.85	7.82
2009	12.78	1.23	22.14	8.48	5.24	7.11
2010	12.38	1.20	21.85	8.29	4.49	4.98

Note: COD = chemical oxygen demand
Source: China Environment Yearbook (2011)

Table 7.4 Treatment efficiency of main industrial pollutants in China 2000–2010 (%)

Year	Wastewater	SO_2	Soot	Dust	Solid wastes*
2000	76.9				45.9
2001	85.2	61.3	67.3	50.2	52.1
2002	88.3	70.2	75.0	61.7	51.9
2003	89.2	69.1	78.5	54.5	54.8
2004	90.7	75.6	80.2	71.1	55.7
2005	91.2	79.4	82.9	75.1	56.1
2006	90.7	81.9	87.0	82.9	60.2
2007	91.7	86.3	88.2	88.1	62.1
2008	92.4	88.8	89.6	89.3	64.3
2009	94.2	91.0	90.3	89.9	67.0
2010	95.3	97.9	90.6	91.4	66.7

* Ratio of utilization for industrial solid wastes

Note: Measured by the proportion of industrial pollutants meeting discharge standards

Source: China Environment Yearbook (2011)

industrial pollution treatment, measured by the proportions of pollutants meeting the national discharge standards, has increased substantially to over 90 %. Such achievements are due to huge investment in pollution treatment projects, technology progression, and, most importantly, the tightened environmental policy in the five-year plan.

Although most rivers and lakes in China are polluted to different extents, surface water quality tended to improve between 2006 and 2010. Table 7.5 shows the water quality of seven river systems in China, measured by the proportions of monitored sections.[17] It shows that in the early 2000s more than 40 % of the monitored sections in the seven river

[17] Water quality is classified into six levels in China, with Grade I the cleanest and worse than Grade V the most polluted. Water of Grades I–III can be used for drinking, Grade IV water is for industrial use, and Grade V is mainly for irrigation; water worse than Grade V is absolutely unsafe. Since heavily polluted water has been used for agricultural irrigation, the soil has been polluted in many places and the quantity and quality of agricultural products have been affected. For drinking water quality standards, many developed countries have devised their own standards, such as the European Drinking Water Directive, and the United States Safe Drinking Water Act. The WHO also has guidelines on the standards for countries without a legislative framework for drinking water quality. China's drinking water quality standards (GB3838-2002) have covered major parameters in the WHO guidelines and, for some parameters, have more rigorous standards. However, comparing with the comprehensive EU standards, some parameters are not included in Chinese standards.

Table 7.5 Water quality of seven river systems in China 2001–2010

		% of monitored section		
Year	No. of monitored section	Grade I–III	Grade IV–V	Worse than Grade V
2000	248	57.7	28.5	13.8
2001	752	29.5	29.5	41.0
2002	741	29.1	30.0	40.9
2003	407	38.1	32.2	29.7
2004	412	41.8	30.3	27.9
2005	411	41.0	32.0	27.0
2006	408	46.0	28.0	26.0
2007	407	49.9	26.5	23.6
2008	409	55.0	24.2	20.8
2009	408	57.3	21.3	18.1
2010	409	59.9	23.7	16.4

Notes: The seven rivers are the Songhua River, Liao River, Hai River, Yellow River, Huai River, Yangtze River, and Pearl River, from north to south. The data in 2000 only included the results of monitored sections in the main rivers while those in the other years included the branches. The proportions of Grade IV–V and worse than Grade V in 2001 are estimated by the author based on the available data that Grade IV accounted for 17.7 %, and Grade V and worse than Grade V for 52.8 %, of all rivers

Source: China Environment Yearbook, various years

systems were severely polluted, while only 30 % of the rivers were drinkable. Conditions started to improve in the following years, when close to 60 % of the monitored sections reached the water quality of Grade III in 2000. Similar distribution and trends can be found when water quality is measured by percentages of evaluated lengths of the rivers. The MEP's overall evaluation of the country's river water quality has been changed from 'moderately polluted' in the early 2000s to 'lightly polluted' in 2009. Among the seven river systems, the Yangtze River and the Pearl River are cleaner than the others. The Songhua River and the Huai River are lightly polluted, the Yellow River and the Liao River are moderately polluted, and the Hai River is heavily polluted. The tributaries of the rivers are usually more polluted than their trunk streams, and the streams across the borders of provinces are usually more polluted than other parts.

The overall air quality of the monitored cities remained in continuous improvement according to the data of the China Environment

Yearbook.[18] In the early 2000s, only one-third of the observed Chinese cities met the national Air Quality Standards Class II, which meant that the majority of urban citizens were living with a serious air pollution problem which was detrimental to their health. However, this proportion significantly increased to 82.8 % by the end of 2010 (Table 7.6).

Overall, all the above indicators demonstrate that 2006 (the beginning of the 11th Five-Year Plan) was a turning point in China's environmental protection. The changes in development strategy and the tightening up of environmental policy has led to industrial upgrading, the stimulation and progression of green technology, as well as enhanced implementation of environmental regulations.[19] For example, from 2005 to 2010, the share of large thermal power units (>300 MW installed capacity) increased from 50 to 73 % in the electric power industry; the production capacity of large blast furnaces (>1000 m^3) increased from 48 to 61 % in the steel industry; and the production of new dry cement clinker increased from 39 to

Table 7.6 Air quality of monitored cities in China 2000–2010

		% of monitored cities		
Year	No. of monitored cities	Class I–II	Class III	Worse than Class III
2000	338	36.5	30.5	33.0
2001	341	33.4	33.4	33.2
2002	343	33.8	35.0	31.2
2003	340	41.7	31.5	26.8
2004	342	38.6	41.2	20.2
2005	522	60.3	29.1	10.6
2006	559	62.4	28.5	9.1
2007	333	60.5	36.1	3.4
2008	519	76.8	21.8	1.4
2009	612	79.5	16.2	1.3
2010	471	82.8	15.5	1.7

Source: China Environment Yearbook, various years

[18] Air quality standards include three classes from the old standards GB 3095-1996. Class I is the cleanest and applies to special regions such as national parks. Class II applies to all other areas, including urban and industrial areas. Class III is for special industrial areas. Worse than Class III means seriously polluted. The revised standards GB 3095-2012 eliminated Class III.

[19] Industrial upgrading refers to 'a process of improving the ability of a firm or an economy to move to more profitable and/or technologically sophisticated capital and skill-intensive economic niches' (Gereffi, "Apparel Commodity Chain", 37–70).

81 %.[20] These developments have greatly improved energy efficiency and contributed to the reduction of pollution emissions. Some environmentally friendly technologies in industrial production have become popular, such as using coke dry quenching technology in the steel industry and low temperature waste heat recovery for power generation technology in the cement industry. In addition, a total of 531 patents were granted for environmental inventions, utility models, and designs, among which 194 were patented inventions of new technologies.[21]

By the end of 2010, China had established a preliminary system consisting of energy saving regulations and standards, emission reduction supervision and management (combining the monitoring of key pollution sources and enforcement of environmental regulations), supporting policies, and technologies. Furthermore, public awareness on energy saving and environmental protection has been enhanced.

The Challenges of Environmental Protection

Although the above mentioned achievements are substantial, challenges still exist in many areas. Air and water pollution is severe and the efficiency in energy consumption is low. Although the consumption of electricity grew much faster than GDP, there were widespread electricity shortages across the country during peak time in 2011, suggesting that China's economic structure was still highly energy inefficient, posing a big threat to sustainable growth.[22]

The Chinese economy has relied heavily on manufacturing for over three decades.[23] In 2011, the manufacturing and construction industries were responsible for 46.8 % of GDP, compared with less than 25 % in many developed countries. In contrast, the service industry was responsible for 43.1 % of China's GDP, compared with over 70 % for most developed economies. Even compared with other BRICS (Brazil, Russia, India, China, and South Africa) economies, China is far more

[20] 12th Five-Year Plan for Energy Saving and Emission Reduction, the State Council of China.

[21] Calculated by the author based on data from China Environment Yearbook, 2007–2011.

[22] Yao, Luo and Rooker, "Energy Efficiency Economic Growth," 99–121.

[23] Yao and Zhang, "Goodbye to Double-Digit Growth."

dependent on the industrial sector. Heavy industry is more capital and energy intensive, though labour extensive, compared to light industry. However, the share of output from light industry in total industrial output declined from 49 % in 1978 to 29.1 % by 2010. Although the industrial sector contributed 40 % of GDP in 2010, it consumed over 71 % of total energy and 95 % of the total coal consumption. In addition, the growth of the six most energy consuming industrial sectors has been faster than that of the others.[24] China has claimed to have adjusted and upgraded its industrial infrastructure for more than a decade; however, its industry is still greatly reliant on the production and exportation of low-tech manufacturing products using cheap labour and energy without the adequate capacity to innovate or the ability to produce high value products. Such over-dependency on low-tech and labour intensive production cannot be maintained forever because of labour shortages, an ageing population, and the rising prices of key commodities, such as iron ore, oil, soybeans, and copper.

There have been several gaps in the formulation of environmental standards. Firstly, existing standards are lagging behind other countries in the world. For example, fine particles ($PM_{2.5}$) are not new for many countries: as early as 2005 the WHO had introduced guidelines on recommended limits for the concentration of $PM_{2.5}$ and other air pollutants, applicable across all WHO regions. Subsequently, most Western countries set their targets accordingly, but China has only recently added them to the updated national air quality standards (GB3095-2012) which will be enforced from January 2016.

Secondly, many environmental standards are outdated and have not been revised for over ten years.[25] For example, it has taken 16 years to revise the existing air quality standard (GB3095-1996). Other standards, such as the Pollution Discharge Standards of Boats and Ships (GB3552-1983) have not been revised for 30 years, and the Soil Quality Standards (GB15618-1995) for almost 20 years. Therefore, such standards do not take into account new pollutants and hazardous substances.

---

[24] The six high energy-consuming industries include: manufacturing of raw chemical materials and chemical products; manufacturing of non-metallic mineral products; smelting and pressing of ferrous metals; smelting and pressing of non-ferrous metals; oil, coking, and nuclear fuel processing; and the production and supply of electricity and heat.

[25] Zhang and Wang, "Problems of China's System," 187–192.

Thirdly, the existing standards focus more on the concentration of the pollutants, rather than total pollution emissions. The concentration of pollutants can be affected by many factors, such as temperature, rainfall, and measuring equipment at the observation site. It is also possible to reduce the concentration whilst not reducing total emissions. For example, the concentration of air pollutants in the city can be reduced by heightening the chimneys of factories or relocating polluting factories out of the city.

Weaknesses in the implementation of environmental regulations also exist. Many places, particularly at the grass-roots administrative levels and in less developed regions, do not possess adequate quantitative management of energy consumption and pollution emissions, which is compounded by insufficient monitoring and supervision capacity. For example, only one-third of cities and counties in Xinjiang have established energy saving supervision bureaus. Few cities have professional energy statisticians and the majority of enterprises do not have a specified energy statistician. Some industrial firms do not even have the energy measuring equipment required by law.[26] Therefore, it is difficult for these regions to monitor and control the energy consumption of large energy users, as well as the emissions of large polluters.

Although many organizations and enterprises are aware that environmental impact assessments have to be carried out before establishing a new project, a substantial number of small and medium scale organizations fail to do so. A greater number of them have no idea about energy saving assessments, which is also required by law and has to be carried out by qualified organizations. A fieldwork study conducted by me in Shandong Province in summer 2013 found that some firms were not aware of the related environmental and energy regulations; therefore, they did not follow the proper assessment procedure. Some were even deceived by unqualified organizations and purchased an expensive but worthless energy saving assessment report. This generated additional costs to the firm which had to redo the assessment, and they also ran the risk of penalties from the energy supervision authority. I also found

[26] General Office of Xinjiang Uygur Autonomous Region (2013) "Energy Conservation, Emission Reduction."

that a large proportion of the firms were still using inefficient models of electric motors listed on the 'Catalogue of Outdated Electromechanical Equipment (Products) with High Energy Consumption to be Phased Out (Batch 2)', which was enforced in 2012 by the Ministry of Industry and Information Technology of China.

In summary, China is lagging behind developed countries and even some developing countries in terms of environmental quality, energy intensity, as well as the enforcement of energy/environmental regulations. In addition to the above inadequate industrial infrastructure and weaknesses in the formulation of implementation of environmental policy, China also faces other challenges in alleviating environmental problems, such as lack of expertise and technology, bureaucracy, and corruption.

Reasons for Failure to Implement Environmental Policies

There are four approaches to implementing environmental measures in China.[27] The first approach is via orders and control, including control of the total amount of emissions, environmental impact assessments, the three-simultaneity system, centralized pollution control, setting deadlines for control of sources, and pollution discharge permits. The second approach is market instruments, such as pollution levies, penalties, SO_2 and CO_2 emission trading, and subsidies for energy-saving products. The third approach involves voluntary actions, for example ISO 14000 standards, eco-model areas, environmental NGOs, and green GDP accounting pilot projects. The fourth method refers to public participation, which means citizens monitor and report environmental issues through, for example, environmental protection hotlines, online reporting systems and complaint mailboxes, and participating in court for some issues. Orders and control used to be the main approach for implementing environmental regulations. Recently, however, methods in the second approach have been widely used, and those in the third and

[27] Matsuno, "China's Environmental Policy."

fourth approaches have also appeared in many places. However, failure to implement these measures also widely exists due to weak enforcement.

The limited power of environmental authorities is one reason for the failure to implement environmental laws.[28,29] Before being upgraded to its current ministerial level, the MEP had limited administrative powers and was not allowed to participate fully in national decision making. After being upgraded, it was granted more power but is still subject to decisions from other ministries and departments. Local environmental authorities are subordinate to local government. They are reliant on the government for both funding and enforcement, making it hard for them to act freely in the local interest and protect the environment. Some local governments set economic growth as a priority and therefore interfere with the environmental protection authority and protect large, polluting enterprises. Current legislation only allows the environmental authorities to make suggestions and issue fines or administrative penalties. They do not have the power to force a violator to make changes or stop production within a certain time limit. Local environmental authorities usually have no powers of enforcement over an unlawful polluting project that has been approved by the environmental authority at higher administrative levels.[30] Also, since the fines are usually small, it may cost more to obey the law than to break it. Many environmental violators receive administrative punishments rather than criminal penalties, as the punishments are not that effective.

Although there is a comprehensive approval process for new industrial projects, and all the projects are required to do an environmental impact assessment, many projects with severe environmental consequences, particularly small enterprises, start construction without environmental investigation or approval. Most of the time, the imposition of punishment to these violators is delayed.[31]

---

[28] Ma, "China's Environmental Governance."

[29] Wang, "Chinese Environmental Law Enforcement," 160–193.

[30] In this case, the local environmental authority can only collect the pollution emission charge, which is paid by all organizations that discharge pollutants, the amount of which is determined by the volume of emissions.

[31] Ibid.

Environmental policy is set by the government, overseen by the environmental authorities, and implemented by various government departments. In principle this is effective, but coordination between environmental authorities and other departments is poor, mainly because of the huge amount of overlap among departments. For example, water pollution is the responsibility of the environmental authorities, but water and groundwater are managed by the Ministry of Water Resource, and sewage is dealt with by the Ministry of Construction, which also has the function of directing the use and protection of groundwater in cities. This problem has been solved in other countries through greater departmental communication, but not in China due to the lack of legislative clarity of each department's role, power, and responsibilities.

Additionally, the public lack of awareness of environmental protection and participation in social supervision is also detrimental to enforcing environmental regulations. Under the current legislative framework, it is difficult for the public actually to participate in the environmental impact assessment process.[32]

Furthermore, decentralization of the environmental regulatory body makes the enforcement of national policy at the local level difficult[33] and the stringency varies between regions. Environmental standards are set jointly by local and national regulators. Levy rates are formally established by a national regulator but the actual levies are decided and collected by local regulators, some of whom tolerate polluting companies for economic interests. Excessive pollution happens in some regions due to the failure of local government. The situation continues because of the lack of awareness by some local government officials about the environment, environmental laws, and the rule of law in general. Therefore, local levies may vary from region to region for identical industries and pollutants. In addition, local regulatory inspections also vary, as some regions have better management systems than others. In some places, the enforcement of environmental and energy laws are mainly by 'urging the rectification supplemented by punishment'. As a result, regulatory strength differs across regions.

---

[32] Ibid.

[33] He et al., 25–38.

Finally, unprecedented economic growth has been the key reason behind implementation difficulties.[34] Rapid economic growth has led to tremendous changes in the economic structure, the concentration of people in major cities, and changes of lifestyles, which have all had environmental impacts. Although China has achieved relative improvement measured by pollution levels or energy consumption per unit of GDP, the absolute environmental improvements are still below the expectations and targets. In addition, the development of other areas of society is lagging behind the development of the economy, for example, legal systems, fiscal and financial policies, education (hence human capital), and technology. These are important factors for the success of the formulation and implementation of environmental policies.

Economic Development and Environmental Protection

There have been a large number of papers, reports, speeches, and official documents addressing the issue of how to balance economic development with environmental protection, which is a big topic covering a broad range of issues. The State Council's 12th Five-Year Plan for Energy Saving and Emission Reduction has provided detailed guidelines on the main tasks, key projects, and safeguarding mechanisms being implemented between 2011 and 2015 (summarized in Table 7.7). This chapter cannot cover every aspect listed and does not intend to repeat those which have already been considered. I prefer to provide additional suggestions on changes in industrial infrastructure and the implementation of environmental policies, which are rarely mentioned in previous studies and reports.

To alleviate the environmental problem whilst maintaining economic growth, short term targets for energy saving and emission reduction can be achieved by eliminating inefficient equipment, closing down out-of-date production capacity, and by curbing the growth of high-energy use and high-polluting intensive industries. Such measures will benefit the environment but will also increase the production costs of firms,

[34] Ibid.

Table 7.7 12th Five-Year Plan for Energy Saving and Emission Reduction

	Main tasks
Adjusting and optimizing the industry structure	• Restraining the excessive growth of high-energy using and high-emission industries • Eliminating the backward production capacity • Upgrading traditional industries • Adjusting the structure of energy consumption • Developing services industry and emerging strategic industries
Improving the level of energy efficiency	• Strengthening industrial energy saving • Enhancing energy saving of buildings • Promoting energy saving in transportation industry • Promoting agricultural and rural energy saving • Strengthening commercial and civil energy saving • Implementing energy saving of public organizations
Strengthening the emission reduction of major pollutants	• Strengthening the construction of urban sewage treatment facilities • Strengthening pollutant emission reduction in key industries • Launching the prevention and control of agricultural sources of pollution • Controlling the pollution emission from automobiles • Promoting the treatment of $PM_{2.5}$

Main projects
• Energy saving renovation projects • Energy saving products to benefit the people • Projects of contracting energy management and promotion • Demonstration of energy saving technology industrialization • Construction of urban sewage treatment facilities • Prevention and control of water pollution in key valleys • Desulfurization and denitration projects • Prevention and control of livestock and poultry breeding pollution • Demonstration of circular economy • Projects related to building energy saving and emission reduction capacity

(*continued*)

Table 7.7 (continued)

Safeguard mechanisms
• Insisting on the green and low-carbon development • Strengthening the objective responsibility assessment on energy saving and emission reduction • Enhancing energy saving management • Perfecting relevant laws, regulations, and standards • Completing the investment mechanism for energy saving and emission reduction • Perfecting the economic policies to promote energy saving and emission reduction • Promoting relevant market-based instruments • Promoting innovations and applications of technology • Enhancing the supervision and inspection and capacity building

Source: 12th Five-Year Plan for Energy Saving and Emission Reduction, State Council of China

the administrative costs of local authorities, and the costs to the local economy, including unemployment and tax reduction. Given the current level of development in China, it is difficult to carry out all these eliminations in one go. A gradual and strategic plan has to be set up in order to make them happen. In the long term, sustainable development is only achievable through changing the industrial infrastructure and upgrading it. Examples of the latter include: improving production quality and using better technology during the production process; moving from the production of cheap labour-intensive and low-tech manufacturing products to more sophisticated and high-value added products and services; and improving the share of environmental protection industry related in industrial sectors and service sectors in the economy. In addition, it is important to promote the commercial use of new clean energy, such as wind power, solar power, shale gas, coalbed methane, geothermal, and biomass energy.[35] The long term strategy not only requires economic development and domestic innovations, but also institutional support, such as an adequate pricing system, fiscal and financial policies, and market-based instruments, in order to restrict the development of high-energy-using and high-polluting industries and

[35] China has been the world leader in the field of solar power and wind power, both in terms of installed capacity and power.

to encourage environmental innovation, clean energy development and utilisation, as well as industrial reform.

The first concern of industrial infrastructure renovation is geographical relocation of traditional polluting industries. Economic development is uneven across regions in China. In general, coastal regions are more advanced than inland regions, but since 2005 the latter have tended to grow faster than the former. Whilst it is good to see the trend of regional convergence, it is a worrying observation that the most energy consuming and polluting industries have been moving from the coastal to the inland regions.[36] These industries include non-metallic mineral products, petroleum, coking and nuclear fuel, paper and paper products, ferrous metals, textiles, non-ferrous metals, chemical materials, and chemical products. Energy production and power generation have also moved towards the inland regions, which have low energy efficiency, so that the relocation of these traditional industries reduces the overall energy efficiency of China's industrial production.[37] This observation has significant implications for environmental protection and economic development policies. Since economic development levels and environmental regulatory stringency are different across regions, profit-maximizing firms have incentives to move their lagging industrial capacities, which have been eliminated in developed regions, to relatively poor regions with lax environmental regulations. At the same time, poor regions may further reduce their regulatory stringency in order to attract more investment from outside. It is widely known that less developed regions usually have the most vulnerable ecological systems. While the immediate results would be to increase energy efficiency and environmental quality in coastal regions, and encourage economic growth in inland regions, the ultimate outcome would be irreversible environmental damage and enormous health and economic losses both locally and nationally. Therefore, in the following decade China should take measures to avoid the geographical relocation of backward capacities in traditional industries when optimizing its industrial infrastructure.

---

[36] Yao, Luo and Rooker, "Energy Efficiency Economic Growth," 99–121.

[37] Ibid.

The second concern is the opportunities and challenges in the development of green industries. Since the 11th Five-Year Plan, both central and local governments have attached more importance to the development of emerging industries in green energy and green technology. The current move towards a global green economy provides China with an opportunity to initiate transition, catch up with emergent green industries, and leapfrog towards an international competitive green economy.[38] China's production capacity of renewable technologies has grown rapidly in recent years. The orientation of the production tends to change from purely exporting overseas to a strategy of servicing both domestic and foreign markets. For example, China is the world's largest producer of solar photovoltaic (PV) cells and modules. In previous years, 99 % of these products were sold in Europe and the USA. However, trade barriers introduced into these countries in 2012 decreased demand. The resulting overcapacity in the industry led to the loss of many PV firms in China. In the first three-quarters of 2013, domestic demand increased and China is expected to become the top country for PV deployment in the year.[39] The boom in domestic demand was mainly caused by government policies on the development of the distributed generation of the solar market segment and the financing support to connecting solar farms to the national grid. China is forecast to become the strongest 'end-market' in 2013, with 50 % of solar PV modules produced domestically, because domestic producers are choosing to focus on the home market, rather than shipping modules overseas. Similar policies and financing support can be applied to the development of other renewable energy and green technologies.

Despite the rapid development of solar PV and other green technology industries in China, some challenges still exist. Firstly, core technologies in the relevant industries are usually monopolized by developed countries. There is a lack of relevant science subjects in universities, and the link between research and industry is not strong, so a lot of research output cannot be commercialized.[40] Therefore, further investment into

---

[38] Fu and Zhang, "Solar-PV Industry," 329–347.

[39] Solarbuzz, "Record PV Demand."

[40] Strangway, Liu and Feng, "Policy Report," 211.

science and technology and in higher education is needed, as well as policies to promote research institutions in the market place.[41] Secondly, a new problem of the green technology industry is that the production process of some green energy or green energy equipment is energy inefficient and can be heavily polluting. For example, silicon tetrachloride, a by-product of producing polysilicon used in solar PV panels, is a highly toxic substance and only a few manufacturers in Germany, the USA, and Japan have the technology for detoxification and recycling at the cost of about $84,500 per ton. However, Chinese companies could produce polysilicon at $21,000–56,000 per ton without proper treatment and recycling of silicon tetrachloride.[42] Additionally, the production of solar PV cells also generates other waste products which pollute water and soil.[43] Therefore, to make the development of such emerging new industries sustainable, China should immediately eliminate the polluting production capacity and then focus on domestic technological innovation in the production of clean energies. It should avoid 'the trap of becoming the new "manufacturing workshop of environmentally damaging industries" for "green" products'.[44]

To implement environmental regulations, China is encouraged to make full use of the four approaches mentioned above. Environmental economic theories tell us that market-based instruments are usually more effective than command and control measures. At present, China has no plan to introduce ecotaxes (or green taxes) and some existing measures of market-based instruments do not work well. For example, a pilot SO_2 emission trading programme started in the 1990s has developed quickly from 2007. Environment and Energy Exchanges opened in many cities but there are many obstacles to further development. Transactions between partners relied on 'forced marriages' imposed by the local environmental protection authority.[45] Many Exchanges have no transactions for as much as half a year or even two years. The reasons

[41] Fu and Zhang, "Solar-PV Industry", 329–347.

[42] Cha, "Solar Energy Firms."

[43] Du and Cao, "Ethical Reflection on Energy," 223–229.

[44] Fu and Zhang, "Solar-PV Industry," 329–347.

[45] ChinaNews, "Several Emission Trading Exchanges."

for this low transaction rate include high costs of emission trading, difficulties in monitoring and supervision, market failure, and most importantly the low penalties for violating environmental regulations (i.e. the pollution levies and penalties are lower than the pollution treatment costs). Therefore, China has to draw on examples in Western countries to optimize environmental laws, regulations, and standards, making the existing measures of command and control, as well as market instruments, play a greater role in environmental protection.

Many things can be done to improve voluntary actions and public participation. A pilot scheme on enterprise energy management systems and standards (ISO 50001) has been undertaken in Shandong Province, which will be used as a prototype for the rest of the country. The green GDP accounting pilot project has not developed well since its launch in 2006; the main obstacles are restrictions in statistical methodology and local protectionism.[46] A more practical system to calculate green GDP as a measure of true economic growth and as a measure of assessing local government official's performance is needed. To encourage the participation and supervision of the public, as well as environmental NGOs, investment in education and publicity campaigns are necessary. In the long term, reforms of the political and judicial systems are required to allow them to participate in decision making; however, this will involve lots more difficulties and obstacles.

To enhance the efficiency and enforcement of environmental regulations, reforms are needed at every administrative level. Firstly, environmental protection authorities need enhanced powers of enforcement. If these measures were put into place, environmental protection departments would be able to act freely to protect the environment. Reforms in the legal systems are needed to increase the financial penalties for those who break the environmental laws. More violators should be prosecuted. Secondly, it is suggested making environmental protection authorities independent.[47] Each such local authority has to be granted the power to determine their own personnel, and more importantly to separate their financial budget from local administration.

[46] Sina, "Green GDP Accounting."

[47] Wang, "Chinese Environmental Law Enforcement," 160–193.

Finally, cracking down on corruption will aid the enforcement of the environmental regulations. The dual-track system for the allocation of resources has been the main source of rent-seeking behaviour and the frequency of corruption in China. The power of approval in many areas of economic activities leads the head officials of various departments to become the targets of lobby groups offering bribes in order to get the inefficient, low-tech, and high polluting projects approved. However, if these projects result in any negative consequences, such as pollution and production accidents, the responsibility is rarely taken by the officials who approved them. The lack of accountability and light punishment have made corruption a high-return, low-risk activity. To combat corruption, these power structures need to be reformed. Two approaches might be taken in the short term: first, reduce the number of items that need to be approved; second, the officials have to be made accountable for their actions. It is known that environmental accountability has been carried out in Shanxi Province, one of the most air polluted provinces in China, from 2006. Officials who had not acted on environmental protection were all investigated and prohibited from being promoted. Thus far over a hundred local officials have been called to account for environmental pollution. This has helped to alleviate the environmental problem, but pollution is still serious in Shanxi. In the long term, radical political reform is necessary.

China is lacking an efficient oversight mechanism in many fields, including environmental protection and food security. However, there are many obstacles in establishing an effective mechanism because the reform will shake the interests of corrupt groups. Lopez and Mitra suggest that for any level of per capita income the pollution levels corresponding to corruption behaviour are always above the socially optimal level, and the turning point of the EKC takes place at income and pollution levels above those corresponding to the social optimum.[48] Therefore, anti-corruption not only strengthens environmental regulation stringency and lower pollution levels but also ensures that China passes the turning point of the EKC at lower income levels, all else being equal.

[48] Lopez and Mitra, "Corruption, Pollution, Environment Curve," 137–150.

Conclusions

In this chapter I have analysed the achievements and challenges in environmental protection along with the rapid economic growth in China, and have discussed the reasons for failure in implementing environmental regulations. The 11th Five-Year Plan has been a turning point in China's energy use and environmental protection, and since 2006 substantial improvements in energy saving and reduction emissions have been achieved. However, China still faces challenges in environmental quality due to its inadequate industrial infrastructure and deficiencies in the formulation and implementation of environmental regulations, which puts pressure on the new group led by Xi Jinping. The State Council's 12th Five-Year Plan for Energy Saving and Emission Reduction suggests that China should look for long term development through improving the industrial infrastructure and upgrading it. But during this latter process, it is suggested that the new leaders adopt measures that avoid the traps of relocating traditional polluting industries to environmentally vulnerable inland regions and the trap of promoting green energy and products that actually produces pollution. In order to enhance the implementation of environmental regulations, a more effective legal system is required as well as the independence of environmental authorities, further environmental accountability, and more participation by the public and civil society. Therefore, radical judicial and political reforms are required.

In his report at the 18th National Congress of the Communist Party of China (CPC), Hu Jintao announced the establishment of the strictest possible systems for protecting farmland, managing water resources, and protecting the environment. China's top legislature, the Standing Committee of the National People's Congress (NPC), has promulgated the revised Environmental Protection Law for the first time since it took effect in 1989. The new legislation reflects stricter measures and more government commitments to protect the already heavily polluted environment. It is expected to grant more actual and effective enforcement powers to the environmental authority, to increase the penalties for unlawful emitters, to put in place more rigid measures to restrain local governments from developing projects while overlooking environmental protection, to increase the importance of environmental protection in evaluating government performance, to encourage and expand the participation of public and non-profit organizations in environmental issues, and to improve the transparency of environmental quality data.

At the Third Plenary Session of the 18th CPC Central Committee in November 2013, Chinese leaders vowed to establish an adequate system to protect the environment and construct an eco-civilization. The communiqué stated that 'the system concerning property rights of natural resources as assets and the administration of their use should be improved'; it also urged 'drawing "red lines" for ecological protection, implementing a system of paid use of resources and ecological compensation, and reforming the system for the protection and administration of the ecological environment'.[49] For the first time, the property rights of natural resource assets are being addressed by Chinese leaders, indicating that the construction of a relevant system will be at the forefront of the reforms of the following ten years. The use of 'a system of paid-use resources and ecological compensation' signifies that there will be new pricing policies on energy and natural resources.

An efficient environmental protection system should be up to date, dynamic, and practicable. It should reflect the needs of environmental management at the current development level, and consider the differences across regions and industries. In addition, to improve the environmental laws, regulations, rules, and standards, many issues have to be included in the system: sound economic policies ensuring sustained investment in environmental protection, a system of environmental accountability and assessment of government officials to ensure the implementation of the system, the oversight mechanisms to improve the transparency and to encourage the public participation in decision making, and so on. Therefore, establishing this system is a protracted process and actions should be taken one step at a time. It is practical to

[49] CNTV, "China Vows Econological Protection."

start by revising and improving the existing systems and then setting up new ones; and pilot projects are usually useful for new systems.

Additionally, investment in education and innovation is as important as the construction of a more effective system. At the 2014 International Conference on Engineering Science and Technology in Beijing, Xi Jinping stressed the leading role of innovation in environmental protection: 'we take the strategy of innovation-driven development as a major national strategy … we will intensify efforts to protect the natural ecosystem and environment, spare no effort to solve issues including the haze and work hard to build a beautiful China with blue sky, green land and clean water'.[50]

To win the 'war' against pollution, China needs to prepare for sacrificing its economic growth to some extent. Although the central government has slightly lowered its economic growth targets to 7.5 % in 2014,[51] it has been criticized by environmentalists that maintaining such a strong growth target will make progress on cleaning up very difficult.[52] China's current wealth level enables the central government to sacrifice a significant part of its economic growth for the sake of the environment. To gain visible improvement in the environment, such as blue skies, more resources need to be put into environmental protection and energy conservation.

Bibliography

Cha, A. E. 2008. Solar energy firms leave waste behind in China. *Washington Post*. [online]. Available at http://www.washingtonpost.com/wpdyn/content/article/2008/03/08/AR2008030802595_pf.html. Accessed 10 Nov 2013.

ChinaNews. 2013. Several emission trading exchanges have a risk to be dilisted with zero transaction. [online]. Available at http://finance.chinanews.com/cj/2013/06-24/4959366.shtml. Accessed 16 Nov 2013.

[50] Li, "Build a Country."

[51] Li, "Work of Government Report."

[52] Li, "Air Quality."

CNTV. 2013. China vows econological protection: Communique. [online]. Available at http://english.cntv.cn/20131112/105404.shtml. Accessed 17 Nov 2013.

Du, P., and Y. Cao. 2010. Ethical reflection on new energy: The case of PV industry. In *High technology developement report of China*, ed. Chinese Academy of Science, 223–229. Beijing: Science Publisher.

Fu, X., and J. Zhang. 2011. Technology transfer, indigenous innovation and leapfrogging in green technology: The solar-PV industry in China and India. *Journal of Chinese Economic and Business Studies* 9(4): 329–347.

General Office of Xinjiang Uygur Autonomous Region. 2013. The notice about forwarding the key emphasis in the work of energy conservation and emission reduction of the autonomous region in 2013. General Office Document No. 85 (2013) of Xinjiang. [online]. Available at http://www.xinjiang.gov.cn/xxgk/gwgb/zfwj/2013/224447.htm. Accessed 13 Nov 2013.

Gereffi, G. 1999. International trade and industrial upgrading in the apparel commodity chain. *Journal of International Economics* 48(1): 37–70.

Grossman, G. M., and A. B. Krueger. (1991) Environmental impacts of a North American free trade agreement. NBER Working Paper No. 3914. National Bureau of Economic Research, Inc. [online]. Available at http://www.nber.org/papers/w3914.pdf. Accessed 1 Feb 2012.

He, G., Y. Lu, A. P. J. Mol, and T. Beckers. 2012. Changes and challenges: China's enviornmental management in transition. *Enviornmental Development* 3: 25–38.

Li, J. 2014a. Only 3 of 74 Chinese cities met air quality. *South China Morning Post.* [online]. Available at http://news.xinhuanet.com/english/special/2014--03/14/c_133187027.htm. Accessed 6 June 2014.

Li, K. 2014b. Report on the work of the government. [online]. Available at http://news.xinhuanet.com/english/special/2014-03/14/c_133187027.htm. Accessed 5 June 2014.

Li, X. K. 2014c. Xi: Build a country with blue skies. *China Daily.* [online]. Available at http://www.chinadaily.com.cn/china/2014-06/04/content_17560481.htm. Accessed 6 June 2014.

Lopez, R., and S. Mitra. 2000. Corruption, pollution and the Kuznets environment curve. *Journal of Environmental Economics and Management* 40(2): 137–150.

Ma, X. 2007. China's environmental governance. [online]. Available at http://www.chinadialogue.net/article/show/single/en/789-China-s-environmental-governance. Accessed 10 Jan 2008.

Matsuno, H. 2009. China's environmental policy: Its effectiveness and suggested approaches for Japanese companies. Nomura Research Institute Paper, No. 140.

MEP's Chinese Academy for Environmental Planning [online]. Available at http://www.caep.org.cn/type.asp?typeid=24. Accessed 27 Aug 2015.

Ministry of Environmental Protection. 2014. China environment bulletin 2013. [online]. Available at http://jcs.mep.gov.cn/hjzl/zkgb/2013zkgb/. Accessed 6 June 2014.

Sina. 2013. Green GDP accounting remained stagnant due to disputable environmental economic statistics. [online]. Available at http://finance.sina.com.cn/china/20130710/011216068499.shtml. Accessed 16 Nov 2013.

Solarbuzz. 2013. Record PV demand from China and Japan marks turning point for solar industry, according to NPD Solarbuzz. [online]. Available at http://www.solarbuzz.com/news/recent-findings/record-pv-demand-china-and-japan-marks-turning-point-solar-industry. Accessed 15 Nov 2013.

Strangway, D., X. Liu, and Z. Feng. 2009. Policy report of China Council for International Cooperation on environment and development. In *Building and environmentally-friendly society through innovation: Challenges and choices*, ed. Chinese Academy of Science, 211. Mimeo.

The World Bank and The Government of the People's Republic of China. 2007. Cost of pollution in China: Economic estimates of physical damages. [online]. Available at http://siteresources.worldbank.org/INTEAPREGTOPENVIRONMENT/Resources/China_Cost_of_Pollution.pdf. Accessed 1 Feb 2012.

Wang, C. 2006–2007. Chinese environmental law enforcement: Current deficiencies and suggested reforms. *Vermont Journal of Environmental Law* 8(2): 160–193.

Wong, E. 2013. Air pollution linked to 1.2 million premature deaths in China. *New York Times*. [online]. Available at http://www.nytimes.com/2013/04/02/world/asia/air-pollution-linked-to-1-2-million-deaths-in-china.html?_r=0. Accessed 5 June 2014.

Yao, S. and J. Zhang. 2011. Chinese economy 2010: Post crisis development. Nottingham University China Policy Institute Briefing Series Issue 67. [online]. Available at http://www.nottingham.ac.uk/cpi/documents/briefings/briefing-67-china-economic-review-2010.pdf. Accessed 10 Nov 2013.

———. 2012. Goodbye to double-digit growth. Nottingham University China Policy Institute Policy Paper, No. 3. [online]. Available at http://www.nottingham.ac.uk/cpi/documents/discussion-papers/discussion-papers-74.pdf. Accessed 10 Nov 2013.

Yao, S., D. Luo, and T. Rooker. 2012. Energy efficiency and economic growth in China. *Asian Economics Papers* 11(2): 99–121.

Zhang, J. 2014. *Foreign direct investment, governance, and the environment in China: Regional dimensions*. Basingstoke: Palgrave Macmillan.

Zhang, Y., and J. Wang. 2012. Problems of China's system of environmental standards and the countermeasures. *China Environmental Science* 32(1): 187–192.

8

Overcoming the Dilemma of China's Growth

Tianyong Zhou

China achieved high GDP growth at an average annual rate of 9.8 % for more than three decades between the start of its reform in 1978 and the opening up of its economy in 2012. Between 1991 and 2012, the average annual GDP growth rate was 10.3 % and between 2001 and 2012 it was 10.1 %. This rapid growth is unprecedented in the economic history of the world; but China cannot sustain it in the long run. Indeed, by 2015 the slowdown had already started, though it is unclear at this stage if it will make the task of rebalancing the economy more difficult or remove resistance to the top leadership's determination to introduce necessary changes.

The law of diminishing marginal utility is a fundamental rule in economics. Correspondingly, the marginal rate of return of the key elements also shows a downward tendency. Moreover, with the recent decline in

T. Zhou (✉)
Institute for International Strategic Studies,
Central Party School, Beijing, China
e-mail: zhouty2005@sina.com

S. Tsang, H. Men (eds.), *China in the Xi Jinping Era*,
The Nottingham China Policy Institute Series,
DOI 10.1007/978-3-319-29549-7_8

China's demographic dividend and environmental pressures, with their related price spiral fuelling ever-rising labour costs, it is inevitable that, under existing technical and institutional conditions, future economic growth will gradually slow down. Since China's economic growth is bound to decelerate gradually, one question remains unanswered. How does one determine the economic growth rate in the future? In other words, is there still potential to be tapped from China's economic future?

China is in a dilemma at present because, on the one hand, with its actual urbanization rate at only 30 %, at the current stage of economic development it cannot afford to allow its growth rate to fall below 7 %, let alone below 6 %, because that would prevent it from realizing the full potential of urbanization. It would also undermine the need for continued development, a balanced revenue, and job creation. On the other hand, is the existing growth model, based on measures like government-led initiatives, increased investment, and rivalries among local governments, still sustainable? If the answer is 'no', from where will the new growth come?

As I explain in this chapter, if China can exploit its full potential by introducing a series of reforms over the next ten years, it is still possible for it to maintain a relatively high growth rate for a sustained period in the future.

Can China's Traditional Growth Model Sustain Its Momentum?

In January 2014, figures published by the National Bureau of Statistics (NBS) showed that China's GDP growth rate in 2013 was 7.7 %, which represented a significant decrease compared with the rates in previous years. The 2013 full-year Hong Kong and Shanghai Banking Corporation Purchasing Managers' Index (HSBC PMI) and PMI National Bureau of Statistics Purchasing Managers' Index (NBS PMI) both picked up after falling earlier in the year, with the lowest points being in the middle of the year. There was a slight rebound in the second half of the year but the indexes disappointed again towards the year end. Although it showed a slight improvement in manufacturing operations on a month-to-month basis, the recovery of the economy remained weak (Fig. 8.1).

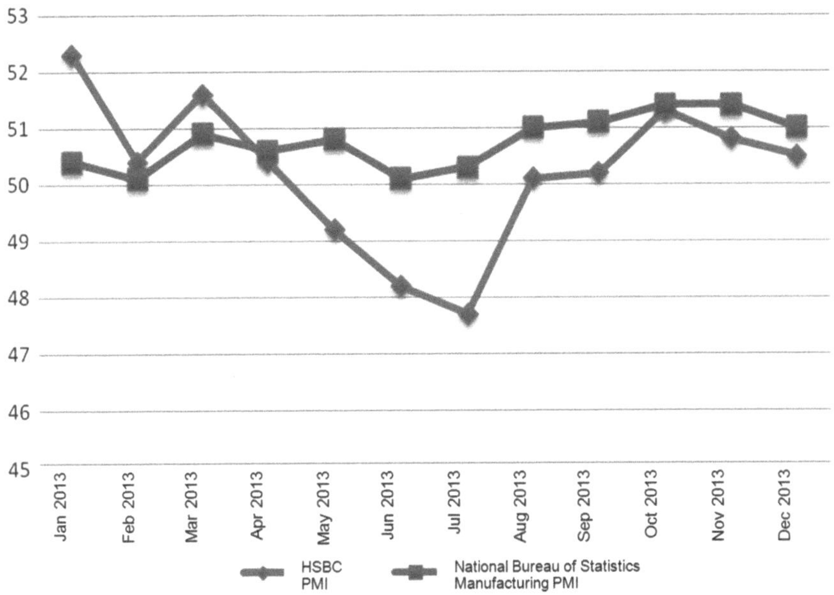

Fig. 8.1 HSBC PMI and NBS manufacturing PMI chart (January–December 2013)

China's overall economic growth has been slowing down since 2013, which has sparked a fierce debate among academics and policy researchers holding divergent theories and contradictory points of view. Liu Shijin, among others, attributed the rebound in August 2013 to a seasonal jump in electricity consumption caused by the use of air-conditioning and other appliances over the summer. He argues that factors such as the development base, resource constraints, and the downward trend in the world economy have allowed China to enter a transitional period during which it can no longer expect its former rapid growth rate of over 8 %. Although he thought that the rate could still possibly reach 7 or even 8 % in the two years leading up to 2015, after that it would likely remain in the 6–7 % range and drop further to around 6 % in 2020. Medium-speed or low-speed growth will become the norm.[1] Others, however, including Justin Yifu Lin, maintain that China will sustain its growth at a rate of

[1] Liu, "8 yue jingji haozhuan."

over 8 % for another 20 years. They advocate the use of investment to foster growth, especially at a time when the growth rate is declining.[2]

To explore the growth potential of China's economic future, we need first to analyse and understand the reasons behind its economic miracle in the past. Only then can we begin to discover why the current slowdown has occurred and why its traditional model was so successful.

Characteristics of China's Traditional Growth Model

China's economic growth since its reform and opening up may be attributed to its traditional growth model whereby, for the last 30 years, the country's high-speed growth in production capacity relied on low cost elements, a high level of investment, and environmental sacrifices. In the eastern regions, an influx of cheap surplus labour into the cities from the rural areas accompanied a growing shift in labour supply from agriculture to the manufacturing sector. The utilization of cheap land and other mineral and energy resources in manufacturing and construction also encouraged economic growth. The arrival of foreign direct investment and technology expanded and enhanced the production capacity of domestic manufacturing industry, though at the same time the virtually uncontrolled squandering of ecological and environmental resources also created many challenges. During the development process, local governments, relying mainly on large enterprises, large investment, large capital, and large projects, vied with each other to attract trade and investment. Meanwhile, large-scale land expropriation and resettlement created land resources and land revenue; and borrowing financed the investment and construction of production capacity and infrastructure. In summary, an increased overall supply gave strong impetus to the high-speed economic growth.

On examining the demand side of China's economic growth over a period of more than 30 years, it becomes clear that investment and export demand were its main drivers. It also becomes clear that: growth owed a good deal to exports; during much of the period of economic growth, but especially when it was starting to slow down, investment demand

[2] Lin, "houfa youshi."

was the main driving force; and consumer demand was gradually losing its power to propel economic growth. China's final consumption expenditure was more than 62 % of GDP in the 1980s, and actually 66 % in 1985. Between 2000 and 2012, however, the contribution to GDP from consumer spending dropped from 62.3 to 49.5 %. At the same time, household consumption expenditure was down from its peak of around 50 % of GDP in 1985 to 36.7 % in 2012. For the period 2000–2013, the growth rate of total retail sales of social consumer goods rose steadily before 2008, though the overall growth rate gradually slowed down between 2010 and 2013. The nominal growth rates of total retail sales of social consumer goods were 18.3, 17.1, 14.3, and 12.7 % for the years 2010, 2011, 2012, and 2013 respectively (as shown in Fig. 8.2).[3]

From the above analysis of supply and demand over China's past 30 years of economic growth, it is evident that, though changes do occur every ten years, the country modelled its growth on government-led initiatives, large-scale labour input, land and other resources, the consumption of ecological and environmental resources, reliance on export-oriented industries, investment, and construction.

Changes in Supply Side Conditions Driving Economic Growth

The Chinese economy had been growing very fast for more than 30 years and during that time many conditions changed drastically. It is therefore important not to fall into the trap of relying too blindly on past performance. The contributions of labour input, capital, and other resources to economic growth gradually decrease in the course of a country's development, and China cannot fly in the face of such an established economic principle. When examining the cost of inputs, a key element in the supply side of economic growth, it is apparent that the rising costs of labour, land rentals, land prices, factory prices, leasing costs, and RMB appreciation were driving up the cost of investment. Land available for projects in the eastern regions is becoming increasingly scarce and usually entails land expropriation and

[3] I obtained these data from the PRC's National Bureau of Statistics website.

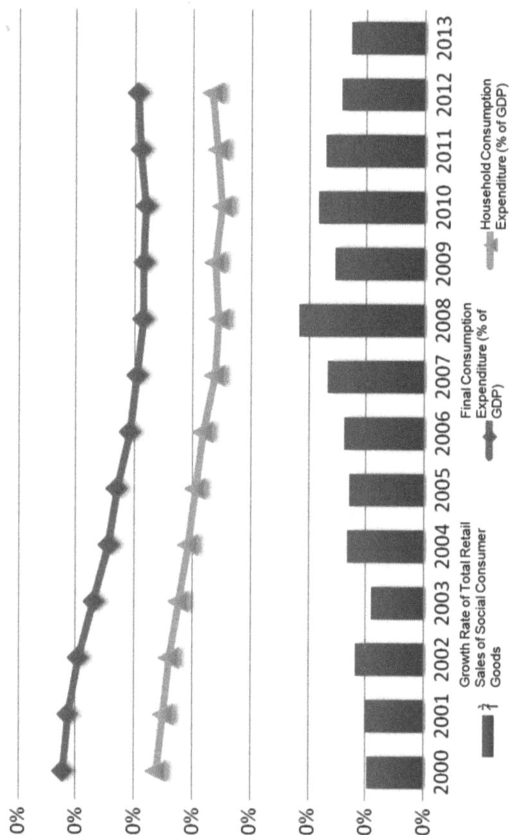

Fig. 8.2 Final consumption expenditure (% of GDP), household consumption expenditure (% of GDP), and the growth rate of total retail sales of social consumer goods between 2000 and 2013

resettlement. In addition, there is mounting pressure on the environment and on resources like fresh water. The people's growing awareness of their property rights and of the adverse effects of these projects on the environment is presenting the government with a new set of challenges.

Demand-Led Growth Is Becoming More and More Difficult

In terms of demand-led economic growth now and in the future, the three key components of the traditional model—exports, investment, and consumption—all appear to be weak. Export-led economic growth has been following a downward trend. In 2013, China's exports rose by 7.9 % and the trade surplus further expanded to RMB1.61 trillion, though high-speed economic growth driven by export demand may have become a thing of the past. This is due to a number of reasons.

First, the import demand of the developed economies will remain weak for a long time. Second, by taking advantage of the relatively cheap labour made available during the financial crisis, Europe and the USA have been revitalizing their manufacturing sectors. In particular, the value added of US manufacturing as a percentage of GDP has risen to nearly 12 % compared with 9 % in 2008, which has a crowding-out effect on imported products. Third, there is protectionism in the USA, which uses the 'non-market economy methodology' to 'impose higher punitive tariffs' against certain Chinese goods 'to protect inefficient domestic industries'.[4] Fourth, the USA is planning new strategies for world trade, which will inevitably crowd out and affect China's trading space in the world. Fifth, the developed economies are implementing a quantitative-easing monetary policy. This excessive money supply means that the depreciation pressure is transferred to other economies and the RMB is forced to appreciate, resulting in the rise in the export cost of Chinese products. From a long-term perspective, the circumstances surrounding China's exports are not looking good.

Investment-led economic growth faces growing constraints, as well as derived problems. Increased investment boosted economic growth in

[4] Watson, "American Protectionism."

2009, but simply replicating this method will only lead to an imbalance between investment and consumption and cause commodity prices and house prices to soar again. The most severe problems with China's traditional investment-led growth model are its government-led nature, fierce rivalries among local governments, and a fondness for large capital, large enterprises, large projects, and large-scale infrastructure. Due to the high organic composition of capital, its ability to attract employment is relatively weak. In addition, the profits gained by large capital and large enterprises by crowding out small and medium-sized enterprise (SME) entrepreneurs have mainly flowed to and are concentrated with the government, central state-owned enterprises (SOEs), and large enterprises of other types of ownership. The majority of the profits are not passed onto households and, as a result, they have not translated into consumer spending power.

Consumption-led economic growth has become difficult and complex. Chi Fulin and other scholars believe that it is vital to transform the investment-led and export-led growth model into a consumption-led one.[5] When using traditional methods to stimulate growth, such transformation is undoubtedly a right choice when restrictions are being placed on exports and when investment is having adverse effects. However, the key to the transformation of the growth model is whether it is able to improve the logical chain of regulatory restructuring→encouraging entrepreneurship→expanding employment opportunities→improving household income→increasing household spending→balancing production capacity on the supply side of the national economy. On the one hand, China is currently experiencing weak growth in household consumption, which means that private consumption cannot replace or compensate for cuts in public spending. On the other hand, 60 % of income is concentrated in the government, financial institutions, SOEs, and other non-public enterprises, while only a small percentage has gone to households. High income earners have a relatively low marginal propensity to consume and, although low income earners have a high marginal propensity to consume, their modest incomes limit their spending power. This is the main reason why it is difficult to drive high-speed economic growth by consumer demand in China and why the

[5] Chi, "Jingji zengzhang."

transformation from the export-led and investment-led growth model to a consumption-led model has been unsuccessful.

Net exports, investment, and consumption are the troika driving economic growth under the Keynesian framework. The above analysis also demonstrates that, because not much potential can be tapped from any of these three directions, the macroeconomic policies based on the Keynesian framework are having very limited scope of operation in China. In summary, the traditional growth model no longer has strong and sustainable momentum for growth. If China continues to adopt the traditional model, it is inevitable that economic growth will continue its downward trend for a long time.

The New Momentum for Economic Growth

The decline of the Chinese economy is logically inevitable under the traditional growth model. Does this mean no new momentum or new drivers for growth in China's future development? The answer is no. We must consider and seek a new growth model capable of delivering an alternative momentum and areas for growth.

Entrepreneurship and Small Businesses as the Driving Force of Employment

From a microeconomic perspective, we should consider the vitality of entrepreneurship and employment in mainstream society as the foundation of public prosperity and strong consumer demand. However, the vitality of entrepreneurship and employment is seriously inadequate in China when measured against international benchmarks. Two important indicators may be used to prove that there is no vitality or momentum in China's microeconomic environment in relation to entrepreneurship and employment. The first is the average number of enterprises per 1,000 inhabitants; the second is the graduate entrepreneurship rate. Compared with other countries, China's number of enterprises per 1,000 inhabitants is only one-third that of developed countries, and half that of developing countries, whereas China's graduate entrepreneurship rate is only one-tenth that of the developed countries.

Compared with the public prosperity and strong consumer demand during the era of high-speed growth in Japan, South Korea, and Taiwan, mainland China lacks the vitality and momentum of entrepreneurship in a microeconomic sense, as well as the means to distribute wealth to those who create it. Without micro-entrepreneurs, it is impossible to form a middle-income group or substantial middle class. Without the small businesses that entrepreneurs create, there will be no substantial demand for employment. Therefore, because of the lack of a substantial middle-income population and household income brought about by full employment, there will be no improvement in household spending power. The Chinese are always complaining about the irrational distribution of income and lack of consumer demand. In fact, the most important thing is to encourage the public to participate in the distribution of wealth while creating it.

Although Japan, South Korea, and Taiwan had a higher population density geographically than China, during their period of high growth the unemployment rate was very low, at around 2 %. They even had to bring in foreign workers from abroad to alleviate the shortage of labour. During their development processes, Japan, South Korea, and Taiwan enjoyed high investment rates and high-speed growth. What is different from China's 30 years of rapid growth is that their Gini coefficient was very low, which means there was relatively fair income distribution. Their savings and investment rates were also high, which suggests that there was no decline in household income or consumer demand. Instead, there was a simultaneous increase in household and national wealth, as well as a positive relationship between investment and consumption. The main reason for this is that active entrepreneurship created a large number of owners of SMEs, which in turn creates a middle class. The rise in the number of SMEs produced a high demand for labour, hence a very low unemployment rate. Because income increased in line with economic growth, the number of people living in poverty through unemployment was relatively insignificant. Japan pioneered the idea of relying on SMEs to build its nation. In the 1970s, South Korea attached great importance to the development of SMEs and adopted relevant strategies. Taiwan also built its economy on SMEs. This shows that large-scale micro-entrepreneurship and a large number of SMEs are capable of creating a strong momentum for growth. It is the best way to promote employment, increase household wealth, reduce income inequality, and create a positive relationship between investment and consumption.

Current data show that, although the sales figures of large and medium enterprises have improved thanks to the investment stimulus, the operating conditions for small enterprises continue to deteriorate. Although the NBS PMI remained above the 50 demarcation line between contraction and expansion in the first four months of 2014, it continued its gradual decline. The HSBC PMI reading, however, was already below the 50 demarcation line for the same period and continued its downward trend (as shown in Fig. 8.3).

China is currently facing an employment predicament. The latest studies by the Southwestern University of Finance and Economics revealed that, as of June 2012, the urban unemployment rate was 8.05 %, up by 0.5 % compared with 2011. Among them, the youth unemployment rate reached a record high of 16.4 % for university graduates. Moreover, the unemployment rate for second-tier cities increased significantly from 6.4 % in 2011 to 8.7 %,[6] which was higher than the officially published figure of around 5 %. It is not possible for a middle-income group to be formed under such employment patterns. What is more, there is no stable employment and it is difficult for the new labour force to find jobs, which means that the whole society lacks a stable foundation.

The current concept, strategies, systems, and policies are limiting. Inertial thinking still deems large investment, large capital, large enterprises, and large projects to be the driving force of economic growth. Furthermore, employment and livelihood issues are still government led and rely heavily on GDP growth and the increase in government revenue. The focus of the actual ideas, strategies, systems, and policies is not on employment and prosperity for the people; and neither is it on the vitality and momentum of entrepreneurship among the public.

Evaluations of the strong vitality and momentum that micro-entrepreneurship and employment bring to economic growth, roughly

[6] The Survey and Research Center for China Household Finance, Southwestern University of Finance and Economics, "Zhongguo chengzhen shiye baogao."

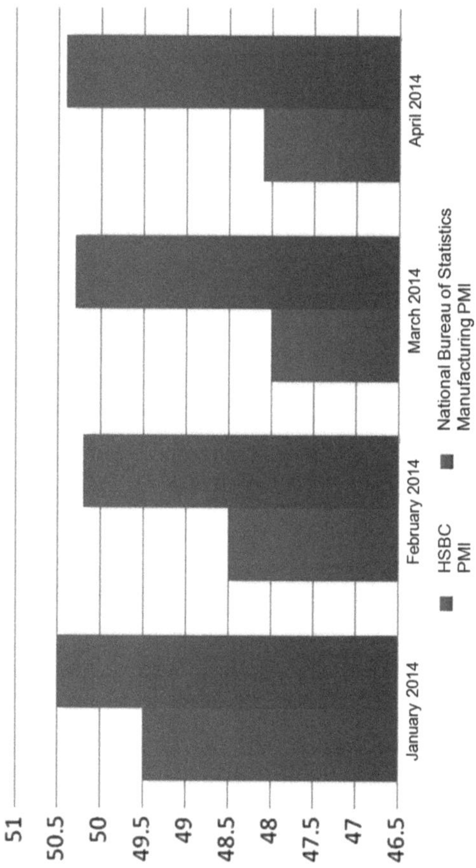

Fig. 8.3 PMI chart, January–April 2014

estimate that if the number of SMEs per 1,000 inhabitants in China reaches the average level in developing countries, namely 30 per 1,000 inhabitants, the number of enterprises will reach around 41 million,[7] 19 million more than the current 22 million. Assuming that each enterprise has ten employees and each employee has an average annual income of RMB36,000 and social security contribution of RMB10,000, the labour remuneration then comes to RMB460,000. When taking into account the proprietors' profit of RMB300,000 and depreciation of investment of RMB200,000, even if the government waives all taxes, the resultant GDP will be in the region of RMB1 million per annum. The above calculation shows that China is potentially losing RMB19 trillion worth of GDP due to its lack of SMEs compared with other developing countries. If there had been a healthy increase in entrepreneurship and SMEs in 2012, GDP attributed to SMEs would have replaced GDP attributed to large-scale investment, large capital, large enterprises, and large projects. This also means that GDP figures would have become less exaggerated and more credible, and the total value of GDP would have been greater. In terms of the distribution of GDP, the proportion of labour remuneration and household income would have increased significantly. If future efforts move in this direction, we will witness an economic and social situation in which the size of the middle-income population increases, the unemployment rate drops, people are living a prosperous life, domestic consumer demand is high, and there is sustainable economic growth and prosperity.

Innovation Creates Momentum for Robust Development

China has reached a stage of development when technological innovation primarily drives economic growth. The theories of developmental economics suggest that a less-developed economy is much more likely to rely

[7] The claim that there are more than 40 million SMEs in China, which is currently being quoted in the news, speeches, and documents on various occasions, is unscientific because the statistics regard a sole trader business operated by two self-employed individuals as an enterprise. In fact, the vast majority of sole traders, for example ice-cream sellers operating their businesses from ice-cream carts, should not be regarded as a true enterprise.

on investment, especially capital investment, to drive economic growth, whereas knowledge and technology are playing a much more important role in driving growth in a more developed economy. China's economic development has reached a transitional stage where growth is to be primarily driven by the advancement in knowledge and technology coupled with industrial innovations, rather than the investment of capital and resources.

China has confidence in an innovation-driven strategy because it has favourable conditions for technological innovations. When examining the conditions conducive to innovation-driven economic growth, the following points should be noted:

- Chinese people are hardworking, diligent, and intelligent, as the results of high school students from mainland China, Hong Kong, and Taiwan participating in annual international mathematics, physics, and chemistry competitions confirm.
- The total size of China's human capital is estimated to be worth between RMB200 trillion and RMB300 trillion, which is a significant figure.
- With economic development, the ability to invest in R & D has greatly improved. The scale of investment is close to 2 % of GDP, accounting for about 14 % of the world's total R & D investment. In addition, it is continuing its high-speed growth at present.
- The equipment used in scientific research has improved considerably, leading to a more complete national innovation system that has strong R & D capabilities.
- China has accumulated a large number of research projects in reserve, and it has the world's largest-scale and fastest-growing market. This has created the optimum market conditions for turning technology into products and pushing forward the development of related industries.

China is currently the leader in many fields of science and technology, such as lasers, super rice cultivation and other crop hybridization, the removal of lifeless satellites from space, comprehensive and integrated high-speed rail, intelligent robots, hovercraft, aerospace, low-speed underground maglev trains, quantum communication, global positioning, mobile communication, fourth-generation nuclear power, cloud computing, the Internet of Things, and sensor networks.

In terms of driving economic growth by technological innovations, China is in a period of strategic opportunity during which low-cost R & D, application, and industrialization are achievable. The remuneration of scientific and technical personnel and other costs are relatively lower than that in developed countries. Moreover, some research equipment developed by China is cheaper than in developed countries. It has the advantage of low-cost development, creation, and industrialization, which means that there is a period of strategic opportunity during which low-cost innovation is viable. Opportunity only knocks once so China should take it when it comes.

During economic downturns, developed countries, especially the USA, have successfully been able to revitalize their economies through the use of technological innovations. Since the 1980s, the number of technological alliances among US companies has increased by an average of more than 10 % a year. During this period, the percentage of high-tech trade in the import and export of manufactured goods almost doubled to over 20 %. The advancement in science and technology was the most important driving force of its continued high-speed economic growth in the 1990s.[8] Since the beginning of the 21st century, further development in information technology and the energy technological revolution involving shale gas and oil have acted as buffers against economic recessions. They also facilitated reindustrialization and revitalized manufacturing industry. As a result, the US economy showed signs of recovery. In December 2013, the US unemployment rate fell to 6.7 %, and manufacturing as a percentage of GDP increased from 9 % in 2008 to the current figure of nearly 12 %. China should pay attention to and learn from the experience of the USA in terms of reviving the economy through technology, and regard the innovation-driven approach as a new way of promoting economic growth.

Innovation is the key driving force of sustained economic growth. If we catch up by accelerating innovation so that the contribution made by technological advances towards economic growth increases by 1.5 % per year from the current level of around 50 %, the incremental GDP as a result of innovation will reach nearly RMB1 trillion in 2013. The economic growth

[8] Mao, "Keji chuangxin."

rate will also increase by 1.8 %, which will build up sustained stamina for further growth. If we attach importance to the value of technological innovations in driving economic growth and effectively implement an innovation-driven strategy, the national economy will grow further at a rate of around 2 % per year, or possibly even more.

Actively Promoting New-Style Urbanization

China's real urbanization rate may at present be only 30 % or at most 35 %. It is still in the middle stage where promoting urbanization is very important for providing momentum to economic growth.

The traditional urbanization model has created a series of issues. The first is the urbanization of land. Although the urbanization level above ground is close to that of Japan, the level of underground infrastructure lags behind Japan and it would take decades to catch up. The second issue is the urbanization of buildings and the failure to achieve real 'citizenization'. The third issue is the lack of coordinated development of urbanization and industrialization. In my opinion, large-scale industrialization leads to agricultural industrialization, especially the ever increasing proportion of the industrial and service sectors. Some cities have developed without industries. This blind pursuit of urbanization based on land construction has created an imbalance between the urbanization of people and the urbanization of land, between employment and entrepreneurship, as well as between the urbanization of industries and the urbanization of spaces or areas. These are the problems associated with traditional urbanization. We now need a new, coordinated way of modernization that is people-oriented, dynamic, and, most importantly, driven by employment and entrepreneurship. Further urbanization is an important driving force in China's future growth. However, it is important to drive urbanization with entrepreneurship and the development of small and micro-enterprises. In addition, we also need to ensure that urbanization provides adequate housing and equal access to public services and social security for all households. Therefore, to gain continuous momentum for growth from urbanization, it is necessary to promote it in the process of system reform.

Regaining Growth Momentum by Deepening the Open-Door Policy

Is there a new driver for China's export-led economic growth in the future? The answer is 'yes'.

First, the new mechanisms of unilateral, bilateral, and multilateral free trade will almost certainly open up space for Chinese imports and exports and provide a new momentum for economic growth. China is currently engaged in talks with 28 countries and regions concerning building 15 free trade zones, for which ten free trade agreements have already been signed. The Mitsubishi Research Institute in Japan predicts that the positive earnings obtained from building a China–Japan–South Korea free trade zone will be higher than those of any other bilateral free trade zone and is certainly within the scope of North East Asia. The GDPs of China, Japan, and South Korea will grow by 1.63, 0.23, and 1.84 % respectively.[9] Other media forecasts are more optimistic and claim that after the establishment of the China–Japan–South Korea free trade zone, China's GDP will rise from 1.1 to 2.9 %, Japan's from 0.1 to 0.5 %, and South Korea's from 2.5 to 3.1 %.[10] I think that China should actively engage in talks to establish multilateral and bilateral free trade zones and that this should include a dialogue with the USA on a bilateral investment treaty. It is also necessary to promote more free trade between China and other countries, as well as to seek new areas of growth under the new pattern and environment of international trade and investment. China has unilaterally started to construct a Shanghai free trade zone and its new strategic quest for unilateral, bilateral, and multilateral free trade zones, as discussed above, will provide the new impetus for economic growth. Such a new trade pattern would contribute at least 1–2 % per annum towards China's future economic growth.

Furthermore, transforming and upgrading exports and implementing the 'Going-out Policy' at a higher level will create new momentum for growth. China needs to focus on a number of areas with respect to upgrading its exports. First, it needs to establish its own marketing system

[9] Xu, "Zhong ri han zimaoqu."

[10] Geng, "Zhong ri han zimaoqu."

for technology brands. Second, it must promote the export of large-scale and integrated high-tech products. Third, it should encourage Chinese investments to go abroad. The strategic significance of the upgrade of exports is to reduce the consumption of China's resources and erosion of its environment and weaken the impact of rising labour costs and the renminbi appreciation on exports. It is hoped that China will gain anti-recession capability and new impetus by trading export quantity for export quality, and the weak competitiveness created by the large-scale export of low-end manufactured products for the strong competitiveness created by the business network of technology brands.

The next task is to seek new momentum for growth from the internationalization of the renminbi, which is a question that has already sparked a certain amount of debate.[11] Given the substantial volume of trade and the large scale of domestic and foreign direct investment, relying on a foreign currency for paying, clearing, pricing, and holding in reserve incurs high transaction costs and considerable losses due to fluctuations in the exchange rate. This puts China at a disadvantage in the context of economic globalization. It will suffer more economic losses by maintaining its current defensive stance on the renminbi than it would if it opted for a steadier and more progressive model.

Current world economic and monetary systems are placing China in an awkward position vis-à-vis other sovereign states in three respects. First, China suffers from the loss of monetary seigniorage and settlement. Second, the renminbi is unfavourably placed in currency wars, which can easily lead to huge losses. And third, countries issuing international currencies have the advantage of low financing costs when borrowing money from the world capital market, thanks to local currency settlements and their right to issue currency.

While it is important to assess and guard against the various risks associated with internationalizing the renminbi, we need to accept some minor risks and costs in the interests of avoiding the far greater losses that a defensive and slow approach to doing so would bring. The internationalization of the renminbi will support the growth of the national economy and neutralize the impact of recession by roughly 1 %. This figure comes from

[11] Wang, "Jianyi zhanhuan renminbi guojihua."

savings gained through monetary seigniorage, the lower costs of settlement, transaction and financing, as well as China's ability to resist currency devaluations and decide its own macroeconomic policies.

New Sources of Growth: Strategic Transformation and Further Reform

It is essential to transform the old mindset, change our way of thinking, establish strategies, reform the system, and introduce new policies if we are to seek new momentum for growth by moving towards a new model. Otherwise, despite our good intentions, it is not possible to achieve growth.

New Growth Strategy: Transforming Macroeconomic Regulation and Control

To create a new momentum for economic growth, it is necessary to address three key tasks: (i) to change our way of thinking about and developing strategies; (ii) to transform the practice of macroeconomic regulation and control; and, in particular, (iii) to change the way we assess our local government leaders.

China's growth model needs fundamental strategic transformation. First, we need to switch the development priority from large-scale economic activities to small and micro-enterprises, thus encouraging entrepreneurship among the people and enhancing the vitality and momentum of society. Second, technological advances and industrial innovations rather than the investment of capital and resources should be driving economic growth. Third, private investors and entrepreneurs rather than the government should move to the forefront of economic growth. Fourth, people must rely on urbanization strategies to promote sustained economic growth. Fifth, we should replace the traditional export-oriented model with a more advanced one in which growth is driven by free-trade, cross-border investment and the internationalization of the renminbi.

The second task is to shift the practice of macroeconomic regulation and control from a demand-oriented to a supply-oriented form of management. China's national economy is currently investment led and export dependent and, for a long time, this has meant that the growth in consumption has been weak and inadequate. Excessive investment leads to high commodity prices and high house prices. However, if the price level is controlled, there will be a sharp increase in unemployment, resulting in a slowdown in economic growth. To tackle the above problems, China needs to find a new model for macroeconomic regulation and control. In my view, this should be more people oriented and should focus more on creating jobs, increasing household income, and expanding consumer demand. In other words, there should be more emphasis on supply and less on demand, and more focus overall on promoting the development of small enterprises and the service industry. Macroeconomic regulation and control should aim to coordinate monetary, fiscal, and other economic policies, while facilitating the transformation of the development model and promoting related reforms. It should also seek to expand domestic consumption, alleviate export dependence, and absorb (or at least offset) the possible impact of the global recession.

A fiscal policy that increased supply and employment opportunities would cut taxes and charges for small enterprises, which would enable them to create large numbers of jobs and reduce the percentage of macro-fiscal revenue in the GDP. In particular, it would reduce the tax burden on micro-enterprises.[12] The purpose of such effective fiscal stimulus is to increase the supply of products and services in the overall society, balance demand, and improve the central government's handling of employment, income, and consumption. Monetary policy should control the currency, liberalize the market, promote the marketization of interest rates, and gradually loosen control of the exchange rate. It should also coordinate its operations with the fiscal policy and, where appropriate, support the reform of the financial system.

---

[12] In fact, within China's tax structure, the proportion of tax paid by small and micro-enterprises is insignificant. Therefore, substantial tax cuts for these enterprises would not greatly affect China's total fiscal revenue, especially the revenue of central and provincial government, but it would make considerable contributions to employment. The resistance to tax cuts and fee reductions for small and micro-enterprises comes mainly from local governments over concerns about possible reductions in revenue, and from various administrative departments and public institutions that rely on fees and fines for their income, as well as from some civil servants and other law enforcement officers over concerns about the loss of benefits.

The third task is to change the performance indicators for assessing senior local government leaders. To transform the growth model successfully, we need to solve a very important issue, namely that of how senior leaders direct and restrict the performance indicators of their juniors. This covers the command structures between central government leaders and provincial officials, as well as between senior and junior office holders at county, city, and provincial level. It is necessary to change the orientation of performance evaluation and design a system of performance indicators that will reflect the new model of growth. Performance evaluation should put more weight on indicators such as people's livelihoods and environmental protection. The assessment, which should focus on the vitality of entrepreneurship and innovation, should place people's livelihoods and the environment at the top of the list and indicators like GDP per capita at the bottom. The statistics and evaluation should be objective and impartial; and extensive efforts should be made to publish the results in the hope of gaining media coverage. The second element is to ensure that the performance evaluation is genuine and objective in that its findings really are linked to the appointment or dismissal of cadres. It is also necessary to allow people more opportunity to have a say in the appointment of these cadres.

The fourth task is to monitor operations closely with a view to eliminating potential financial risks. Over the next five years, Chinese macro-control must pay close attention to the impact that a possible sudden burst of debt or asset bubbles might have on the steady growth of the national economy. On 16 April 2013, international rating agency Moody lowered its outlook for China's sovereign rating from 'positive' to 'stable', within a week of Fitch downgrading the long-term local currency credit rating from AA– to A+.[13] If a crisis due to systemic risks hits the financial system, the Chinese economy will go into a medium or even long-term period of slow growth.

In my opinion, there are five reasons why we should not take China's debt problem and its potential risks lightly. First, the central and local government debt to GDP ratio was close to the critical value of 60 % at the end of 2012. The central bank currently calculates the liability component of foreign exchange reserves. Had the fiscal authorities included it

[13] Su, "Liangda jigou xiatiao."

in their balance sheets, an extra $3.31 trillion worth of debt would have been added, the equivalent of RMB20.52 trillion, which means that the overall debt ratio of all levels of the Chinese government would have reached a staggering high of 96.7 %.[14] In particular, local government debts are very large, which is an indication of high risk. Let me explain the risks posed by the liability component of the foreign exchange reserve. Compared with currencies like the US dollar, the renminbi has been appreciating for a long time. The foreign exchange reserve has suffered large losses in the past, and is likely to depreciate in the future. Because of its large size, as well as the appreciation of the renminbi, foreign exchange reserves put high inflationary pressures on consumer goods and real estate in China. When there were problems like the financial crisis or debt ceiling in the USA and Europe, the security of the US dollar and other claimable assets in foreign currency in China's foreign exchange reserves would be adversely affected by defaults.

Second, by the end of 2012 the size of China's shadow banking system had reached RMB14.6 trillion (based on official data), or RMB20.5 trillion (based on market data). The latter accounted for 40 % of GDP, or 16 % of the total assets of the banking sector.[15] In recent years, local governments have accumulated mounting levels of debt, both through normal banking channels and through the shadow banking system; and 'borrowing new debt to pay for old debt' acts as a master key for relieving short-term pressure on loans raised on financing platforms. The main concern for the market now is that, when central government confiscates the master key, it is likely to cause a domino effect and lead to a financial crisis.

Third, the high level of debt incurred by enterprises is affecting the stability of the entire financial system. This means that China's domestic non-performing loans (NPL) ratio is likely to rise sharply in the future, which will pose even greater systemic risks than shadow banking.

Fourth, we need to monitor closely the risks posed by the potential bursting of the property bubble. A fall in house prices would have a negative

[14] At the end of 2012, Japan's foreign exchange reserves were $1.268125 trillion, GDP was $5.963955 trillion, foreign exchange reserves to GDP ratio was 21.3 %, and public debt to GDP ratio was 214.3 %.

[15] Zhongguo hangye yanjiu wang, "Jinrong anquan yinhuan."

impact on the banks and stock market, and bring instability to the financial system. Nobel Prize winning economist Robert Shiller has expressed concern about this bubble, which poses an especially serious risk to places like Shanghai and Shenzhen. He believes that if the bubble were to burst, as it did in the USA, it would deal a huge blow to the Chinese economy.[16]

Fifth, the pension gap poses a debt risk for the future. A study by Cao Yuanzheng and Liao Shuping revealed that the actual pension shortfall in 2013 was RMB18.3 trillion. If the current pension system remains unchanged, the gap will gradually widen year by year. Assuming an annual growth rate in GDP of 6 %, by 2033 the pension shortfall will be RMB68.2 trillion, or 38.7 % of GDP for that year.[17] If China resorts to borrowing to solve the problem, the national economy will soon fall into welfare and debt traps.

It is essential to take a number of measures to alleviate these financial risks. The central government should continue to maintain a low debt ratio by strictly controlling and absorbing local government debts, whether explicit or implicit. It is also important to keep a close eye on debts in other government areas, businesses, and households because problems of overcapacity, a rise in the debt ratio of the real economy, and the excessive debts incurred by real-estate companies are likely to cause bad debts for the banks. In terms of household debt, we need to pay close attention to issues such as falling house prices, failures to meet mortgage repayments, and defaults on credit card payments. The aim is to control the continuing increase in debts that have little prospect of being repaid while tapping the idle assets. Within an acceptable range, moderate price fluctuations should be utilized to reduce debts.

With regard to the relationship between welfare and risk, we should not misinterpret recognition of people's livelihoods as an attempt to advocate populism. Both central and local government must be practical about livelihood projects and ensure that any promises or arrangements they make are realistic and in scale. Everybody must live within their means according to the level of economic development and the financial capabilities of the system. We must learn from the serious political,

[16] Shen and Li, "Zhongguo fangdichan paomo yanzhong."

[17] Jingji cankao bao, "Yanglaojin quekou."

economic, and social crisis that excessive welfare debt caused in the USA and Europe and avoid such pitfalls by establishing sustainable economic development; and we should curb our spending to avoid passing heavy debts on to future generations.

From the standpoint of macroeconomic management, the following measures are recommended:

- Maintain adequate economic growth; guard against any significant decline in the national economy; sustain healthy relations between businesses and banks, between different businesses, and between households and banks; keep the bad debt ratio in the financial system as low as possible.
- Adjust the local fiscal system; replace land transfer fees with property taxes and property transaction fees; and establish a stable source of income for local government finance.
- Encourage private enterprise; loosen foreign currency controls for households; manage foreign exchange reserves in a more relaxed manner; and avoid foreign reserve losses caused by currency devaluations of the US dollar, euro, and Japanese yen.
- Form a bad debt reserve from seigniorage revenue generated by the central bank, gains from refinancing, a percentage of bank profits, and, under special circumstances, some state-owned assets in order to eliminate all possible financial risks.
- Adjust the family planning policy, which would help to secure future pension provisions, transform the age structure of the population, and change the current demographic trend of population ageing; also, acknowledge the reality of an urban–rural dual structure and the differences in pension provisions; encourage a variety of pension provisions, including relying on children for pension support and the house-for-pension scheme; consider the relationship between youth employment and sustainable social security payments; set a reasonable retirement age and number of qualifying years for pension contributions; raise pension funds from multiple channels, including the privatization of state-owned assets; and create a plan to ensure the sustainable supply of pension funds.

A number of institutional mechanisms are also required to prevent or alleviate various financial risks. For example, it is vital to establish a comprehensive, statistical early warning system for recognizing debt in the national economy. An indicator system is required to carry out statistical analyses and to compare government debts, corporate debts, household credit debts, house price to earnings ratios, and bank balance sheets. Such a system would regularly evaluate the overall risks in the national economy and provide trend estimation and early warning.

We need a set of indicators against which to assess county-level leaders and cadres. These will include their financial debt ratio and other implicit debts such as financing platforms, land reserve loans, and the debt ratios of local SOEs. High debt ratios should be regarded as a negative factor when measuring the performance of the cadres. When senior county-level leaders leave office, they should be subjected to auditing and evaluation to assess their debt situation. Those found to have engaged in construction projects supported by excessive debts should be held accountable rather than praised for their achievements.

In view of the worsening debt problem in China, when the NPC and CPPCC supervise the government, an annual debt budget and financial report on debts should be drawn up in addition to the financial budget already published by government leaders at all levels. When borrowing for construction projects and issuing bonds, the debt budget needs to be submitted to the higher level financial authority and the National Development and Reform Commission (NDRC). Any borrowing that exceeds the economic and financial capacity of the system should be stopped. The budget and financial reports need to be submitted to the NPC and CPPCC. They should be open to the public and discussed, reviewed, and approved.

Because the use of administrative means to control house prices has proven ineffective, we must abandon that idea. Instead, there are other economic measures available to stabilize house prices, bring the house-price to earnings ratio to a reasonable level, and avoid the financial risks of a bursting property bubble. These include extending the supply of land by making use of undeveloped sites, bringing rural construction land into the market, breaking local government's monopoly on land sales, replacing land transfer fees with taxes, levying property taxes, and protecting farmers' rights to receive income from assets during the urbanization process.

Overcome Resistance to Growth and Gain New Momentum Through Reforms

From the perspective of institutional economics, reform per se can provide a new momentum for growth. There are six key tasks that China must discharge to achieve this objective.

The first is to cut taxes and charges, reform the taxation system, and establish new fiscal policies. In terms of macroeconomics and fiscal expenditure, a medium to long-term fiscal policy should:

- Reduce the fiscal revenue to GDP ratio to less than 30 %, ideally around 28 %, as opposed to the current level of 35 %;
- Limit party and government public expenditure to less than 18 % of all fiscal revenue (all inclusive), and reduce it by 2 % each year, as a matter of urgency;
- Amend the budget law or pass a temporary one to ensure that the fiscal revenue to GDP ratio is cut to no more than 30 % within 15 years, and that party and government public expenditure is reduced to 18 % within a set period at an annual rate of deduction of 2 %.

The above should be enshrined in law and never breached by the State Council or the fiscal or taxation departments.

The State Council recently introduced a microeconomic policy change exempting small businesses with monthly sales of less than RMB20,000 from VAT and turnover tax. In my opinion, this policy is over conservative in that the threshold is too low. In addition, local taxes and various charges in place of taxes will probably offset the benefits of the tax exemption. I suggest it would be advisable:

- To implement a fiscal policy based on supply-side economics to stimulate economic growth. Each year the fiscal department should arrange to cut the taxes of small and micro-enterprises, as well as in the manufacturing and service sectors generally, to the tune of 3–4 % of the budget. If starting from 2014, this would cut taxes by RMB400 billion, RMB500 billion, and RMB600 billion respectively for three consecutive years.

- To raise the tax threshold for small businesses, so that those with monthly sales of less than RMB100,000 are exempt from paying taxes.
- To make it illegal for any government or public institution with administrative functions to charge fees to small and micro-enterprises and to hold accountable any person who breaches the above regulation.
- To lower the ratio of social security payments for 'five kinds of insurances from one fund' (social insurance, pensions, occupational injury, health care, and housing) to average gross earnings from the current level of 40–50 % to around 35 %.
- To suspend or amended certain laws and regulations so that trade union funds and funds for the disabled are collected on the basis of voluntary membership payments, government funding, and social charitable donations. These must not be financed by levying taxes on small and micro-enterprises.

The second task is to neutralize administrative resistance and broaden access for entrepreneurship and for small and micro-enterprises. The current institutional barrier to entrepreneurship and investment in small businesses is that there are too many access restrictions and too much bureaucracy. It is necessary to relax the system more. We need:

- A system whereby privately owned businesses can file rather than register their intention to trade, thus encouraging unconventional entrepreneurship and more flexible employment for people running street stalls, mobile vendors, and small shops. There should also be provision for training, education, and guidance on food safety.
- To streamline or abolish pre-entry regulations for the registration and record keeping of sole trader businesses and enterprises.
- To relax the restrictions on capital funds to allow non-movable assets and intangible assets to become registered capital.
- To relax the restrictions on registering premises, so allowing businesses that cause no trouble in the neighbourhood to register residential properties as business premises.
- To abolish the annual inspection system whereby the administrative department for industry and commerce, or other government

departments or public institutions with administrative functions, inspect traders and businesses.

- To detach the associations of privately owned businesses and private enterprises from their affiliation to the department for industry and commerce and waive their membership fees.
- To encourage the department for industry and commerce to focus on education, training, and service in the course of their duties, and regard seizures and severe punishments as a last resort.

The old belief in a restricted private economy is no longer fit for purpose. It is now the responsibility and duty of the government to promote the development of the private sector.

The third task is to promote entrepreneurship, finance small and micro-enterprises, and reform the banking system. Regulating the financial system should happen alongside the reforms and development, rather than be introduced at a later stage. In my opinion, banking regulatory departments should not only assess financial risks, but also share in the burden of curbing the risk of social instability. I think that the marketization of interest rates is the right way forward because that would provide the foundation for reforming the monopolistic banking system. If we are to boost urbanization, we need to encourage and promote entrepreneurship and employment in the cities. The key therefore is not to develop banks in the rural areas, but rather to broaden access by developing small community banks in urban areas. The idea is to create a channel through which cash can flow to fund small businesses, which in turn will increase output, provide employment, and raise income and consumption sufficiently to make credit available at an appropriate rate of interest. Government departments should actively encourage the fiscal authorities to build a financial system capable of providing finance to individuals, micro, and small enterprises both now and in the future.

The fourth task is to introduce the reforms and policies required to implement the innovation-driven strategy. Institutional arrangements to facilitate technological innovations must be set up, for the government must protect intellectual property and crack down on any infringement of intellectual property rights. Consequently, various systems are needed to facilitate market valuation, transactions, investment, and loans in relation to intellectual property rights. Furthermore, guidance and training from government departments, NGOs, or other bodies on how to start up a company, either alone or in partnership with others, is essential because only by forming a company can the technology be expeditiously turned into products. In addition, staff need training in enterprise and business theory. Alternatively, they may team up with business professionals to develop their capacity in manufacturing, marketing, financial management, resource integration, and risk management.

Another requirement is to adapt to technological advances, adopt an innovation-oriented business model, and create an environment conducive to business operations, all crucial preconditions for the industrialization and commercialization of the new technology, for the technological and financial climate must be open to innovation. Current studies show that a key obstacle in the way of the successful industrialization of technology in China is the lack of sufficient financial support for innovation in the chain of technology—funding—testing—funding—small-scale production—funding—large-scale output—marketing. This situation needs to be addressed.

To encourage innovation it is also essential to reform the taxation system and introduce new fiscal policies. VAT credit should be offered to technology enterprises and corporate R & D investment. The marginal rate of income tax should ideally be reduced to 30 %, and the ratio of social security funds to income should also be lowered to 30 %.

Furthermore, to implement an innovation-driven strategy, some important relationships need better management, including those between knowledge stocks, expert authority and theoretical innovations, inter-disciplinary work, fringe knowledge, and technological newcomers. Where enterprises are at the forefront of innovation, the relationship between government-driven strategies and those driven by non-government and market forces can be difficult to handle. It is essential to ensure that a new institution put in place for innovation complements what is already there. Also, in terms of the industrialization of new technologies, it is important to deal with the relationship between market development needs and government guidance, and between the purchase demands from government and from national defence departments.

The fifth task is to reform land and housing policy while protecting the ecological environment, developing water-saving technologies, establishing farmers' property rights, and preventing fake development. On this basis, the government should develop its unused land, including deserts, saline and intertidal areas, hilly plains, and gradual slopes. It should also face up to the inevitability of urbanization and the consequent decline of villages in the overhauling of the use of village land. To increase land supply, the government should consider disregarding the red line it set to guarantee that arable land never shrank below 1.8 billion *mu* (120 million hectares). Government sales of public land and the administrative 'tender, auction, and listing' of land should end. China needs to suspend and abolish the collective ownership of rural land by bringing it into state ownership and extending the terms of people's usufructuary rights. Such rights to woodland, arable land, recovered desert, saline land, and intertidal land should be set at 1,000 years and 500 years for rural homesteads and residential land. Meanwhile, industrial, commercial, and financial organizations should be given a 300-year term for land use, which is akin to having land ownership rights. The above mentioned terms of land use should be confirmed by certificates and legally regarded as akin to property rights. These may be inherited, sold, pledged, bought as shares, or rented just like any other property.

The system of land transfer fees, as well as other fees related to land development and commercial residential properties, should be abolished. Some taxes on land and housing transactions should be merged into value-added or property taxes. A progressive transaction tax and individual income tax should be levied on those who become rich overnight through the sale of land. Finally, government incentives based on availability, interest rates, and taxes should be used to regulate the supply and demand for land. In summary, land reform should expand the supply of land, extend the terms of state-owned land, grant rights akin to property rights, allow different types of land equal rights to enter the market, replace fees with taxes, and manage planning and regulation.

The sixth task is to introduce more open policy. The international economic landscape has changed radically since 2008 and China needs to take advantage of the new momentum for growth that economic globalization has provided. To achieve this, it must establish free trade mechanisms, internationalize the renminbi, and encourage overseas investment; or, as they call it, 'deepening the Going Out Strategy'.

In sum, China's traditional model of economic growth has gradually lost momentum and this can only be regained by promoting entrepreneurship, innovation, new-style urbanization, and a very much more 'open' policy.

The six reform measures discussed above are geared towards rejuvenating the economy from the supply side, so they are a move away from the traditional demand-led approach towards stimulating growth. Like traditional Chinese medicine, a supply-oriented policy is slow acting, but it treats the root causes of the problem rather than the symptoms. In the next five to ten years, promoting reforms in the above six areas will help solve the endogenous problems of the Chinese economy and generate new ways of maintaining relatively fast economic growth. The old demand-driven form of growth is no longer viable and, without new measures, the Chinese economy risks slipping further into recession, or even, God forbid, stagflation.

Bibliography

Chi, F. L. 2012a. Jingji zengzhang cong zhengfu zhudao zhuanxiang xiaofei zhudao. [The transformation from government-led to consumption-led economic growth]. *Nanfang Ribao.* [*The Southern Daily*] 25 July 2012.

——— 2012b. Zouxiang xiaofei zhudao de zhongguo jingji zhuanxing yu gaige zhanlue. [Moving towards consumption-led economic transformation and reform strategies in China], GMW.cn, 16 November 2012. [online]. Available at http://www.gmw.cn/xueshu/2012–11/16/content_5699910.htm.

Geng, Y. B. 2013. Zhong ri han zimaoqu jiang shi Zhongguo GDP duozeng 1–3 ge dian. [The China–Japan–South Korea free trade zone will bring 1–3% GDP growth for China]. *21 shiji jingji baodao.* [*21st Century Business Herald*], 20 June.

Jingji cankao bao. [*The Economic Information Daily*]. 2012. Yanglaojin quekou de N ge banben. [N versions of the pension], 23 July.

Li, K. Q. 2013a. Shenhua jingji tizhi gaige yiwu fangu. [No turning back from deepening economic reforms], Xinhuanet, 16 October 2013.

——— 2013b. You nengli you tiaojian wancheng jinnian jingji shehui fazhan renwu. [We have the ability and conditions to complete the task of economic growth and social development for this year]. Speech at the opening ceremony of the 10th China–ASEAN Expo and China–ASEAN Business and Investment Summit, China.org.cn, 3 September 2013. [online]. Available at http://finance.china.com.cn/news/special/2013dmblh/20130903/1782934.shtml.

Lin, J. Y. F. 2013. houfa youshi dailai zengzhang qianli quebao 'liangge fan yifan'. [Latecomer's advantages bring growth potential to ensure 'doubling for both']. *Jingji cankao bao*. [*The Economic Information Daily*], 8 October 2013.

Liu, S. J. 2013a. Zhongguo jingji zengzhang sudu huoyi chuyu zhuanzhe shidian. [China's economic growth rate may have reached at a turning point], Tencent Finance, 23 March 2013. [online]. Available at http://finance.qq.com/a/20130323/001517.htm.

——— 2013b. 8 yue jingji haozhuan shu cunhuo tiaozheng, 7% jiang cheng zengsu changtai. [Economic recovery in August is due to inventory adjustment, 7% growth rate will become the norm]. [online]. Available at http://www.caijing.com.cn. Accessed 16 Sep 2013.

Mao, L. 2013. Keji chuangxin – meiguo zhouqixing jingji shuaitui de huanchong qi. [Technological innovations – the buffer against US periodic economic recession]. *Xinhuanet* 31 January.

National Bureau of Statistics. 2012a. *Zhongguo tongji nianjian 2012 nian*. [*China statistical yearbook 2012*]. China Statistics Press, Beijing.

———. 2012b. *Zhongguo tongji zhaiyao 2013 nian*. [*China statistical abstract 2013*]. Beijing: China Statistics Press.

———. 2013. *Zhongguo jingji jingqi yuebao 9*. [*China Monthly Economic Indicators Issue 9*].

National Bureau of Statistics of China. [online]. Available at http://www.stats.gov.cn/english/.

Shen, W. Q., and L. Li. 2013. Nuobeier jingjixue jiang dezhu zhiyan zhongguo fangdichan paomo yanzhong bixu jingti. [Nobel laureate in economic sciences warns that we must be vigilant against China's dangerous real estate bubbles]. *Xin jing bao*. [*The Beijing News*] 15 October.

Su, M. D. 2013. Liangda jigou xiatiao zhongguo pingji zhanwang danyou xindai guodu kuozhang. [Two agencies downgraded China's outlook over concerns of excessive credit expansion]. *21 shiji jingji baodao*. [*21st Century Business Herald*] 18 April.

Tencent Finance. 2013. Linyifu piping kanshuai zhongguo zengzhang de pubian beiguan qingxu. [Justin Yifu Lin criticized widespread pessimism in China's growth outlook], 30 July 2013. [online]. Available at http://finance.qq.com/a/20130730/000765.htm.

The Survey and Research Center for China Household Finance, Southwestern University of Finance and Economics. 2013. Woguo chengzhen shiyelv da 8.05%. [China's urban unemployment rate reached 8.05%]. Zhongguo chengzhen shiye baogao. [Report on China's urban employment], 9 December.

Wang, J. 2013. Jianyi zhanhuan renminbi guojihua. [It is recommended to postpone internationalization of the RMB]. *Yingcai.* [*Talents magazine*] July 2013.

Watson, B. 2014. American protectionism threatens US–China trade. *The Diplomat*, 28 October. [online]. Available at http://thediplomat.com/2014/10/american-protectionism-threatens-us-china-trade/. Accessed 21 Sep 2015.

Xi, J. P. 2012. Gaige bu tingbu kaifang bu zhibu. [Never cease to reform or open up], Xinhuanet, 12 December 2012. [online]. Available at http://news.xinhuanet.com/politics/2012-12/11/c_113991112.htm.

——— 2013a. Baoyou 'sida xinxin', paichu zhongguo jingji shisu fengxian. [Have 'four faiths' and eliminate the risk of China's economic slowdown]. Xinhuanet, 10 October 2013. [online]. Available at http://news.xinhuanet.com/politics/2013-10/10/c_117659385.htm.

——— 2013b. Chuangxin qudong buneng dengdai buneng guanwang buneng xiedai. [To become an innovation-driven nation, we cannot wait, watch and wait or slack off], Xinhuanet, 1 October 2013. [online]. Available at http://news.xinhuanet.com/politics/2013-10/01/c_117582862.htm.

Xu, J. J. 2012. Zhong ri han zimaoqu: yichang chaoyue jingji de boyi. [The China–Japan–South Korea free trade zone: a game beyond the economy]. *Sanlian shenghuo zhoukan.* [*Sanlian Life Weekly*], 26 October.

Zhongguo hangye yanjiu wang. [*China Industry Research Network*]. 2013. Jujiao 7 da jinrong anquan yinhuan. [Focus on the 7 greatest threats to China's financial security], 10 October.

Zhou, T. Y. 2011. Cong xuqiu tiaokong zhuanxiang gongji tiaokong qiafeng qishi. [It is the right time to steer towards supply regulation and control from demand regulation and control]. *China Business Times*, 22 August 2011.

Zhou, T. Y., and X. J. Guo. 2013. Zhongguo weilai tudi zhuzhai tizhi gaige kuangjia fangan. [Reform plan of China's future land and housing system]. Research topic of China Urban Development Research, 10 October 2013.

9

Tradition, Cultural Modernization, and Soft Power

Yingchun Sun

Modernization is a worldwide historical process characterized by the universal force of Western culture pulling societies with different traditions into a more homogeneous modern world. Apart from transforming modes of production, economic arrangements, social organizations, and political systems, new conflicts and inconsistencies between local traditions and modern ways still continue to come forth from obscurity, not only to compete for control of cultural consumption, lifestyles, and public values, but also to influence the mentalities and choices of different demographic groups.

China has achieved rapid economic growth in recent years, yet this has failed to translate into a simultaneous advance in the cultural self-confidence of the Chinese people. The demand for cultural

Y. Sun (✉)
School of Political Science and Law, Communication University of China, Beijing, China
e-mail: sunychun@sina.com

S. Tsang, H. Men (eds.), *China in the Xi Jinping Era*,
The Nottingham China Policy Institute Series,
DOI 10.1007/978-3-319-29549-7_9

modernization has created many difficult issues and raised numerous questions at different levels in contemporary China. These include:

- How should people regulate their own cultural traditions and understand and interpret local values, ideological frameworks, and discourses?
- How should they approach the relationship between tradition and modernization or respond to the dilemmas that the tension between modernity and post-modernity create?
- How can they find the right balance between tradition and modernity to converge and further integrate local and global communities?
- Given the directions and patterns of human history and the modernity-oriented values of liberty, equality, and rationality, what would be a feasible path for Chinese culture to follow?
- Can Chinese culture offer some kind of universal value to the 'virtuous life' of mankind? In other words, does the modernization of Chinese culture have a global significance?

Tradition and Modernity

Tradition and modernity are contradictory yet closely related categories. They are the seeds from which modernization theories have grown and are at the forefront of the critiques and debates these theories spark. In attempting to proceduralize the social life and cultural sustainability that modernization demands, modernization theories have at different times produced very different characterizations of the notions of tradition and modernity. The relevant theoretical procedures and conceptual transitions have already blended into the global ethos of 'cultural consciousness', which deserves a rethink by Chinese scholars.

Western modernization studies and related schools of thought have undergone significant changes since the 1950s and these have influenced a number of disciplines, including economics, political science, history, and sociology. The transition from the classical modernization theory of Talcott Parsons to the new modernization theory of Cyril Black demonstrates that the historical orientation and humanistic concerns of modernization studies have been gradually recognized and reinforced. Tradition is no longer seen as the antithesis of modernization. Moreover, following in the footsteps of Western countries is no longer considered the only route to modernization. Correspondingly, the attitudes of non-Western countries towards tradition and modernity have become more rational. Now, when a country explores development options or considers the prospect of modernity, it places far more weight than ever before on the importance of tradition. Academics working on East Asia attribute the successful modernization of countries like Japan and South Korea to the support and application of traditional factors, and argue that their success proves that modern and traditional systems coexist quite happily and that traditional attitudes and forms of behaviour can have a positive influence on modernization. There is a growing consensus among global mainstream intellectuals that we should look upon modernization as a progressive process of practice and understanding, and that there is more than one model of modernization from which each country must seek the most suitable one for itself. Furthermore, the very notion of modernity is determined by the cultural forms rooted in various traditions. Regardless of whether a country is Western or non-Western, the presence of tradition in modernity has almost become a law, and all cultures and countries can find resources within their traditions that can make a positive contribution to modernity.

The Chinese cultural tradition is a mixed array of various elements that have blended into and permeated each other over generations of integration and selection. China has a ubiquitous and comprehensive cultural heritage that has stood the test of time. Despite rises and falls in its history the country's cultural lineage has continued to thrive and grow increasingly harmonious. During this process, the cultural tradition, in the sense of the 'Chinese community' as that created by an integrated multicultural ethnic structure, continued to foster the spiritual and moral characteristics of the people and allowed the civilization to retain its leading position in East Asia and in the world for a very long time. However, at the beginning of the modern era, the West began to exert a strong influence through cultural domination and its claim to political, economic, and military superiority. Consequently, we need to address the tension between China's cultural tradition and modernity from the commencement of modernization in Chinese society. Debates about different cultural values—for instance radicalism vs fogyism, liberalism vs conservatism, and tradition vs modernity—have been ongoing. They started with the notion that Yan Fu proposed of 'learning from foreigners in order to control them', then continued with the cultural integration theories of Liang Qichao and his colleagues about the establishment of a 'new culture system' to reconcile the various key elements of the East and West. Wu Mi, with other scholars from the Xueheng School, insisted that the most effective way of building a new culture was to 'assimilate new knowledge' by 'promoting the quintessence of Chinese culture'. Chen Duxiu and other early communists attempted to solve China's problems by turning to Marxism. Liang Shuming proposed 'cultural pluralism' in a bid to counter the cultural monism of 'complete Westernization'.

China had achieved cultural autonomy through revolution, and there was a point after the founding of the PRC when it abandoned any wish to gain entry to the modern world that the Western countries had built. Under the influence of its ideology, Chinese society and culture became exceptionally homogeneous, as testified by the imbalance between its cultural mentality and social structure, as well as the constant marginalization (even threatened disintegration) of its traditions. This inevitably made the spirit of contemporary Chinese culture narrow-minded and extreme. So, although 30 years have elapsed since China's reform and opening up, its attitude to the West is still ambivalent, tainted with a combination of goodwill and animosity, and with periodic displays of self-abasement and arrogance towards the international community. The global spread of Western culture is a challenge to China in the 21st century, as it is to other non-Western countries. Modernity, post-modernity, and, especially, the culture of consumerism are transforming the cultural and spiritual ethos in China and causing the whole society, including the intellectual elite, to lose touch with its spirituality and to become anxious about making cultural choices.

There are no fundamental differences between the choices China faces now and those it faced more than a century ago. If the country chose to reject modernity and modern culture, it would be unable to keep up with the progress of world civilization; but if it chose to abandon tradition altogether it would be equally unable to maintain the identity of its indigenous civilizations. Some scholars in recent academic debates in China have adopted the liberal attitude towards tradition that Yan Fu, Hu Shi, Chen Xujing, and others have been advocating since the dawn of the modern era. They criticize Chinese traditions, hold anti-traditional views, and, in a bid to rebuild Chinese culture within the framework of Western modernity, advocate wholesale Westernization. However, their position is unconvincing because it fails to take China's social reality into account and to address its problems. Liu Junning reminds us that nobody has successfully tried to combine the two ideological systems of Confucianism and liberalism; and studies in this area 'have failed to interpret the modernization path of Confucian societies from the perspectives of Eastern and Western civilizations'. He believes that it will take a lot more scholars a lot more research, a lot more debate, and a lot more time to find a rational solution to these problems.[1]

Cultural conservatism, as opposed to liberalism, has a relatively strong following. It supports traditional values, but without confining them to conventional practices. It sees the relationship between tradition and modernity as the unity of two opposing ideas that complement and mutually stimulate each other. Mou Zongsan stresses that Confucianism forms the core of Chinese culture and that the Chinese people can only achieve modernization through exploring the essence of Confucianism using the correct methods. This is because 'Confucianism and modernization do not contradict each other. In other words, it does not passively 'adapt to' or 'cope with' modernization, but plays an active role in it'.[2]

Tu Weiming, who supports this assertion, believes that modernization is pluralistic and that it is wrong to interpret tradition and modernity as two parallel yet unrelated phenomena. He argues that tradition and modernity, Eastern culture and Western culture, popular culture and elite culture, and modernization and regionalization exert mutual influences over one another. The right way forward, he claims, is to address these interactive relationships properly rather than devalue tradition in the interests of modernization. Tu hopes that Confucian culture will stand

[1] Liu, "Ziyou zhuyi."

[2] Mou and Zheng, *Daode lixiang zhuyi chongjian*, 4.

by the principle of 'communicative rationality' and looks forward to the modernization and globalization of Chinese culture.[3]

Yu Ying-shih argues that in the past century intellectuals had such divergent views and showed so much ideological confusion that the fundamental values of Chinese culture were given no opportunity to undergo a modern makeover in a systematic and conscious manner. As a result, rational thinking is overshadowed by entangled emotions over whether to use Western culture to subvert Chinese tradition or to use Chinese tradition to resist Western culture. In his view, because real life is not separated from culture but rather the materialization of it, modernization will not cause the Chinese value system to collapse. To rebuild Chinese culture, it is necessary to address properly 'the question of how to adjust and transform the fundamental values and core concepts of Chinese culture under the requirements of modernization'.[4]

Geertz, through his concept of 'local knowledge', sees culture as of special significance because it embraces diversity. Irrespective of the culture in question, local traditions are still the most apparent determinants of social order in everyday life. In recent years, more and more Chinese scholars have been applying Geertz's concept to the postmodern critique of the grand narrative and to the postcolonial critique of Western cultural hegemony. They believe that not only should 'local knowledge' be put on an equal footing with Western knowledge, but that it is also of irreplaceable value to the potential of human knowledge. Even in a modernized world, people need the moral and spiritual sustenance that local traditions sustain. Tradition, which encapsulates the moral and emotional content of 'local knowledge', must not be ignored or thoughtlessly abandoned. More importantly, we cannot equate the status and influence of tradition in China with that of any other country or nation, for its differences are precisely what reflect the value, function, and significance of Chinese tradition. This is because, compared with other major countries, Chinese culture has a more time-honoured heritage and a more distinctive evolutional logic. It is the 'spiritual chain' connecting generations of Chinese people throughout history. Once it is broken beyond repair, Chinese

[3] Tu, "Ruxue fazhan."

[4] Yu, *Zhongguo sixiang chuantong*, 45–52.

civilization will inevitably collapse and the resultant shock, suffering, and cost of such a misfortune would be unimaginable.

We cannot ignore the fact that, despite its ups and downs, the pursuit of modernity has been the main theme in debates on Chinese culture in modern times. In addition, contemporary Chinese society is familiar with the value orientation and ideological framework of modern culture. In particular, under the guidance of the intellectual elite, the rational spirit, not a salient feature of Chinese tradition, made a significant breakthrough in this period. The traditional sources are filled with modern concepts such as science and democracy, which intellectuals, at least those who are open to modern culture, have consciously or unconsciously been absorbing for generations. Traditional practices that diametrically oppose the modern spirit have, throughout different periods of history, always been ignored, criticized, or rarely promoted.

Li Xianghai argues that, 'in terms of the fundamental value orientation, Chinese culture has generally completed the transition from pre-modernity to modernity, and modern concepts such as science, democracy and liberty have been internalized into Chinese culture as its intrinsic requirements'. He also notes, however, that the rise of postmodernism and all that goes with it has made it more difficult for Chinese culture to survive in the contemporary era. While Chinese culture is waiting to enjoy the full fruits of modernization, the West is already discussing its drawbacks. This reveals a time lag in the contemporary era between the development of Chinese culture and its Western counterpart. As Li explained, 'the cultural phenomena of pre-modernity, modernity and post-modernity, which appeared diachronically and sequentially in the development of Western culture, have been introduced into contemporary China in a synchronic manner to a certain extent. As a result, we will inevitably be faced with profound dilemmas and serious challenges in the future development of Chinese culture'.[5]

Although Chinese tradition retrogressed significantly during the modernization process, its importance remains in society today, especially in the many secular traditions that people still practise and that, despite being fragmented and incomplete, have a huge number of supporters and

[5] Li, "Zhongguo wenhua xiandaihua lichen," 63, 65.

defenders from different mindsets. Depending on the circumstances or region, tradition is either fighting a losing battle against modernity, or it has successfully resisted the ingress of modernity, or, better still, tradition and modernity have learned to live together in an integrated and mutually beneficial way. As Raymond Firth argued, we cannot overlook the importance of traditional forces because, after long exposure to external forces, there is apparently a radical alteration in people's way of life or thinking, though 'they often break back once again to their ancient practices, or mingle ancient practices and beliefs with modern forms'.[6]

In 1996, Cao Jinqing, who conducted fieldwork on the effect of modernization on Chinese rural communities, pointed out that Chinese society had to face changes at two levels—the ideological and material. In other words, the beliefs of the common people and of the intellectuals influenced by Western learning were changing, as were the characteristic features of urban and rural areas, and of coastal and inland regions. When looking at the beliefs of the intellectuals and at life in the urban and coastal areas, it seems that China has already 'almost been modernized'. When looking at the beliefs of ordinary people and at life in underdeveloped inland and rural areas, however, 'China has hardly made any progress from its original point of departure'.[7]

Many studies have also noted that, although major changes have taken place in Chinese society since the 1950s, in rural areas and in most central and western regions, people's daily lives, how they interact with each other, their social relations, and core cultural values have not undergone any structural changes. In fact, some scholars have noted the emergence of an accelerating trend towards 'regression' in recent years.

In 1988, however, Arthur Barnett described the western region of China as a vast 'mixture of old and new' where 'modern civilization is gradually but steadily penetrating and changing previously undeveloped areas'. He wrote that 'radical changes are indeed taking place, but it [the western region] is still strongly fettered and influenced by traditional ideologies; from what I can see, the idea of modernization has been firmly built on the basis of the past'. He went on to say that 'although the

[6] Firth, *Human Types*, 159.

[7] Cao, *Huanghe bian de Zhongguo*, 757, 763, 764.

majority of people have seen a notable improvement in their standard of living, a small minority … are still living in extreme poverty'.[8]

A study that Ma Chunhua and others undertook in 2010 noted that families across China have their own unique value systems and ways of life. This means that, although China is following in the footsteps of the West by adopting industrialization and urbanization as its overall development model, families across the different regions are embracing modernization in distinctive and diverse ways. In other words, there is a trade-off between tradition and modernity.[9]

Cultural modernization is a solemn and sacred undertaking. Not only is it dedicated to China's past, but it is even more dedicated to its future. Its purpose is not only to save Chinese tradition from imminent threats, but also to promote its history and culture to a higher and more mature plane.[10] From a cultural standpoint, the only way to preserve the tradition is to address the need to reconcile Chinese and foreign cultures and to appease conflicts between different political and cultural values and between the mainstream culture and various subcultures in Chinese society.

Modernizing the Confucian tradition is a complicated and difficult task. After centuries of refinement, Confucianism can undeniably take its place as a dominant tradition in Chinese culture. It informs the cultural approach and values of most Chinese people; and it influences and imposes boundaries on all ethical aspects of people's everyday secular lives. Characteristic of the reforms in East Asia, which started in the 1970s, is a coexistence, or even complementarity, between the Confucian tradition and modernization. There is growing consensus among the intellectual elite that the Confucian tradition need not present an obstacle to China's modernization and that it is possible to modernize without destroying the tradition. Thus, through reinterpreting and restoring Confucianism with a view to placing Chinese culture on the world stage, China will seek to establish a unique place for itself in the pluralistic structure of the global community. It is also the primary cultural resource brought to dialogues between China's intellectual elite and the West. Tu Weiming, commenting

[8] Barnett, *China's Far West*, 247, 326.

[9] Ma et al. "Zhongguo chengshi jiating bianqian."

[10] Jin, *Cong chuantong dao xiandai*, 3.

on the universal importance of the cultural contributions of Confucianism, suggested drawing on its main tenets to open up dialogues with other cultures. If the teachings of Confucianism are to be enriched and strengthened, it needs to find a voice outside China or East Asia; it needs exposure to foreign cultures if it is to 'receive more nourishing support'.[11]

All the same, it is advisable to conduct a proper evaluation of the contemporary value of Confucianism rather than overstate its importance. Many scholars hold that, although it has made a valuable contribution to disciplines such as moral philosophy, its influence is less pronounced in the scientific, political, and religious spheres.

Cao Jinqing believes that 'to understand the contemporary significance of the Confucian tradition, we should not seek answers from the Confucian classics, but rather from the evolution of Chinese families and China as a country in the last century, especially in the last 50 or even 20 years'.[12] In his view, 'Chinese families' and 'China as a country' are both constantly changing and, since the shift is away from moral questions and more towards contractual arrangements, Confucian ethics will have little significance in the real world. In addition, given the present gap between China and the West, it would be unwise to overstate the role of Confucianism in the development of modern Chinese culture because, since ancient times, Chinese tradition has always been pluralistic. Confucianism, Taoism, Buddhism, and the cultural traditions of various ethnic groups are all to a greater or lesser extent the carriers of Chinese tradition and the vital resources for the construction of a contemporary socio-cultural community. On all accounts, the 21st century will be characterized by a range of different cultures flourishing and prospering alongside one another, so the Confucian culture will neither become the dominant one in the world, nor will it act as the only mainstream one in China.

For a while, China's mainstream ideology has been focusing on 'realizing the great revival of the Chinese nation' as the goal of cultural modernization, which shows that much importance is attached to cultural traditions and indigenous ideological resources. However, emphasizing the prophetic nature of ancient concepts and their applicability

---

[11] Tu, "*Dongya jiazhi*," 214.

[12] Cao, *Huanghe bian de Zhongguo*, 757.

for solving real-world problems can be problematic. Some people believe that ancient Chinese thoughts contain true solutions to real-world problems, for example, the belief that 'the harmony between nature and the human' can save mankind.[13] Given the modernization experiences of other non-Western countries, it is unfitting to appropriate the modern value of local traditions as counters to globalization; it could lead to a vicious rise in nationalism and generate many negative consequences. Wang Ning and other scholars argue that when dealing with the global community, the best option is not to adopt an indigenization strategy fuelled by strong nationalist sentiment, because 'this is likely to exacerbate existing regional conflicts and consequently result in political and cultural rivalry between the Eastern and Western nations'.[14]

From the above discussion, one might assume that properly handling the relationship between tradition and modernity entails adopting the Confucian 'doctrine of the mean', which encourages a middle path that 'does not bend one way or another'. However, the advocacy of tradition should not mean being confined to a deficient and ossified cultural structure. Nevertheless, overstating the importance of tradition will inevitably lead to a religious pursuit of romanticism and nostalgia, which is merely temporary escapism and that hardly has any constructive contribution to make to complex modernization practices.

Soft Power and Its 'Discourse Trap'

When Joseph Nye articulated his concept of soft power, it attracted the ongoing attention of Chinese scholars and government departments. The importance of soft power is not only acknowledged in academic discussions, but it has also been incorporated into social practices. In addition, 'based on existing cultural resources and ideology, the notion of soft power has been given a very different interpretation'[15] and has been built into China's foreign and domestic policies. On the one hand, China is

[13] Zhao and Gan, "Wenhua rentong weiji."
[14] Wang, "Wenhua lunzheng," 266–267.
[15] Shi and Shao, "Quanqiu 'zi' li," 87.

actively seeking support from other developing countries; on the other hand, it is prioritizing culturally related national interests by placing equal emphasis on ideology and business.

Shi Yinhong describes how, in foreign relations, China has found a way in which 'peaceful international exchanges and "soft power" in a broad sense, especially peaceful trade, international negotiations and "smile diplomacy", are to be predominantly relied upon under most circumstances and in most areas'. The characteristics of such an approach are that 'its non-violent, incremental and widespread properties and primarily reciprocal nature suggest that such force is the most difficult to resist, the least likely to trigger strong resistance, and with the ability of incurring minimal cost while delivering the most acceptable outcomes'.[16] Domestically, the exercise of soft power is mainly through national policy makers deciding on conscious and culturally informed choices about the large-scale development of the cultural industry and the promotion of cultural products.

Since 2011, the Chinese government has been fomenting a strategic plan to build 'a culturally strong nation'. This plan aims to encourage the production of cultural artefacts, promote cultural branding, and help cultural products gain entry to the international market by improving access, fostering capable and competitive cultural industries, increasing investment in such industries, and developing emerging industries like the cultural and creative industry, animation, and games. China's approach to this differs from that of other countries in that it sees building soft power as an important component in the expansion of national economic transformation and in balancing the relationship between cultural and economic social development. Chinese people from all walks of life have been paying increasing attention to discussions and debates on the issue.

Joseph Nye constantly updates his interpretation of soft power. One of his latest arguments is that a country's soft power rests on three resources—its culture (where it is attractive to others), its political values (when it lives up to them at home and abroad), and its foreign policies (if seen as legitimate and having moral authority).[17] Based on Nye's revised view, some Chinese scholars have proposed the idea of 'cultural

[16] Shi, "Chengjiu yu tiaozhan," 82–83.

[17] Nye and Wang, "Zhongguo ruanshili."

soft power', which they see as a country's spiritual charm and influence, or a blend of its traditional and modern culture that reflects its distinctive national ethos. This ethos will extend to its political and value systems, its capabilities in science, technology, and education, its cultural heritage and cultural products, the quality of its population and their moral standards, as well as other factors such as the people's creativity and the wisdom they bring to their decision making and diplomacy. These scholars contend that cultural soft power is what a country brings to the international stage and that inevitably expresses the nation's mainstream ideology and values, together with a subtle sense of competitiveness that exemplifies its distinctive spiritual charm.[18] Recently, with a view to protecting mainstream ideology and the socialist value system from the impact of internal and external forces, some Chinese scholars have taken the discussion further by linking cultural soft power to cultural security, thus guaranteeing China's full and complete cultural sovereignty and maintaining the cultural, ethnic, and national identity of the people.

The Western discourse on the world order and soft power assumes a specific set of political systems and social patterns. For countries that had a late start in the modernization process, it is also a kind of 'discourse trap' that needs to be handled with wariness and sensibility. Actors should analyse critically the context of soft power building and the means through which it is manifested. China should establish its own independent theoretical discourse on soft power that reflects its values, national conditions, and long-term interests. More specifically, the discourse should centre on the actual objectives of Chinese cultural revival, at home and abroad, rather than on chasing so-called influential power. Although there have been changes in Nye's discourse on soft power, one point remains unchanged—a country must have a set of core values that will inspire confidence at home and convince others abroad. For the moment, however, China needs to prioritize its own national issues—social instability, imbalances in the domestic economy, infrastructural problems, and pressures of political transformation—rather than pay too much attention to the manifestation of its soft power in a global setting. After all, it is a big step from being a form of local knowledge to becoming global knowledge

[18] Huo, "Wenhua ruanshili."

with global influence. Moreover, culture is not only a type of soft power; it is also a realistic choice based on the real-life experiences of individuals and groups. It is inextricably linked to the vital interests, personal aspirations, and ways of life of every citizen, rather than merely the country's pursuit of wealth and influence.

Historical evidence suggests that when a nation tries to modernize by imposing a cultural or national identity on its people, the society is likely to resist by delaying the transformation process in a number of ways. It is evident from the history of the PRC, from its founding to its reform and opening up, that the suppression and obliteration of 'local knowledge', which is essentially based on historical traditions, makes the newly built top-down cultural system totally unfit for purpose, unable to benefit the society at grass-roots level, and unable to improve the everyday lives of common people.

Some Chinese intellectuals hold that the current large-scale construction of soft power is in need of an overhaul. They argue that its development should not be regarded merely as a means of participating in the game of international politics, but should rather be directed towards serving the long-term benefits of the country and its people. It is an inescapable fact that, in its blind pursuit of GDP growth and political achievements, the Chinese government's 2011 strategic plan to build 'a culturally strong nation' is falling into the trap of developmentalism. In 2012, I wrote an article expressing the concern of Chinese intellectuals about the development of the cultural industry. This kind of development should be a gradual process of accumulation, which takes time and calls for tolerance and pluralism. It cannot be activated solely through the guidance and interference of the government or relevant departments. We must go beyond utilitarianism and short-sightedness, for the continuing development of the cultural industry cannot be achieved merely through the market-oriented operations of some cultural institutions or business sectors.[19] Furthermore, the rise and decline of cultural soft power is directly linked to the spiritual senses and pursuits of society as a whole at a particular point in history. Although the data suggest that the Chinese cultural industry is continuing to grow, this does not mean that there has been any genuine improvement in the influence of

[19] Sun, "Wenhua fanrong de jichu."

Chinese culture over the international community. In addition, there are dangers inherent in putting too much emphasis on the expansion of cultural industries and the production of a consumer culture. A new round of attempts to commercialize culture could backfire. As different political groups and stakeholders hijack the various cultural propositions, we might well see the disintegration of the debate on modernity and tradition igniting a long-lasting 'ideological civil war'.

We should recognize that, as a large but not wealthy country, in recent years China has more than fulfilled its obligation to donate international aid, and its own development has also provided the world with important opportunities. However, its extensive growth and export-oriented development strategy have exacerbated worldwide competition for resources and markets, and altered the pattern of profit distribution in the world. The interests of some countries and groups have also been affected. Although China has received wide praise and recognition in some developing countries, it still has to wade into the morass of its unsatisfactory moral appeal, for its image and influence continue to decline in Western countries. As a large country with complex historical traditions and different local situations, there are many drawbacks to relying solely on the state to enhance cultural soft power. These include a lack of operational space, insufficient persuasiveness, and the risk of being misinterpreted as harbouring covert hegemonic ambitions. As Shi Zhiyu pointed out, 'whether China's soft power is strong or weak depends on its ability to cultivate social relations and make selfless policy compromises in order to prevent being perceived as a mutual threat by other countries, where lives, languages and values may be completely different from those of China, and peaceful coexistence can thereby be secured'.[20]

Prevailing attitudes about its interests and destiny can present a country trying to construct its own culture with a real challenge. Giving up its long-term interests for the immediate approval of the outside world is not in keeping with the objectives of soft power building. These are not only to seek trust, understanding, and respect from foreign countries, but also to protect the welfare of its citizens at home, with greater importance attached to the latter. Modernization is not a perfect process during

[20] Shi and Shao, "Quanqiu 'zi' li," 69.

which all parties are able to enjoy its fruits; China needs to look calmly and rationally at the shifts in cultural soft power of the major countries in the international community. It cannot possibly meet all the expectations of the other countries and groups in the world. Although to some extent world opinion needs to be taken into account, it is more important to consider the expectations of the Chinese people and the requirements of their society. In September 2013, speaking at the opening of the Davos Forum, Li Keqiang clearly articulated this position, which we may take as a new departure on the topic of China's soft power: the country's modernization will be a long and arduous process during which the international responsibilities and obligations that it undertakes must be commensurate with the level of its own development.

The Local and Global Community

No country is isolated in our rapidly changing global community. In observing the world and solving our problems, we need to take both the global and local contexts into account. We need to foster an open and comprehensive approach to understanding ourselves and the world around us. The experiences of different countries have shown that, in evaluating local traditions with a view to achieving modernization, we cannot hold back the advancement of culture without losing freedom or ossifying the culture. Moreover, despite the urgency of China's social development in many areas, it is important not to bypass a stage of history by repealing the main components of modern culture and the global community.

In relation to China's cultural modernization and intention to build soft power, the pressure for change inevitably associated with global exchanges calls for a new framework through which to reinterpret the complex structure of the local and outside world. As mentioned earlier, confinement to a narrow national perspective is not conducive to understanding the outside world and ultimately leads to an insular and isolated imagination. Chinese society is presently undergoing a complex transition characterized by strong social differentiation and a serious moral panic at home. Some of China's more sceptical elites are turning to Western culture for critical ammunition and are paying close attention to whether local material and spiritual resources can indeed maintain a sustainable modernization process. The main choice China faces, therefore, is how to deal with the trend towards multiculturalism in the local and global community. It needs to decide whether to participate in the global community or stick to its insularity; whether to get lost in the antagonistic conflict between tradition and modernity, or revive some type of heterogeneous culture embedded in national cultural identities. It is important to recognize that the lead of Western culture in the world's political and economic arenas is due on the one hand to its comprehensive strength and on the other to its 'modernity' and policy of cultural dialogue. Not only is the West effectively, from a legal perspective, able to restrict unbalanced growth and unbalanced power relationships, but it is also, like a magnet, able to draw other societies into emulating its practices. Furthermore, Western culture will continue to respond to a pluralistic global cultural market with a wide range of diverse cultural and commercial solutions. No matter what forms of resistance other cultures choose to adopt, a pattern of 'hybrid cultures' may eventually materialize.

In the light of these broader trends, Chinese cultural ideals cannot simply be pinned to a fixed tradition. The Chinese need to consider carefully the costs of social progress before gradually establishing a rational and tolerant structure. They should set up institutional arrangements to introduce tradition to all aspects of social life, learn from the experiences of countries like Japan and South Korea, and help the public accept a way of life commensurate with 'living in the tradition'. This means that China's path to cultural modernization must neither veer towards further Westernization nor relapse into the old traditional ways. Rather, the country should retain its emphasis on the pluralistic development of a spiritual life and cultural awareness, but with tradition 'embedded' in the key elements of modernity. This would provide a local framework for Chinese people from different cultural backgrounds to observe the world. Its strength is that, while helping people inherit domestic traditions, it does not restrict their exploration of the outside world. It also provides a form of reproduction after the breakdown of tradition. It is not the inheritance of ready-made ideas, but rather the product of institutional arrangements, which also includes an understanding of tradition by contemporary society.

The modernization process entails making constant changes to the institutional structure. Its success or failure depends on how systems and institutions are reformed and how the modern ideology that advocates social and individual liberty gets established and expanded. The wisdom of the process lies in its attitude to problem-solving, which advocates using a combination of technical and moral approaches rather than relying on one of them alone. The same applies to the further development of soft power, which requires cultural and institutional responses. It is a mistake to ignore the interdependence of the relationship between institutions and culture in China's modernization process, and this is something that has yet to be fully rectified. Furthermore, there is an urgent need to resolve conflicts between institutions founded on Western models and those that have evolved from the local and national culture. Such a reform, which entails reconstructing relations between the state and society, needs to take into account the relationship between sociocultural development and social costs, the establishment of a civil society, the development of private autonomy, and the consequences of income concentration, social stratification, and the breakdown of the social structure. Moreover, these issues should be considered in relation to the social and moral structures, social control mechanisms, and legislation.

In Chinese society, the idea of forming an alliance between modern culture and the state is still relatively new. In fact, modernization is driving a complex social transformation of contemporary China that involves not only a change from traditional to modern ways, but also a change from modernity to tradition. The country is going through a transition from pre-modernity to modernity, as well as from old modernity to new modernity. This is undoubtedly a profound social shift to which its policy makers and intellectuals should adopt a realistic rather than hasty approach. To deal with the concept and the various proposals that modernity presents, and to grasp the current applicability and transformational potential of tradition, it might consider adopting the idea of 'following principles and maintaining impartiality' and 'adapting oneself to changing situations', which form part of the Confucian 'doctrine of the mean'. It is essential to draw on the balanced values and ethical resources of both traditional and modern cultures. Some major issues of our time still need to be resolved. For example, there is a need to prevent the further stratification of the social structure and division of value systems, as well as to safeguard against the irreversible secularization and vulgarization of the whole society.

Offsetting the grim historical inertia associated with earlier civilizations and cultures, such a systemic change should see the implementation of a truly prudent and stable, all-inclusive, cultural policy based on facts, knowledge, and openness. Also, in its ability to regulate multiculturalism, it would offset the clumsiness and inefficiency of the current political, economic, and social order. It also points to the need for China to improve and harmonize the balance between itself as a cultural tradition and itself as a complex national political system. The Chinese government is capable of developing and regulating policies that influence the quality and characteristics of contemporary culture; and it is also capable of bringing various practices to a halt that seriously damage its cultural heritage and cultural diversity.

This systemic change also means that for a relatively long time China will have to grapple with trying to reconcile the differences between two contradictory systems of meaning, the first of which is between cultural traditions and pluralistic development. Because the far-reaching transformation of Chinese society unleashed such a wide and irreversible assortment of attitudes and behaviours, simplistic prescriptions like becoming Westernized or going back to ancient times are neither realistic nor suitable for the new, multi-faceted, hybrid, local culture. Moreover, the focus of this type of coordination involves proper handling of the relationship between what the Chinese call 'small tradition', namely different geographical areas, ethnic groups, and ordinary people, and 'large tradition', which encompasses state ideology, laws and regulations, and elite culture. The object of this approach is not only to protect domestic cultural diversity, but also to provide a foundation for the future development of Chinese culture.

The second set of differences in need of reconciliation is between local standpoints and the global community. Needless to say, modernity is inseparable from intercultural openness and dialogue. The prospects of Chinese cultural modernization and soft-power-building depend on whether they have contributions to make to the existence and development of global culture. If Chinese culture is to be able to fit in with the development trends of global culture, it must seek useful ideological resources and common values from different cultural systems in the world, and this includes re-establishing a new consensus on the 'universal values' of Western countries. We cannot simply regard these universal values as a tool for the preservation of hegemony or as a monopoly over cultural power; neither can we look upon them as 'reactionary' thoughts in conflict with the values of Chinese society that undermine its political stability and the authority of the Communist Party.[21]

Furthermore, to help the state implement effective institutional arrangements with which to mobilize the nation's willpower and traditional resources, we need to give deep thought to our modern way of life, to our cultural trends, and to our value systems. Here, we are not restating compromises like 'Chinese learning for fundamental principles and Western learning for practical application', but rather seeking to create a new cultural system based on China's pluralistic tradition that can effectively respond to the major issues of the day, as well as replicate and absorb the common values and ethics of mankind. In the 1980s, Daniel Bell, reflecting on ongoing economic, political, and cultural conflicts and the serious decoupling of social structure and culture in the West, especially the USA, proposed 'returning to some sort of religious values' in the hope of rebuilding the basics of morality and culture, and achieving some sort of reconciliation between tradition and modernity.[22]

Although, from a Western cultural point of view, the ideas it can offer might seem rather remote, such a school of thought at least encourages more open and rational thinking. In the 21st century China faces the urgent task of coming up with a value system that is not only applicable to its own cultural development but that will also have a positive contribution to make to the rest of the world. I call such a value system, or cultural ideal, a 'China dream'.[23] My dream, which is similar though not identical to the one the government proposed in 2012, describes the home that contemporary Chinese people strive to find. It is, however, envisaged as a

[21] On 24 September 2013, Wang Sanyun, Secretary of the Provincial Party Committee of Gansu in China, commented at the Provincial Propaganda and Ideological Work conference that 'we must take a clear-cut stand against reactionary ideas such as Western universal values, and boycott anything that is non-Marxist or negative' (*Yao qizhi xianming de fandui xifang pushi jiazhiguan deng fandong sichao, dizhi fei makesi zhuyi, xiaoji fumian de dongxi*).

[22] Bell, *Cultural Contradictions of Capitalism*, 17.

[23] Sun, "Zhongguo guojia xingxiang."

model for human existence in the future with which 'outsiders' would also feel comfortable. It is therefore not a Chinese monodrama, but a production in which all members of the global community would have a part.

After comparing the theory of soft power with the successes and failures of its various practices, China should make further adjustments to its traditional thinking on security, attach greater importance to the cultural dimension of national security, and regard cultural security as an important part of overall national security and the achievement of various strategic objectives. In the light of the above, such efforts should take into consideration all the political and cultural aspects of Chinese society and imbue the country's future development objectives with their ethos. The aim is to draw on China's cultural traditions, core contemporary values, and global ethics to build the country's cultural soft power and create a new future-oriented concept of cultural security that is 'pragmatic, self-confident, open and pluralistic'.[24] This is not only a requirement for dealing with the influence of foreign culture and maintaining cultural independence, but also a tool with which to create a favourable international environment for China's future development.

To be 'pragmatic' in this context means practically and realistically assessing the numerous challenges and choices that Chinese culture faces—the many social and cultural changes that have taken place as well as, and especially, the various destabilizing influences of modern development. Being pragmatic also calls for a targeted approach to formulating relevant cultural policies and designing projects.

Being 'self-confident' refers to the fact that, alongside its economic and social development, 'the tables have turned' on the power balance between Chinese and Western culture. Consequently, China is now in a position to bring its tradition into its cultural independence equation. In other words, the Chinese have acquired a contemporary cultural consciousness with the distinctive feature of self-assertiveness.

An 'open' concept of cultural security is especially necessary in the light of China's former insularity. It cannot be denied that part of the reason why modernity and change in the global community damaged, even disrupted, Chinese culture is because its self-containment was unable to

[24] Sun and Wang, "Ruan shili lilun."

deliver values and consumer satisfaction commensurate with those of a globalized modern world. Western culture has become 'invincible' in recent years, not only because of its association with 'strong gunboats and powerful artillery' but also because it is an open system representing modern values and ethics of universal importance. As a country that started its development process late, it is reasonable that China should objectively compare the respective positions and values of its and Western culture before opening itself up to the global ethics conducive to intercultural exchanges and the common interests of mankind. Assessing Chinese tradition, modernization and soft-power building is inextricably linked to understanding the global ethics, shared values, and interests of mankind. In other words, Chinese culture must establish a common ground with the values of other cultures, as well as with their emotional, aesthetic, and ethical perspectives. Meanwhile, China should identify ethics and values from its own tradition for absorption into the global ethical order. It can then gradually establish a 'balanced cultural ecology' conducive to positive interaction between it and the outside world, build the international community's confidence in it, and ensure that it is sustainable, and promote understanding between it and the world.

At the same time, it is necessary to establish a 'pluralistic' concept of cultural security that encompasses the ideology and core values that legitimate national sovereignty, as well as the cultural policies that effectively meet the needs of the people by approaching tradition and modernity as an organic whole. Meanwhile, it is vital to implement a policy that protects cultural diversity in different geographical areas and among different ethnic groups. It is also important to curb the 'homogenization' of different domestic cultures caused by rapid economic and social development, and maximize efforts to save the cultural heritages of different geographical areas and ethnic minority groups that are going downhill. Being 'pluralistic' in this context includes learning from the experiences of Western countries like the USA regarding diversifying the main carriers and maintainers of cultural security. There are many drawbacks to relying solely on the state, including the lack of operational space and flexibility; and the state may mistakenly be suspected of harbouring covert hegemonic ambitions of its own. Furthermore, as international exchanges veer in a pluralistic direction, the participants themselves are bound to become more diverse. The development of information and communication technology has made nation-states ideologically less unitary, which has brought unprecedented advances to civil organizations and individual citizens alike.

Conclusion

Different countries' experiences of modernization have shown that the destruction of tradition does not necessarily mean the realization of modernity. On the contrary, it may lead to the disintegration of value systems and the loss of cultural identities, even to the detriment of the very process of building a modern social order. There is abundant evidence from China since the mid-20th century that it is impossible to achieve sweeping social or cultural reforms if there is a fundamental mismatch between the reform and the cultural orientation or traditions of society. Whether to enhance the competitiveness and influence of the country, to oppose Western centrism and hegemony, or to respond to modernity induced difficulties and problems, it is necessary, through effective and collective efforts, to reproduce and revive tradition. Only then can it become an effective form of resistance capable of effortless integration into a cultural value system compatible with China's contemporary modernization process.

China's current extensive drive towards constructing soft power calls for appropriate institutional arrangements and a more future-oriented vision. Soft power is not only about participating in international politics; it is also about benefitting the country and its people in the long term. China is a large country with highly complex historical traditions and equally complex contemporary situations. The twists and turns of the last century dealt repeated blows to the people's cultural traditions. The extraordinary economic development currently taking place is further eroding the culture and creating an endless list of social problems. While ever more frequent global exchanges bring opportunities, they also put China under increasing pressure to reconcile its own and foreign cultures, not to mention the conflicts at home between different political and cultural values, as well as between the mainstream and various subcultures in its society. Under these circumstances, it is vital to safeguard the nation's cultural security, protect the spiritual values the Chinese people need to secure their stability and subsistence, and seek support from historical traditions for further development.

Modernization is a journey not merely from the West to China but also from China to the world. China's history over the last century shows that, given the vast array of subcultures vying with mainstream Chinese culture and the numerous conflicts between different political and cultural values, cultural advances have never been easy there. All this makes it virtually impossible to predict the future prospects of its culture, yet we still need to be mentally prepared for our entry onto the world stage, however far away that might seem at present. Meanwhile, we should always remain open to exploring new avenues for further research and discussion.

Bibliography

Barnett, A. D. 1998. *China's far west: Four decades of change*. Beijing: Oriental Press.

Bell, D. 1989. *The cultural contradictions of capitalism*. Beijing: Joint Publishing.

Cao, J. Q. 2000. *Huanghe bian de Zhongguo*. [*China along the Yellow River*]. Shanghai: Shanghai Literature and Art Publishing House.

Firth, R. 1938. *Human types*. London: Nelson.

Huo, G. H. 2011. Wenhua ruanshili de zhexue fansi. [Philosophical reflections on cultural soft power]. *Xueshu yanjiu* 3.

Jin, Y. J. (King, A.) 1999. *Cong chuantong dao xiandai*. [*From traditional to modernised*]. Beijing: China Renmin University Press.

Li, X. H. 2002. Zhongguo wenhua xiandaihua licheng de zhexue xingsi. [Philosophical reflections on the Chinese cultural modernization process]. *Zhongguo shehui kexue* 6: 63–65.

Liu, J. N. 2010. Ziyou zhuyi yu rujiao shehui. [Liberalism and Confucian society]. [online]. Available at http://www.21ccom.net/articles/sxpl/sx/article_201001201043.html. Accessed 7 Jan 2014.

Ma, C. H., J. Q. Shi, et al. 2011. Zhongguo chengshi jiating bianqian de qushi he zuixin faxian. [Changes in China's urban households: Trends and latest findings]. *Shehuixue yanjiu*, no. 2.

Mou, Z. S., and J. D. Zheng. 1992. *Daode lixiang zhuyi de chongjian*. [*Reconstruction of moral idealism*]. Beijing: China Radio and Television Press.

Nye, J. S. Jr., and J. S. Wang. 2009. Zhongguo ruanshili de xingqi jiqi dui Meiguo de yingxiang. [The rise of China's soft power and its impact on the United States]. *Shijie jingji yu zhengzhi* 6.

Shi, Y. H. 2008. Chengjiu yu tiaozhan: zhongguo heping fazhan, hexie hexie shijie linian yu duiwai zhengce xingshi. [Achievements and challenges: China's peaceful development, the concept of a harmonious world, and foreign policy situation]. *Dangdai shijie yu shehui zhuyi* 2: 82–83.

Shi, Z. Y., and X. L. Shao. 2013. Quanqiu 'zi' li: shijian fuzeren daguo de wenhua ziyuan. [Global "self" care: Fulfil the cultural resources of a responsible great power]. In *Zhongguo zhanlue baogao. [China strategy report]*, ed. H. H. Men, vol. 1, 87. Beijing: People's Publishing House.

Sun, Y. C. 2010. Zhongguo guojia xingxiang de wenhua jiangou. [Cultural construction of China's national image]. *Jiaoxue yu yanjiu*, no 11.

——— 2012. Wenhua fanrong de jichu shi baorong. [Inclusiveness is the foundation of cultural prosperity]. *Xuexi Shibao* 12 May. [online]. Available at http://xlt.ccmedu.com/bbs12_169241.html. Accessed 28 Aug 2015.

Sun, Y. C., and Y. Wang. 2014. Ruan shili lilun fansi yu zhongguo de "wenhua anquan guan". [Reflection on the soft power theory and China's "cultural security standpoint"]. *Guoji anquan yanjiu* no 2.

Tu, W. M. 1995. Wei ruxue fazhan buxie chencl. [Be untiringly remarking on the development of Confucianism]. *Dushu* no. 10.

——— 2001. *Dongya jiazhi yu duoyuan xiandaixing. [East Asian values and pluralistic modernity]*. Beijing: China Social Sciences Press.

Wan, S. Y. 2013. Yao qizhi xianming de fandui xifang pushi jiazhiguan deng fandong sichao, dizhi fei makesi zhuyi, xiaoji fumian de dongxi. [We must take a clear-cut stand against reactionary ideas such as Western universal values, and boycott anything that is non-Marxist or negative]. Comment at the Provincial Propaganda and Ideological Work Conference. 24 Sept 2013.

Wang, N. 2002. Quanqiuhua shidai de wenhua lunzheng he wenhua duihua. [Cultural debates and cultural dialogues in the era of globalization]. In *Quanqiuhua: Xifanghua huanshi zhongguohua. [Globalization: Westernization or Chinalization]*, ed. K. P. Yu, 266–267. Beijing: Social Sciences Academic Press.

Yu, Y. S. 1989. *Zhongguo sixiang chuantong de xiandai quanshi. [Modern interpretation of traditional Chinese thoughts]*. Jiangsu: Jiangsu Renmin Chubanshe.

Zhao J. Y., and C. S. Gan 2005. Xiandaixing yu jindai yilai zhongguoren de wenhua rentong weiji ji chonggou. [Modernity and the crisis and reconstruction of cultural identity for Chinese people in modern times]. *Xueshu yuekan* no. 1.

10

Defining and Safeguarding Priorities in China's National Security

Xi Xiao

Security is crucial to national strategic planning and policy design for any country. China is in the process of changing from a regional to a global power, and will then transform further into a leading global power. During this transition, China's national strategic interests are rapidly expanding worldwide; it is attracting international attention and there is an increase in cultural and ideological infiltration. Combined with other factors, including the acceleration of its overall domestic restructuring, the enhancement of the interaction between domestic and international factors, and the blurring of boundaries that define what falls into the category of its national interests, China's national security environment has become ever more complex. In addition, there is a structural contradiction in its security because its national interests are expanding while its capacity to defend them remains relatively weak; the vulnerability and

X. Xiao (✉)
School of Administration, Jilin University, Changchun, China
e-mail: Xiaoxijlu@163.com

S. Tsang, H. Men (eds.), *China in the Xi Jinping Era*,
The Nottingham China Policy Institute Series,
DOI 10.1007/978-3-319-29549-7_10

sensitivity of this contradiction has become evident. Therefore, in safeguarding its national security interests China faces ever more constraints and challenges. Optimizing a national security strategy and strengthening its ability to shape its international environment have become major strategic issues currently facing China.

Since its 18th Party Congress, China has been committed to establishing a National Security Council. It sees this as an opportunity to overhaul and improve the entire framework of its national security strategy. Determining how to safeguard national security is something on which Chinese policy makers and the wider strategic research community are particularly focused. Currently, the core issues of national security planning are:

- To pay close attention to both domestic and international situations;
- To judge the trends of international situations in a forward-looking manner;
- To recognize the external threats and challenges facing China's national security;
- To assess China's national security and put forward relevant policy recommendations accordingly.

These issues are also the core focus of national security studies.

A Rapidly Changing International Environment

The economic recovery from the global financial crisis is unbalanced. Revolutionary changes have taken place in the international order and the situation is becoming increasingly complex. Changes, whether gradual, quantitative, or qualitative, are affecting the international situation and are likely to last into the long term.

While world peace and development are still the main themes of the international arena, a majority of countries still prefers to address international relations through cooperation and coordination. Since all countries need to join forces to deal with the profound impact of the current financial and economic crisis, they should all, particularly the global powers, consider development to be the core objective, and cooperation to be the primary means of achieving it. Thus, through coordination and compromise, they endeavour to serve their common interests. Peace is an important prerequisite to development for all countries. Hence, the international system contains stabilizing mechanisms to help facilitate development.

In the meantime, factors causing revolutionary change in the international system are increasingly evident. Significant changes in the national strength of global powers have taken place and this has had a dramatic impact on the outlook of the world.[1] These changes have included a comparative waning in the overall national strength of developed powers and a concomitant rise of a group of emerging powers, which have begun to make a conscious effort to carry out a policy of strategic coordination. Therefore, traditional relations among global powers have shifted, meaning the previous international order has been shattered, the competition between global strategic forces has become unprecedentedly fierce, and strategic relations among the global powers are increasingly complex.[2]

With the progress made towards global governance, countries no longer need be bound together in both positive and negative situations. The global powers have reached a consensus on securing coexistence and mutual prosperity through the convergence of common interests and institutionalization, with the traditional practice of shifting problems onto others now cast aside. The majority of countries are open to diversity and use democratic methods when dealing with international relations. This means that with the acceleration of globalization, a new international paradigm is emerging and the conditions for peaceful change are starting to take shape.

[1] Qin, "Guoji tixi yanxu biange," 7.
Yu, "Guoji tixi biange tezheng," 1–8.

[2] With regard to changes in the world order, three theories generally dominate, namely transfer theory, diffusion theory, and equilibrium theory. Transfer theory asserts that the centre of gravity of world powers has shifted from the West to the East, and from the Atlantic to the Pacific, while diffusion theory argues that this centre has shifted from the West to emerging powers, and equilibrium theory claims that the rapid development of developing countries, especially emerging global powers, contributes to the increasingly balanced distribution of global forces. See Le, "Guoji xingshi Zhongguo waijiao," 1–10.

However, these changes have not significantly altered the international situation China faces. China's rise has been so fast that neither it nor the rest of the world has been sufficiently prepared for it. Against this backdrop, it has become the main focus of global change and, in 2010, surpassed Japan to become the world's second largest economy in terms of GDP. As its national interests expand throughout the world, China is shifting its domestic focus towards becoming a player on the international stage, and the competition between it and other countries, particularly the great powers, is becoming increasingly fierce. Its national strength has improved dramatically compared with that of its neighbouring countries. Therefore, the future orientation and execution of its strategic plans has become a sensitive issue and some great powers are responding to its rise by trying to coordinate among themselves. China's neighbours, especially Japan and some ASEAN countries, are taking advantage of the period before it becomes a leading global power to seize control of certain key interests. Some separatist elements within China are causing instability by trying to cooperate with the anti-China forces to disrupt its development plan, contain its development prospects, and promote 'peaceful evolution'. Their rather suspect and destructive activities are presenting China, which has long been a leader among the emerging powers, with major challenges.

Major External Threats and Challenges

Because China's rise occurred at approximately the same time as the transformation of the rest of the world, it has become the most important of the current global changes. The rapid intensification of its strength and dramatic increase in its international influence, particularly since the 2008 global financial crisis, is beginning to encroach on the former world system of one superpower and several great powers. At the 18th Communist Party of China (CPC) National Congress in 2012, General Secretary Xi Jinping launched 'the China Dream [which is] to achieve the great rejuvenation of the Chinese nation'. Through its rich content and grand vision, this concept outlines an ideal blueprint to guide and mobilize the whole of China to achieve a higher stage of modernization.

Chinese policy makers, who insist on adopting a low profile in their quest for ever greater achievements, place equal emphasis on deepening reform and extending China's international influence. They aim to transform the country into a major global power; and its ambitions are causing considerable concern to the international community, especially to the great powers, which will have to make some strategic adjustments. Consequently, the external threats to and challenges facing China's national security are expanding rapidly and becoming increasingly more complex.

As China's national interests become increasingly international, current geopolitical, economic, and security matters are also becoming subjects of concern for Chinese national security; and the gap between its national and international security is narrowing.[3] To begin with, there is a conflict between China's overseas interests and the traditional interests of the Western powers, especially those of the USA in Latin America and West European countries in Africa. In particular, there exists a structural contradiction in which China's strategic interests are irreconcilable with those of the USA. After several years of debate about China's impending threat to US hegemony,[4] the USA has now agreed to pursue a policy of both containment and engagement, with increasing weight given to the containment of both its soft and hard power. It is now employing various means, including military, economic, and security coordination in China's neighbouring territory, to speed up its attempts to surround China with a containment belt.[5] Meanwhile, China's integration into the world economy has produced mutual interdependence between the two countries. However, while China's direct and indirect influence on the world economy has increased, external factors are severely constraining the country's economic and financial security. Therefore, we can conclude that, with the acceleration of globalization, global issues, especially non-military factors and other key strategic elements, have further increased

[3] Some scholars have pointed out that the expansion of national interests also results in an increasing number of external threats to these interests; so the nation has a responsibility to assess and respond to these threats. See Song, "Guoji guanxi liliang yunyong," 66–75.

[4] Goldstein, "China's Emerging Grand Strategy," 57–106.

Segal, "Constraintment of China," 107–35.

Kang, *China Rising*.

[5] Zhu, "Chongfan Yazhou zhanlue," 1–4.

the constraints on and threats to China's security. For example, the acceleration of its economic development has deepened its dependence on energy resources. However, the issue of its offshore energy transportation channels has become one of the external factors constraining its development planning, while the construction of inland channels has not yet achieved satisfactory results.

China shares more borders with other countries and has more territorial disputes than any other nation. For various reasons, including historical factors, different conflicts of interests and the possible trajectory of future strategic considerations, China is facing an increasingly severe and complicated security situation. Traditional geopolitical thinking still plays a dominant role, but the idea of containment against China is also gaining traction. Furthermore, neither the new notion of a China Dream, nor the proposal to shelve differences and seek joint development in order to resolve disputes, has received proper recognition. On the contrary, in some respects these ideas have served only to hinder China's own development. Because in the past China did not designate land borders, it has had long-standing boundary disputes with many of its neighbouring countries, with the disputes over islands and territorial waters attracting much regional and global attention in recent years. As a consequence, conflicts of interest between China and its neighbouring countries will continue for a long time and the potential for intervention from various powerful external forces, including the USA, provides the country with new security challenges.[6]

In respect of land security, the regions to the north and north-west of China are relatively stable, while those to the south-west still face uncertainty. The area from South Asia to the Persian Gulf in particular has become a new geostrategic focus, which is crucial to China's land security. To some extent, India has replaced Japan as China's main regional rival in Asia and, between these two countries, there is a structural conflict of strategic interests. India has intensified its cooperation and coordination with both the USA and Japan, which has some strategic implications for China's national security. The situation in North Korea appears stable but is increasingly uncertain.

[6] With regard to the adjustment of the US strategy, see Clinton, "Remarks on Regional Architecture."

In the field of maritime security, the contradictory structural security situation between China and both the USA and Japan is becoming increasingly prominent. China's north-east access to the sea has been blocked and the territorial dispute between China and Japan over the Diaoyu Islands is becoming increasingly tense. While quasi-alliances are being formed against China in its south-east region towards the sea, its space for strategic development has been compressed. The South China Sea has been termed a 'second Persian Gulf', and disputes over sovereignty and the right to exploit natural resources are becoming the new hot spots of this region. Various direct and indirect interferences from other countries, including the USA and Japan, have had a significant effect on China's national security situation and development strategy. The development of cross-strait relations has shown a positive and peaceful trend, but there remains a significant possibility that the Taiwan issue will not be solved for some time. In China's current predicament, forming a viable and forward-looking maritime strategy has become a litmus test for the wisdom of its policy makers and strategists.

Although there is no longer any threat of a foreign invasion, there are increasing attempts from destructive external forces to infiltrate China ideologically and politically. Also, external forces have become more adept at exploiting various ethnic separatist movements, which could pose a threat to China's national security. Given these circumstances, China's main national security priority is to safeguard its long-term cultural security and its short-term social stability.

These external threats and challenges show that there are many areas in which China could improve its national security strategy. First, its decision to prioritize economic development has stood in the way of efficient and comprehensive strategic planning. In particular, its strategic adjustments have taken insufficient account of new international situations and of its overall development prospects. The frameworks of China's security and cultural and national strategies, which need to be able to deal efficiently with the development of international powers by the middle of the 21st century, have not yet been properly formulated. Although it has taken a few security initiatives (for example, the People's Liberation Army (PLA) Navy's escorting missions in the Gulf of Aden), its general strategy remains a passive one.

Second, for the foreseeable future the main focus of its national security should be on East Asia, but currently China has no clear strategy for deciding which region to prioritize in the deployment of its security, and it has failed to put East Asia—where the USA, Japan, India, the ASEAN member states, and China all have great influence—at the centre of its national security policy. Countries such as the USA, Japan, and India see China as their major competitor in the region and have increased their presence to the south and east of the country, laying siege through their soft strategy to constrain its overall influence in the region. This should change.

Third, China has no clear maritime strategy. Through lack of naval planning and experience, as well as no overall naval defence strategy, its interests in this sphere are severely constrained.

Fourth, China's comprehensive growth at home has extended its national interests to every corner of the world and its military power is playing an increasingly important role in safeguarding its national interests.[7] However, its military prowess for a long time lagged behind its economic performance, so its role in supporting the country's national interests is inadequate.

Fifth, in an era of international interdependence, a mature great power should be able to draw on a combination of diplomatic, military, economic, cultural, and other resources to deal with conflicts between countries. China has been unable to employ these means effectively and its ability to utilize combined measures to deal with conflicts is particularly weak compared with that of other great powers.

State Security Council and Strategic Planning

China needs a State Security Council to coordinate and manage the increasingly diverse and complex challenges to its national security that its rapid rise has brought. To achieve more comprehensive, systematic, and forward-looking planning on major strategic issues China needs to improve its decision-making ability and coordinate its diplomatic,

[7] Men, "Zhongguo zhanlue liyi tuozhan," 88–9.

military, economic, intelligence, and communication facilities. The country faces several serious national security challenges in such strategic areas as territory, territorial waters, resources, social stability, and national unity. Some Western countries, including some of China's neighbours, frequently try to penetrate these defences to undermine its core national interests. China must therefore maintain its long-term stability and sustainable development in a globalized world by strengthening its capacity for overall national planning and strategic decision making. It is normal for major countries to pay close attention to their national security and many have established their own State Security Councils, which are able to put forward, coordinate, and carry out national security and foreign policy decisions. These councils serve as pivotal institutions, in charge of national security and foreign policy, and their existence can be viewed as a sign that a particular country's national policies are maturing.

In November 2013, the Third Plenary Session of the 18th Central Committee of the CPC announced its decision to establish a State Security Council to improve and safeguard China's security.[8] The main aims of this council should, I believe, include:

- Researching the important strategic issues pertaining to China's national security, including studies on territory, territorial waters, diplomacy, the military, natural resources, the economy, and people's livelihoods;
- Establishing the important major strategies;
- Overseeing the implementation of national security strategies;
- Producing efficient and effective responses to domestic and international emergencies.

The Third Plenum of the 18th Party Congress put out an official statement that the establishment of the State Security Council was a reflection of the rapid growth of China's national strength and that, given that the country faced increasingly complex foreign policy, strategic, and security challenges, it urgently needed such an institution to centralize power at the highest level and to coordinate the various government departments.

[8] Xinhuanet, "Shibajie zhongyang weiyuanhui gongbao."

The State Security Council will improve the efficiency of the national security strategy and policy.[9]

The Standing Committee of the Politburo should take the lead in establishing how the State Security Council should be established and in determining that its principles and structure comply strictly with the requirements of the PRC constitution. The CPC Central Committee should retain absolute control over any issue regarding China's national security, while encouraging relevant research and promoting coordination among all government departments.[10] While establishing its State Security Council, China should learn from the experiences of other countries and, in so doing, establish a council that befits its national circumstances and in which the CPC General Secretary plays the leading role.

Based on the above proposed principles, the main development orientation of the State Security Council should be:

- To institutionalize the management of its central leading committee;
- To focus the role of this committee only on national security issues;
- To actualize its proposed functions and institutions;
- To further expand and improve these functions.

This new State Security Council should thus be committed to increasing the importance of national security and foreign affairs. It should provide the CPC Central Committee with a powerful tool with which to exercise its leadership and decision-making authority in the field of national security and it should centralize the management of politics, military affairs, foreign policy, internal affairs, the economy, and intelligence. The Council should communicate and coordinate with government departments in these fields to form an overall integrated system responsible for the overall planning, strategic coordination, management, and containment of any crises that may arise. Finally, to safeguard national security and to secure

[9] Shi Yinhong, a counsellor of the State Council of China and professor in the School of International Studies at Renmin University of China, believes that the State Security Council should be an organization with flexible institutional settings.

See *People's Daily*, "Guojia anquan weiyuanhui."

[10] When talking about methods of work, Mao Zedong pointed out that 'the central party must retain absolute control over major issues, while decisions on less major issues can be decentralized. The Central Party Committee makes final decisions regarding major issues, while local governments should execute them. See Mao, "Gongzuo fangfa 60 tiao," 355.

the country's long-term interests, the Council should be able to provide consultancy services, make decisions, and execute relevant policies.

China's president, Xi Jinping, chairs the State Security Council, while Premier Li Keqiang and Zhang Dejiang, chairman of the National People's Congress (NPC) standing committee, are its two vice chairmen. Because of the complexity of the issues facing the council, a member of the Politburo should serve as its general secretary and be in charge of its day-to-day work. The statutory members of its committee consist of a deputy chief of the general staff in the PLA General Staff Department and ministers from key governmental departments, including the Ministry of Foreign Affairs, the Development and Reform Commission, the Ministry of Defence, the Ministry of Public Security, the Ministry of State Security, the Ministry of Commerce, the International Department of the Central Committee of the CPC, the Taiwan Affairs Office of the State Council, and the Publicity Department.

China should, in my opinion, set up three sub-institutions within the State Security Council, namely a ministerial committee, a vice ministerial committee, and a policy coordinating committee. The ministerial committee, which would be responsible for reviewing, coordinating, and supervising the establishment and implementation of national security strategy and policies, would be chaired by the secretary general of the State Security Council and attended by its statutory members as well as invited heads of various departments.

The vice ministerial committee, which would be responsible for suggesting how to formulate and implement national security policy, would also supervise and review work in the State Security Council that involves interdepartmental collaboration. The executive deputy secretary general of the State Security Council would chair its committee meetings, which the deputy heads of the relevant departments would attend. The latter would also attend the separate committee meetings of sub-departments on economic security, financial security, internal affairs, and international security.

A policy coordination committee would operate at both the global and regional level to deal with issues such as Sino-US relations, Sino-Japanese relations, the nuclear issue on the Korean Peninsula, as well as specialist matters such as handling major infectious diseases and energy security. This committee would be responsible for advising decision makers on how to frame and implement national security policy in particular fields.

The general secretary of the State Security Council, who is in charge of its day-to-day operations, should act as the president's representative in organizing and supervising appropriate research on national security. Inside the Council, various functional departments should be established in line with its strategic objectives, including a strategic planning bureau, a policy coordination bureau, a crisis management bureau, and a secretariat. The Council is an inter-departmental advisory body dealing with national security, directly under the leadership of both the Standing Committee of the Politburo and the President of China. It is a key department of both the CPC and the state system. The following are its principal functions.

First, it provides strategic planning and consultancy on national security issues and is responsible for formulating long-term strategies and policies, which is crucial at a time of rapid and unpredictable change in the world. This generally relies on the in-depth analysis of internal and external security situations, as well as on strategic thinking about the country's long-term interests and national security objectives. It includes formulating major principles and security strategies and advising the president about them. It is responsible for producing the 'Outline of China's National Security Strategy', a report detailing China's medium and long-term plans, as well as 'China's National Security Strategy Report which provides a five-year strategic assessment and formulates planning in the field of national security.

Second, it liaises with other key governmental departments, which is beneficial to the overall planning of national security in that it enables the relevant government departments to act in a more united and coordinated manner.[11] As an advisory body acting at the behest of China's leader, the State Security Council is responsible for both formulating and implementing security policy. It is also responsible for coordinating and unifying the views of various government organizations. It encourages research, seeks interdepartmental collaboration, submits occasional

[11] Qu Xing, President of the China Institute of International Studies, pointed out that, with the development of high technology, the national security issues facing China are changing and becoming more complex. Therefore, various governmental departments need to work together effectively to protect national security.
See *People's Daily*, "Guojia anquan weiyuanhui."

national security analysis reports, and organizes meetings attended by relevant governmental officials and experts.

Third, it is responsible for dealing with any national security crisis that may arise and develops an emergency response mechanism and technical support system with which to do so. Because threats to China's national security are likely to be unpredictable, it is crucial to manage and contain them. The State Security Council is responsible for collecting information on any potential crisis or emergency and then using it to inform and advise the president.

The following are the main focuses of the State Security Council's work:

- Formulating strategic planning for national security in the medium and long-term (about 10 to 15 years);
- Regularly bringing out a National Security Report (every five years);
- Occasionally publishing national security strategic analyses and other related reports;
- Alerting decision makers to any major issues concerning national interests and national security, as well as recommending clear policies to address such issues;
- Coordinating and supervising tasks that require cooperation with other governmental departments;
- Dealing with any emergency concerning national security, including managing and controlling a crisis on behalf of the president.

China's National Security Strategy and the Bottom Line

The core objectives of China's national security strategy include:

- Preparing for its emergence as a leading global power;
- Steadily promoting its national security;
- Actively participating to safeguard international security;
- Maintaining and expanding China's security interests.

The next ten years will be crucial to China's development into a leading global power, and a period when its national security will face serious challenges. When meeting these challenges, there are five things that China needs to do.

First, it should safeguard its national interests within its territory, both on land and in its territorial waters. It should keep its land borders with its neighbouring countries safe and stable, while continuing to compete and cooperate with the other leading global power over its maritime boundaries. It should also consolidate and promote its security interests as well as improve its strategic environment.

Second, China should promote its reunification, maintain its territorial integrity, and oppose independence movements. It should stick to a policy that uses political, economic, and cultural means to promote consensus and military means to combat Taiwanese independence. It should also do everything it can to oppose the independence of both Xinjiang and Tibet; in particular, to prevent the secession of these or any other regions, it should clamp down firmly on any rioting from within these movements.

Third, China should shape and maintain an international environment that is conducive to its peaceful development. It should seek to avoid creating a vicious circle of confrontation, containment, and a cold war with the USA, to prevent the formation of any alliance against it, and to prevent hotspots in neighbouring regions from getting out of control.

Fourth, China should maintain and expand the scope of its national strategic interests. It should promote multilateral security cooperation with other countries, participate in the establishment of security systems involving China and its neighbouring countries and, under certain circumstances, play a leading role in this process, while also participating in the establishment of wider international security systems with a view to expanding its own interests.

Fifth, China should expand its military power to protect its national security. To safeguard this, it must steadily increase military spending and speed up the modernization of its conventional armed forces. It must also strengthen its military cooperation between and exchanges with other countries. In addition, it must emphasize its peaceful military mission, while displaying its military capacity when appropriate.

Currently, China's national security situation is relatively stable. It has unswervingly maintained its strategic focus on improving its national strength and, as this increases, the threat of military invasion will decrease and eventually cease altogether. Its enhanced international economic influence has increased its capacity to maintain its economic security, while the acceleration of its overall restructuring has developed its standing as a leading global power. Meanwhile, China should continue to improve its national strength and strive to convert this into international influence. It should also maintain a modest and calm attitude, actively taking on its share of international responsibilities, devote itself to shaping an international environment conducive to peaceful development, and strive peacefully to transform itself into a major world power.[12]

China has to improve its attitude if it is to become a leading global power. It must abandon the victim mentality it formed during the 'century of humiliation' and instead become a mature power able to deal with volatile international situations. Recently, China has responded more actively to external pressure and a clearer framework on national security is gradually taking shape. The White Paper on China's Peaceful Development, which the State Council's Information Office published in September 2011, pointed out that the world is becoming smaller because of closer contact between countries, which in turn can increase the chances of friction, or even conflict, especially during periods of dramatic change. China has also strengthened its interaction with the outside world, thus showing its commitment to illustrating the scope of its core national interests and the trajectory of its development.[13] On 28 January 2013, at the Politburo's Third Plenary Session for collective study, General Secretary Xi Jinping emphasized that 'China should improve its strategic perspectives, increase its strategic focus and coordinate both its domestic situation and the global situation in a more effective manner. … China should adhere to its peaceful development policy. However, it should never give up its legitimate rights or sacrifice its core national interests'.[14]

[12] Xiao, "Zhongguo anquan zhanlue sikao," 51–4.

[13] Guowuyuan bangongshi, "Zhongguo de heping fazhan."

[14] Xi, "Genghao tongchou liangge daju," 1.

This shows that China is beginning to recognize itself as a mature, leading, global power. Signs that this is happening include a country's ability to:

- Define the scope of its national interests and unswervingly safeguard its core ones;
- Respond calmly to criticism and discuss its problems frankly;
- Consider the national interests of other countries from the long-term perspective of its own national interests.

However, China has not yet completed the process. Its long-term strategic vision is insufficient and it lacks overall objectives and specific, viable strategies. It does not know enough about national strategy, cannot deal with strategic issues in an open and objective manner, has insufficient understanding of the reasons for its rise, and so does not really know what domestic and international factors might contain it.[15] It has also been unable to define its core interests clearly. 'China's policy makers have endeavoured to shape its international image as a responsible and benevolent leading global power, departing from the *Tianxia* (Under the Heaven) worldview',[16] but many countries neither recognize nor properly understand China's worldview, which will obviously have an effect on its foreign relations.[17]

As it builds itself up to become a leading global power in the new world order, China must seize the strategic high ground. The present system is unable to keep up with the rapidly changing international landscape, and handling the transformation will require cooperation between countries. China has already been integrated into the international system and is widely recognized as a future superpower. It should seize the

[15] Men, "Zhongguo jueqi," 9–16.

[16] Black and Hwang, "China and Japan's Quest," 431–51.

[17] Joshua Cooper Ramo pointed out that if China wants a peaceful rise, an essential prerequisite is to persuade other countries to accept its view of the world. Barry Buzan also believes that if China wants to achieve its peaceful rise, there is an urgent need for it to explain its understanding of the international community and how it views its own position in the current and future international community.

See Ramo, *The Beijing Consensus*, 28.

Buzan, "China in International Society," 1–32.

opportunity that the current situation presents to help construct a fairer and more rational world order.

Since the transformation of the world order entails competition between global powers, one of the aims of China's strategic planning must be to ensure that the regional changes already taking place in East Asia move in favour of its own strategic national interests yet also accommodate the convergence and institutionalization of the common interests and responsibilities of the other East Asian countries.[18] China must reinforce its domestic order to establish a harmonious socialist society in which democracy, the rule of law, and justice reign; it should be a place where people are honest and kind and the whole of society is full of vigour, where people's lives are stable and orderly and where the human race coexists harmoniously with nature. It should also build a solid foundation for the construction of a harmonious international society.

China's spectacular rise will inevitably disturb the existing world order and cause concern to the international community, particularly to the great powers with global interests. Since the latter are likely to respond with measures that may constitute obstacles to its rise, China should establish, promote, and extend communities of interests in the international arena. Certain traditional alliances, free trade zones, and measures to bring about regional integration, however, have been in existence for centuries, thus allowing countries to work together with others in both positive and negative situations in the context of globalization. These communities have been formed not only by putting this idea into practice but also by regularizing and institutionalizing it.[19]

In establishing communities of interest, it is important to focus on both the global and regional levels. At the global level, China should seek to promote global cooperation and, when dealing with international crises, make effective use of existing arrangements while strengthening its own agenda-setting capability. At the regional level, China should demonstrate its positive attitude and show that it can play a role in establishing such communities. It should take the initiative in developing economic, security, military, and ecological cooperation with its neighbouring coun-

[18] Men, "East Asian Order Formation," 47–82.

[19] Men, "Zhongguo anquan liyi jiedu," 54–8.

tries and enhance its capacity to shape the geopolitical landscape and focus on establishing institutional frameworks for regional cooperation.

An effective way to safeguard national security and expand national interests is to develop transport networks and ensure they remain unimpeded. With the process of globalization ongoing, this is an issue that has attracted increased attention from every country and is a major task facing China. Globalization and the expansion of the Internet have created huge increases in the flow of goods, which must rely on these transport networks. China is now more closely connected than ever before to the international market, but its domestic resources are failing to meet its development requirements. Consequently, its imports are increasing each year and shortages of resources pose a threat to its economic security.

With its maritime lifeline reliant on the Taiwan Strait, the South China Sea, the Strait of Malacca, the Indian Ocean, and the Arabian Sea, China needs to strengthen its naval forces and actively develop and expand its large ocean-going commercial fleets. It should increase its strategic investment in the major oil-producing regions around the world, including the Middle East and Africa, and strengthen its relationship with oil-producing countries to secure a stable supply of energy. In addition, it should maintain good relations with the ASEAN countries to ensure the safety of its sea lanes, with appropriate naval capacities for this purpose. In short, China needs to minimize the vulnerability inherent in its dependence on maritime transport.

To implement the national security strategy, China needs to uphold the following six principles. The first is that it should pay attention to its own area, for Asia Pacific will be the world's key region in the future, before reaching out to the developing countries of Asia, Africa, and Latin America. It should endeavour to manage its territorial waters and exclusive economic zones, develop good relationships with countries that have abundant resources, as well as rely on developing countries. It should also take on its international responsibility to play a more active role in global hotspots. In particular, it should work towards establishing a new type of great-power relationship with the USA.

Second, China should place the same amount of emphasis on establishing a formal national security system as on promoting its 'partnership diplomacy', namely maintaining flexible partnerships with other countries, particularly its key strategic partners. It has already established partnerships of various sorts with more than 57 countries and international organizations around the world. These (see Table 10.1) include 'comprehensive strategic cooperative partnerships', 'strategic partnerships of coordination', 'strategic cooperative partnerships', and 'strategic partnerships'. 'Partnership diplomacy' has played a key role in safeguarding China's overall position in the world and ensuring that it does not, in general, face enemy states. It also provides stable, institutionalized channels through which to extend China's national interests. Since the 18th CPC National Congress, China has continued to build multilateral relationships, but it needs to return further to its traditional strategy of bilateralism. Specifically, it should commit to a multilateral security system, but use its bilateral relations with other countries where they specifically benefit it, while constraining those that do not.

Third, to improve its agenda-setting capability, China should place as much emphasis on defence as it does on developing international cooperation. Bearing in mind that 'peace comes from national strength', it is especially important in the face of an increasingly complex security situation to strengthen its defensive capacity.

Fourth, China should place equal emphasis on traditional and non-traditional security threats. With regard to the latter, it needs to employ measures to deal with the diversity of such threats and their extended targets.[20] Territorial disputes and ethnic separatist movements pose the main traditional security threats, which are serious matters on which China can make no concessions. As globalization deepens and the speed of its integration into the world increases, China is facing a growing number of increasingly serious non-traditional security threats and, when dealing with these, it needs to show not only resolution and determination but also international cooperation. With public opinion now expressed more explicitly and the dissemination of information across borders becoming easier, tightening its control over cross-border interaction between domestic and international extremists has become an important part of its national security strategy.

[20] Lu, "Fei chuantong anquan lun," 42–8.

Table 10.1 China's strategic and cooperative partnerships (1993–2014)

Type of partnership	Countries or international organizations	Number of partners
Comprehensive strategic partnership of coordination	Russia	1
All-weather strategic cooperative partnership	Pakistan	1
Comprehensive strategic partnership for cooperation	Vietnam, Cambodia, Myanmar, Laos, Thailand	5
Strategic partnership of cooperation	South Korea, India, Sri Lanka, Afghanistan	4
All-round strategic partnership	Germany	1
Comprehensive strategic partnership	UK, Italy, France, Brazil, Spain, Denmark, Portugal, Kazakhstan, Mexico, South Africa, Greece, Indonesia, Belarus, EU	14
Strategic partnership	UAE, Angola, Uzbekistan, Tajikistan, Turkmenistan, Mongolia, Argentina, Poland, Nigeria, Canada, Serbia, Chile, Ukraine, Venezuela, Peru, Kyrgyzstan, ASEAN, African Union	18
Strategic partnership for mutual benefit	Ireland	1
All-round partnership of friendship	Belgium	1
Comprehensive partnership of friendly cooperation	Romania, Bulgaria	1
Comprehensive cooperative partnership	Republic of Congo, Croatia, Nepal, Tanzania, Bangladesh, Ethiopia	6
Partnership of friendly cooperation	Hungary	1
Partnership of traditional cooperation	Albania	1
Partnership of important cooperation	Fiji	1
Friendly partnership	Jamaica	1
Total		57

Source: Men Honghua and Liu Xiaoyang, 'China's Strategy for Partnering, 1993–2014', *World Economy and Politics* (2015), no. 2, p. 21

Fifth, China should give equal attention to defending its land and maritime borders, including its territorial waters. It has traditionally prioritized defending its land borders over its coastline, but under current circumstances, the importance of defending the sea borders needs emphasizing. Meanwhile, it should increase its naval patrols in the East China Sea and South China Sea to retain its sovereignty over these waters.

Sixth, China should give equal weight to diplomatic and military solutions, relying mainly on diplomacy to reduce animosity towards it, while strengthening its military capabilities. It should also improve cooperation between its foreign affairs and domestic affairs departments, so that they can work together to safeguard and expand its national interests. In addition, the pattern of public diplomacy has slowly changed in recent years with the role of the government diminishing and that of the general public becoming increasingly important. The primary task of its public diplomacy in the new era is to dispel doubts and fears over its rise among people in other countries.

To implement these principles effectively China needs to have a proper understanding of both its own national situation and of world development trends. To do so effectively, it needs: (a) to assess its own national strength; (b) to outline its national strategic interests; (c) to define exactly what the concept of national security means to it; and (d) to assess the risks to its national security.

How the national strength of a country should be assessed has become one of the most discussed topics in strategic studies within China. An assessment should recognize the impacts of globalization and of the information revolution, the relative and dynamic natures of national strength, the importance of international comparisons in an objective judgement of that strength, and the level of self-discipline exercised during displays of strength.

A country's core national strategic interests are economic, political, and security related, though international and social interests are now also playing an increasingly important role. The 'rank ordering method', which ranks interests according to their priority, is now the standard tool for measuring national interests. An alternative approach sees the achievement of national interests as a dynamic process, in which a nation has a different focus at different times. Different interests play different roles under different domestic circumstances and in different international situations.

Since the notion of national security has gradually expanded in scope from its traditional military, political, and economic meaning to include non-traditional connotations such as society, the environment, and culture, a much broader concept has gradually come to depict the mainstream orientation of international security. Xi Jinping has set out the core values of this new concept of security to include mutual trust, mutual benefit, equality, and cooperation, which need to be studied from both their theoretical and practical perspectives.

Finally, China needs to assess carefully the risks to its national security. A well-known quotation from *Master Zuo Qiuming's Spring and Autumn Annals* (左传) reminds us that 'to be alert to danger in times of peace means mental preparedness, which in turn ensures security'. China must therefore establish systems for assessing and regulating its national strategic objectives that are in line with international development trends and appropriate for its own domestic situation.

Bibliography

Black, L., and Y. J. Hwang. 2012. China and Japan's quest for great power status: Norm entrepreneurship in anti-piracy responses. *International Relations* 26(4): 431–451.

Buzan (2010). China in international society: Is 'peaceful rise' possible? *The Chinese Journal of International Politics*, 3(1): 1–32.

Clinton, H. R. 2010. Remarks on regional architecture in Asia: Principles and priorities. US Department of State. [online]. Available at http://www.state.gov/secretary/rm/2010/01/135090.htm. Accessed 12 Jan 2010.

Goldstein, A. 2007. An emerging China's emerging grand strategy: A neo-Bismarckian turn? In *International relations theory and the Asia-Pacific*, eds. G. J. Ikenberry, and M. Mastanduno, 57–106. New York: Columbia University Press.

Guowuyuan bangongshi. 2011. Zhongguo de heping fazhan. [China's peaceful development]. [online]. Available at http://politics.people.com.cn/GB/1026/15598619.html. Accessed 6 Sep 2011.

Kang, D. C. 2007. *China rising: Peace, power and order in East Asia.* New York: Columbia University Press.

Le, Y. C. 2010. Dui guoji xingshi he Zhongguo waijiao de yixie kanfa yu sikao. [Some views and thinking on the international situation and China's diplomacy]. *Waijiao pinglun* 6: 1–10.

Lu, Z. W. (ed.). 2003. *Fei chuantong anquan lun.* [*Non-traditional security theory*]. Beijing: Current Affairs Press.

Mao, Z. D. 1999. Gongzuo fangfa 60 tiao (cao'an). [60 methods of work (draft)]. *Mao Zedong wenji* 7: 355.

Men, H. H. 2003. Zhongguo guojia zhanlue liyi de tuozhan. [The prolongation of China's national strategic interests]. *Strategy and Management* 2: 88–89.

——— 2004. Xin anquanguan, lihai gongtongti, zhanlue tongdao – Guanyu Zhongguo anquan liyi de yizhong jiedu. [The new security concept, interest community, strategic transportation channels – An interpretation of China's security interests]. *Jiaoxue yu yanjiu* 8: 54–58.

——— 2010. East Asian order formation and Sino–Japanese relations. *Indiana Journal of Global Legal Studies* 17(1): 47–82.

——— 2012. Zhongguo jueqi jiqi zhanlue duiying. [China's rise and its strategic response]. *Guoji guancha* 3: 9–16.

People's Daily. 2013. Sanzhong quanhui jueding sheli guojia anquan weiyuanhui. [The 3rd Plenum of the 18th Congress of the Chinese Communist Party Decided to Establish the State Security Council]. [online]. Available at http://military.people.com.cn/n/2013/1113/c1011-23521979.html. Accessed 12 Nov 2013.

Qin, Y. Q. 2010. Guoji tixi de yanxu he biange. [The continuity and change of the international system]. *Waijiao pinglun* 1: 7.

Ramo, J. C. 2004. *The Beijing consensus.* London: The Foreign Policy Centre.

Segal, G. 2007. East Asia and the 'constraintment' of China. *International Security* 20(4): 107–135.

Song, D. X. 2010. Guoji guanxi zhong de liliang yunyong: cezhong yu Zhongguo fangmian de fenxi. [The use of power in international relations: A case study of China]. *Waijiao pinglun* 6: 66–75.

Xi, J.P. 2013. Genghao tongchou guonei guoji liangge daju, hangshi zou heping fazhan daolu de jichu. [Coordinating both China's domestic situation and the global situation in a more effective manner, China should adhere to its peaceful development policy]. *Renmin Ribao*, p. 1. 30 January 2013.

Xiao, X. 2010. DongbeiYa feichuantong anquan: wenti lingyu yu hezuo moshi. [Non-traditional security in northeast Asia: Problem areas and cooperation models]. *Dongbeiya luntan* 2: 42–48.

——— 2011. Guanyu Zhongguo anquan zhanlue de ruogan sikao. [Some thoughts on China's security strategy]. *Lilun shiye* 6: 51–54.

Xinhuanet. 2013. Zhongguo Gongchandang di shibajie zhongyang weiyuanhui disanci quanti huiyi gongbao (cao'an). [The Communiqué of the Third Plenary Session of the 18th Central Committee of the Communist Party of China (draft)]. [online]. Available at http://news.xinhuanet.com/house/suzhou/2013-11-12/c_118113773.htm. Accessed 12 Nov 2013.

Yu, Z. L. 2010. Lun dangqian guoji tixi biange de jiben tezheng. [On the basic characteristics of the transformation of the current international system]. *Shijie jingji yu zhengzhi* 6: 1–8.

Zhu, F. 2010. *Chongfan Yazhou zhanlue yu Aobama zhengfu de DongYa qiangshi waijiao*. [The return-to-Asia strategy' and the Obama administration's strong diplomacy in East Asia]. *Guoji zhanglue yanjiu jianbao* 49: 1–4.

11

China as a Leading State in the International System

Christopher R. Hughes

Since China emerged from the 2008 global financial crisis with its economic power relative to the USA considerably strengthened, the question has arisen as to how its leadership role in the international system will develop. This discussion has been made more urgent by perceptions of increasing Chinese assertiveness across a range of issues, from the Copenhagen conference on climate change to reaction to the sale of arms to Taiwan by the USA, but especially in the conduct of maritime territorial disputes. When Xi Jinping was appointed General Secretary of the Communist Part of China (CPC) in November 2012 and President of the People's Republic of China (PRC) in March 2013, further questions arose when he made a number of policy statements advocating preparing

C.R. Hughes (✉)
Department of International Relations, London School of Economics, London, UK
e-mail: c.r.hughes@lse.ac.uk

S. Tsang, H. Men (eds.), *China in the Xi Jinping Era*,
The Nottingham China Policy Institute Series,
DOI 10.1007/978-3-319-29549-7_11

the military for battle and articulating the new ideological slogan of fulfilling the 'China Dream'.[1]

At first sight, it might seem inappropriate to ask about China's international leadership role, given its long-standing claim to uphold the principle of state sovereignty, oppose international 'hegemony', and locate itself as part of the developing world. Yet the country has long occupied a special position in the international system. Legally, this is most obvious in its status as a permanent seat on the United Nations Security Council (UNSC). Militarily, the PRC had started to consolidate a special status by becoming a nuclear weapons power even before it took over the China seat from the Republic of China (ROC) in 1971. Politically, the period of revolutionary diplomacy under the leadership of Chairman Mao Zedong can also be seen as an attempt to exert a form of international political leadership that was partly forced on China by exclusion from the United Nations (UN) system. China continued to play a special role after the demise of Mao's revolutionism, when it became one of the corners of the strategic triangle with the USA and the Soviet Union that shaped the political dynamics of the late Cold War system. At present, it is trying to gain more political influence through the development of 'soft power'.

Now that China has the second biggest economy in the world and the second largest defence expenditure, the question arises as to whether its growing power will be used in the service of its special position to shape more actively the international system. Inside China, much of the discussion on this topic is still rooted in the exceptionalist claim that it will be different from previous rising powers. Much of this has focused on the insistence that China's rise will not be like that of militaristic Germany and Japan because it will be characterized by 'peaceful development' leading to a 'harmonious world', and that its role will be different from the negative 'hegemonic way' (*ba dao*) of the USA because it will be legitimated by a special kind of 'righteous way' (*wang dao*).[2]

Broad discussions of the rise of China by political activists, academics, and popular writers inside the country thus propose a range of

[1] Xinhuanet, "Xi Guangzhou zhanqu kaocha."

[2] For a survey of recent literature to this effect see Hughes, "Reclassifying Chinese Nationalism," 601–620.

exceptionalist arguments. There has also been a flourishing of advice on how it can develop a reserve of 'soft power' that will allow it to be able to lead by attraction. These include the possibility that influence can be exerted through a Chinese economic model that is better than the Washington Consensus for the developing world and superior to the 'casino capitalism' practised by the advanced industrialized economies. Others look to China's particular cultural heritage to propose that it can forge models of international stability that are very different from the post-Westphalian system of equal sovereign states by returning to the kind of hierarchical order characterized by the *tianxia* tribute system of the imperial tradition.[3] Straddling these poles is the attempt by Tsinghua University's Professor Yan Xuetong to combine the practices and principles of Chinese tradition with those of the modern state system to arrive at a theory that combines hierarchy with legal equality between states.[4] Even those who believe that it is necessary to divert more resources into building hard power for an inevitable conflict with the USA and its allies claim that this will still follow the *wang dao* because it will be a necessary measure to create international stability in the face of foreign aggression.[5]

One of the biggest problems for observers of Chinese foreign policy is establishing the degree to which any of these views are held by key decision makers and feed through into policy initiatives and strategic thinking. In this chapter an attempt will be made to establish this by looking at recent developments in the practice of Chinese foreign and security policy at the level of regional policy in the Asia Pacific, relationships with major powers at the global level, and behaviour in international organizations. First, however, it is necessary to look at how the position of the Chinese government increasingly reflects the fundamental tension between an old attachment to a conception of the international system based on a conservative understanding of state sovereignty on the one hand, and the pressures for a more assertive leading role that arise from rapid economic growth on the other hand.

---

[3] Zhao, "Rethinking Empire," 21–36.

[4] Yan, Ancient Chinese Thought.

[5] Liu, Zhongguo meng.

Grand Strategy and 'Core Interests'

The general shift away from foreign policy conservatism towards more assertiveness can be seen first of all by looking at recent developments in China's grand strategy. It is somewhat surprising that a number of scholars propose that the country does not have such a strategy, because its government and the Communist Party have always gone to great efforts to rationalize foreign policy actions in terms of guiding principles and objectives. This used to be summed up by formulas such as the Five Principles for Peaceful Coexistence and an emphasis on creating a peaceful environment for economic development under Reform and Opening. Since 2008, the most significant development in this grand strategy has been the enumeration of non-negotiable 'core interests'. These were stated most systematically by State Councillor Dai Bingguo at the China–US Strategic and Economic Dialogue in Washington, July 2009, as:

- Defend fundamental systems and national security;
- Preserve national sovereignty and unification;
- Maintain steady and sustainable development of the economy and society.[6]

To some degree, this list shows continuity with China's long-established emphasis on rejecting actions that might be seen as interference in the country's internal affairs and insisting on the goal of national unification. Yet there are some very important new implications. For example, whereas the call to preserve national sovereignty and unification tended to focus on gaining control of Taiwan in the past, in recent years it has been increasingly applied (if ambiguously at times) to the broader issues of maritime territorial disputes with neighbouring states in South East Asia and Japan.

This expansion of the scope and importance of territorial claims gains additional significance from labelling the 'steady and sustainable development of economy and society' a 'core interest'. Because a geopolitical case can be made that access to the natural resources that feed China's industrialization requires control over maritime territories, such a principle

[6] People's Daily. "Respect China's National Interests."

effectively institutionalizes a non-negotiable linkage between the economic growth that is necessary to keep the CPC in power and the politics of domestic nationalism. In other words, as China's economy grows, an assertive foreign policy becomes ever more tightly linked to the legitimacy of the CPC, not just for nationalistic ideological reasons, but also for material reasons linked to growing wealth. How this shapes strategic thinking can be seen in the security challenges listed in the 2010 Defence White Paper, which go well beyond the expression of long-standing fears over the activities of forces for 'independence' in Taiwan, Xinjiang, and Tibet to include the need to secure 'vast territories and territorial seas', 'maritime rights and interests', 'non-traditional security concerns', and 'external suspicion and interference towards the rise of China'.[7]

It is crucial to understand these linkages between domestic politics and foreign policy to assess whether China will be able to follow the path of 'peaceful development' that began to be espoused under the leadership of CPC General Secretary Hu Jintao. Whether such an outcome is sustainable will depend not only on managing relationships with regional and global powers but also on how the pressures that arise from the conflation of nationalism with a growing perception that the legitimacy of CPC rule should be judged by not compromising on issues that fall under the rubric of 'core interests' which now extend well beyond older problems such as the pursuit of the claim to Taiwan, to the disputed maritime territories in the East and South China Seas, and even the security of sea lanes vital for maintaining economic growth.

Various options are available for trying to reconcile this dilemma between a diplomatic stance that advocates 'peaceful development' and the mission of protecting 'core interests' that is driven largely by concerns over the CPC's domestic legitimacy. These range from working with and shaping existing international institutions and regimes to unilateral deployment of the various foreign policy instruments that are given potency by the country's growing reserves of economic, military, and possibly soft power. How these options are being experimented with can be seen, first of all, by looking at how China's regional policy is shaped by the combination of its grand strategy and the need to respond to domestic pressures.

---

[7] State Council, "China's National Defense."

Regional Leadership

After the 1997 Asian Financial Crisis, China surprised most observers by departing from the state-centric foreign policy it had clung to during the Cold War to promote actively regional multilateralism. This proved to be a remarkably effective dimension of its foreign policy because it generated substantial economic power and influence through integration with neighbouring states. Equally important is that it also enhanced China's soft power, as credit could be claimed for taking a leading role in initiatives that stabilized the regional financial system through measures such as the Chiang Mai currency swap scheme and the promotion of trade liberalization through the China–ASEAN Free Trade Agreement. On the security front, China could also claim to be building multilateralism as a member of the ASEAN Regional Forum (ARF), as a founding member of the Shanghai Cooperation Organisation (SCO) and as host of the Six Party Talks to address the stability and denuclearization of the Korean Peninsula.

Even though Beijing continued to reject the idea of great power politics, such initiatives to avoid and control cries that could lead to larger conflicts are compatible with the behaviour of a great power as defined by Hedley Bull of the English School of International Relations. Theory, such as Hedley Bull. From a constructivist perspective, China was also successful in shaping international norms at the regional level because its restrictive vision of state sovereignty and the principle of non-interference is mirrored by the values enshrined in the ASEAN Charter. It was thus possible to use largely diplomatic instruments to form a common front with authoritarian regimes to block the more liberal visions espoused by democratic states.[8]

The general result of these initiatives was to make China a diplomatic and economic partner for South East Asia, but in an increasingly asymmetric relationship as the rapid deepening of regional economic integration provided it with new instruments for the pursuit of non-economic goals. This has become increasingly clear with the growth in Chinese assertiveness over maritime territorial claims in the South China Sea. The reasons for this are complex, with the immediate trigger being the submission

[8] Hughes, "China's Membership of ARF," 54–71.

of claims by Vietnam and the Philippines to the UN in accordance with the May 2009 deadline set under the United Nations Convention on the Law of the Sea (UNCLOS). Yet China's responses have involved the use of both hard power and economic influence, with the despatch of a combination of paramilitary coastguard vessels and People's Liberation Army Navy (PLAN) vessels and the use of economic sanctions. Most remarkable among these was the targeting of the Philippines by using customs inspections to slow its exports of bananas to China and warnings to Chinese tourists that their safety could not be guaranteed.

These actions are significant not only because they were effective in forcing Manila to soften its stance, but also because economic sanctions had not been used in this way before and China's tough posture was a long way from the low profile and 'good neighbour' policy that had previously prevailed. Moreover, the linkage between domestic politics and a foreign policy based on the pursuit of 'core interests' could be seen in the way that Beijing's tough rhetoric was echoed by a rising tide of domestic nationalist passions that had found a new target in the Philippines, with commentators calling for military action against this relatively weak state so as to send a signal to more powerful adversaries, such as India and Japan.

A similar dynamic can be seen in China's relationship with Japan. Managing the territorial disputes between the two countries in the East China Sea presents a far more sensitive issue for China's leaders, partly because Japan is far more prosperous and powerful than any of the South East Asian states. Yet the situation is complicated even more by the way in which frictions between the two countries are politicized by a nationalistic public opinion, shaped by memories of Japan's wartime aggression and the atrocities that the CPC has done much to keep alive as part of the legitimating narrative of the party that claims to have 'saved China'. This dynamic can be seen in the reaction to the arrest of the skipper of a Chinese trawler that had rammed two coastguard vessels in waters near the Senkaku/Diaoyu islands in September 2010. While this dispute has flared up periodically since China (and the ROC on Taiwan) began to claim the islands in the early 1970s, what was new this time was the way in which China was able to use its economic leverage to punish Japan, in the form of veiled threats to suspend the export of rare earth metals and divert the flow of Chinese tourists.

Such actions in the maritime territorial disputes give a clear indication of whether China is moving towards a foreign policy in which challenges to 'core interests' will be managed through international regimes and the attraction of soft power or by the exertion of the country's growing economic and military power. That the movement is towards the latter is shown by China's refusal to go to arbitration, despite the growing alarm of its neighbours. Instead, a strategy has been developed of asserting China's claims by taking measures that can call into question the claims to legal title over the territories based on the principle of effective control, through actions such as patrols by Chinese coastguard vessels around the Senkaku/Diaoyu Islands and naval patrols and the building of permanent structures on islands in the South China Sea.

This, of course, raises serious concerns over the drift of China's regional policy away from its successful multilateralism and towards something more in tune with the hegemony (*ba dao*) that its leaders and diplomats claim to eschew. This tension, and the seriousness with which the Xi Jinping administration views this perception, can be gauged from the fact that the CPC Central Committee held a conference at the end of October 2013 in Beijing to hammer out a diplomatic strategy towards neighbouring countries for the next five to ten years.[9] Xi's speech at this event encapsulates the dynamic tension between the economic dimension and nationalism, calling on the one hand for diplomatic work with neighbouring countries to serve the needs of realizing the 'centenary goals' of economic development,[10] while on the other hand advocating the nationalistic ambition of achieving the 'great rejuvenation of the Chinese nation'.

His emphasis, however, was firmly on reassuring neighbouring states that his leadership will stay true to the path of 'peaceful development' and the regional policy of his predecessor and the assertion that China has a friendly and mutually beneficial relationship with most of its neighbours. The basic principle of diplomacy towards them, he stressed, should be to treat them as friends and partners, make them feel safe, and help them

[9] Nation, "Xi Stresses Diplomatic Work."

[10] The first of the 'centenary goals' is to double both GDP and per capita income by 2020 on the basis of the 2010 level by the centenary of the establishment of the CCP in 1921; the second is to turn China into a socialist modernized country that will be 'rich, strong, democratic, culturally advanced and harmonious' by the centenary of the establishment of the PRC in 1949.

to develop, winning China more friends and partners by highlighting friendship, sincerity, benefit, and inclusiveness. His concrete initiatives also remained firmly fixed on the belief that economic integration will lead to regional stability, especially through infrastructure connectivity under projects such as the building of the new Silk Road economic belt, a 'Maritime Silk Road of the 21st century', and the acceleration of the implementation of a free trade zone strategy. He also made what looks like an overture to the USA by stressing that the Asia-Pacific region is big enough for all countries to develop and that countries in the region must promote regional cooperation with an open mind and with greater enthusiasm.

The tension between such reassuring diplomatic statements and actions in the arena of foreign and security policy, however, was dramatically illustrated in the month following Xi's speech when the PRC made the unilateral declaration of an Air Defence Identification Zone (ADIZ) in the East China Sea. Despite PRC claims that this was a legitimate measure that would help to prevent military accidents, it was viewed by Japan as a highly provocative act due to the lack of prior consultation, the inclusion of territory claimed by Japan, and for giving China's armed forces the responsibility to adopt defensive emergency measures against aircraft that do not declare their identity or refuse to follow instructions. This was only the most recent reason for the countries of the region to be concerned over China's willingness to resort to hard power, following on from incidents such as the fixing of a fire-control radar on a Japan Maritime Self-Defense Force vessel in January that year and the development of projects such as the commissioning of the aircraft carrier *Liaoning* in September the previous year, as well as the development of a new generation of fighter planes that would be most useful in a conflict with Japan.

To borrow Bull's terminology,[11] this type of behaviour might be described as symptomatic of a state that is moving from a position of primacy, in which other states are increasingly conceding leadership, towards one of domination through an increasing tendency to use force and economic coercion. As would be expected by both the English School and realist international relations theory, this is leading to power-balancing by neighbouring states through the acquisition and deployment of

[11] Bull, The Anarchical Society, 213–215.

beefed-up defence and coastguard capabilities and the strengthening and forging of new bilateral and trilateral modes of defence cooperation.

This growing sense of threat in the region presents the USA with a dilemma. Any signal that Washington is conceding to Beijing's demands threatens to undermine its credibility as a stabilizing force in the region in the eyes of its allies. Under the rubric of President Obama's 'Asia pivot', Washington has thus overseen a revival, confirmation, and strengthening of old defence commitments with its allies, and there has been a remarkable improvement in the relationship with Vietnam. Japan, the USA's most powerful ally, is finally responding to Washington's long-standing call for it to take on more of the security burden. The new national security strategy unveiled by the Abe administration thus openly declares the mission to develop military capacity that is specifically aimed at countering the threat from China. On the diplomatic front, Prime Minister Abe has also invested more time in touring the region and ploughing large amounts of foreign investment into the relatively impoverished South East Asian states, such as Myanmar and Cambodia, which had previously fallen under largely Chinese influence.

A 'New Type of Great Power Relationship'?

China has had to respond to these reactions to its assertiveness by trying to develop ways to manage its interaction with the USA under the formula of a 'new type of great power relationship'. That the USA is the main focus of this slogan can be seen from the fact that it was first aired by Xi when he visited Washington in February 2012, preparing the ground for his appointment as Chairman of the CPC the following November. Following that, it was raised in May 2012 by then President Hu Jintao and State Councillor Dai Bingguo at the US–China Strategic and Economic Dialogue in Beijing. After he had been appointed Chairman of the CPC and President of the PRC, Xi again brought it up in a discussion with President Obama at the informal meeting between the two leaders at Sunnylands, in June 2013.[12]

---

[12] Wacker, "China-Europe Relations."

So far, what the new type of partnership will involve has been explained more in terms of attitudes than concrete policy measures. These include: respecting each side's 'core interests and major concerns'; deepening mutually beneficial cooperation; and enhancing cooperation and coordination in international affairs and on global issues. An article co-authored by Beijing's ambassador to Washington in 2012, was slightly more specific in proposing that the lack of strategic mutual trust can be overcome if core national interests can be accommodated, the principle of treating each other as equals can be implemented, and the composition of trade can be restructured.[13]

In addition to the lack of detail on how this list of aspirations might be put into practice, what the new formula says about China's international role is made more problematic by the tendency of Chinese commentators and policy makers to expect Washington to take positive measures rather than Beijing. China naturally wants the USA to respect its 'core interests' through measures such as ceasing arms transfers to Taiwan and giving up the idea of 'peaceful evolution' (the belief that the USA is trying to undermine China's political system through the use of soft power). But the Americans take a more pragmatic stance based on confidence building, summed up when White House security advisor Tom Donilon tried to interpret the new formula in terms of military–military relations, economic relations, and the problem of cyber-security during a visit to China in May 2013. The lack of clarity has ultimately led to confusion, with some academic commentators in the USA hoping that the formula can produce a durable foundation for a good relationship, while others cannot see much difference from the old mantra of the Five Principles of Peaceful Co-existence.[14]

Concerns that there is little to distinguish the formula from traditional notions of great power politics and the carving out of spheres of influence are only exacerbated when Chinese leaders seem to imply that a new Monroe Doctrine is in the making, as when Xi Jinping remarked in Washington that the Pacific Ocean is big enough for both China and the USA. This also seems to imply a new hierarchy of great powers, which creates the danger of alienating some of the states with which China has

[13] Cui and Pang, "China-US Relations."

[14] Wacker, "China-Europe Relations."

been striving to build strategic partnerships to promote a multipolar global system since the end of the Cold War. Russia is particularly sensitive in this regard, being China's main arms supplier and diplomatic ally in the UNSC. That Xi Jinping is aware of the danger of alienating this would-be great power was made clear when he made it the destination of his first overseas visit after becoming Chairman of the CPC and President of the PRC. While there, he explained how the relationship was one of China's most important and also the best of its relationships with the major powers, serving as an important guarantee of international strategic balance and world peace and stability.

The same problem arises with groups of states such as the European Union and the BRICS. Yang Jiemian, president of the Shanghai Institutes for International Studies, has thus argued that although the formula of the new type of major power relationship has originated from thinking about US–China relations, it can also embrace both traditional major powers such as Europe and Japan and emerging powers like the BRICS. The relationship with Russia can thus be taken as a model, with the USA as the focal point, the BRICS as the growth point, the EU as the effort point, and Japan as the hard point.[15]

Yet such complex arguments are more a reflection of an awareness of the problems inherent in trying to formulate a new model of great power politics than a sign of clarity over who is to be included in this privileged relationship. Qu Xing, President of the China Institute of International Studies (CIIS), for example, argues that the BRICS states cannot fall under the category of the 'new type of great power relationship' because they are not established powers. The status of the EU also appears to be problematic because, although Qu sees it as an established great power, it does not perceive the development of China as a threat, but primarily as an economic competitor. Qu says nothing about whether Russia and Japan should also be seen as great powers by China.[16]

If Bull is right to say that one of the roles of a great power in maintaining international order is to limit the likelihood of war by reducing misunderstandings and misinterpretations between great powers and to

[15] Yang, "Xinxing daguo guanxi."

[16] Wacker, "China-Europe Relations."

settle disputes through negotiations,[17] then it seems unlikely that the idea of a 'new type of great power relationship' will do much to alleviate the fears that are growing over the rise of Chinese power. According to more liberal theorists, such as John Ikenberry, the way to avoid such dilemmas is for a rising power to engage in building the kind of international regimes and organizations that will effectively constrain its own room for manoeuvre in ways that assuage the concerns of potential rivals and thus avoid the appearance of the security dilemmas that so often lead to international instability and conflict. When assessing the nature of China's growing international role it is thus important to look at the third dimension of its foreign policy, namely its approach to international organizations and regimes.

International Organizations and Regimes

How China behaves in the UN is a good place to start, because its veto-holding power in the Security Council gives it a special power to uphold, promote, and shape norms that is shared by only four other states in what is supposed to be the supreme arena for international politics. Despite its long-standing claim to be an advocate of a restrictive view of state sovereignty and non-interference and its claim to be protecting states in the developing world from creeping interventionism, in practice China has been reluctant to use this privilege in ways that confront or antagonize the other major powers. Apart from occasional cases in which it perceives a direct threat to its national interests, it has preferred to abstain from resolutions to impose sanctions or engage in military intervention, rather than cast its veto.

That the globalization of China's economy is making this stance increasingly anachronistic, however, has become quite apparent as the country has been called on to take a stance on issues around the world in which it now has direct material interests. This first dilemma initially emerged when international non-governmental organizations (INGOs) revealed the activities of its oil industry in the Darfur region of Sudan, where a civil war was degenerating into what many observers labelled genocide.

[17] Bull, The Anarchical Society, 213.

Beijing resisted calls for the UN to impose targeted sanctions against Sudan's political leaders in 2005, but by 2008 the crisis was threatening to spoil the propaganda coup of the Beijing Summer Olympics. The Chinese government was also facing domestic calls to do more to protect Chinese assets and personnel in the world's hot spots. It finally reacted by dispatching a special representative to mediate between the warring parties, resulting in a peace process that led to the partition of the country and the establishment of an independent South Sudan by referendum. China then became one of the first countries to recognize the independence of the new state, in July 2011, and establish an embassy at the capital, Juba. Its role did not stop there, as investments in Sudan's oil industry made it the target of South Sudanese anger over disagreements between the two sides over access to oil resources.

That these interventions show a move away from the old orthodoxy of the Five Principles of Peaceful Coexistence is indicated by the fact that some Chinese commentators now present this as a positive example of the way in which their country is playing the kind of responsible role that inevitably accrues from being a major international economic presence. Moreover, involvement in Sudan set the context for China's role in the Arab Spring. The evacuation of some 32,000 out of 37,000 Chinese citizens working for around 75 Chinese firms in Libya's oil, transport, and industrial infrastructure sectors again reveals how out of date it is to claim that China is not involved in the domestic affairs of other states. Yet formulating a response to the popular movement for political change in the Middle East and North Africa (MENA) presents a number of problems for Beijing. Primary amongst these is the concern that support for international intervention could be turned against China itself if a similar type of domestic protest movement were to erupt there.

Despite these fears, maintaining a stance of 'non-interference' has been particularly problematic because pressure for intervention in Libya came not only from the Western powers but also from the Arab League. Faced by calls in the Security Council for a vote on armed intervention to protect the opposition to the Gaddafi regime, China abstained instead of using its veto. While this avoided a head-on clash with significant sections of the international community, it still left China shouldering the burden of bad publicity with the opposition forces that eventually replaced the Gaddafi regime. Despite this, concerns over the spectacle of Western intervention leading to regime change combined with geostrategic calculations about the implications of new international alignments in the Middle East led Beijing to revert to its more conservative stance when the political unrest spread to Syria and to join with Russia to block three Security Council resolutions designed to put pressure on the Assad regime.

Yet this successful action should not be understood as just a reversion to the old principle of non-interference, when China had nothing like today's global reach. Instead, it is an indication of the kind of leadership that the country is beginning to play in shaping global norms, a position that was made quite clear when the Presidents of Russia and China, buoyed by the failure of President Obama and UK Prime Minister Cameron to secure their own domestic support for the use of military force, met at the Asia-Pacific Economic Cooperation (APEC) summit in Bali in October 2013 and presented their veto of Western interventionism as an example of how the bilateral relationship could be deepened to 'resolve urgent and acute international and regional issues'.[18]

This great-power alignment with Russia in the UN is a good example of how China is using its growing influence to revert to rather traditional power-balancing in international organizations. Yet this great power approach also raises new dilemmas with elements of the Global South, with which China has traditionally identified itself. Rather than give up such a status, China is attempting to adapt to the world of globalization by aligning with a broader coalition of developing states to shape international organizations and regimes under the rubric of South–South relations. The most advanced manifestation of this is the BRICS club that brings Brazil, India, and South Africa into alignment with China and Russia. Claiming to represent about one-quarter of global GDP and wielding significant financial and trade power when working together, these states have been trying to cooperate on an increasing range of global issues.

On the diplomatic front this has already matured into the stage of convening a regular BRICS summit. In September 2013, the members of this club came up with a concrete proposal to establish a BRICS development bank, to be capitalized with $50 billion, as part of a foreign exchange

[18] Jazeera, "China, Russia at APEC."

reserve pool of $100 billion. That there is a geopolitical dimension to such economic measures was made clear when New Delhi also proposed cooperation in establishing a reinsurer for large infrastructure projects. While such projects are economically important for emerging markets, it was also presented as a way to respond to sanctions imposed by Western countries, such as those related to Iran—an important supplier of oil to both India and China.[19] Yet the fact that China's contribution of $41 billion to this pool dwarfs those of any of the other states (all will contribute $18 billion, with South Africa only adding $5 billion) shows that it may be more accurate to call the BRICS phenomenon more of a recentring of global economic power than a rebalancing between North and South. When it was announced in July 2014 that the headquarters of the bank would be located in Shanghai rather than New Delhi, Brazilian President Dilma Rousseff had to fend off suspicions that it was merely replacing the US hegemony with a Chinese hegemony.[20] In other words, the rapid growth of the Chinese economy, coupled with the size and structure of the Chinese market, makes it increasingly difficult to present the formation of a South–South alignment as a partnership of equals.

As well as presenting China with a dilemma in its attempts to continue presenting itself as a part of the developing world against the developed, the emergence of a new type of export dependency also creates problems for how China is perceived within the states of the Global South. This has become particularly clear in Africa. Since this relationship came to the attention of many scholars with the grand spectacle of the 2006 Forum on China–Africa Cooperation (FOCAC) in Beijing, much attention has been focused on the tension that is developing between elites who benefit from Chinese investment and the grass roots of societies in which workers, farmers, and small businesses and traders have felt no benefit at best and have been driven out of their own jobs and markets at worst. Such tensions have already broken the surface in episodes such as strikes in Chinese-owned companies, attacks and kidnappings of Chinese employees, and the use of anti-Chinese sentiments to mobilize popular support in election campaigns. The fact that China's influence on socio-

[19] Economic Times, "BRICS Nations."

[20] Leahy and Rathbone, "China Hovers Over Brics."

economic development may be as exploitative and distorting as that of the old imperial and hegemonic powers makes it difficult to present its growing footprint in the developing world in terms of a rhetoric that is still rooted in the revolutionary anti-colonialism of the 1950s.[21]

Policy Making and International Leadership

The above brief survey of recent developments in China's foreign policy should be sufficient to illustrate the complex nature of the challenges that arise for a rising power in an age of globalization. How Beijing will manage this process, however, depends not only on stated goals but also on the capacity of its political system to deliver those goals. In his groundbreaking neo-classical realist analysis of the rise of US power in the 19th century, Fareed Zakaria points out the need for a state to have effective, centralized policy-making processes and institutions in place if it is to be able to marshal its economic resources behind its foreign policy.[22] This is equally true for China as it grapples with the kinds of dilemmas outlined above, although on a much larger scale. While the central government in Beijing has clarified the nation's core interests and the CPC is good at drawing up the long-term economic strategies that are supposed to determine the broad parameters of foreign policy, implementation on the ground has appeared to be increasingly haphazard. When trying to understand Xi Jinping's slogan of the 'China Dream', it is thus hard to reconcile the lack of consistency between proclamations of 'peaceful development' and 'harmonious world' on the one hand, and calls for a stronger military and the implementation of assertive actions towards Japan and several South East Asian states on the other.

One possible explanation for this inconsistency is a lack of coordination between the growing number of actors with an interest in foreign and security issues in an increasingly pluralistic society. Leading Chinese international relations scholars have in fact been calling attention to the need for better foreign policy coordination to deal with this problem for

[21] Alden and Hughes, "China's Africa Strategy," 563.

[22] Zakaria, From Wealth to Power.

many years. In their seminal article on new actors in Chinese foreign policy, Jakobson and Knox have developed this argument further, pointing to the likelihood that an increasing number of new actors is having an impact on foreign policy making.[23] Most obvious at the regional level is the danger of miscalculation that arises from the actions regarding the maritime territorial disputes launched by low-level agencies, the proliferation of which has been well documented in a report on the South China Sea tensions by the International Crisis Group.[24]

If this is occurring, then it is having a seriously detrimental effect on efforts by organizations such as the Ministry of Foreign Affairs and various propaganda organs of the Chinese state to accumulate soft power by presenting an image of China as following a path of 'peaceful development'. This is shown by a new public opinion survey by the Pew Research Centre on global attitudes towards the USA and China, published in July 2014. Even at a time when the USA is seen as weakened by economic crisis and political partisanship and discredited by the Snowden revelations about Internet surveillance, its positive perception across Asia still boasts a regional median of 66 %, against China's 61 %. Only Malaysia bucks the trend and has a higher positive perception of China among the countries surveyed. What should be of most concern to advocates of China's peaceful rise is that all the states surveyed showed a majority who are concerned that territorial disputes with China will lead to a military conflict, with even Pakistan only just bucking the trend at 49 % believing in such an eventuality.[25]

Particularly significant, given their country's history of warfare with it, is that even 76 % of Vietnamese have a more positive opinion of the USA than of China, with 84 % concerned about a military conflict. This underlying public concern was demonstrated in dramatic fashion with the eruption of anti-Chinese protests and riots in response to the movement of an oil rig by the China National Offshore Petroleum Corporation to waters near the disputed Paracel Islands in the South China Sea on 2 May 2014. This grass-roots explosion was a reaction to a Chinese action

[23] Jakobson and Knox, "Foreign Policy in China."
[24] International Crisis Group, "South China Sea."
[25] Pew Global, "Asia Worry About Conflict."

that was widely seen as a response to a commitment by President Obama to the defence of the Senkakus in a speech in Tokyo on 24 April, during a tour of regional allies, designed to present his vision of a 'rebalancing of the world's largest region'; and modernizing alliances[26] may serve as a stark illustration of the dilemmas that arise from playing the global balance of power while simultaneously trying to develop soft power. To get such a balancing act right requires remarkable capacities for intelligence gathering at all levels and for policy coordination.

Policy dislocation might also explain why the attempt to build the 'new model of a great power relationship' with the USA has been badly implemented. One of the most notorious examples of conflicting messages in this respect was the unveiling by the Chinese air force of a new stealth fighter plane during a confidence-building mission by Defence Secretary Robert Gates, only for President Hu Jintao to deny any awareness of the event. Gates's own account of the incident makes it clear he was certain Hu was genuinely non-plussed.[27] Not surprisingly, Gates asked his host to clarify whether the increasing number of hawkish books and articles that have been appearing in China represent the views of elements of the military.

China's reputation has also suffered from an apparent lack of coordination when dealing with international organizations. Little confidence is generated in its ability to comply with agreements by incidents such as Beijing's denial of any knowledge that a Chinese company was selling arms to the Gaddafi regime during the Libyan revolution, in breach of the UN sanctions that China had itself tacitly accepted. Far more serious for the country's reputation was the behaviour at the Copenhagen conference on climate change. Despite having made efforts to improve performance by sending a delegation composed of experts on the domestic dimensions of the issues drawn from the National Development and Reform Commission (NDRC) and experienced negotiators from the Ministry of Foreign Affairs, the discussion descended into debacle when it was hijacked by a higher ranking delegation that parachuted in under Premier Wen Jiabao.[28] The net result was that China was blamed for the

[26] White House, "The President's Trip."

[27] Gates, Call of Duty, 527–528.

[28] Conrad, "China in Copenhagen," 435–455.

failure of the conference to reach agreement on the crucial problem of climate change, antagonizing not only the developed world but also the states of the developing world.

Just short of six months after Xi Jinping became President of the PRC, the importance of improving policy coordination was addressed in an article entitled 'Innovations in China's Diplomatic Theory and Practice Under New Conditions', by State Councillor and former Foreign Minister Yang Jiechi, who now heads the Central Committee Leading Group on foreign policy. A large section of this focuses on proposals on how to uphold 'core national interests' by improving top-level design and strategic planning in diplomatic work and on 'the need for enhanced coordination in diplomatic work to ensure unified central leadership over the operations'. Pointing out that Xi Jinping had repeatedly called for stronger top-level design and medium to long-term strategic planning in diplomatic work, Yang goes on to elaborate how the Central Committee attaches great importance to a holistic management of foreign affairs, balanced considerations, overall planning, unified command, and coordinated implementation. More specifically, he points out that this requires the central and local governments, NGOs, and all foreign-related agencies to work together to form a synergy, with each performing their respective functions. Central to this task, according to Yang, is the striking of a balance between fully motivating all the parties involved and sparking their creativity, while subjecting their activities to unified management guided by national interests.[29]

Xi Jinping also focuses on these themes in his October 2013 speech on regional diplomacy, where he describes coherent policies and strategies as 'the lifeline of the Party' and stresses the need to analyse and deal with issues from a strategic perspective and improve the abilities in overall planning and operational execution. It is also important to note that Xi draws attention to the fact that effective diplomatic work requires bearing in mind both the overall domestic and the international situations. This is important because it recognizes that foreign policy is increasingly to be put to the service of domestic politics by achieving the two 'Centenary Goals' of economic development and the nationalist discourse of 'the

[29] Yang, "Innovations China's Diplomatic."

great rejuvenation of the Chinese nation'. It is this relationship between economic pragmatism and nationalistic ambitions that is central to Xi's 'China Dream', as evident when he goes on to explain in his speech how foreign policy will have to both 'fight for good external conditions for China's reform, development and stability' and 'safeguard China's sovereignty, security and development interests, to safeguard world peace and stability, and to promote common development'.

Assuming that these goals will not change, the shape of China's international role will depend in large part on how successful Xi Jinping is when it comes to implementing the kind of institutional reform that will allow an effective management of the dilemmas that arise when nationalism comes into conflict with pragmatism. Yang Jiechi could claim that the Central Committee had already engaged in institution-building in foreign-related work in the six months before he wrote his article, involving the sorting out of relevant systems and mechanisms and formulating clear-cut regulations. This process was already put in train when Xi was consolidating his supreme leadership over the Party and the State, most notably with an attempt to control the growing number of coastguards involved in the maritime territorial disputes under a new State Oceanographic Administration in March 2013.

Such issue oriented reforms are unlikely to be effective, however, without more central concentration of decision-making power. A highly significant step was taken in this respect in November 2013, when the Third Plenum of the CPC's 18th Central Committee announced the formation of a State Security Council (SSC). In his contribution to this volume, Xi Xiao provides the most detailed account of this noes organ to date. As she makes clear, this is a response to the failure of China to change effectively its thinking in a period of bewildering domestic and international change, where domestic threats of secessionism come together with shifts in the global and regional balance of power in unpredictable ways. The new organization is thus designed to draw on and coordinate several ministries and areas of policy making, from foreign policy to economic development, that have a special impact on national security because they span the domestic–international divide. Yet, as Xi Xiao herself points out, the aim is to harness national power in ways that will not only create a stable situation but will also enhance China's ability to conduct international 'struggle' (*dou zheng*). An early indication of what this means in practice can be seen from the fact that the ADIZ was declared just 11 days after the SSC was announced. If this was not the result of lack of policy coordination but symptomatic of a longer-term integrated strategy, it will offer little comfort to China's neighbours.

Unfortunately, this means that a greater concentration of power in the hands of Xi may not offer much comfort to those on the receiving end of Chinese assertiveness. While Zakaria may be right to argue that the rise of the USA shows how effective, centralized institutions are necessary to convert national wealth into foreign policy power, the history of other rising states that concentrate power in the hands of strong political elites is replete with warnings. Looking at the rise of German and Japanese imperialism; for example, Jack Snyder draws on the work of historians to illustrate the political dynamics that push leaders to resort to international expansion when society is being torn asunder by competition between old and new interest groups and rising demands for popular representation and organization.[30] In such situations, the logic of domestic politics can trump the rationality of the international system, causing even the best-informed leaders to make irrational decisions, such as Germany's wars against Britain, Russia/the Soviet Union, and the USA, and Japan's attack on Pearl Harbor.

From this perspective, it is important to observe that the establishment of China's SSC is part of a broader package of policies announced at the Third Plenum, which are designed to accelerate the introduction of market mechanisms into the economy and try to reform the existing interest groups that have grown up around the state owned enterprises (SOEs). In the short term, at least, such policies are likely to intensify further the existing tensions in Chinese society over issues that range from the daily life experiences of growing inequality, environmental degradation, and job insecurity to broader concerns over the lack of political reform. It may well be the case, therefore, that Xi Jinping's 'China Dream' involves an intensifying of the relationship between economic liberalization and the strengthening of state security, legitimized by the propagation of nationalism that has always been at the heart of 'Reform and Opening'.

[30] Snyder, Myths of Empire.

Conclusion

International relations provides a number of perspectives on what it means to take a leading role in international politics. A rich debate has taken place amongst academics over which perspective is most appropriate for China. The pessimistic predictions of neo-realists like John Mearsheimer, for example, are challenged by liberal international relations theorists such as John Ikenberry, who point to the ways in which states that suddenly find themselves with unexpected degrees of power are able to build international stability and avoid the perils of power-balancing and security dilemmas by building institutions that bind their own freedom of action to some degree.[31] An irony of the current debate over China's rise, though, is that a growing number of voices inside the country argue that conflict with the USA and its allies will be hard—if not impossible—to avoid.

It has been argued above that such arguments are of little use unless they can look at how domestic politics impacts on foreign policy in ways that may lead to outcomes that appear to be irrational from the perspective of the international system. At present, China's leaders operate in a domestic environment of social dislocation caused by rapid economic and technological change that is similar to that of other late industrializing powers in history, such as Germany and Japan. Like those cases, the absence of more effective political structures of accountability and legitimacy means that the political elite has to hold on to power by challenging powerful interest groups, from industrial cartels to the military. This requires building coalitions and mobilizing nationalism to gain popular support and political capital. As those other cases show, even though nationalism may be used instrumentally in the first place, after several generations it becomes an article of faith that shapes perceptions of the world as divided into friends and foes that cannot be questioned.

This primacy of domestic politics has costs for foreign policy. Most immediately, the degree of soft power that had been so assiduously cultivated by China in the wake of the 1997 Asian Financial Crisis has

[31] John G. Ikenberry gives a more recent version of the argument, drawing on a number of historical examples, in Ikenberry, After Victory.

been squandered. Whether one concludes that these domestic dynamics are pushing China towards 'hegemony' or 'empire' in the longer term will depend to a large degree on how one understands such concepts. It seems safe to say that 19th-century-style colonization is unlikely at the start of the 21st century. Yet much of the expansion of European and American power has involved the building of informal empires. In the most aggressive cases, these have often been driven by the need to put in place counter-cyclical measures to alleviate the domestic political pressure that arises from economic imbalances, rather than by the economic fundamentals of international trade and investment.[32] It is not hard to see how China's policies of subsidizing export offensives, creating 'reserve markets' to absorb excess production, tying down natural resources, and ensuring that the nation has sufficient hard power at its disposal to protect overseas assets and supply lines fit this pattern.

Looking at Chinese foreign policy in this way is more likely to provide explanations for what appears to be inconsistencies between rhetoric and practice, whether it be in regional politics, the great power politics, or working through international regimes. Assuming that the main dynamics of the international system are not going to change in the near future, tracing the root causes of assertiveness to domestic politics also has the advantage of looking for solutions where there is more space for change. As students of the rise of Germany and Japan point out, even when policy making is driven by economic expansionism, options to avoid military conflict are still available. What ultimately pushes decisions in an aggressive direction is capture by a certain type of nationalistic ideology. Few would dispute that nationalism has played an increasingly important role in shaping Chinese foreign policy making since 1989 and shows little sign of decline as the economy has grown to near super-power status. Unless political reforms are undertaken to reduce the reliance of the political elite on this ideology, the outcome of China's global economic expansion and increasing defence budgets is likely to be closer to the negative hegemony of *ba dao* than the righteous way of *wang dao*.

[32] Smith, Origins of Nazi Imperialism, 64–65.

Bibliography

Alden, C., and C. R. Hughes. 2009. Harmony and discord in China's Africa strategy: Some implications for foreign policy. *The China Quarterly* 199: 563.

Bull, H. 1977. *The anarchical society*. Basingstoke and London: Macmillan.

Conrad, B. 2012. China in Copenhagen: Reconciling the "Beijing climate revolution" and the "Copenhagen climate obstinacy". *The China Quarterly* 210: 435–455.

Cui, T. K., and H. Z. Pang. 2012. China-US relations in China's overall diplomacy in the new era: On China and US working together to build a new type relationship between major powers. [online]. Available at http://www.fmprc.gov.cn/mfa_eng/wjb_663304/zzjg_663340/bmdyzs_664814/xwlb_664816/t953682.shtml. Accessed 28 Aug 2015.

Economic Times. 2013. BRICS nations keen to set up reinsurance company. [online]. Available at http://articles.economictimes.indiatimes.com/2013-11-11/news/43929958_1_brics-development-bank-reinsurance-crude-purchases. Accessed 11 Nov 2013.

Gates, R. M. 2014. *Call of duty: Memoirs of a secretary at war*. Random House. London: W. H. Allen.

Global, P. 2014. Global opposition to US surveillance and drones, but limited harm to America's image: Many in Asia worry about conflict with China. Pew Research Centre. [online]. Available at http://www.pewglobal.org/files/2014/07/2014-07-14-Balance-of-Power.pdf. Accessed 17 July 2014.

House, W. 2014. The president's trip to Japan, the Republic of Korea, Malaysia and the Philippines. [online]. Available at http://www.whitehouse.gov/issues/foreign-policy/asia-trip-spring-2014. Accessed 17 July 2014.

Hughes, C. R. 2009. China's membership of the ARF and the emergence of an East Asian diplomatic and security culture. In *Cooperative security in the Asia-Pacific: The ASEAN regional forum*, eds. J. Haacke, and N.M. Morada, 54–71. Abingdon: Routledge.

——— 2011. Reclassifying Chinese nationalism: The geopolitik turn. *Journal of Contemporary China* 20(71): 601–620.

Ikenberry, J. G. 2001. *After victory: Institutions, strategic restraint and the rebuilding of order after major wars*. Princeton and Oxford: Princeton University Press.

International Crisis Group. 2012. Stirring up the South China Sea. ICG, Asia Report No 223. [online]. Available at http://www.crisisgroup.org/~/media/Files/asia/north-east-asia/223-stirring-up-the-south-china-sea-i.pdf. Accessed 28 Aug 2015.

Jakobson, L., and D. Knox. 2010. New foreign policy actors in China. SIPRI Policy Paper 26.

Jazeera, A. 2013. China, Russia congratulate each other on Syria at APEC. Al Jazeera America. [online]. Available at http://america.aljazeera.com/articles/2013/10/8/china-russia-congratulateeachotheronsyriaatapec.html. Accessed 9 Oct 2013.

Leahy, J., and J. P. Rathbone. 2014. China's shadow hovers over $100bn Brics bank. *Financial Times* 16 July. [online]. Available at http://www.ft.com/cms/s/0/9bdd1f68-0cda-11e4-90fa-00144feabdc0.html#axzz3k6dYiWYO. Accessed 28 Aug 2015.

Liu, M. F. 2012. *Zhongguo meng: hou Meiguo shidai de da guo siwei yu zhanlue dingwei.* [*China dream: Great power considerations and fixing strategy in the post-American era*]. Beijing: Zhongguo youyi chubanshe.

Nation. 2013. Xi Jinping stresses diplomatic work with neighbouring states. *The Nation.* [online]. Available at http://www.nation.com.pk/international/01-Nov-2013/xi-jinping-stresses-diplomatic-work-with-neighbouring-states. Accessed 1 Nov 2013.

People's Daily. 2009. Senior Chinese official calls on U.S. to respect China's core national interests. [online]. Available at http://english.people.com.cn/90001/90776/90883/6713167.html. Accessed 17 July 2014.

Smith, W. D. 1986. *The ideological origins of Nazi imperialism.* New York and Oxford: Oxford University Press.

Snyder, J. 1991. *Myths of empire: Domestic politics and international ambition.* Ithaca and London: Cornell University Press.

State Council. 2014. China's national defense in 2010. Beijing: Information Office of the State Council. [online]. Available at http://english.gov.cn/official/2011-03/31/content_1835499.htm. Accessed 17 July 2014.

Wacker, G. 2013. China-Europe relations and the European perspectives on the "new type of major power relations. [online]. Available at http://www.swp-berlin.org/fileadmin/contents/products/projekt_papiere/Taiwan2ndTrack_Wacker_2013.pdf. Accessed July 2013.

Xinhuanet. 2012. Xi Jinping zai Guangzhou zhanqu kaocha qiangdiao jianchi fuguo he jiangjun xiang tongyi nuli jianshe gonggu guofang he qiangda jundui. [Xi Jinping during inspection of Guangzhou military region stresses building consolidated defence and strong army by striving to combine national wealth and a strong army]. [online]. Available at http://news.xinhuanet.com/politics/2012-12/12/c_114003822.htm. Accessed 7 Aug 2015.

Yan, X.T. 2011. *Ancient Chinese thought, modern Chinese power.* Oxford and Princeton: Princeton University Press.

Yang, J. C. 2013a. Innovations in China's diplomatic theory and practice under new conditions. Ministry of Foreign Affairs of the PRC. [online]. Available at http://www.chinese-embassy.org.uk/eng/zgyw/t1066869.htm. Accessed 28 Aug 2015.

Yang J. M. 2013b. 'Xinxing daguo guanxi: Lilun, zhanlue he zhengce jiangou' ['The New Model of Great Power Relationship: Theory, Strategy and Policy Structure'], Guoji wenti yanjiu, (1 May). Online referred to 30 May 2016, http://www.ciis.org.cn/gyzz/2013-05/30/content_5993566.htm

Zakaria, F. 1998. *From wealth to power: The unusual origins of America's world role*. Oxford and Princeton: Princeton University Press.

Zhao, T. Y. 2011. Rethinking empire from the Chinese concept of 'all-under-heaven'. In *China orders the world: Normative soft power and foreign policy*, eds. W. A. Callahan, and E. Barantseva, 21–36. Baltimore: Johns Hopkins University Press.

12

China's Position in the World and Orientation of Its Grand Strategy

Honghua Men

In the era of globalization, the central issues for any country seeking to safeguard its national dignity and achieve its historical missions are to determine its own national identity, promote national integration through its national identity, and involve itself in world affairs by using an integrated and unambiguous national identity in the international community.

A nation often derives its national identity from its national power, which the international goals it pursues and the international community's responses to these goals directly influence. China's national identity has always largely reflected the relationship it has with the world at a particular time or during a specific historical period. In the agrarian era,

H. Men (✉)
School of Political Science and International Relations,
Tongji University, Shanghai, China
e-mail: menhonghuacanran@163.com

S. Tsang, H. Men (eds.), *China in the Xi Jinping Era*,
The Nottingham China Policy Institute Series,
DOI 10.1007/978-3-319-29549-7_12

China was one of the most developed countries in the world. Confucian ethics, which encapsulate the core values of Chinese civilization, were introduced more than 2,500 years ago. Therefore, for a significant period China was positioned at the centre of world culture.

In the mid-19th century, China fell victim to an international power transfer and at one point was on the verge of collapsing into a failed state. The key imperial powers, with their advanced technology in the form of powerful warships armed with cannons and the dissemination of their Western Christian ideology, had forced their way into China and turned it into a semi-colonial country. The collapse in the early 20th century of a monarchy that had lasted for millennia paved the way for the transformation of China's social system. After a couple of unsuccessful experiments with a bourgeois democracy and bourgeois constitutional system, China finally chose the socialist path.

The 20th century was a pivotal time for China. In the first half, it was at the bottom of an unstable international system, seeking to win back the independence and sovereignty it had lost in the 19th century; in the second half, it began its historic transformation into a prosperous country with realistic expectations of rejuvenation. In the last two decades of the 20th century, in particular, it seized the opportunity of a new wave of globalization to begin to integrate into the international system and redefine its national identity. It has gradually grown into a responsible, constructive, and predictable great power, committed to promoting the transformation of international society and intending to play a constructive role in the process. It has become one of the beneficiaries of an international shift in power relations.[1] In the 21st century, particularly since the global financial crisis of 2008 and the consequent debt crisis in Europe and the USA, China has accelerated the pace of its rise, which has brought positive global changes and garnered much attention around the world.

China's national identity rests on 5,000 years of civilization, a century of humiliation, and its current rise towards great power status. Since its reform and opening up began, it has gradually progressed from being a traditional great power to a modern power; from a large closed power to an open one; and from a great power with a small international role to an important great player. This period has seen China's national power and international influence continue in an upward trend

[1] Men, "Goujian Zhongguo zhanlue kuangjia," 2.

with a corresponding rise in pessimistic, even alarmist, views towards it, embodied, for example, in labels such as 'the China risk', 'China collapse', 'China split', and 'China threat'. The majority of strategic analysts, however, predicted that its rapid rise would eventually turn it into a leading global power.

Ever since the Asian financial crisis of 1997, Chinese leaders have on numerous occasions publicly committed the country to taking on more international obligations and responsibilities. This has attracted widespread attention from around the world, especially since 2006 when the G2 meeting (between the USA and China) launched China as an emerging superpower. In 2010 it surpassed Japan as the second largest economy in the world, and it has overtaken the USA as the world's top trading nation. Its rise has triggered great changes in the world. The country has moved rapidly from being a regional power to being a global power and in the future it is likely to become a leading global power. This transformation of its national identity presents the Politburo Standing Committee, led by Xi Jinping, General Secretary of the Communist Party of China (CPC), with new opportunities and challenges.

A New Type of Socialist Great Power

While China is currently the only great power with a socialist political system, it is not socialist in a traditional sense. Its form of socialism has gradually developed from a combination of traditional Chinese characteristics, world trends, reflections on the histories of other socialist countries, and the pursuit of its national development goals. As a political system, it is underpinned by three integrated elements:

- The socialist road with Chinese characteristics, which serves as the method through which the goal is pursued;
- The theoretical framework of socialism with Chinese characteristics, which acts as a guide to action;
- The political system of socialism with Chinese characteristics, which is the fundamental political foundation.[2]

[2] Hu, *Shibaci daibiao dahui baogao*, 13.

These distinctive characteristics are reflected in the following areas. First, as its Five Principles of Peaceful Coexistence and independent foreign policy of peace reflect, China is a large, peaceful, socialist country. At the third Plenary Session of the 11th Central Committee of the CPC, Deng Xiaoping decided to change China's outdated focus on war and revolution to one of peace and development—in other words, it would follow a path of cooperation and not conflict. With Deng Xiaoping's declaration, in which 'China advocates peaceful socialism', the country completed its transformation from a revolutionary to a status quo country, from an opponent of the international system to a reformer, even defender, of it.[3] Its response to anti-socialist forces would be to take whatever measures were necessary and justifiable to safeguard its interests, but basically to act with restraint; 'the only other measure is to continue to strengthen friendship and cooperation for development with them'.[4] This approach is reflected in the following principles that China established:

- Learning a lesson from the Soviet Union;
- Committing itself to peaceful development;
- Adhering to the concept of peaceful diplomacy;
- Using its own development to promote international peace, cooperation, harmony, and peaceful development.

Second, China is a large developing socialist country and its policy makers recognize that it 'will continue to be in the preliminary stage of socialism for a long time. … China's international status as the world's largest developing country remains unchanged and in all circumstances this status, which is the most important domestic factor, should be taken into consideration'.[5] Its policy makers also believe that the most important contribution that socialist countries can make to the world is to run their own countries successfully and display to the world the overall advantages of socialism in various fields, including politics, the economy,

[3] Johnston, "Zhongguo guanxi yanjiu gaishu," 48–53.
Men, "Zhongguo zhanlue wenhua chonggou," 57–63.

[4] Deng, *Deng Xiaoping wenxuan*, 328, 349.

[5] Hu, *Shibaci daibiao dahui baogao*, 16.

culture, society, and ecology. It is of fundamental strategic significance that socialist counties concentrate on their overall development, coexist peacefully with all countries, including capitalist ones, and work together for world peace and development.

Third, China is an open socialist country. By overcoming obstacles in its ideology and reducing the institutional constraints on its social system, the country has turned from being an almost completely closed one to an active participant in the world market. As it becomes a more open global power, its interdependence with the international community will deepen and its capacity to shape the international system will continue to increase. China has extended its policy of opening up to the outside world to one of opening up both domestically and internationally.

Fourth, as a socialist great power devoted to developing a socialist market economy, China must now move from a planned to a market economy. To integrate into the international system, which is its development trajectory, it needs to understand market economics and act accordingly. In a speech during his 'Southern Tour' in 1992, Deng Xiaoping stressed that 'whether China should focus more on a planned economy or on a market economy is not the fundamental difference between socialism and capitalism'.[6] This sparked China into formulating its own theory of socialist market economics and thus began the construction of its remarkable socialist market economy. As a result, it has improved socialist theory and ushered it into a new stage of development.

Fifth, China is a socialist great power devoted to pursuing prosperity for all. Its change of direction started when Deng Xiaoping recognized that China, as an underdeveloped country with a long-established leftist ideology, was ill equipped to embark on reform and opening up in a comprehensive manner. Deng Xiaoping had hoped that 'when Chinese people reach[ed] a moderately high standard of living at the end of the twentieth century, this issue ... [would have been] outlined and resolved'.[7] At the beginning of the 21st century, however, China's new leaders recognized that, while the country faced many and varied strategic development opportunities, it also had to confront an increasing number of

[6] Deng, *Deng Xiaoping wenxuan*, 73.

[7] Ibid., 374.

new challenges. They consequently set forth a strategy that involved the constant promotion of social harmony. They also announced the concept of scientific development and abandoned the 'get rich first' theory, initially introduced as an innovative way of revitalizing the economy, in favour of a policy of 'common prosperity'.

The notion of socialism with Chinese characteristics fits the country's current position in the era of globalization. The socialism to which it adheres differs from the socialism that Karl Marx envisaged, as well as that of the Soviet Union.[8] China has learnt lessons from the successes of capitalism and its market economy, but has not been assimilated into it. Socialism with Chinese characteristics aims to combine the best of socialism with the best of capitalism with an emphasis on continuous adjustment and improvement. Its pursuit of peace, development, cooperation, and mutual prosperity is an indication of its confidence in its future trajectory.

China's identity as a new type of socialist great power faces both domestic and international challenges. The domestic challenges lie in the understanding of the nature of socialism and the institutionalization of common prosperity. International challenges stem mainly from some Western countries attempting to highlight the differences between their political systems and that of China, implying that China poses a threat. Meanwhile, China continues to consolidate and promote its overall 'five in one development strategy', namely the all-round development of its economy, politics, culture, society, and ecology. It continues to emphasize the philosophy of 'advocating harmony without uniformity' and to interact further with Western countries. The relations that China intends to achieve with these countries are:

- The pursuit of harmony without being identical;
- Being different without triggering conflict;
- Coexisting and developing together in a harmonious manner;
- Complementing each other's differences.

[8] Of course, the exploration of the construction of socialism in the Soviet Union has provided an important reference for China, and its experiences and lessons in this regard have also provided significant inspiration for building socialism with Chinese characteristics. Professor Steve Tsang's analysis of consultative Leninism in this book gives a deep understanding of the lessons China has learnt in this regard from the experiences of the Soviet Union. See Chap. 2, 'Consolidating Political and Governance Strength'.

A Developing Great Power

In general, developing countries are still undergoing the transformation from being traditional agricultural societies to becoming modern industrial ones; their levels of economic and social development, as well as people's living standards, are consequently relatively low.[9] As research into development has deepened, new statistical indices for measuring a country's level of development, apart from the traditional (absolute and per capita) gross domestic product (GDP), have been introduced; these include the Global Competitiveness Index, the Human Development Index (HDI), and balanced development. The indices measuring GDP focus on economic factors and the overall scale of a country's economy, while the Global Competitiveness Index puts the emphasis on gauging a nation's efficiency, endurance, and development trends. The indicator measuring the balanced development of a nation emphasizes the level of its sustainable development, while HDI focuses on the comprehensive factors of a country's social development and includes life expectancy, adult literacy rates, and GDP per capita.

In the early 1980s, during negotiations for China to join the General Agreement on Tariffs and Trade (GATT), serious disagreements arose between China and the West over whether to class China as a developed or a developing country. These negotiations lasted for more than a decade. Even when China joined the World Trade Organization (WTO) in 2001, the report of the 'Working Party on the Accession of China' did not fully recognize the country's status as a developing one, thus denying it across-the-board preferential treatment.[10] At the start of the 21st century, with China now the largest emerging economy, the developed countries specifically asked China to relinquish its status as a developing country to stop it being one of the biggest 'free riders' of those preferential treatments. After the global financial crisis of 2008, it became popular to say that 'in 1949 socialism saved China, in 1989 China saved socialism, while in 2009 China saved capitalism'. In general, China has received a great deal of praise from the international community, but this has also resulted in pressure from the same quarters.

[9] Liu et al., "Fazhan zhongguojia shenfen Zhengyi," 6–10.

[10] Xu, "Xinxing guojia jueqi," 186–204.

Many countries emphasize that it has become a world power and a potential superpower, with some even brandishing the notion of the 'G2'. Thus, there are continuous calls for China to give up its status as a developing country.

According to the WTO's conventional definition, developing countries are those with a GDP per capita of less than $3,000. China's GDP per capita reached $3,315 in 2008, which was ranked 106th highest in the world; in 2009 the figure was $3,678, ranked 97th in the world; in 2010 it was $4,520, ranked 90th; and in 2011 the figure was $5,414, ranked 89th.[11] Although the pace at which its GDP per capita has increased has been particularly fast, it is equally striking that it remains so far down the global rankings in this regard. China must realize that the global average GDP per capita is rising (for example in 2010 it was $8,985, twice as high as its own). It should also be aware of the seriousness of its own unbalanced development. For example, according to the definition used by the United Nations (UN), those with an income of less than $1 a day are considered to be living in poverty. This currently applies to 150 million people in China.

In view of this, China should, economically and socially, calmly position itself as a developing great power. A report to the 18th National Congress of the CPC reaffirmed that 'China's international status as the world's largest developing country remains unchanged'. Its quest to become a modern country continues, though the process is not always smooth and is frequently complex. Through industrialization and modernization a developing country endeavours to eradicate extreme poverty, escape backwardness, improve the level of its development, and eventually attain the status of a developed nation. China's modernization and industrialization are accelerating, but while it reduces its underdeveloped areas to shed its image as an underdeveloped country, and increases its developed areas to enhance its credentials as a developed one, the underdeveloped and developed areas of the economy must necessarily coexist. This is a dynamic process in which quantitative changes lead to qualitative improvements. In other words, China is striving to transform itself from a developing, to a moderately developed, to a developed country.

China's overall GDP has been ranked second in the world since 2010, while its international competitiveness ranking in 2008 was 30th in the

[11] Wenku.

world, 29th in 2009, 27th in 2010/2011, and 26th in 2011/2012. It is the only nation among the BRICS (Brazil, Russia, India, China, and South Africa) to be ranked among the top 30 in the world. These two indicators show its economy among those at the top of the global rankings, which makes it very difficult to define it as a standard developing country. Other indices, however, show it far down the global rankings. For example, in developed countries economic and social progress is relatively balanced, with rather small gaps between urban and rural areas and between regions. China's development, by contrast, is not balanced. There are large gaps between its urban and rural areas and among its various regions and, in some areas, these gaps are widening. Such features are typical of developing nations. China has many underdeveloped regions, particularly in its rural areas, while its big cities and coastal areas are becoming increasingly modern. These advanced regions are competing with developed countries in an increasingly wide range of fields. In terms of the UN's HDI, however, China is ranked in the lower reaches and is on a downward trend. Its HDI was ranked 81st in the world in 2008, 92nd in 2009, and 89th in 2010. The ranking fell to 101st in 2011. These figures show China is still in the middle or lower level of human development.

In summary, in various aspects of development, including the economic, social, political, and cultural, China is still at the preliminary stage and, as the above analysis shows, the picture is not static. China is not a typical developing country; nor is it a developed or a moderately developed country. It has underdeveloped features that are being reduced and developed ones that are expanding. Yet, despite being a developing country, it has transformed itself into one that plays a leading role in the world. This makes it impractical to deal with its issues as if it were a developing country, for that would negatively affect the formulation and implementation of important economic and fiscal policies. The 21st century has brought rapid modernization to an increasing number of areas in society and to people's lifestyles. Against this backdrop, China is trying, at a rapid but steady pace, to pass the middle point of its preliminary stage of socialism. The explicit objective of its overall restructuring is to complete its modernization process and thereby establish a modern nation. The current situation has made it difficult to achieve this objective. Therefore, it is vital for it to improve its development philosophy, optimize its development models, and adjust its development strategy. In particular, it is imperative for it to complete its path from unsustainable to sustainable, from inequitable to equitable, and from uneven to balanced.

A Great Power with a Rich Cultural Heritage

The culture of a nation is its heart, soul, and character, the source of its national cohesion and solidarity, and the solid foundation for its national identity. In general, the modernization of a nation includes economic, political, and cultural modernization, with the latter presenting China with a particularly difficult challenge. As Tu Weiming pointed out, 'for China's rise to be complete, it needs to rise in the field of culture'.[12]

Globalization has not only increased the integration of numerous cultures around the world but it has also triggered cultural disintegration, along with various conflicts. A nation's cultural traditions are frequently treated as the core symbols of its national identity, and China's culture is of great significance to it. As British philosopher Bertrand Russell pointed out, China is a cultural rather than a political entity: it was not originally the name of a country per se, but the perceived geographical centre of the world; it was an advanced, enlightened civilization and its common values formed the basis of the identity of the Chinese nation. It is now more than 30 years since China started to reform and open up, but its cultural modernization lags behind its economic modernization, with the reform of its cultural system still in its infancy. Its cultural security is profoundly threatened at present.

Both the historical evolution of Chinese culture and its international influence give China an inherent advantage in terms of its cultural soft power. This advantage lies in the advanced level of its ancient culture, which has Confucianism at its core, and the significant influence of this culture on the surrounding regions. This advantage is also reflected in the role Confucianism played in promoting economic development in several East Asian countries, including Japan, the 'Four Asian Dragons' (Hong Kong, Singapore, South Korea, and Taiwan), the ASEAN four

[12] Tu, "Zhongguo jueqi wenhua zhicheng," 35–9.

(Indonesia, Malaysia, Thailand, and the Philippines) and China itself. In the last 100 years, Eastern civilizations have faced enormous challenges from the West. However, this situation has started to change since China's reform and opening up shifted the world's centre of gravity to the Asia–Pacific region. China's traditional culture is again being actively promoted, while Western countries have begun to reflect on and adjust their own cultures. East–West cultural integration is likely to reach a new stage in the near future and China is becoming the centre of this assimilation. As Wang Meng put it, 'Chinese traditional culture has responded efficiently to grave challenges, caught up with the international development trend and increasingly regained its vitality. It is a culture that is able to communicate with and complement global mainstream cultures, modern cultures and advanced cultures. It is also a living culture that is able to keep pace with the times'.[13]

China's cultural problems have historical roots. The country failed during the era of industrial modernization and, as a result, the foundation of traditional Chinese culture was gradually eroded. In particular, China suffered a series of defeats in the mid-19th century, which forced it to begin to reflect on and restructure its culture. Chinese elites were wondering why such a great country had fallen into such a sharp decline and many turned to the West, first to learn how to make powerful warships and weapons, but later to reflect on its own traditional culture—and this has been going on ever since. The question of whether Chinese tradition or Western learning should play the leading role in China's development has been a consistent topic of hot debate.

China's modernization began in the 20th century with the Revolution of 1911 and the 'May Fourth Movement'. Since then, there have been many different approaches to dealing with China's cultural identity. 'The New Culture Movement' was deeply critical of traditional Chinese culture and advocated wholesale Westernization, with such self-criticism particularly evident in the anti-Confucian movement that gathered momentum during the Cultural Revolution. The idea of the wholesale Westernization of China then disappeared from the horizon, only to reappear intermittently, but each time triggering political turmoil. When China's overall

[13] Meng, "Chuantong wenhua ruan shili," 6.

national strength started to diminish, its people became increasingly disenchanted with their traditional culture and blindly started copying Western cultures. At the start of the reform and opening up in 1978, China began to import products and technology from the West on a large scale and actively adopted many Western cultural values. For the West, China's reform and opening up is a process of Westernization; while for China, it is a process in which Chinese culture integrates with Western cultures, and the principle of 'advocating harmony without uniformity' will continue to determine the future prospects of the world. The other mainstream idea in this field, which supports China's traditional culture, is represented by Liang Shuming, who believes that 'the future of global cultures lies in the revival of Chinese culture',[14] and his view has continued to attract support, particularly in non-political academic circles.

Through its reform and opening up, China seized the opportunities the new wave of globalization presented and reforming existing rules and practices to create something new became a popular cultural pastime. China achieved its economic rise in unison with the rapid development of the Asian economies, thus sparking a reassessment of the huge influence of its traditional culture, the core of which is, of course, Confucianism. Traditional culture has started to play a positive role in suggesting solutions to various global problems. These include:

- Reshaping the international political and economic order;
- Resolving escalating international conflicts;
- Eradicating blatant materialism, which hinders cultural development;
- Dealing with the increasingly evident global crisis of faith.

Chinese policy makers recognize the importance of culture in determining their own national identity, hence they advocate its use as a tool with which to lead social trends, educate people, serve society, and boost development.

Notwithstanding the above, China lacks cultural influence and urgently needs to modernize its customs and develop its rich array of traditional resources; the disappearance of social values and traditional ethics is responsible for many of its most serious social ills. When it pre-

[14] Liang, *Liang Shuming quanji*, 543–6.

viously showed an eagerness to learn from foreign cultures, it tended to overlook its own and even to belittle it. However, if a nation loses its cultural identity, it will also destroy the foundations of its national independence. Across the world, in modern and ancient times alike, no country has ever achieved modernization through the wholesale import of other countries' solutions. As China integrates into the world, it is as essential for it to maintain and develop its culture as it is to enhance its economic and military strength. There are two ways in which China might achieve this objective. The first is through the revival of Confucianism, which emphasizes the fundamental values of Chinese traditional culture. It is an extension of the concept Zhongti Xiyong (中体西用), meaning turning to Chinese learning for fundamental principles and Western learning for practical matters. The other is to emphasize that traditional Chinese and Western cultures can complement one another, learn from and merge into each other, though bearing in mind that no global power has ever been founded on foreign cultural values. Chinese culture grew from and gestated in its own soil; its modernization, therefore, cannot be achieved without recourse to its traditional culture. It should emphasize the concept of Zhongti Xiyong by overlooking those elements that disparage Western culture, treating them instead in an open manner and absorbing their beneficial aspects, but discarding those that are unhelpful. Western culture has an impulsive desire to penetrate and transform other cultures. During its transition into a modern industrial society, China has, consciously or unconsciously, absorbed Western culture and values, including some negative characteristics, such as excessive selfishness, extreme consumerism, value disorientation, and other immoral tendencies. These negative aspects are subverting the essence of Chinese culture, adversely affecting the appeal of traditional Chinese ethics, destroying the cohesion of the national culture, and seriously threatening its cultural security.

In recent years, Chinese policy makers have come to recognize the strategic importance of—and urgent need for—a cultural reconstruction, which has previously failed to keep pace with overall development. The 18th Party Congress report stated that China should continue to develop the whole nation's cultural creativity, as well as safeguard people's basic cultural rights and increase the international influence of its culture. It has already decided to use its culture as an instrument for transforming itself into a leading global power. This strategy involves:

- Adhering to its cultural traditions;
- Promoting its cultural traditions;
- Deepening the reforms of culturally rooted industries;
- Developing itself as a cultural power;
- Advocating dialogue between different cultures.

With its strategy of vigorously promoting the modernization and development of its culture, China is embarking on an important period of its development.

A Responsible Great Power

Taking on international responsibilities is a requisite for all countries in a global world. A surge in the number of global issues, and the concomitant need to find solutions to them, requires all countries, regardless of their size or importance, to accept their share of responsibilities. Domestically, this means delivering the public good to their populations; internationally it means abiding by international norms, safeguarding international rules, and fulfilling international responsibilities. As the world's second largest economy, a major Eastern nation, and one of the strongest global powers, China should play an important international part in safeguarding the common interests of mankind. Being a 'responsible great power', which it continues to emphasize it is, implies taking on that role; and to that end it has already repositioned itself in the international community.

Sun Yat-Sen pointed out that 'if China becomes strong and prosperous, we will not only want to restore the status of our nation, but also take on a large responsibility for the world'.[15] The construction of its image as a responsible great power is closely related to its reform and opening up, as well as to the depth of its integration into the international community. In the 1980s, China turned away from its 'war and revolution' approach to the world and began the process of integrating into it. It has now transformed itself from an outsider and opponent to a participant in (and architect of) the international system.[16]

[15] Sun, *Sun Zhongshan xuanji*, 691.

[16] Jiang, "Guoji zuzhi guanxi," 52.
Qin, "Sange jiashe,"10–15.

There is a link between China's opening up and its increasing participation in the international system. In fact, since the early 1980s, China has actively supported a number of international economic organizations and this has, directly and indirectly, made a positive contribution to the world. It has conveyed new perspectives, influenced diplomatic decision making, and been involved in other kinds of international institutions.[17] Since Deng Xiaoping's speeches in early 1992 ushered in an era of overall international participation, China has engaged in world affairs in an all-around, strategic, and long-term manner and has endorsed almost all the major international institutions.

After the end of the Cold War, China's economy continued to develop rapidly and the pace of its political democratization accelerated, as did its desire and capacity to accept more international responsibility. In November 1997, President Jiang Zemin gave a speech at Harvard University in which he said that China and the USA 'share broad common interests and shoulder common responsibilities' to safeguard human survival and development.[18] Since then, its leaders have frequently referred to China as a responsible great power. For example, on 4 March 2006 Premier Wen Jiabao declared that 'China has become a responsible country'[19] and, on 29 April 2010, at a joint press conference with the president of the European Commission José Manuel Barroso, Wen said that 'China will take on more international responsibilities, which is not only the expectation of the international community, but is also in its own interest'.[20] The 18th Party Congress report stressed that 'China will assume a more positive attitude towards participating in international affairs, play its role as a responsible great power and deal with global challenges together with other countries'.

For China to position itself as a responsible great power means that it has undergone a tremendous change of national identity. This new identity combines its traditional conceptualization of itself as an independent power and its new one as a responsible great power, increasingly regulated by international rules and an active and responsible participant in the international system.

[17] Men, "Yali, renzhi guoji xingxiang," 17–22.

[18] Jiang, *Jiang Zemin wenxuan*, 64.

[19] Guangming Ribao, "Wen da jizhe wen," 1.

[20] Sina.

Meanwhile, the international community, particularly the USA and some Western countries, has been putting pressure on China to take on even more responsibilities. Huang Jing identifies three specific forms of this pressure:

- To put more money and effort into dealing with international affairs;
- To open its financial market to allow entry to foreign companies and to abandon all governmental control over it;
- To behave gradually in compliance with Western values and rules.[21]

Some scholars see the notion of 'China's responsibility' as a new kind of soft containment, which, while giving it opportunities to cooperate internationally, also contains a level of deception which might be potentially difficult to deal with.[22] Because China is both a rising global power and the only socialist country among those powers, it needs to be cautious when accepting international responsibilities. When emerging powers take these on, other global powers are highly likely to misinterpret their actions negatively. Furthermore, China's status as a socialist great power makes the prospect of Western countries adopting an antagonistic stance towards it more likely. Domestically, there is some level of disagreement over China positioning itself as 'a responsible great power', which stems from conspiracy theories, a belief that China has insufficient capability and a desire to focus on domestic rather than international issues.

China's development is inseparable from that of the world, and world development needs China's contribution. Looking ahead, China should calmly assess its own international position, actively assume international responsibilities in accordance with its capabilities, promote its common interests with other countries, strike a balance between its capabilities and responsibilities when dealing with international issues, and continue actively to seek more international rights.

---

[21] Huang, "Xifang yiwei pengsha Zhongguo," 10.

[22] Guo, "Xifang duihua 'ruan ezhi," 71–5.

A Major Asia–Pacific Power with Global Influence

Henry S. Kissinger believes that every century sees the rise of a country with the strength, will, wisdom, moral force, and intent to reshape the international system according to its own values. This is almost a law of nature.[23] Many Chinese and foreign elites are inclined to believe that in the 21st century China is such a country and evidence of this lies in the G2 concept that some American strategic thinkers have proposed.

China has always been a major power. Even during the decline of the later Qing dynasty it never lost that status. Napoleon called it a sleeping lion and warned that 'once China wakes, she will shake the whole world'.[24] Since 1978, China's national strength and international influence have continued to increase and the whole international community recognizes its ascent. Most strategic analysts believe that it is only a matter of time before it becomes a leading global power. Since the Asian financial crisis of 1997, China has actively been taking on international obligations and it is attracting growing attention from the world community. Since 2006, the G2 has become a popular topic for discussion and even more so since 2010 when China overtook Japan as the world's second largest economy in terms of GDP.

The academic community frequently discusses what criteria are appropriate for assessing whether or not a country is a leading global power. German historian Leopold von Ranke held that it must be able to fight other global powers without being defeated, even when the other powers have formed an alliance against it.[25] Wang Jun of China's State Administration of Taxation believes that it must have significant national strength, a far-reaching influence on the world, and a profound influence on history. By 'significant national strength' he means that, compared with other countries in the same historical period, its economy is more developed, its military force more powerful, its culture more thriving, and its territory broader; by 'far-reaching influence on the world' he means being able to alter profoundly the complexion of the world and to

---

[23] Kissinger, *Diplomacy*, 17.

[24] Khanua, "Impact of China's Ambition," 9.

[25] Ranke, *Theory Practice of History*, 86.

influence strongly or even control the development of world culture; by 'profound influence on history' he means it has a long-standing influence across time and space.[26] Michael Oksenberg and his co-authors believe that the basic criteria are being the most economically developed and militarily powerful country in the world, as well as having worldwide cultural and political influence.[27] Brzezinski argues that such a status requires a genuine and absolute military advantage in the world, great international financial and economic influence, a clear lead in the field of technology, and a way of life that others view as attractive. All these factors must be combined to form worldwide political influence.[28]

Considered against these criteria, one can argue that, since history began to be recorded, China has been a significant country, at least in East Asia and perhaps across the whole of Asia. The concepts of *Tianxia* (Under the Heaven), the Chinese perception of world order, and *Chaogong Tixi*, the tribute system in ancient China, are reminders of China's former glory.[29] However, China has never been a world power because no world power existed before the 19th century. There had only been major regional powers, with real world powers arising through various others competing for greater influence around the world.[30] During that period, the rise of great powers in Europe sharply contrasted with the decline of China. The establishment of the People's Republic of China (PRC) halted the decline in its international status, which had lasted for more than a 100 years, and it quickly re-established its place as a major political and military power.

As I mentioned earlier, since China's reform and opening up in 1978, its economic status has risen rapidly. Its overall national strength has increased; it has paid more attention to its maritime interests; and its influence has been extended to the entire Asia–Pacific region, as well as to the rest of the globe. Now, China's active participation is an essential ingredient in all major Asia–Pacific affairs. It meets many of the requirements of a world power; it is the third largest country by land area; it is the most heavily

[26] Wang, "Qiangguo xingsheng zhilu," 2–16.

[27] Funabashi, Oksenberg, and Weiss, *An Emerging China*, 2.

[28] Brzezinski, "Ruhe yu Zhongguo gongchu," 12–13.

[29] Dreyer, "The Tianxia Trope," 1–2.

[30] Britain was a world power, but it was not a superpower. I thank Professor Steve Tsang for pointing this out.

populated nation in the world; and it has abundant natural resources. It is a permanent member of the UN Security Council and plays important roles in the International Monetary Fund and the Group of Twenty (G-20), so is a verifiable political power. It is also a leading global power in terms of its economy, trade, and foreign investment. With its high defence spending and modernization attracting the world's attention, it is generally regarded as a global military power. However, it faces challenges, including a shortage of per capita resources, uneven economic development, and limited cultural influence in the world. In addition, because of its history of having been a militarily defensive country, it lacks adequate overseas interests and international privileges. In short, China defines itself as a major Asia–Pacific power with significant world influence.

In a traditional geopolitical sense, China is located in the heart of Asia and is a representative of the East. With the deepening economic interdependence between China and its neighbouring countries, it has become the geo-economic centre of the Asia–Pacific region; its role in the economic development of the region is now greater than that of either the USA or Japan. Since a peaceful and stable regional environment is the primary prerequisite for China's modernization, it focuses its attention on cooperation within East Asia and its surrounding areas, while continuing to pursue and expand its global responsibilities to the best of its ability.

China's positioning is not without domestic and international challenges. The domestic challenges come mainly from rather impulsive eruptions of nationalist fervour and an immature parochial mentality. Evidence of a mature mentality in a country would include:

- The ability to define unambiguously the scope of its national interests;
- The ability to respond to criticism in a calm manner and hold frank discussions about any problem in which it is involved;
- The ability to give due consideration to the core national interests of other countries, viewed within the context of its own long-term national interests.

China has yet to reach this point, which would affect its national identity in general.

Its international challenges come mainly from the other global powers in the Asia–Pacific region and their various, competing, vested, national interests and strategies to contain its emergence as a leading global power. In particular, the USA has refocused on East Asia, while Japan, among others, has strengthened its strategic collaboration with the former. In addition, China faces major security challenges and much uncertainty from its neighbouring region, the U-shaped strip stretching from the north-west of Central Asia, through South Asia, South East Asia, and the South China Sea to the Korean Peninsula. China regards its effort to stabilize this area as a strategic priority. This will entail:

- Reconfirming the core position of East Asia in its overall strategy;
- Committing itself to turning East Asia into a source of strength on which China can rely to support its strategic development;
- Positioning itself as a major Asia–Pacific power and maritime nation;
- Extending its national interests on land and sea in this region.

The Orientation of Its Grand Strategy

China is basing its national status on the idea that it is a new type of socialist great power pursuing a policy of overall opening up, transformation, and development in all areas. It is dedicated to creating a new system, new development model, and new global culture based on the revival of traditional Chinese culture. There is a wide gap between these objectives and the present reality, but China is actively involved in global issues in the following three areas.

First, as it endeavours to play a leading role in East Asia and to become the main engine of the world economy, it is participating actively in economic globalization. Its strategic economic objectives focus on building an international environment that is conducive to its own economic development and to the expansion of its own economic interests. It is aware that deepening globalization and regionalization expose a country to external factors, so to safeguard its economic security it needs to build a solid economic foundation and engage further in international economic cooperation.[31] It is also expanding its overseas markets and increasing the share of Chinese goods in the international market. Furthermore, it is maintaining and broadening the channels through which it obtains its foreign technology, capital, energy, and various other strategic resources from the international market. Finally, through enhanced cooperation and the exploitation of resources, it is penetrating the surrounding regions to establish an area of strategic economic influence.

Second, China is steadily improving its national security and actively participating in the maintenance of international security. It treats the peace and stability of its land borders (with Russia, Central Asia, Afghanistan, India, and Pakistan) as its strategic foundation. It is cooperating with countries on its coastline to maintain peace and stability in North East Asia and to develop a mutually beneficial Sino-Japanese strategic alliance. It is strengthening its cooperation with ASEAN countries, starting with economic cooperation, and actively promoting the development of the ASEAN–China Free Trade Area (ACFTA). China is actively reforming its military capacity through the application of science and technology. It is steadily increasing its military spending, effectively transforming its economic strength into military capability, establishing a reliable nuclear deterrence, accelerating the modernization of its conventional armed forces, and transforming its numerically superior army into a qualitatively efficient one. It opposes independence movements and is resorting to military measures to counter the independence of Taiwan, Xinjiang, and Tibet, promote cross-strait exchanges, and maintain and promote its one-China policy. It is taking the initiative to promote multilateral cooperation and to help establish security systems to serve itself and its neighbouring countries.

Third, while adhering to the principle of cultural diversity, China is promoting its traditional culture, increasing international cultural exchanges, and learning from the achievements of various civilizations at different periods of history. It is also promoting universal values and endorsing the international influence of its culture as a solid foundation for its rise.[32] The culture of a nation is roughly equivalent to its soft power

---

[31] Qiu, "Jingji quanqiuhua," 3–13.

[32] Qin, "Shijie zhengzhi wenhua lilun," 4–9.

and, while economic and military strength are important indicators of global power, culture plays an equally important role. Globalization is changing China's traditional way of thinking and it should, therefore, adjust its cultural strategy to keep up with this trend and shape a Chinese culture fit for the 21st century,[33] especially since the advent of the knowledge economy increases the importance of a nation's cultural strength.[34]

The above analysis has shown China:

- Holding high the banner of peace, development, cooperation, and mutual prosperity;
- Using scientific methods to pursue domestic development and contribute towards a peaceful international environment;
- Working with other countries in pursuit of harmonious development;
- Rejuvenating the Chinese nation;
- Growing into a globally recognized world power.

China will continue to consolidate its national identity, the strategic orientation of which is reflected in four main areas—citizen consensus; soft power; linking its national, regional, and global identities; and providing a bridge between developing and developed countries.

First, China, like any other country, should focus on improving its people's sense of nationhood.[35] During this process, nurturing citizen consensus, which is the ideological foundation of nationhood, must be prioritized.[36] It includes the sense of belonging to a nation as well as a sense of honour and responsibility as its citizens. Strengthening it requires citizens of all ethnic groups to develop a sense of nationhood, on which China should build to forge a national identity that embraces everyone's cultural differences. Obviously, in the era of globalization,

[33] Huang, *Zonghe guoli xinlun*, 12.

[34] Johnston, "Thinking About Strategic Culture," 32–64.

[35] Facing challenges regarding European identity, Daniel Tarschys, former Secretary General of the Council of the European Union, was clearly aware of the importance of European education and called for including it as an important part of its political education. See Ma and Kuang, *Ouzhou rentong yanjiu*, 246.

[36] Han, "Guojia minzu wenhua renting," 106–13.

citizen consensus is not a closed concept; China should aim to transform its people into citizens with both national and global consciousnesses and identities.

Second, China should develop its soft power. National identity is founded on national strength, whereas soft power determines the stability of that identity. For a long time China focused on increasing its hard power to the detriment of some aspects of its soft power. As a result, the uneven development of the two has had a negative effect on the country's potential for further development. Internationally, China is still in a weak position in many respects. It is unable to persuade other countries to follow its lead, seems incapable of proposing and setting agendas or guiding public opinion in international affairs, so has been unable to set the framework of international discourse. The development of its national soft power has a bearing on how it might exploit its appeal in both international and domestic situations. To gain international understanding and recognition, it must broadcast and sell its outstanding culture, its development model, and its diplomatic philosophy to the rest of the world.

Third, China should strengthen the links between its national, regional, and global identities, thus seeking not only domestic consensus but also international understanding and recognition. In other words, it should pay attention to how other countries affect its national identity. In an era when globalization and regional integration go hand in hand, it should focus on changes in its international position as well as on strengthening the connection between its national, regional, and global identities. Because the international community expects China to assume more responsibility, yet is suspicious of its increasing national strength, the most prudent way forward would be to find the common ground between them. To realize their mutual goals, enhance international recognition of Chinese national identity, and achieve its full participation in international affairs, China should seek to:

- Involve itself further in global governance;
- Place more emphasis on converging the interests of the different actors on the world stage to enhance its ability to further its own regional and global agendas;

- Improve the quality of the interactions between its national, regional, and global identities;
- Build and develop communities of interest in different areas and levels with other countries.

Fourth, China should actively position itself as a bridge between developing and developed countries. To strengthen its national identity, it must understand global development trends, especially the interactions between world and emerging powers. Gui Gu Zi, an ancient Chinese philosopher, said that 'statesmen who were considered wise and able were those who had tried to consider the strength of other states and understand their situations'.[37] Many of the major conflicts of the current world order stem from interactions between developed and developing countries. China, at the juncture between the two, is ideally placed to form an 'international bridge' between them. Consequently, it will continue to play a more active role and take on more responsibility for international issues.

Bibliography

Brzezinski, Z. 2000. Ruhe yu Zhongguo gongchu. [How to live together with China]. *Zhanlue yu guanli* 3: 12–13.

Deng, X. P. 1993. *Deng Xiaoping wenxuan.* [*The selected works of Deng Xiaoping*], vol. 3. Beijing: Renmin chubanseh.

Dreyer, J. T. 2015. The "Tianxia trope": will China change the international system? *Journal of Contemporary China* 24(91): 1–2.

Funabashi, Y., M. Oksenberg, and H. Weiss. 1994. *An emerging China in a world of interdependence.* New York: The Trilateral Commission.

Guangming Ribao. 2006. Wen Jiabao Zongli zai shijie quanguo renda sici huiyi jizhe zhaodaihui shang da jizhe wen. [Premier Wen Jiabao answers reporters' questions during the press conference at the Fourth Session of the Tenth National People's Congress], 15 March, p. 1.

Gui, G. Z. 2015. Guiguzi: Liangquan [Gui Gu Zi, assessing the world's situation]. [online]. Available at https://books.google.co.uk/books?id=ryFaBAAAQBAJ&pg=PA199&lpg=PA199&dq=%E9%AC%BC%E

[37] Guiguzi, *Liangquan.*

8%B0%B7%E5%AD%90%C2%B7%E9%87%8F%E6%9D%83&source =bl&ots=QBGV11CikD&sig=Xf6VYYwe7HfMr5qYEqu_t17uBgY&hl=en &sa=X&ved=0CDsQ6AEwBWoVChMIjovP4OnLxwIVi9gaCh2AUgSM# v=onepage&q=%E9%AC%BC%E8%B0%B7%E5%AD%90%C2%B7% E9%87%8F%E6%9D%83&f=false. Accessed 28 Aug 2015.

Guo, S. Y. 2008. Lun xifang duihua 'ruan ezhi' zhanlue jiqi duice sikao. [Thinking on the Western countries' strategy of "soft containment" and its countermeasures]. *Mao Zedong, Deng Xiaoping lilun yanjiu* 12: 71–75.

Han, Z. 2010. Lun guojia rentong, minzu rentong ji wenhua rentong – yizhong jiyu lishi zhexue de fenxi yu sikao. [On national, ethnic and cultural identity – An analysis and thinking based on the philosophy of history]. *Beijing Shifan Daxue xuebao (shehui kexue ban)* 1: 106–113.

Hu, J. T. 2012. *Jianding bu yi yanzhe Zhongguo tese shehui zhuyi daolu qianjin wei quanmian jiancheng xiaokang shehui er fendou – zai Zhongguo Gongchandang di shiba ci quanguo daibiao dahui shang de baogao (2012 nian 11 yue 8 ri)*. [*Firmly March on the path of socialism with Chinese characteristics and strive to complete the building of a moderately prosperous society in all respects – Report to the Eighteenth National Congress of the Communist Party of China on 8 November 2012*]. Beijing: People's Publishing House.

Huang, S. F. 1999. *Zonghe guoli xinlun*. [*New theory of comprehensive national strength*]. Beijing: China Social Science Press.

Huang, J. 2010. Xifang renchao Zhongguo moshi yiwei pengsha Zhongguo. [The real reason for Western countries hyping China's model is suspected to be disguised flattery intended to shoot China down]. *Guangzhou Ribao*, 24 January: 10.

Jiang, Y. E. 2001. Meiguo xuezhe guanyu Zhongguo yu guoji zuzhi guanxi yanjiu gaishu. [A summary of American scholars' research on relations between China and international organizations]. *Shiejie jingji yu zhengzhi* 8: 52.

Jiang, Z. M. 2006. *Jiang Zemin wenxuan*. [*The selected works of Jiang Zemin*]. Beijing: People's Publishing House.

Johnston, A.I. 1995. Thinking about strategic culture. *International Security* 19(4): 32–64.

——— 2001. Meiguo xuezhe guanyu Zhongguo yu guoji zuzhi guanxi yanjiu gaishu. ['A summary of American scholars' research on relations between China and international organizations]. *World Economics & Politics* 8: 48–53.

Khanua, R. P. 1999. Impact of China's ambition to be a regional power. *Asian Defense Journal* 6(9): 9.

Kissinger, H. 1994. *Diplomacy*. New York: Simon & Schuster.

Liang, S. M. 1989. *Liang Shuming quanji.* [*The complete works of Liang Shuming*], vol. 1. Jinan: Shandong People's Publishing House.
Liu, S. J., et al. 2011. Ruhe zhengque renshi zai Zhongguo fazhan zhongguojia shenfen shang de Zhengyi. [How to correctly understand the debates in China on the identities of developing countries]. *China Development Observation* 7: 6–10.
Ma, S. L., and Y. Kuang. (eds). 2008. *Ouzhou rentong yanjiu.* [*A study on European identity*]. Beijing: shehui kexue wenxian chubanshe.
Men, H. H. 2005. *Goujian Zhongguo da zhanlue de kuangjia: guojia shili, zhanlue guannian yu guoji zhidu.* [*China's grand strategy: National power, strategic concepts and international institutions, a framework analysis*]. Peking University Press Beijing.
Men, H. H. 2006a. Yali, renzhi yu guoji xingxiang – guanyu Zhongguo canyu guoji zhidu zhanlue de lishi jieshi. [Pressure, cognition and international image – On the historical interpretation of the strategy of China's participation in the international system]. *World Economics & Politic Shiejie jingji yu zhengzhi* 4: 17–22.
——— 2006b. Zhongguo zhanlue wenhua de chonggou: yixiang yanjiu yicheng. [The reconstruction of China's strategic culture: A research agenda]. *Teaching and Research* 1: 57–63.
News Sina. 2012. [online]. Available at http://news.sina.com.cn/c/2010-04-30/0102174443735.html. Accessed 22 Dec 2012.
Qin, Y. Q. 2003a. Guojia shenfen, zhanlue wenhua he anquan liyi – guanyu Zhongguo yu guoji shehui guanxi de sange jiashe. [National identity, strategic culture and security interests – Three assumptions regarding relations between China and the international community]. *Shiejie jingji yu zhengzhi* 1: 10–15.
——— 2003b. Shijie zhengzhi de wenhua lilun – wenhua jiegou, wenhua danwei yu wenhua li. [The cultural theory of world politics – Cultural structure, institutions and power]. *Shijie jingji yu zhengzhi* 4: 4–9.
Qiu, Y. L. 1999. Jingji quanqiuhua yu Zhongguo guojia liyi. [Economic globalization and China's national interests]. *Shijie jingji* 12: 3–13.
Ranke, L. V. 1973. *The theory and practice of history.* Indianapolis: Bobbs-Merrill.
Sun, Z. S. 1981. *Sun Zhongshan xuanji.* [*The selected works of Sun Yat-sen*]. Beijing: People's Publishing House.
Tu, W. M. 2011. Zhongguo de jueqi xuyao wenhua de zhicheng. [China's rise requires the support of its culture]. *Studies on the Socialism with Chinese Characteristics* 6: 35–39.

Wang, J. 2003. Jiangshan dai you qiangguo chu – shijie qiangguo xingsheng zhilu tanxi jiqi dui Zhongguo fazhan de qishi. [Great powers rise in every generation – The exploitation and analysis of the rise of major global powers and its inspiration to China's development]. *Jingji yanjiu cankao* 49: 2–16.

Wang, M. 2011. Zhonghua chuantong wenhua yu ruan shili. [Chinese traditional culture and soft power]. *People's Daily* (*Overseas Edition*), p. A 6. 2 November 2011

Wenku. 2012. [online]. Available at http://wenku.baidu.com/view/d0bd643531126edb6f1a10b9.html. Accessed 22 Dec 2012.

Xu, C. L. 2012. Xinxing guojia jueqi yu guojian guoji jingji xin zhixu – yi Zhongguo de lujing xuanze wei shijiao [The rise of emerging countries and the building of a new international economic order – From the perspective of China's choice for its development path]. *Zhongguo shehui kexue* 10: 186–204.

13

Megatrends of the Xi Decade

Steve Tsang and Honghua Men

When Xi Jinping took over the stewardship of China in late 2012, the Communist Party had already delivered a longer period of sustained fast growth than any government had achieved anywhere in human history. The approach the Party had adopted hitherto was essentially a kind of pragmatic experimentalism that Deng Xiaoping introduced after the end of the Mao Zedong era in the late 1970s. As the 21st century unfolded questions were raised as to whether the same model would still be suitable. But they were not addressed head on immediately. Since the established

S. Tsang (✉)
School of Contemporary Chinese Studies, University of Nottingham, Nottingham, UK
e-mail: steve.tsang@nottingham.ac.uk

H. Men
School of Political Science and International Relations, Tongji University, Shanghai, China
e-mail: menhonghuacanran@163.com

S. Tsang, H. Men (eds.), *China in the Xi Jinping Era*,
The Nottingham China Policy Institute Series,
DOI 10.1007/978-3-319-29549-7_13

way had delivered spectacular results for several decades, the power of inertia was entrenched. Indeed, under Xi's predecessor, Hu Jintao, the Party largely stayed the course and focused on maintaining stability and a fast rate of growth. While the Party under Hu was officially committed to deepening reform, its 'instinct' was to avoid risk, which dampened the scope and scale of reform.

Xi is much more ambitious than his predecessor. Staying the course and making small incremental improvements is not an option that he considers appropriate. He seeks to steer China through an 'exciting' or eventful decade that will transform the goals and rhetoric of the 'China Dream' into reality. Xi has not yet outlined a detailed plan for reform and how he proposes to deliver it, but the goals for his decade-long tenure have been articulated. He aims to deliver national rejuvenation, which will involve the Communist Party being sufficiently revitalized to function efficiently and effectively in implementing the reforms and other wishes of the top leadership, as well as commanding the appropriate level of respect and admiration from the international community for a more assertive China. The range of policy issues that he will take on is wide. So far he has demonstrated the confidence, courage, and commitment to push for significant changes. The directions and depth of changes Xi seeks to deliver essentially define the megatrends that will distinguish his tenure from that of his two most recent predecessors. Xi has embarked on a quest to move China forward and change it on a scale that can be compared to what happened under Deng Xiaoping.[1]

Reinforcing the Consultative Leninist System

While the instigation and conclusion of formal proceedings against former Politburo Standing Committee member Zhou Yongkang shows Xi's commitment to the anti-corruption cause and his preparedness to let this reach the very top layer of the retired leaders, it does not imply that

[1] During the commemoration of Deng's 110th birthday, the Chinese authorities under Xi describes him as a torchbearer of Deng as a reformer. The implication is clear.
Xinhuanet, "Xi carries Deng's torch."

he plans on changing the basic political system. As Tsang highlights in Chap. 2, Xi remains fully committed to making the existing consultative Leninist political system work better. This will require considerable governance reform and a rectification of the Party, but such efforts are directed to making the system work effectively and efficiently to its full potential, not to replace it. Like Deng Xiaoping, Xi sees a need to overhaul the system in place in China but fundamentally rejects North American or European constitutionalism or democracy or any other liberal democratic system as appropriate for China.[2] Xi also shares Deng's confidence that the Communist Party is fit for purpose provided certain reforms are implemented. Curbing corruption is essential for this purpose. The anti-corruption theme is therefore not going to be just a political campaign, which always ends after a period of time. It will remain as the first megatrend of the Xi decade, by which corruption is meant to be tamed and contained on a sustained basis.

The continuation of the anti-corruption campaign should not, however, be seen as an attempt to eradicate corruption with Zhou Yongkang being the first of many other former or current top level leaders to be publicly humiliated and punished. No state where systemic corruption has existed for a significant period can afford a vindictive approach to punishing corrupt officials to the last man, as such an approach will, at least in the short to medium term, delegitimize the regime, gravely undermine its stability and capacity to govern effectively for some time, and overload the judicial system to beyond breaking point. It may also provoke a collective fight back by those feeling vulnerable in the establishment. This goes against the most basic requirement of the consultative Leninist system, which is to ensure the stability and endurance of the system, and Xi will therefore try to avoid this in China. Successful anti-corruption efforts in a state that has suffered from systemic corruption generally require some form of a partial amnesty, be it proclaimed formally or not.[3] For Xi to secure the support or at least the passive acceptance of his colleagues at the Politburo and the rest of the establishment to embrace his anti-corruption

---

[2] Zhongguo Xinwenwang, "Xi tichu 'diwuge xiandaihua.'"

[3] Hong Kong went through this in the 1970s; see Tsang, *Documentary History Hong Kong*, 191, 175–94.

commitment, he cannot but reach an understanding with them on the scope and extent of this commitment. This is likely to imply criteria for not instigating investigations against certain acts beyond a certain point in time in the past or certain individuals, with little or no tolerance for offences or new offenders outside of the agreed perimeter—a de facto partial amnesty. In return, Xi will use this to leverage against some Party elders to secure his objective of greater political institutionalization.

Indeed, to maximize the capacity and effectiveness of the consultative Leninist political system, Xi needs to press on with greater institutionalization. His ambition to deliver changes or progress comparable to what Deng managed can often lead to observers suggesting that Xi is trying to take on the mantle of a strongman, the last of whom in the People's Republic of China (PRC) was Deng Xiaoping.[4] As Tsang has demonstrated in Chap. 2, Xi has created new institutions at the top level of policy making, such as the State Security Council and the Leading Small Group for Deepening Reform, to enhance the effectiveness of the consultative Leninist system, not to assert himself as a strongman. Whatever understanding Xi may reach with the establishment in arranging for a de facto partial amnesty in the anti-corruption efforts, it will almost certainly involve requiring most if not all retired elders to fade out of key decision making or the personnel change process after a face saving interregnum. This should mark a major step forward in political institutionalization, as it should significantly reduce the clout of retired top leaders asserting themselves behind a bamboo curtain. Hence, the second notable direction of change is the deepening of institutionalization and the fading away of the dominant influence of the Party elders.

A corollary to such governance changes is a commitment to enhancing credibility and transparency through judicial reforms. As Wang has argued powerfully in Chap. 3, the commitment of the Chinese government under Xi is real but it needs to be understood in the context of the Chinese political environment. The greater importance being put on the judicial system and process was reflected in the trial of former Politburo member Bo Xilai. Although the Bo case came up before Xi took over the leadership of the Party and of the country, he and his

[4] Tsang, *China after Deng Xiaoping*, 78.

colleagues at the Politburo Standing Committee ultimately decided on how the Bo case should be handled. They chose to put it through a relatively open judicial process rather than the Party disciplinary route or a secret trial. Xi's commitment to enhancing credibility and transparency through judicial improvements is, nonetheless, balanced by a desire to keep important matters under control. His use of the court proceeding to show defiance meant he and his colleagues preferred to avoid the possibility of something similar happening in the Zhou Yongkang case, the trial of whom was kept under tight control. Xi's commitment to enhancing credibility and transparency of the judicial system should not be taken to imply a commitment to judicial independence as it is understood and practised in countries like the UK or the USA. The judicial reforms under Xi are not meant to benefit dissidents but to improve the administration of justice and minimize abuse of the system for ordinary people in China.

As Wang explains, judicial reforms will be introduced and implemented under the leadership of the Party. The objective is not to transform the judiciary into a branch of government independent of the executive (or, for that matter, the legislative) branch. The curbing of corruption and improved management of the judiciary are the key instruments for such a purpose. What is being put forth under Xi are efforts to deliver higher quality judgements and sentencing through a greater monitoring of the process, in order to secure results that the Party deems appropriate and the general public embraces as credible.

Carefully recalibrating the relationship between the government and the people is another key feature that will help to define the Xi decade. 'The people' in the PRC is a complex concept. At one level it incorporates all ethnic groups that make up the Chinese people. At a different level it distinguishes between the Han and those ethnic minorities who have embraced Sinification and the Party's brand of patriotism on the one hand and those who refuse to accept Sinification or others who are simply deemed unpatriotic on the other hand. Both elements need to be carefully managed, and the overwhelming majority, whose loyalty is not in doubt, requires only routine social management. The restless minorities who are seen to challenge the unity and territorial integrity of China will face special measures beyond the standard social management approach.

This approach, adopted since Hu Jintao's time, is likely to be modified and improved by a greater focus on social governance. The main difference here rests in a more top-down approach inherent in social management, against the social governance approach which aims to engage with the general public more. For simplicity we have generally used the term 'social management' in this book. In Chap. 4 Fulda has shown that such a general approach is not in fact unique to China. Something similar had previously been tried in the newly united Germany under Otto Von Bismarck towards the end of the 19th century, where rapid transformation created social conditions and challenges not incomparable to those in China today. Fulda reminds us that in both cases the two governments that adopted variations of the social management approach have delivered impressive results in the short term. But if there is a particularly poignant lesson to be drawn from the German case it is that the changes unleashed by the tremendous progress made following rapid industrialization often require a much more collaborative relationship being forged between the government and the people. In the context of the 21st century it means a government needs to work well with civil society or the non-governmental sector. The shift in emphasis from social management to social governance under Xi suggests that he and his advisers are aware of this requirement, though whether what is needed will be implemented successfully or not only time will tell.

All the difficulties and complications inherent in managing the relationship between the government and the people in 'China proper' exist in the western parts of the country, homeland to some of the most important visible minorities. As has been revealed in Zhao's incisive study in Chap. 5, the Chinese authorities are acutely aware of the scale of the challenges and have examined the experience of other countries, big or small. The approach that Zhao sees as particularly appropriate for China in the present circumstances is to promote ethnic integration, for example by promoting intermarriages, not assimilation or Sinification. This implies the treating of the minority groups as partners in the Chinese nation, where their cultural heritage is better respected and their special advantages or discrimination are removed. What Zhao advocates is important. But the ultimate test rests in making the minorities want to be proud of being constituent parts of the Chinese nation. Notwithstanding Zhao's advocacy and the Xi Administration's apparent disposition in principle to move towards adopting a policy of integration, the odds are that this will not emerge as a dominant trend that will define the Xi decade.

Since Xi took the helm of state, long standing deep ethnic cleavages, the lack of trust between some ethnic groups and the government, particularly its security forces, in the western part of the country, have resulted in a spiral of escalating violence, particularly in Xinjiang. Knife attacks mounted by disaffected members of the Uighur community, mostly but not exclusively directed against the Chinese security forces, have resulted in the latter responding with overwhelming force. Whether the many knife attacks, which differ markedly from the al-Qaeda brand of indiscriminate suicide bombing, should be seen in terms of Islamist terrorism of the post 9-11 type is a matter open to interpretation and debate. But the reality is that the Chinese Government sees such attacks as inspired, if not organized, by Islamist terrorists aimed at splitting China. By the autumn of 2015 the spread of violence is at risk of becoming a vicious circle, which will eventually radicalize elements of the Uighur communities and transform some of them into Islamist terrorists. The risk here is heightened by the impending withdrawal of the North Atlantic Treaty Organization (NATO) forces from Afghanistan where the Taliban has so far avoided attacking the Chinese in order to focus on the Americans and Europeans. Once all NATO troops have left Afghanistan, the Taliban will have less incentive to avoid or minimize support for the radicalized elements of their 'Uighur brothers' in resisting the secular or 'infidel' government in control of Xinjiang.

This drift to a vicious circle cannot be stopped or reversed by the social management approach successfully adopted so far elsewhere in China. It only stands a chance of being stopped if the Chinese Government takes an approach fundamentally different from the one it has been following. What is needed is to eliminate the appeal of radical Islam to the Uighurs or other Muslims in the country.[5] However, the Chinese Government under Xi has shown no more inclination or ability to do this than the US Government, for example, has in preventing American Muslims from being attracted to join radical Islamist causes since the attacks on the World Trade Center in

[5] For a critical assessment of what would be needed to tackle the al-Qaeda brand of transnational terrorism, see Tsang, *Intelligence and Human Rights*, Chaps. 1, 7, 8 and 11.

New York in 2001. Regrettably the Chinese Government and its security forces will maintain their current policy and persist in tackling this problem as an emerging terrorist threat that requires an escalating use of force as the challenge gets more entrenched. In response, elements of the Uighur communities will resort to greater violence. A spiral of such escalation, feeding on each other, is likely to constitute a feature of the Xi decade, though Chinese security forces will no doubt keep Xinjiang under control.

A More Balanced Approach to Deepening Reform

Maintaining stability and order cannot be a security and social management issue alone. In the context of China it is about creating the conditions for sustaining or even deepening reform which, in turn, needs to take into account its implications for stability and order. They are therefore closely interwoven into other important strands of policies that will shape the Xi decade. The obvious ones that are domestic policy oriented concern the implications of demographic changes, urbanization, the search for a sustainable model of development, and calibrating the pace of economic growth. These are important subjects that have been examined in some detail by Han and Qi in Chap. 6, Zhang in Chap. 7, and Zhou in Chap. 8. They are in an important sense so closely intertwined that they need to be addressed together.

The success of China's reform in the last three decades was based in no small measure on its government making the most of the demographic dividend and a ruthless commitment to sustain a high rate of growth, even at the expense of the environment, knowing full well the time will come for cleaning it up. Such an approach cannot be sustained indefinitely. How to finesse the conflicting demands of poverty alleviation, improving living standards, and promoting rapid development and growth on the one hand, and environmental protection and sustainability of the developmental trajectory on the other hand, is a key challenge that the Xi Administration will have to tackle. Muddling through, as a policy option, is one that Xi clearly does not intend to adopt.

Han and Qi have demonstrated in Chap. 6 that the Chinese Government is very much aware of the conflicting demands and is seeking to strike the right balance, as the end of the demographic dividend has already started and the need to make development sustainable can no longer be pushed back a lot longer. The Xi Administration's emphasis on a carefully calibrated approach to urbanization that focuses on incorporating agricultural workers into enlarging towns, and not building megacities, takes centre stage. Such a policy is meant to dovetail other complementary policies designed to confront the problems of China getting old before it gets wealthy and of the drift of manpower from farms to factories. It seeks to utilize the advantages of urbanization based on towns as the instrument to enable the ageing population to remain economically active for longer, in order to moderate the effect of demographic changes and population movements.

The crux of the matter for sustainable development is environmental protection, a requirement fully recognized by the Xi Administration. The Party under Xi reiterated its commitment 'to protect the ecological environment' at the Third Plenum in November 2013.[6] As Zhang's cogent analysis in Chap. 7 shows, this is of great importance, as the scale of environmental degradation in China in the last three decades has been extremely serious, despite considerable progress being made by the government to slow down the process. The reality remains that if the environmental costs are fully included in assessing the real rate of growth in recent decades, this would reduce it by as much as 4 % per annum. This underlines the significance of the issues that the Xi Administration must confront. Zhang's research also shows that three different sets of key factors are responsible for the environmental degradation. They are the inefficiency in the use of energy, the ineffectiveness of the political infrastructure in enforcing government set targets, as well as inadequate public recognition and commitment to rectify the problems. They are issues that the Chinese Government knows it must tackle at some stage. Xi's commitment to a more balanced approach in development means that there will be less emphasis put on growth and more on quality of life in the coming decade, though it does not imply that sustaining a good rate of growth is now irrelevant.

In the context of China the sustainability of its development model goes beyond the more conventional sense of the term, however. It also

[6] Xinhuanet, China vows ecological protection.

raises questions about whether the particular approach, as an economic developmental model, can be sustained on the same trajectory for very much longer. The high rate of growth in the last three decades has already surpassed that achieved in any economic miracle that ever happened in any country in human history. The question thus raised is one that a top leader who merely wants to keep the country on an even kneel can dodge, but one that will be put on the political agenda by a leader who sees himself in a transformational light. Xi Jinping belongs to the latter category. With this in mind Zhou has raised, in Chap. 8, important and highly pertinent questions that he thinks the Xi Administration must address. It is not just about rebalancing the economy, important as it is. It is also about assessing how much longer China can or should focus on export and investment driven growth, and how it should move beyond the existing paradigm for development. Zhou argues forcefully that this is needed because of marginal diminishing returns and the changed environment in which China's economy now operates. Zhou makes a case for the economy to shift its focus to promoting entrepreneurship, real innovation, and smart urbanization, and to provide new and much more appropriate incentives for economic cadres to steer the economy to develop in a balanced and sustainable way.

What Zhou has outlined in his thoughtful chapter are basic issues that can affect the evolution of China's development model. They are also complementary to addressing some of the issues raised by Han and Qi in Chap. 6 and by Zhang in Chap. 7. The early indications are that Xi is in principle willing to explore them, as implied in his advocacy for the market to play a decisive role in shaping the economy. Whether Zhou's prescription for the Xi decade will materialize is too early to tell—state intervention to stop a free fall of the Shanghai stock market in the summer of 2015 suggests there are limits to this policy. Xi is rectifying the Party to make it fit for such a management role, but the politics of Party rectification cannot be predicted on the basis of a linear projection. Ultimately Xi needs to finesse the inherently contradictory requirements of allowing market forces to play a decisive role and requiring the Party to take the lead in steering the country to hold on to its chosen course. At this stage it is not realistic to foretell where China will be at the end of the Xi decade, but there is little doubt that he will explore the kind of questions raised by Zhou and, in this sense, depart from the approach taken by his immediate predecessor and take greater risk in pushing for more far reaching reforms.

A More Assertive China in the International Community

The rise or re-emergence of China as a great power of the first rank has come to be accepted widely since the global financial crisis revealed that the leviathan of the capitalist West headed by the USA has clay feet. While this process started in the latter half of Hu Jintao's second term of office, it became unmistakable by the time Xi succeeded Hu in 2012. This basic change in China's global standing has provided a strong impetus for the Chinese Government to put aside quietly Deng Xiaoping's dictum on foreign policy, which can be summarized in 24 words. They are: 'observe carefully, secure our position, handle the rest of the world calmly, bide our time, perfect hiding our capacities, and desist from claiming leadership'.[7] While the Chinese Government has not officially put an end to the Hu Jintao policy of promoting a harmonious world based on this Dengist dictum, Xi's articulation of the 'China Dream' in 2012 marked the de facto replacement of it by one that promotes national rejuvenation. China under Xi sees itself as a top tier great power that likes to command appropriate respect from the rest of the world. The new kind of great power relationship that Xi and President Barack Obama of the USA agreed to forge in their Sunnylands summit of 2013 confirms where Xi sees China belonging in the global order.

While the goals have been set, how best to achieve them is still an open question, about which the Chinese authorities and intellectuals are exploring and debating. The range of issues that needs to be addressed

[7] Deng Xiaoping's original '24 character strategy' in Chinese is: 冷静观察,稳住阵脚,沉着应付,韬光养晦,善于守拙,决不当头. They were not used together in one document. The first 12 characters were used by Deng in a talk outlining his plan for retirement to top level leaders in September 1989; Zhonggong Zhongyang Wenxian Bianji Weiyuanhui, *Deng Xiaoping Wenxuan*, 321. The rest were compiled and attributed to Deng as a strategy by the Chinese Foreign Ministry in the mid-1990s. Translated by Tsang, "China's Place East Asia," 85.

in recalibrating China's policy towards the outside world covers not only conventional foreign policy issues (examined by Hughes in Chap. 11), national security considerations (scrutinized by Xiao in Chap. 10), and the orientation of its grand strategy (expounded by Men in Chap. 12) but also the projection of soft power (studied by Sun in Chap. 9).

Even though the concept of soft power was coined by an American Harvard professor and former senior Department of Defense official, Joseph Nye, the Chinese Government takes it at least as seriously as any other great power. For over a decade the Chinese Government has invested considerable resources and energy in projecting soft power. While it is debatable how much of China's rise in its standing in the world is due to such efforts, the Government will persist in projecting soft power through the existing bureaucratic infrastructure, like the Hanban.

Sun puts forth an alternative approach to understanding how China can exert greater soft power more effectively. He has rightly stressed in Chap. 9 that soft power really needs to be based on a country and its people being comfortable and proud of its own civilization, history, and achievements, a view that is shared by Men in Chap. 12. Thus, as Sun argues, the building up of soft power is not particularly dependent on creating a bureaucracy to design and support policies that aim at making the country appealing to foreigners, though having an appropriate bureaucratic infrastructure is an advantage. A more effective approach is to promote and support the revival of China's tradition and values that sit comfortably with modernity and the country's quest for development. The values thus revived and promoted should not have an exclusive flavour. Indeed, it should incorporate ideas and inspiration that originate from the outside world as well. A modernized version of Chinese culture that benefits the country and its people in the long term is one that is more likely to generate soft power. In other words the projection of soft power needs to be based on an effective revival and modernization of China's tradition and culture.

Since foreign policy is about protecting and enhancing a country's national interest its starting point is to ensure national security. This gets more complex and complicated under Xi, not because, as Xiao reminds us persuasively in Chap. 10, China faces a 'clear and present danger' in terms of any external threat. It is because China is in a stage of transition, from having largely played the role of a regional power to becoming a world power. From the perspective of Beijing, China's rise has resulted in measures taken by its neighbours and the USA that have important security implications for it. The Chinese Government therefore sees real challenges to its national security. The most basic is the need to secure energy and resources from distant parts of the world to sustain the economy, a cornerstone for stability, order, and prosperity. The challenges to China's territorial and in particular maritime positions are also seen as a priority issue in foreign and security policy terms. Xiao further highlights that, from Beijing's vantage point, China faces a threat from external forces that seek to subvert its developmental approach for ideological reasons. The same forces are also seen as trying to exploit ethnic separatist forces to undermine China's national unity and territorial integrity. This explains why Xi has created the State Security Council as he started his second year as leader, as he saw a need for China to have a top level policy coordinating body to enable him to pull together the various strands of foreign and security policy issues, and take a strategic approach. It implies that Xi is working out a comprehensive national security strategy that will steer China to assert itself as a world power on the one hand, and to consolidate the internal security situation in the coming decade on the other.

The complexities in which Chinese foreign policy under Xi have to operate in fact go beyond that highlighted by Xiao above. As Hughes aptly points out in Chap. 11, the Chinese Government has to make and conduct its foreign policy against an external environment and a domestic political context that do not always fit in with how they would like them to be. While Xiao has expounded on the problems as they are seen from the Chinese perspective, most of the same problems are perceived differently by other countries. How others approach these issues, such as the maritime disputes in the South China Sea and the East China Sea or the American policy to 'pivot' back to Asia, will become policy challenges that the Chinese Government under Xi has to take into account. Likewise, while the Government is working on steering to transform itself from a regional power to a world power, much of the rest of the world already sees China as the second most powerful country, with an expectation that it will play a more proactive and constructive role in world affairs. Xi cannot ignore this. Domestically the rise of nationalism, a trend that is being accentuated by Xi, poses constraints on what the Chinese Government can do in some foreign policy matters, such as the maritime disputes. Shortcomings in the institutional or political setup within the country have also, as underlined by Hughes, caused problems. For example, Xi's predecessor Hu Jintao was deeply embarrassed when the Chinese military unveiled a new stealth fighter without his knowledge when he was hosting the American Secretary of Defense Robert Gates. Xi will not tolerate a similar implicit challenge to his authority.

Hughes agrees with Xiao (Chap. 10) and Tsang (Chap. 2) that the founding of the State Security Council was clearly an attempt by Xi to create an institution to strengthen China's capacity to coordinate and manage its foreign and security policy better. In the rest of Xi's tenure there is clearly a trend to reinforce this process in order to enable China to play a more proactive and assertive role in global affairs under his own direction, though it will still focus primarily on its neighbourhood or East Asia.

To understand what drives China in its approach to relations with the international community, it is essential to probe deeper into its sense of self-identification with the world, and how this has shaped its world view and grand strategy. Men's lucid and perceptive analysis in Chap. 12 has forcefully reminded us of the need to understand how China under the Communist Party perceives itself in the world. Since the Dengist reforms, as Men puts it, the Chinese Government sees China as a new type of socialist great power which is still a developing (in contrast to being a developed) power, one which has a great cultural heritage that is, particularly within the last decade, conducting itself as a responsible great power. Juxtaposing this against Xi's concept of the 'China Dream', one can see the implications more clearly. In Men's words, what China now strives to become 'is a new type of socialist great power that is pursuing a policy of overall opening up, transformation and development in all areas', one that 'is dedicated to creating a new system and development model as well as a new global culture based on the revival of traditional Chinese culture'. As a great power China remains focused primarily on its region, as it is aware that being still in a developmental stage it faces certain inherent weaknesses that must be addressed. Thus, despite the general perception in the wider world of China's rise, the Government is still concerned about potential challenges to internal security and national unity. It is also aware that, despite the impressive improvements in its military capabilities in the last two decades, China does not as yet have global power projection capabilities that are normally associated with a world power. Here, Men's analysis dovetails with that of Hughes (Chap. 11) in that the long standing default position of China being a premier power in East Asia or Pacific Asia will continue to play a key role in shaping its foreign and security policy in the coming decade.

Conclusions

The megatrends for China under Xi Jinping are all about taking calculated risks to deepen reform significantly and to play a more proactive role in world affairs. Xi's willingness to take risks contrasts starkly against his predecessor's proclivity to play safe. It is easy and tempting to suggest that Xi may be reckless in his approach, but he is taking risks for a reason. He is working to implement transformational changes to take China to the next stage of reform, in a scale that can be compared to what happened under Deng Xiaoping. Xi can see that the experimental approach of Deng, epitomized in the description of 'crossing a stream by feeling for rocks under the surface' is now out of date. The easy options had already been taken. It is like finding out the 'stream' that needs to be crossed has become a deep river. One can no longer cross it by feeling for rocks below. Careful routing and a better instrument that will enable China to cross are now needed.

To secure them Xi is rectifying the Party in order to revitalize its capacity and effectiveness as a Leninist instrument of control and governance. Whether the changes in the political arena will also end up delivering to him power akin to that of a strongman when the process is completed is a moot point. What he has so far done is to try to make the Party fit for the new purpose. When the Communist Party has largely cleansed itself of systemic corruption and the politics of elders, Xi should have the capacity and confidence to take more risk in taking on more dramatic economic and other reforms. Given the nature of the consultative Leninist system in place, allowing market forces to play a decisive role in shaping the economy can only happen if the Party feels confident that this will not result in such forces unwittingly causing an unravelling of the economy and destabilization of the party-state. The need to strengthen a Leninist instrument to allow market forces the scope to work their magic may seem self-contradictory to scholars from the Anglo-American tradition, but it can make sense if one looks at it from a Hegelian dialectic perspective.

The deepening of reform domestically is meant not only to enable the Party to stay in power but also to deliver the national rejuvenation encapsulated in the concept of the 'China Dream'. China under Xi can be expected to claim its place under the Sun, play a more proactive role in world affairs generally, but it will still focus primarily on its neighbourhood. Xi's China will go some way to meet the expectations of its rising standing in the world but the long time lag in building the necessary capabilities to function as a true world power means that there is a limit to its preparedness to take on global responsibilities beyond focusing on its core national interests and projecting soft power in the coming decade.

Bibliography

Tsang, S., ed. 1995. *A documentary history of Hong Kong: Government and politics*. Hong Kong: Hong Kong University Press.

——— 2008a. China's place in East Asia. In *China, Japan and regional leadership in East Asia*, ed. C.M. Dent, 85. Cheltenham: Edward Elgar.

———, ed. 2008b. *Intelligence and human rights in the era of global terrorism*. Stanford: Stanford Security Studies.

——— 2014. China after Deng Xiaoping: The search for a non-democratic development model. In *Democracy or alternative political systems in Asia: After the strongman*, ed. M.H.H. Hsiao, 78. London & New York: Routledge.

Xinhuanet. 2013. China vows ecological protection: Communique. [online]. Available at http://english.cntv.cn/20131112/105404.shtml. Accessed 18 Aug 2014.

———. 2014. Xinhua insight: To reignite a nation, Xi carries Deng's torch. [online]. Available at http://news.xinhuanet.com/english/indepth/2014--08/20/c_133569033.htm. Accessed 20 Aug 2014.

Zhonggong Zhongyang Wenxian Bianji Weiyuanhui, ed. 1993. *Deng Xiaoping Wenxuan*, vol 3. Renmin chubanshe: Beijing.

Zhongguo Xinwenwang. 2014. Wai mei: Xi Jinping weihe tichu "diwuge xiandaihua". [online]. Available at http://politics.people.com.cn/n/2014/0814/c1001-25464570.html. Accessed 15 Aug 2014.

Index

S. Tsang, H. Men (eds.), *China in the Xi Jinping Era*,
The Nottingham China Policy Institute Series,
DOI 10.1007/978-3-319-29549-7

FSC
www.fsc.org
MIX
Papier | Fördert
gute Waldnutzung
FSC® C083411

Kolibri 360 GmbH
Ferdinand-Jühlke-Straße 7
99095 Erfurt, Deutschland
produktsicherheit@kolibri360.de